PLUTO

URASAWA X TEZUKA

A NEW VISION BASED ON ASTRO BOY – *'THE GREATEST ROBOT ON EARTH'*

BY NAOKI URASAWA AND OSAMU TEZUKA

001

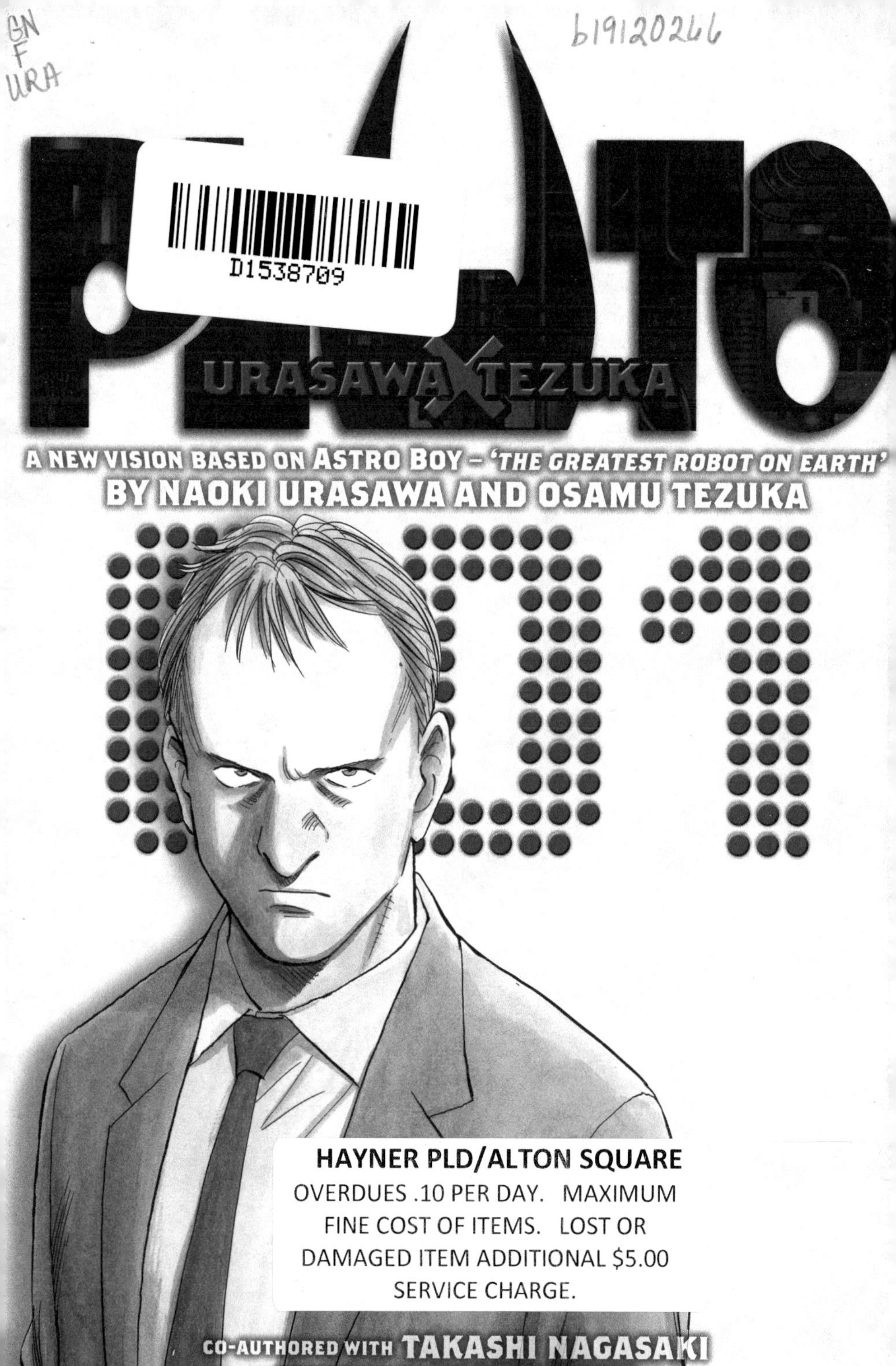

CO-AUTHORED WITH **TAKASHI NAGASAKI**

SUPERVISED BY **MACOTO TEZKA**

WITH THE COOPERATION OF TEZUKA PRODUCTIONS

ACT 1   MONT BLANC 3

ACT 2   GESICHT 35

ACT 3   BRAU 1589 61

ACT 4   NORTH NO. 2 (PART 1) 87

ACT 5   NORTH NO. 2 (PART 2) 111

ACT 6   NORTH NO. 2 (PART 3) 135

ACT 7   BRANDO 165

Act 1 Mont Blanc

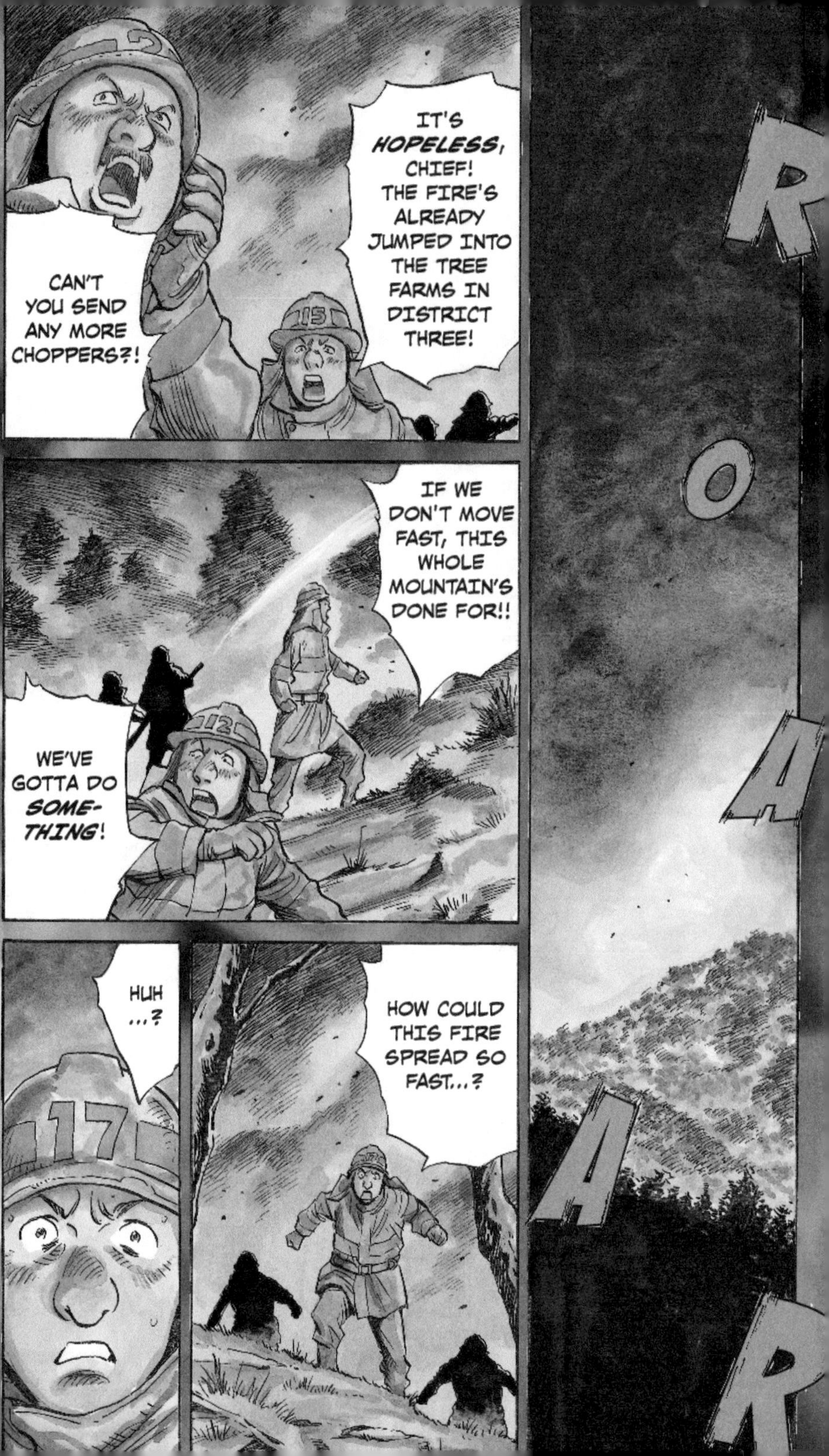

ROAAR
IT'S *HOPELESS*, CHIEF! THE FIRE'S ALREADY JUMPED INTO THE TREE FARMS IN DISTRICT THREE!
CAN'T YOU SEND ANY MORE CHOPPERS?!
IF WE DON'T MOVE FAST, THIS WHOLE MOUNTAIN'S DONE FOR!!
WE'VE GOTTA DO *SOME-THING*!
HOW COULD THIS FIRE SPREAD SO FAST...?
HUH ...?

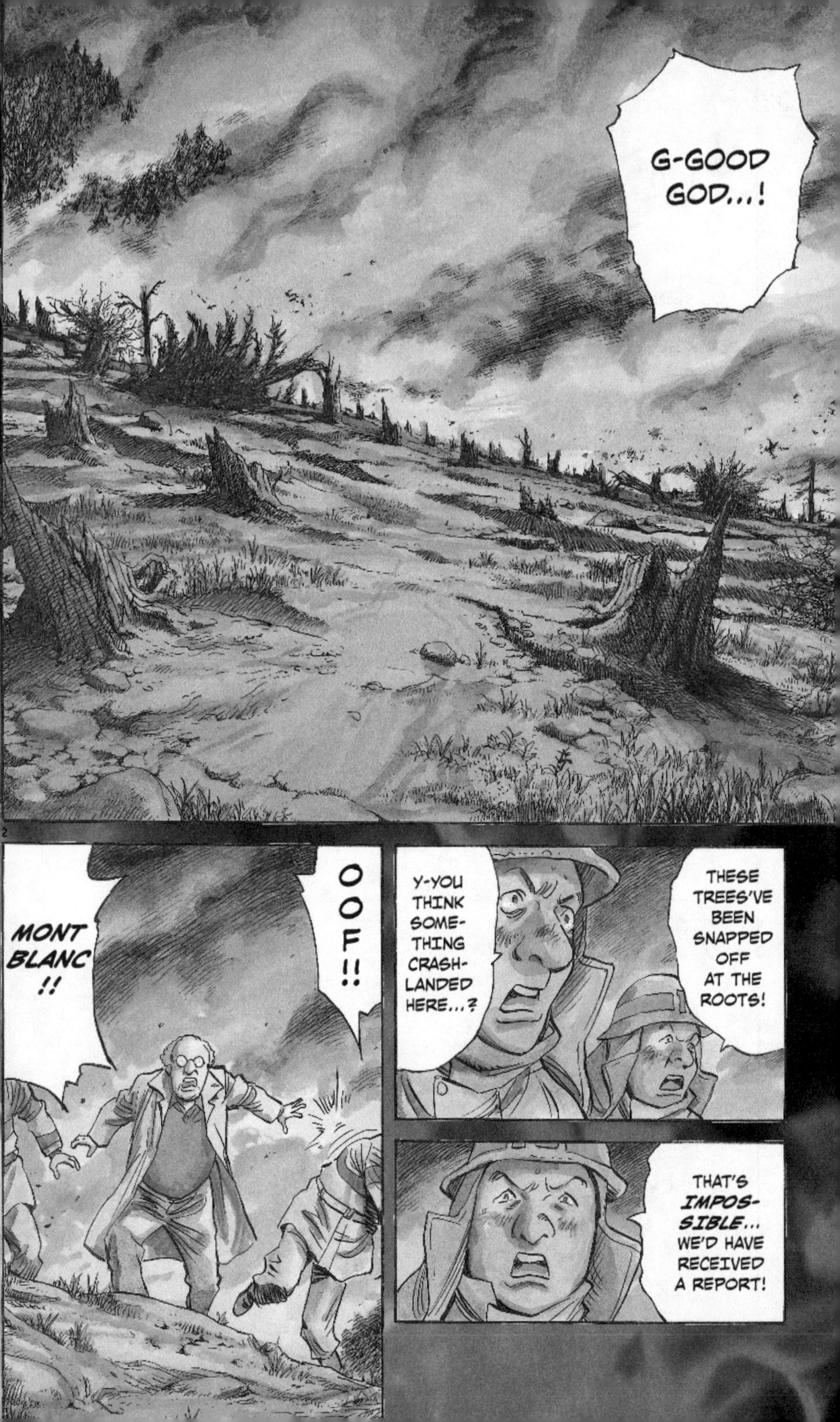
G-GOOD GOD...!
THESE TREES'VE BEEN SNAPPED OFF AT THE ROOTS!
Y-YOU THINK SOME-THING CRASH-LANDED HERE...?
THAT'S *IMPOSSIBLE*... WE'D HAVE RECEIVED A REPORT!
OOF!!
MONT BLANC!!

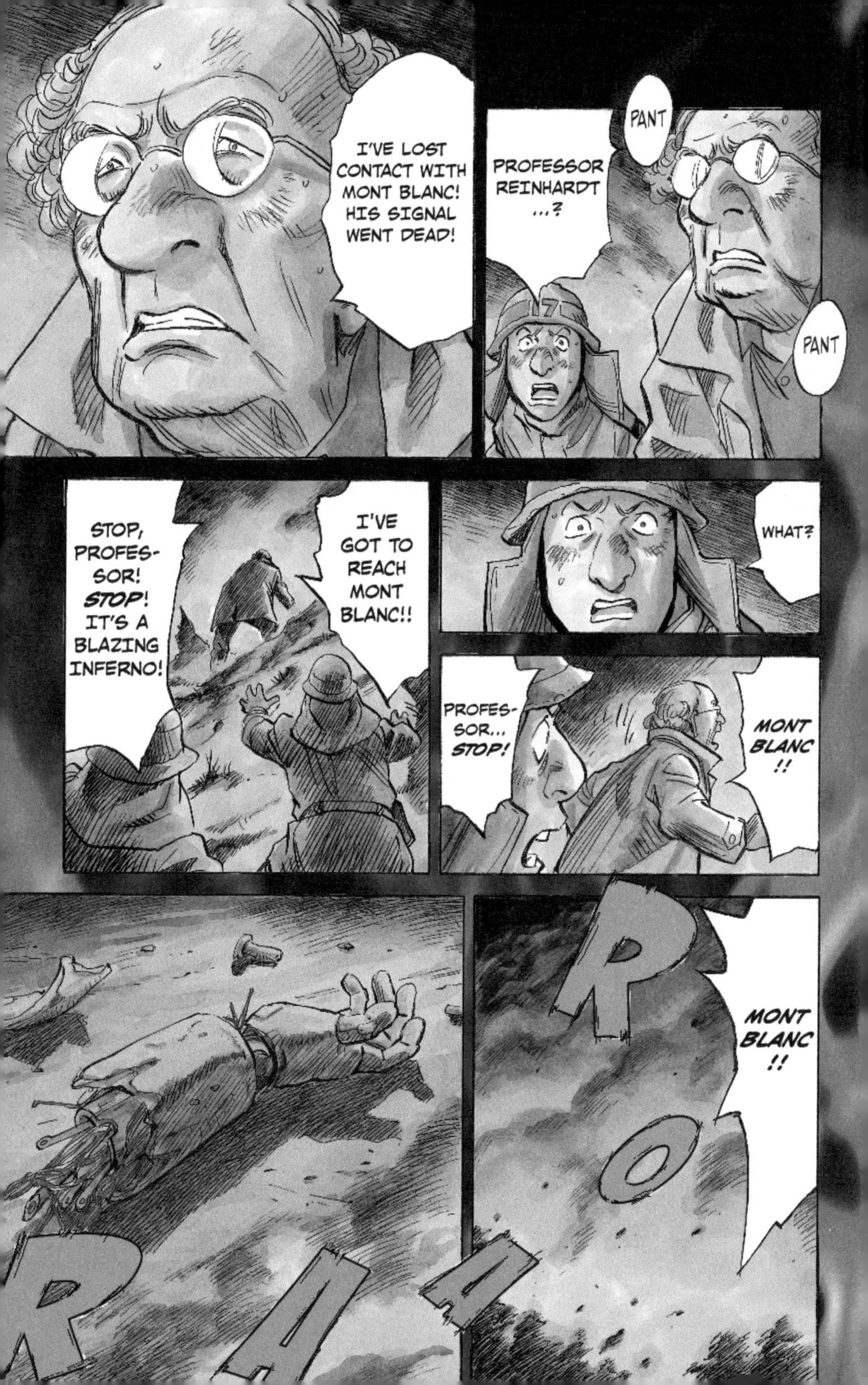
PANT
PROFESSOR REINHARDT ...?
PANT
I'VE LOST CONTACT WITH MONT BLANC! HIS SIGNAL WENT DEAD!
WHAT?
MONT BLANC !!
PROFES-SOR... STOP!
I'VE GOT TO REACH MONT BLANC!!
STOP, PROFES-SOR! STOP! IT'S A BLAZING INFERNO!
MONT BLANC !!
ROAR

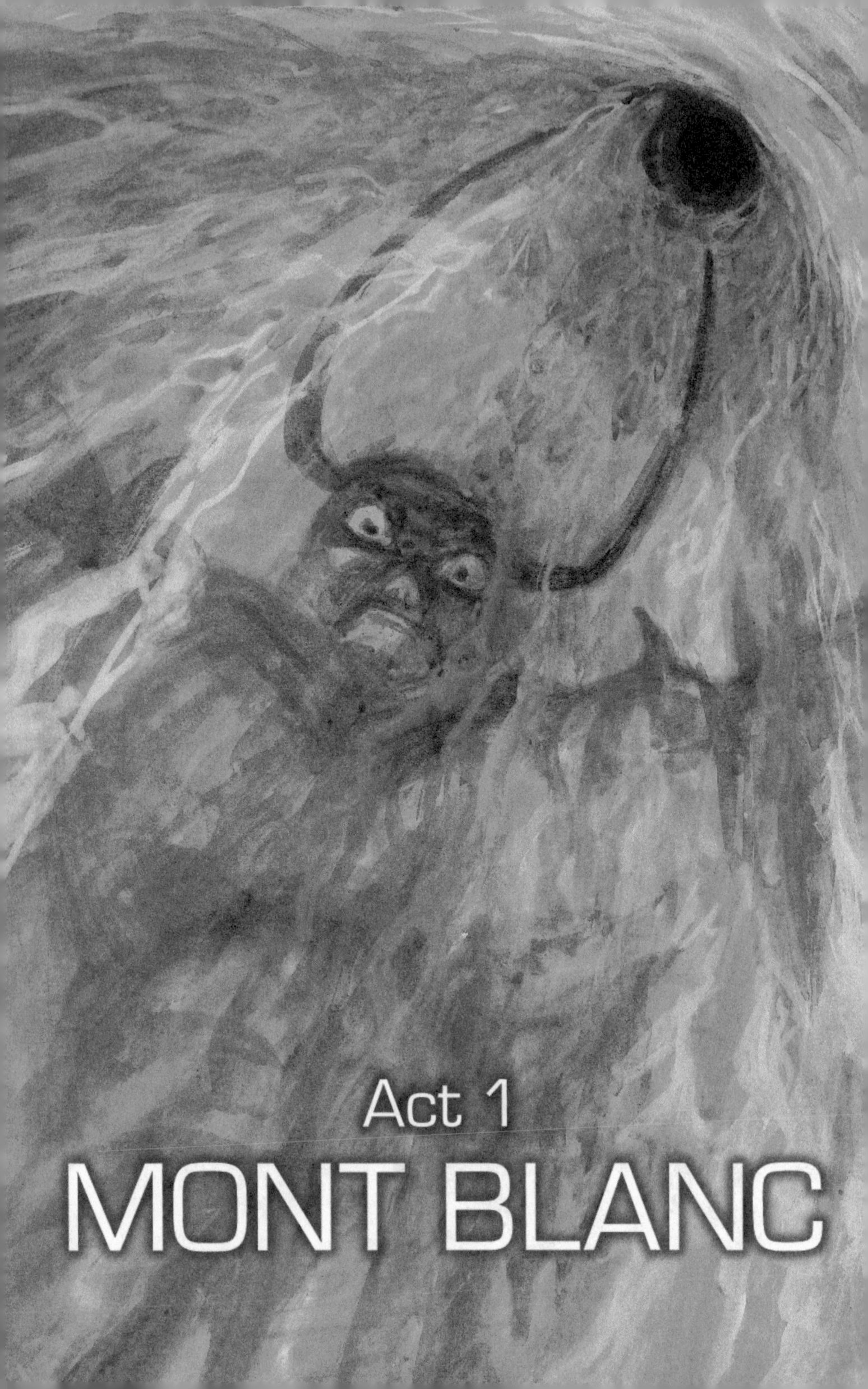

Act 1
MONT BLANC

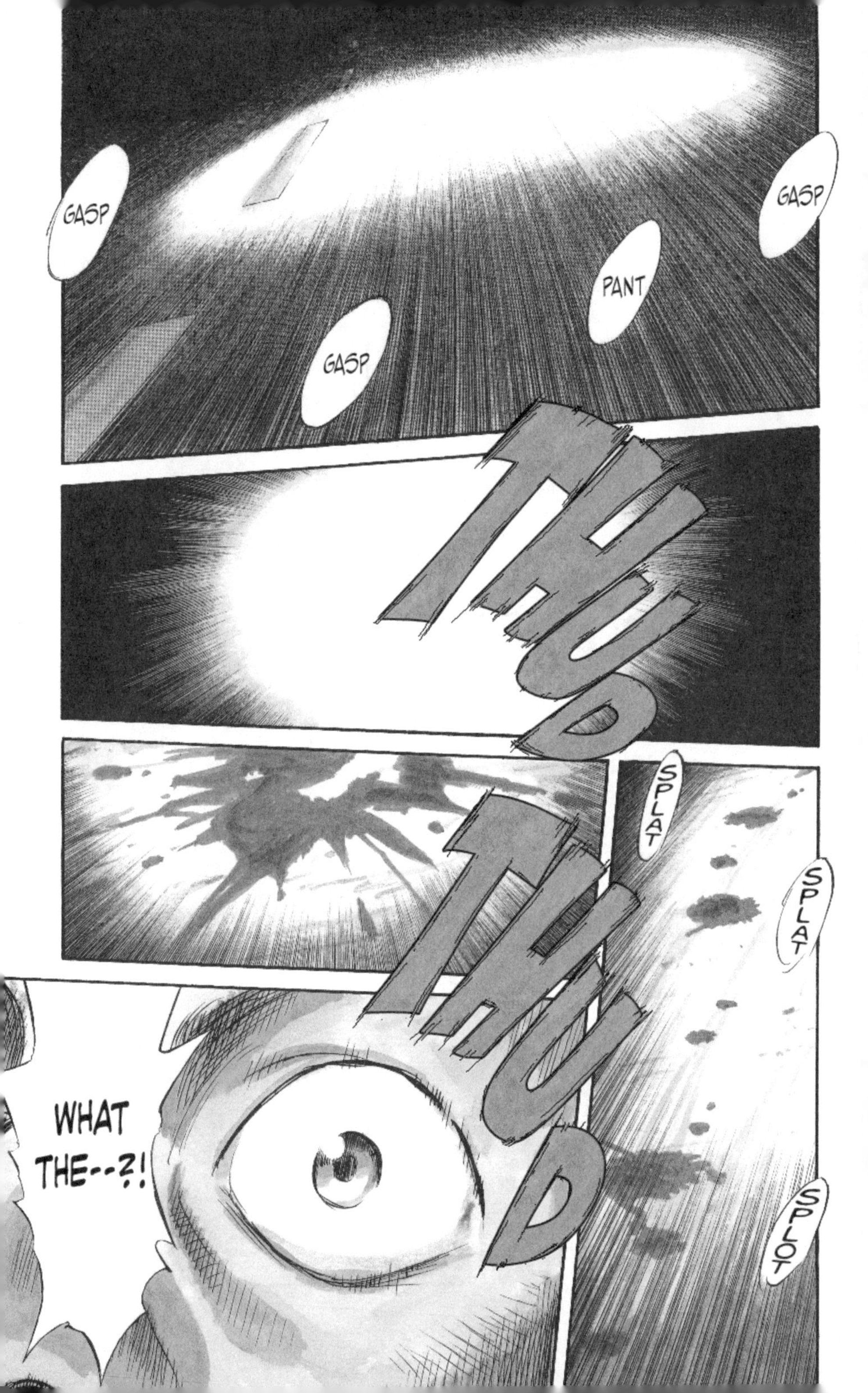
GASP
PANT
GASP
GASP
THUD
SPLAT
THUD
SPLAT
SPLOT
WHAT THE--?!

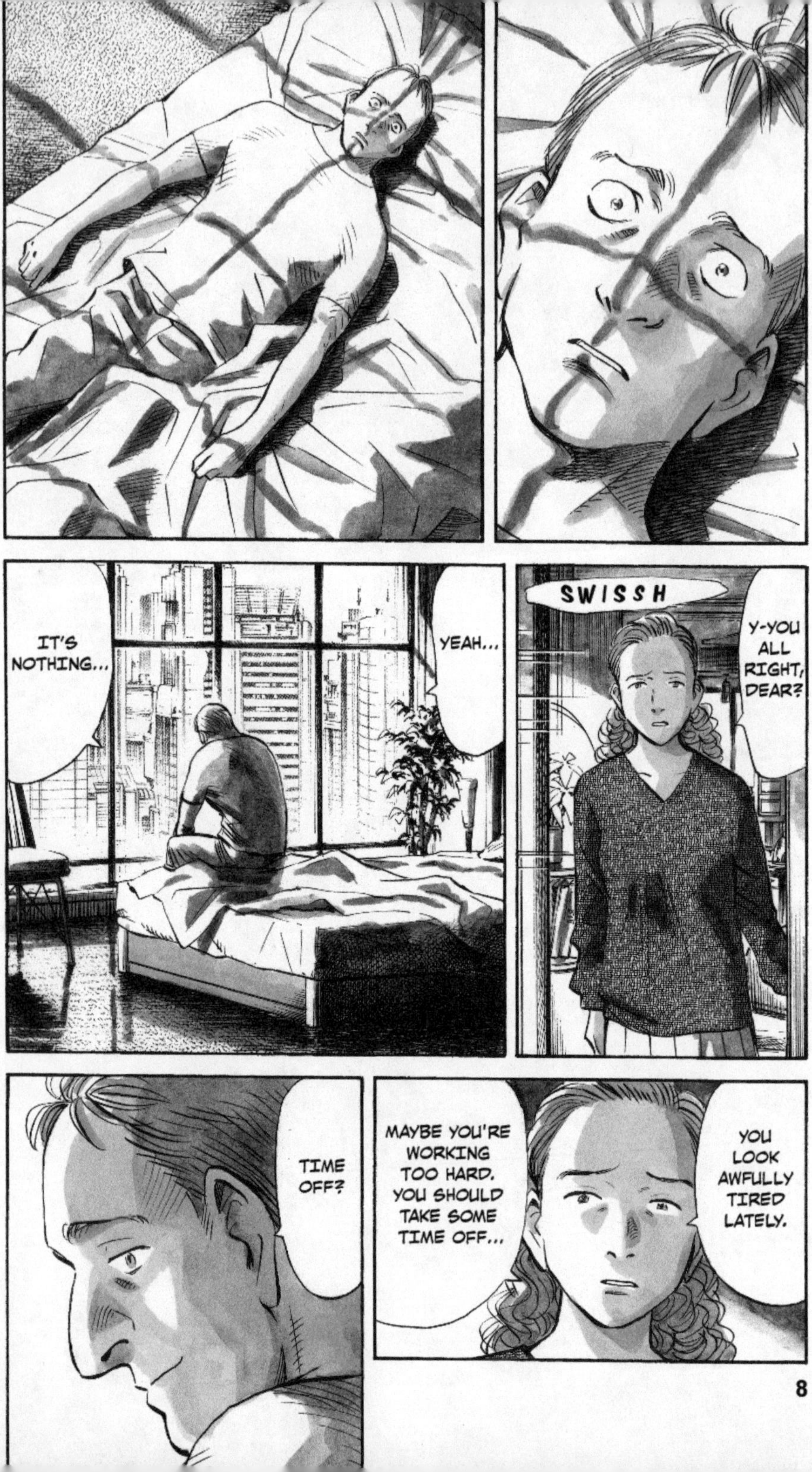
SWISSH
Y-YOU ALL RIGHT, DEAR?
YEAH...
IT'S NOTHING...
YOU LOOK AWFULLY TIRED LATELY.
MAYBE YOU'RE WORKING TOO HARD. YOU SHOULD TAKE SOME TIME OFF...
TIME OFF?

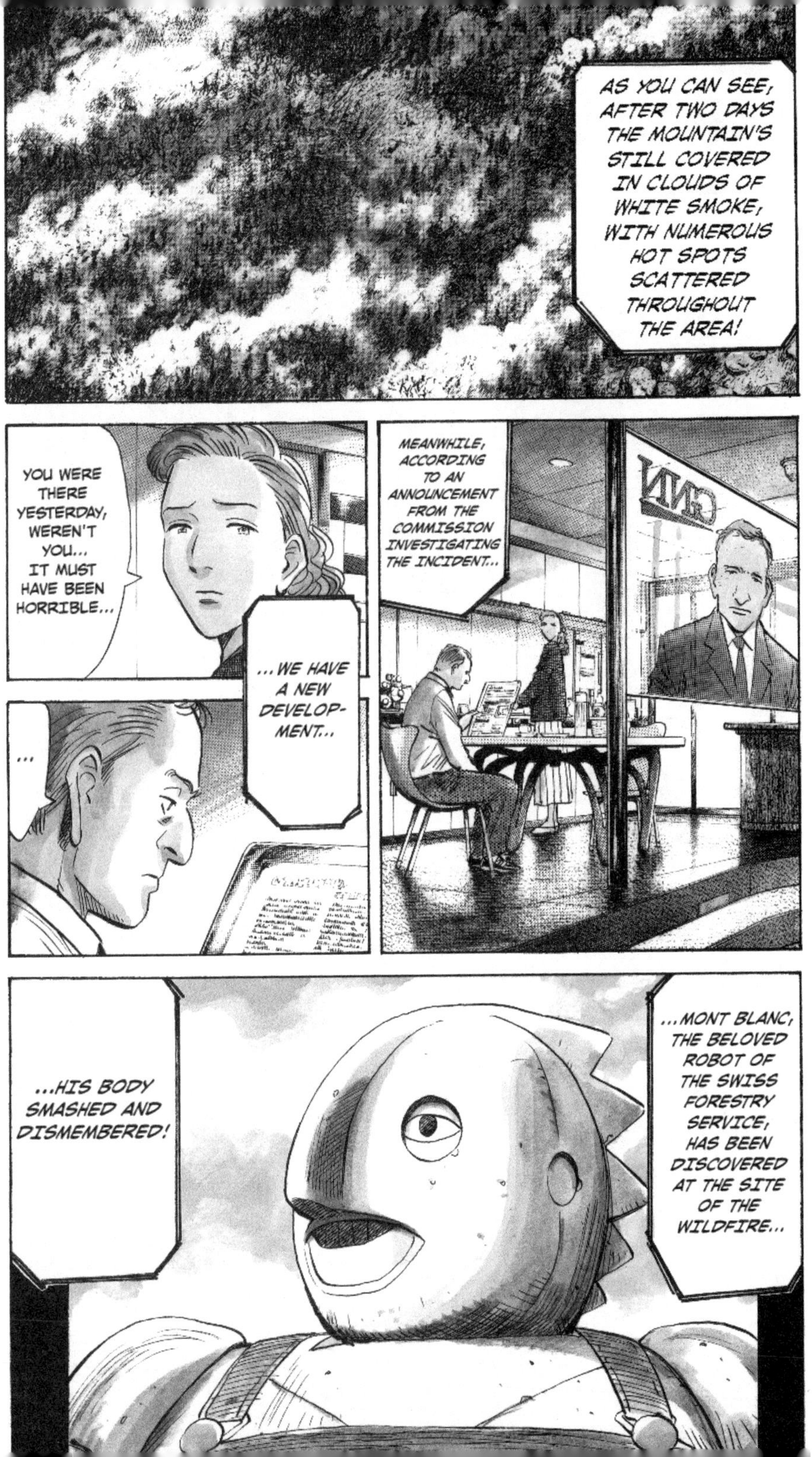
AS YOU CAN SEE, AFTER TWO DAYS THE MOUNTAIN'S STILL COVERED IN CLOUDS OF WHITE SMOKE, WITH NUMEROUS HOT SPOTS SCATTERED THROUGHOUT THE AREA!
MEANWHILE, ACCORDING TO AN ANNOUNCEMENT FROM THE COMMISSION INVESTIGATING THE INCIDENT...
YOU WERE THERE YESTERDAY, WEREN'T YOU... IT MUST HAVE BEEN HORRIBLE...
...WE HAVE A NEW DEVELOPMENT...
...
...MONT BLANC, THE BELOVED ROBOT OF THE SWISS FORESTRY SERVICE, HAS BEEN DISCOVERED AT THE SITE OF THE WILDFIRE...
...HIS BODY SMASHED AND DISMEMBERED!

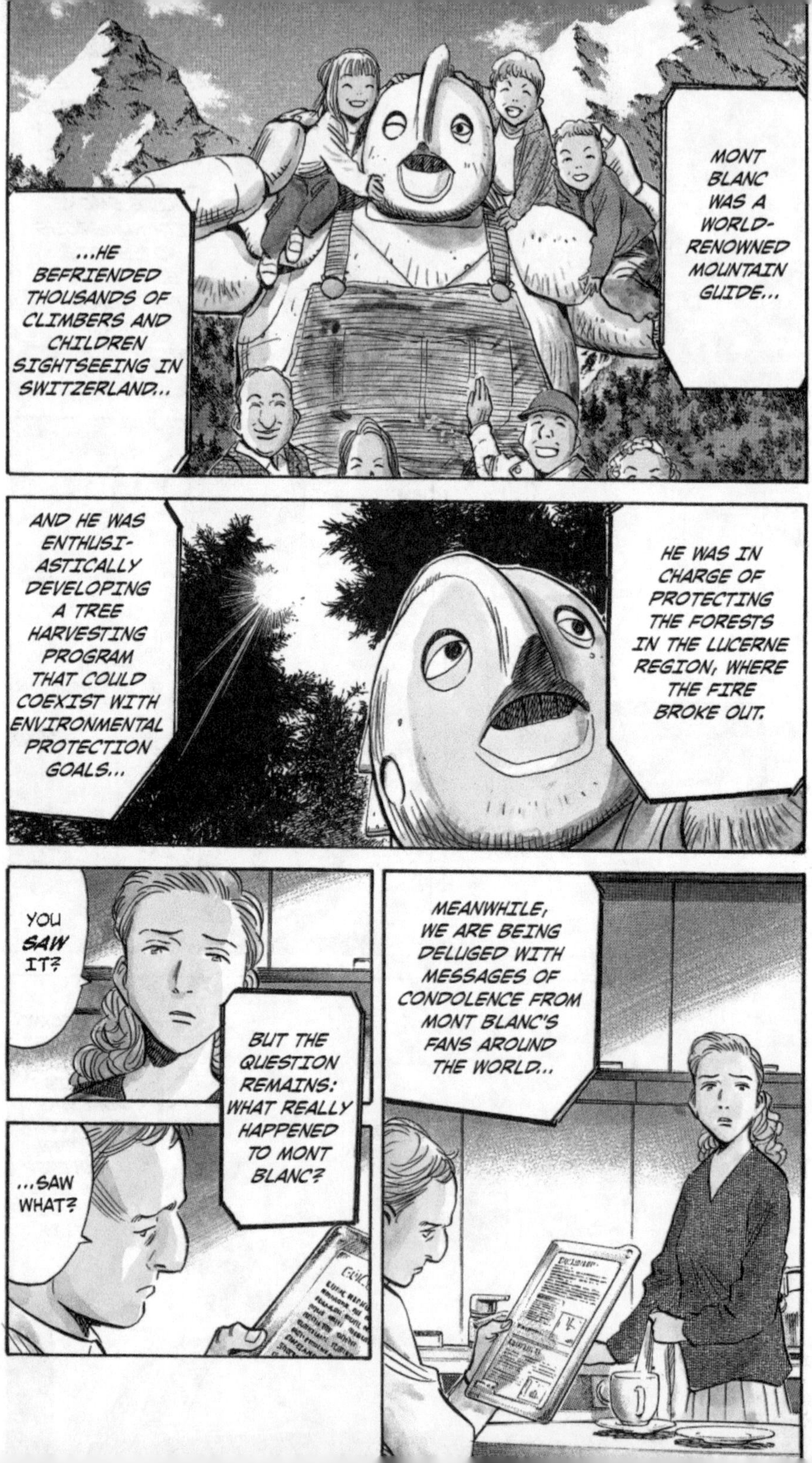
MONT BLANC WAS A WORLD-RENOWNED MOUNTAIN GUIDE...
...HE BEFRIENDED THOUSANDS OF CLIMBERS AND CHILDREN SIGHTSEEING IN SWITZERLAND...
HE WAS IN CHARGE OF PROTECTING THE FORESTS IN THE LUCERNE REGION, WHERE THE FIRE BROKE OUT.
AND HE WAS ENTHUSI-ASTICALLY DEVELOPING A TREE HARVESTING PROGRAM THAT COULD COEXIST WITH ENVIRONMENTAL PROTECTION GOALS...
MEANWHILE, WE ARE BEING DELUGED WITH MESSAGES OF CONDOLENCE FROM MONT BLANC'S FANS AROUND THE WORLD...
BUT THE QUESTION REMAINS: WHAT REALLY HAPPENED TO MONT BLANC?
YOU SAW IT?
...SAW WHAT?

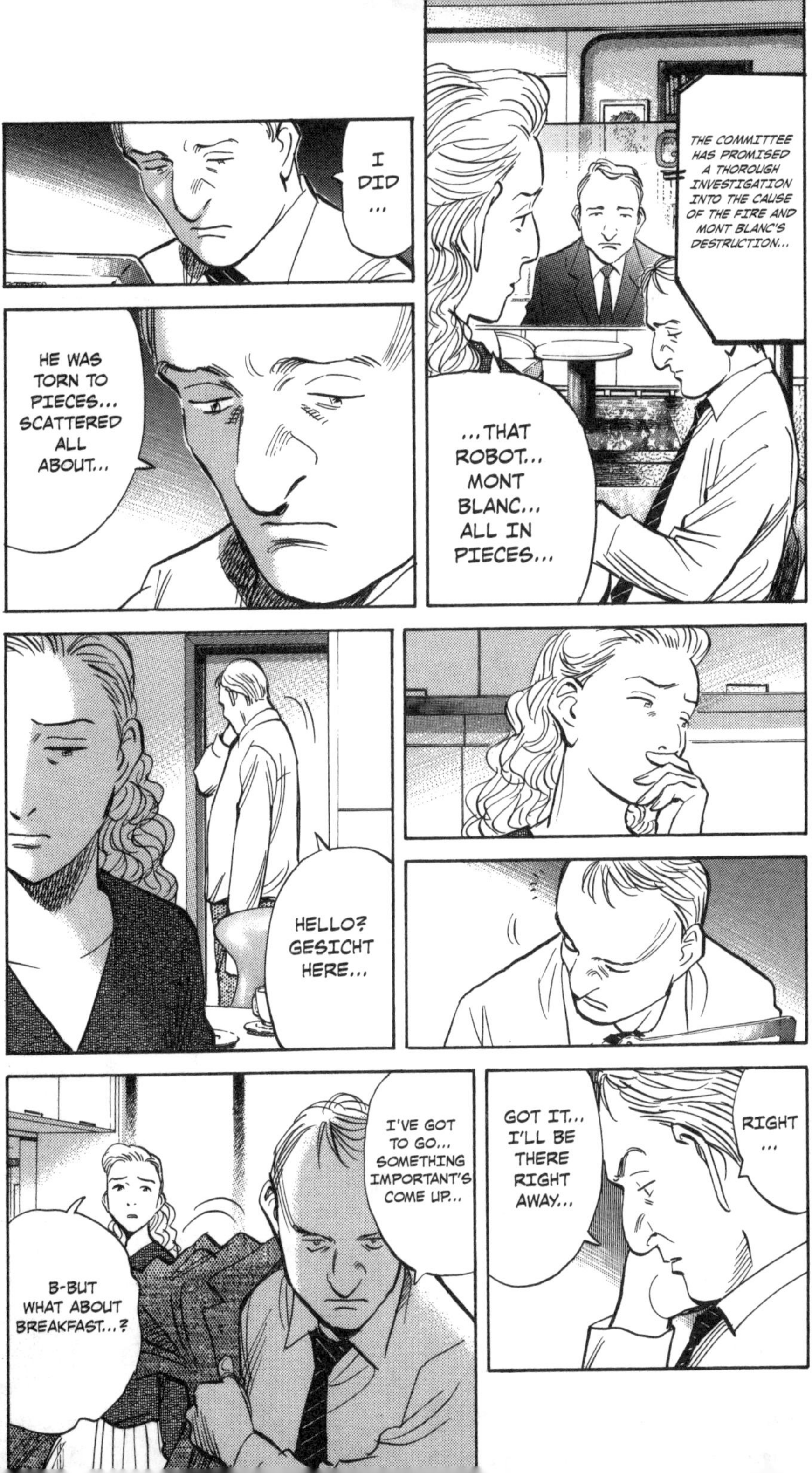
THE COMMITTEE HAS PROMISED A THOROUGH INVESTIGATION INTO THE CAUSE OF THE FIRE AND MONT BLANC'S DESTRUCTION...
...THAT ROBOT... MONT BLANC... ALL IN PIECES...
I DID...
HE WAS TORN TO PIECES... SCATTERED ALL ABOUT...
HELLO? GESICHT HERE...
RIGHT...
GOT IT... I'LL BE THERE RIGHT AWAY...
I'VE GOT TO GO... SOMETHING IMPORTANT'S COME UP...
B-BUT WHAT ABOUT BREAKFAST...?

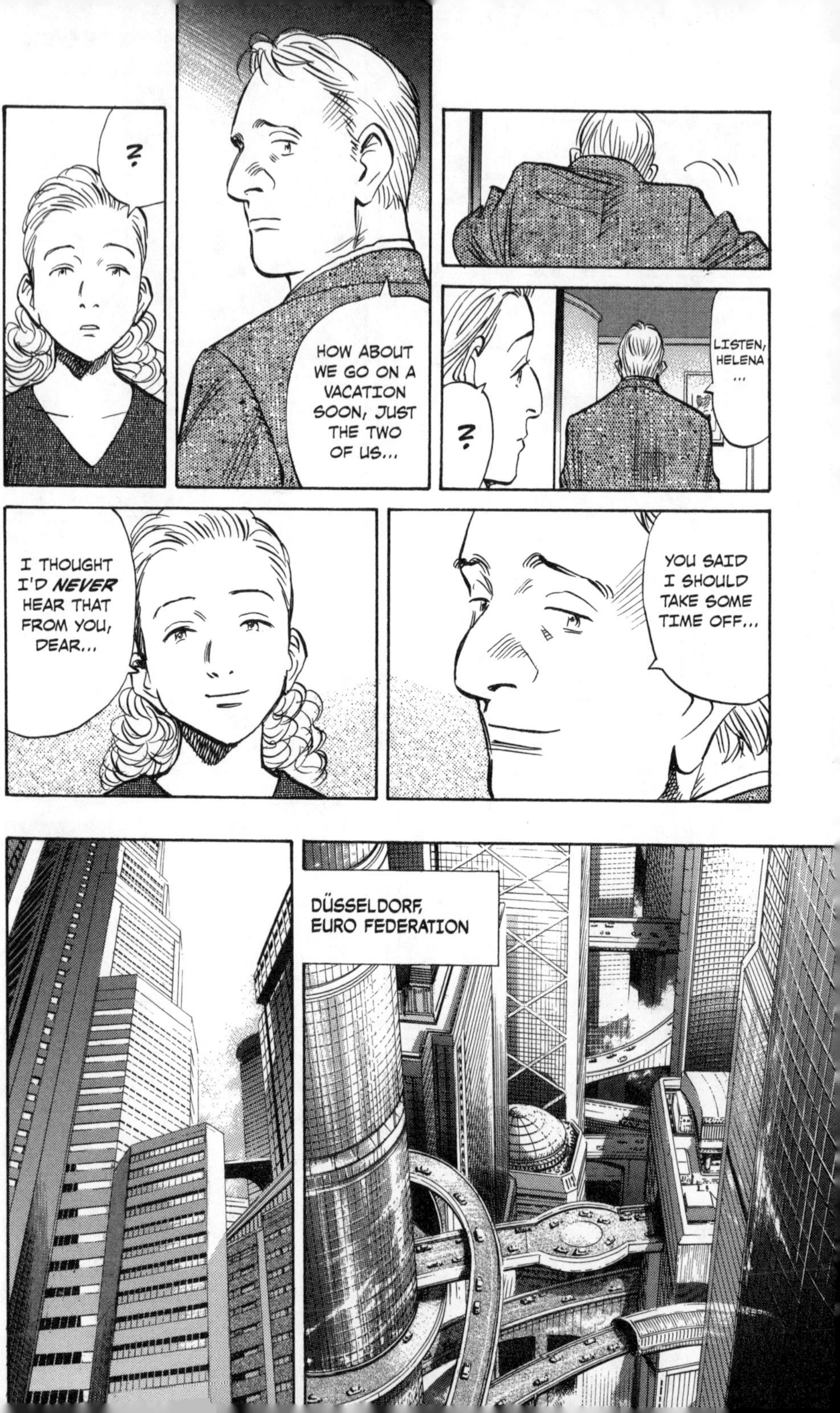
LISTEN, HELENA ...
?
HOW ABOUT WE GO ON A VACATION SOON, JUST THE TWO OF US...
?
YOU SAID I SHOULD TAKE SOME TIME OFF...
I THOUGHT I'D *NEVER* HEAR THAT FROM YOU, DEAR...
DÜSSELDORF, EURO FEDERATION

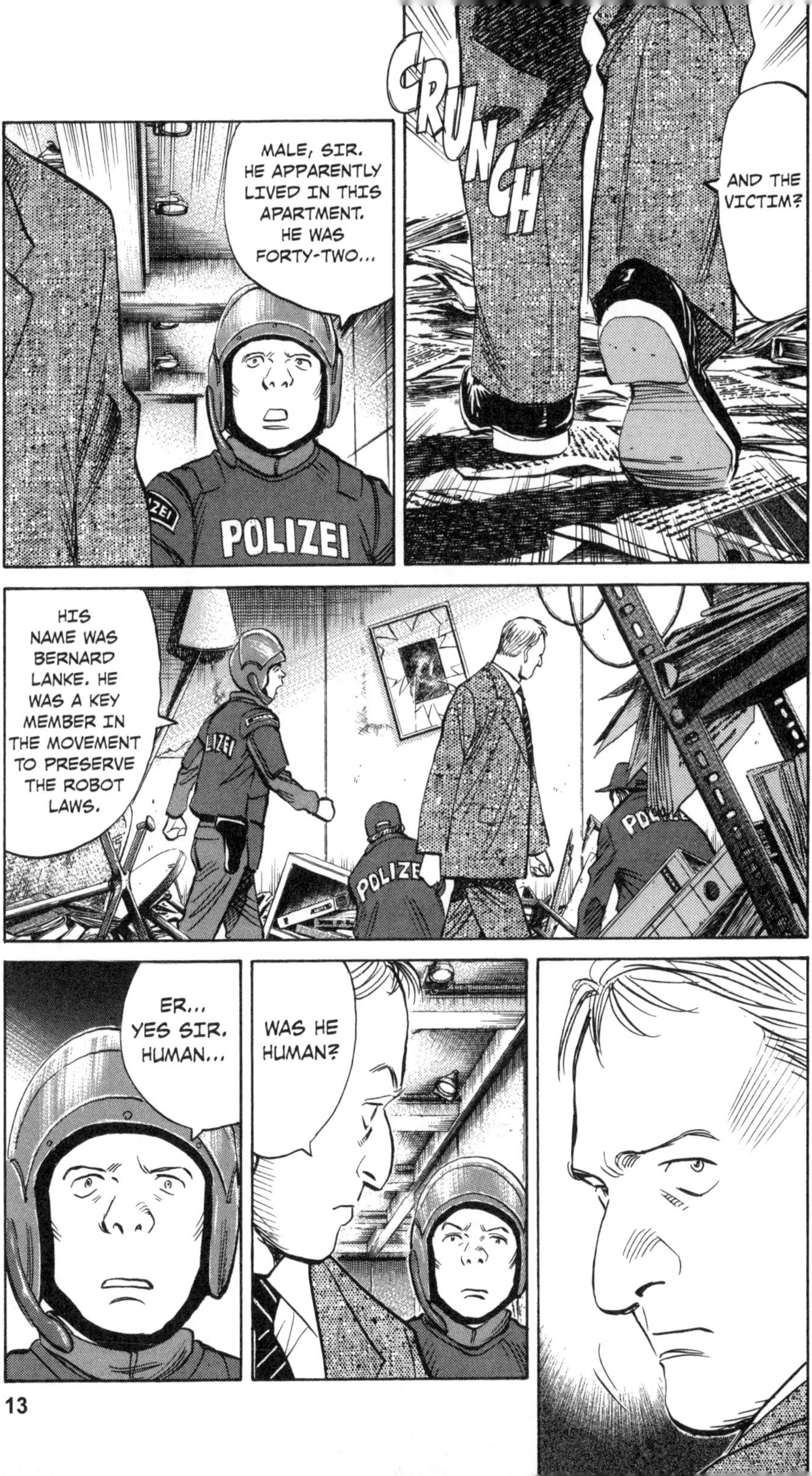
CRUNCH
AND THE VICTIM?
MALE, SIR. HE APPARENTLY LIVED IN THIS APARTMENT. HE WAS FORTY-TWO...
POLIZEI
HIS NAME WAS BERNARD LANKE. HE WAS A KEY MEMBER IN THE MOVEMENT TO PRESERVE THE ROBOT LAWS.
WAS HE HUMAN?
ER... YES SIR. HUMAN...

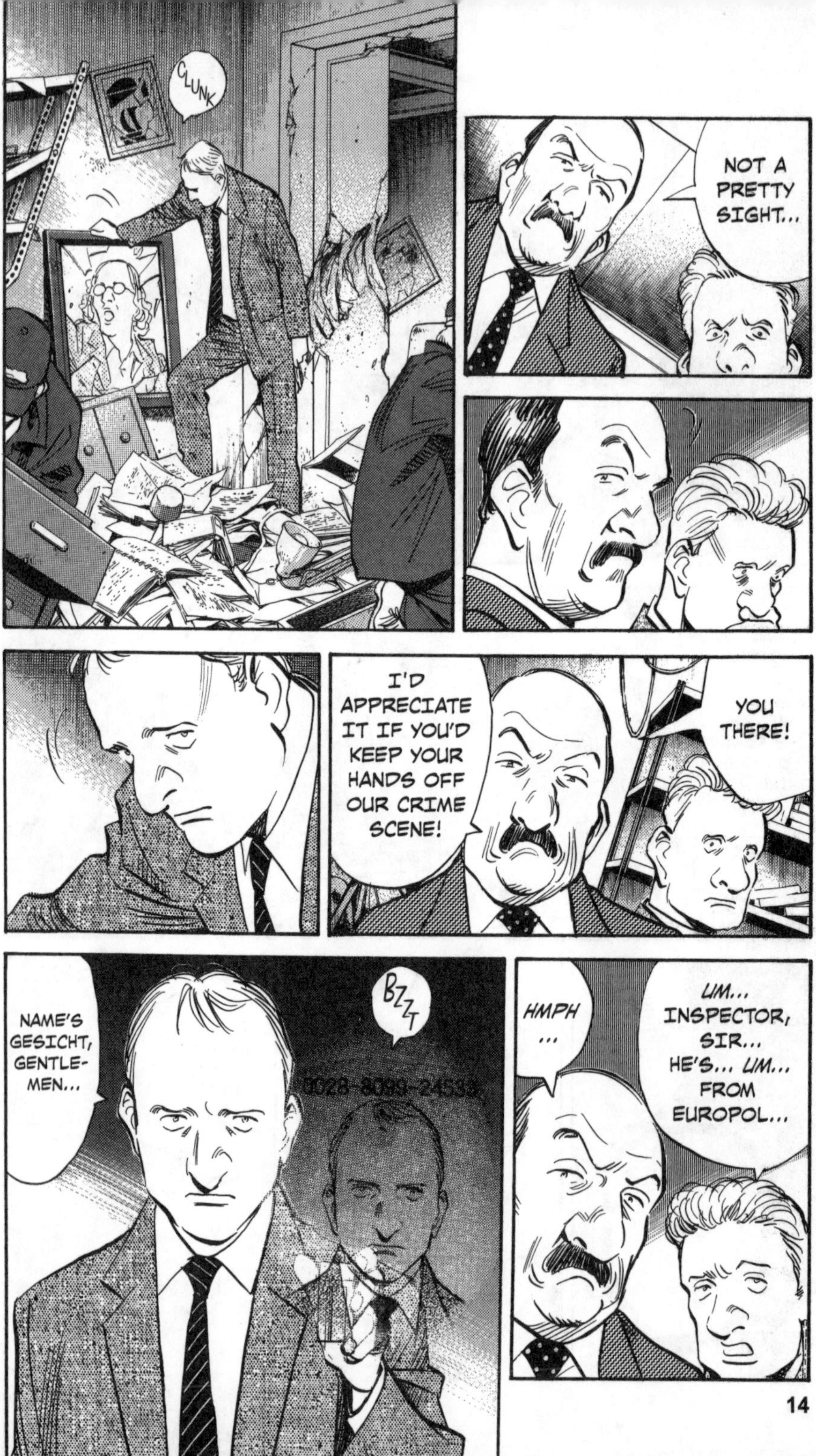
NOT A PRETTY SIGHT...
CLUNK
YOU THERE!
I'D APPRECIATE IT IF YOU'D KEEP YOUR HANDS OFF OUR CRIME SCENE!
UM... INSPECTOR, SIR... HE'S... UM... FROM EUROPOL...
HMPH ...
BZZZT
0028-8099-24533
NAME'S GESICHT, GENTLE-MEN...

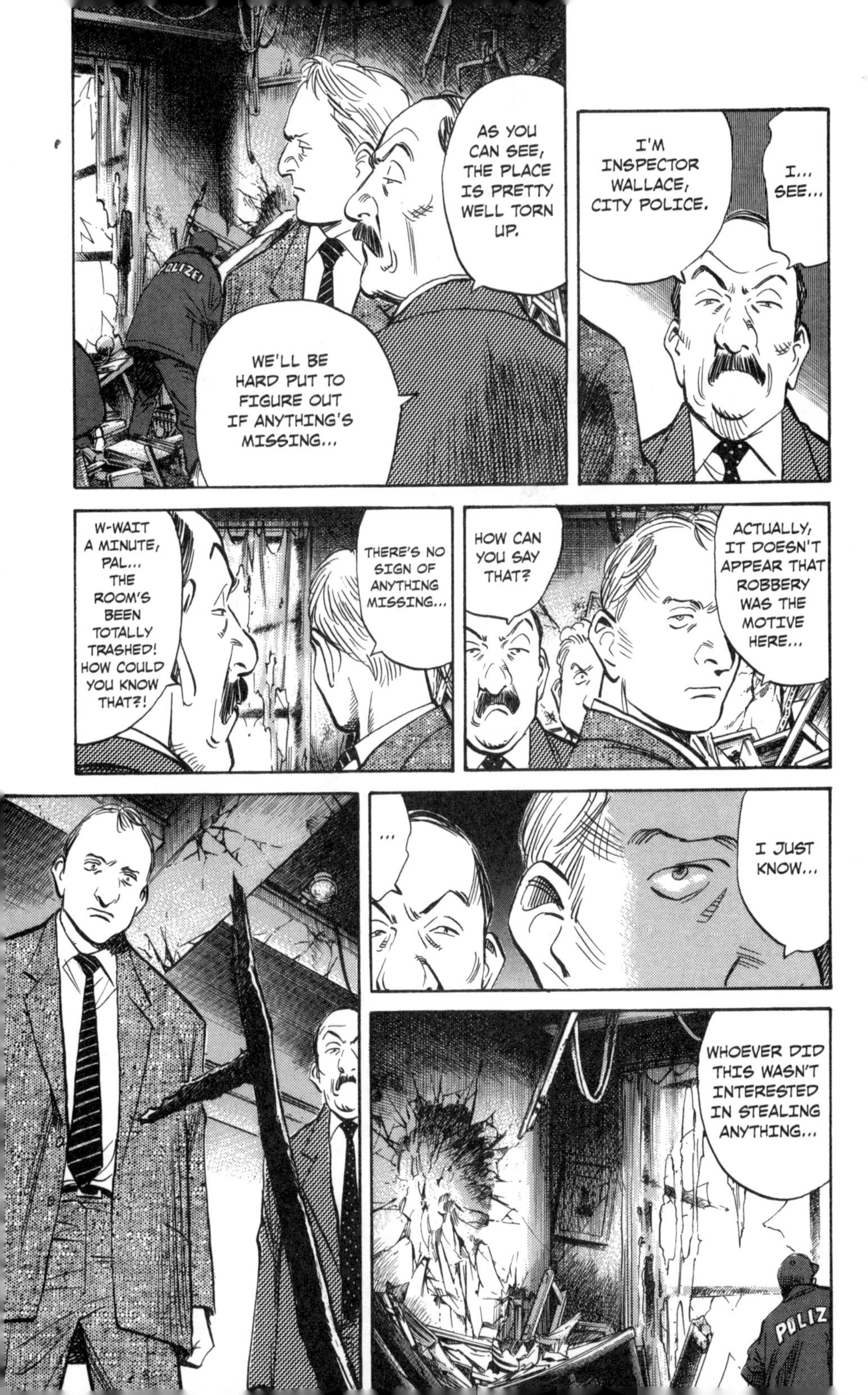
I... SEE...
I'M INSPECTOR WALLACE, CITY POLICE.
AS YOU CAN SEE, THE PLACE IS PRETTY WELL TORN UP.
WE'LL BE HARD PUT TO FIGURE OUT IF ANYTHING'S MISSING...
ACTUALLY, IT DOESN'T APPEAR THAT ROBBERY WAS THE MOTIVE HERE...
HOW CAN YOU SAY THAT?
THERE'S NO SIGN OF ANYTHING MISSING...
W-WAIT A MINUTE, PAL... THE ROOM'S BEEN TOTALLY TRASHED! HOW COULD YOU KNOW THAT?!
I JUST KNOW...
...
WHOEVER DID THIS WASN'T INTERESTED IN STEALING ANYTHING...
POLIZ

WHAT DO YOU MAKE OF THESE ITEMS SHOVED INTO THE VICTIM'S HEAD? KIND OF STAGED TO LOOK LIKE HORNS...

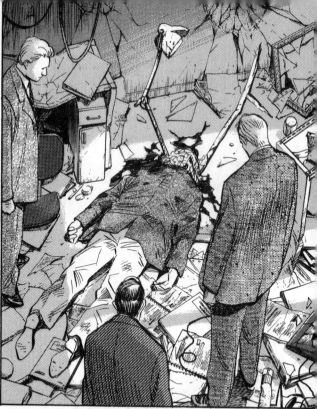

...

WHAT?!!

HELLO? YEAH, IT'S ME...

RING RING ♪

!!

INSPECTOR... SOMEONE'S BROKEN THROUGH ONE OF OUR CHECKPOINTS!

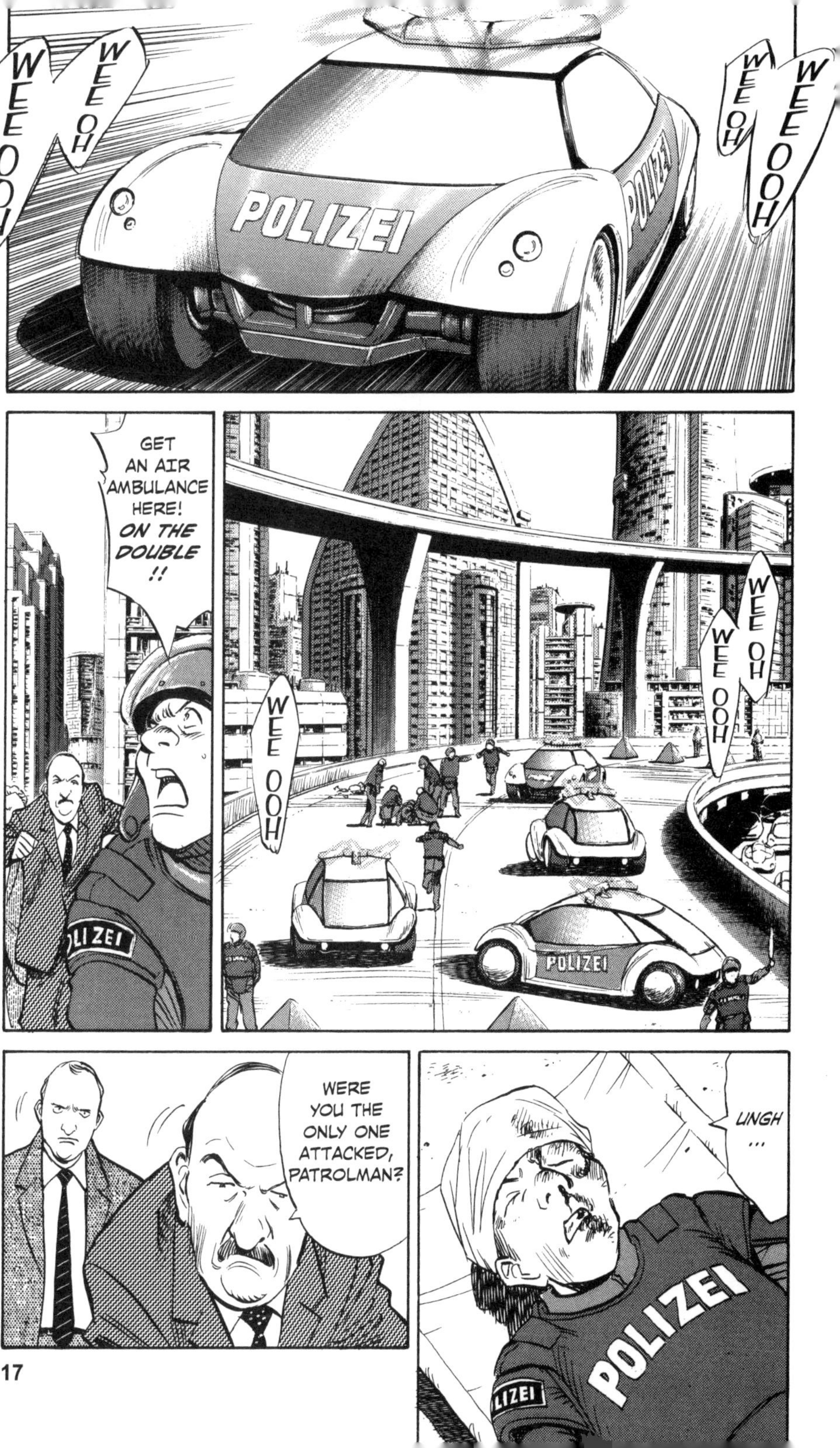
WEE OOOH
WEE OH
POLIZEI
POLIZEI
WEE OH
WEE OOOH
WEE OH
WEE OOH
WEE OOOH
POLIZEI
GET AN AIR AMBULANCE HERE! *ON THE DOUBLE!!*
POLIZEI
UNGH ...
POLIZEI
POLIZEI
WERE YOU THE ONLY ONE ATTACKED, PATROLMAN?

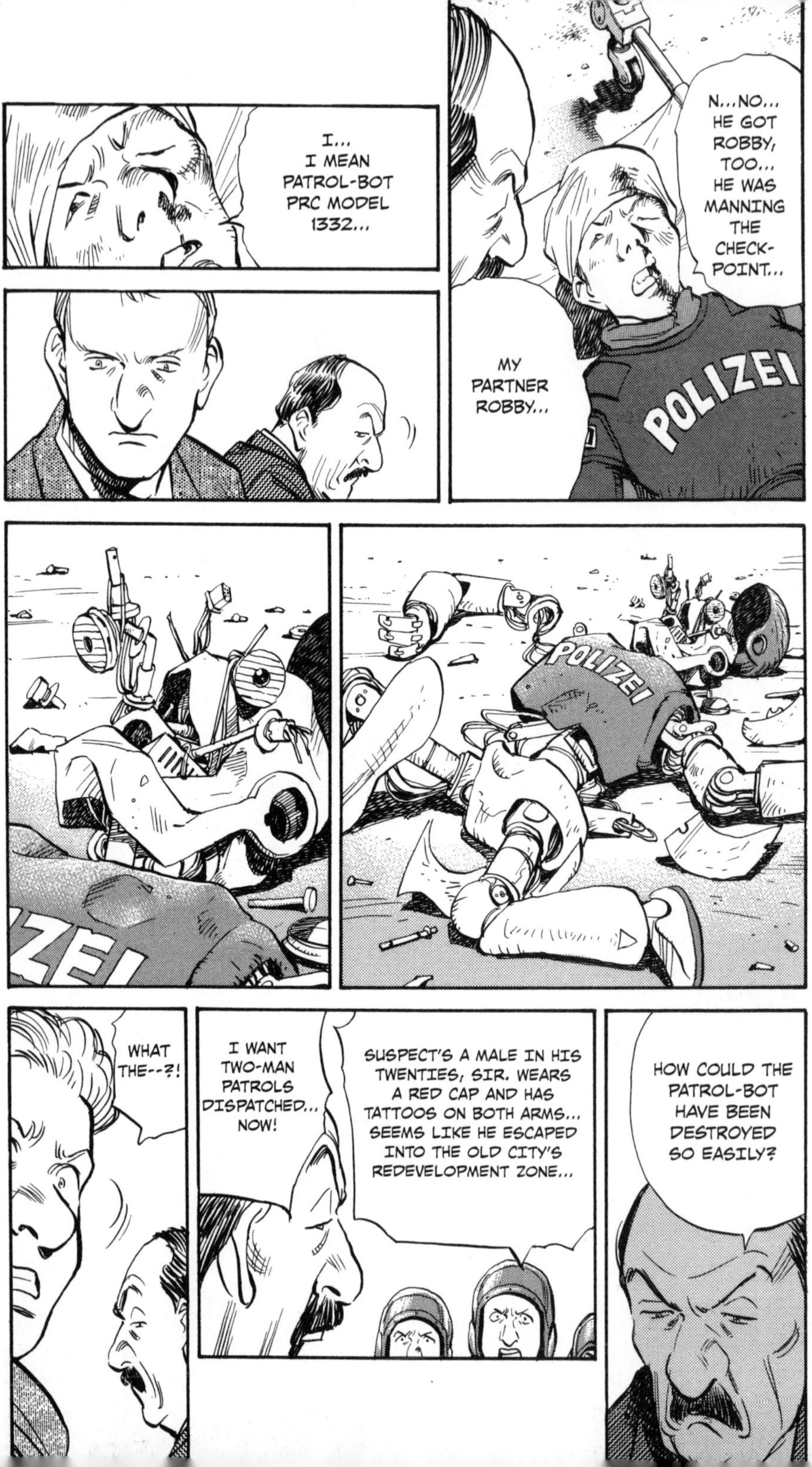
N...NO... HE GOT ROBBY, TOO... HE WAS MANNING THE CHECK-POINT...
MY PARTNER ROBBY...
POLIZEI
I... I MEAN PATROL-BOT PRC MODEL 1332...
POLIZEI
ZEI
HOW COULD THE PATROL-BOT HAVE BEEN DESTROYED SO EASILY?
SUSPECT'S A MALE IN HIS TWENTIES, SIR. WEARS A RED CAP AND HAS TATTOOS ON BOTH ARMS... SEEMS LIKE HE ESCAPED INTO THE OLD CITY'S REDEVELOPMENT ZONE...
I WANT TWO-MAN PATROLS DISPATCHED... NOW!
WHAT THE--?!

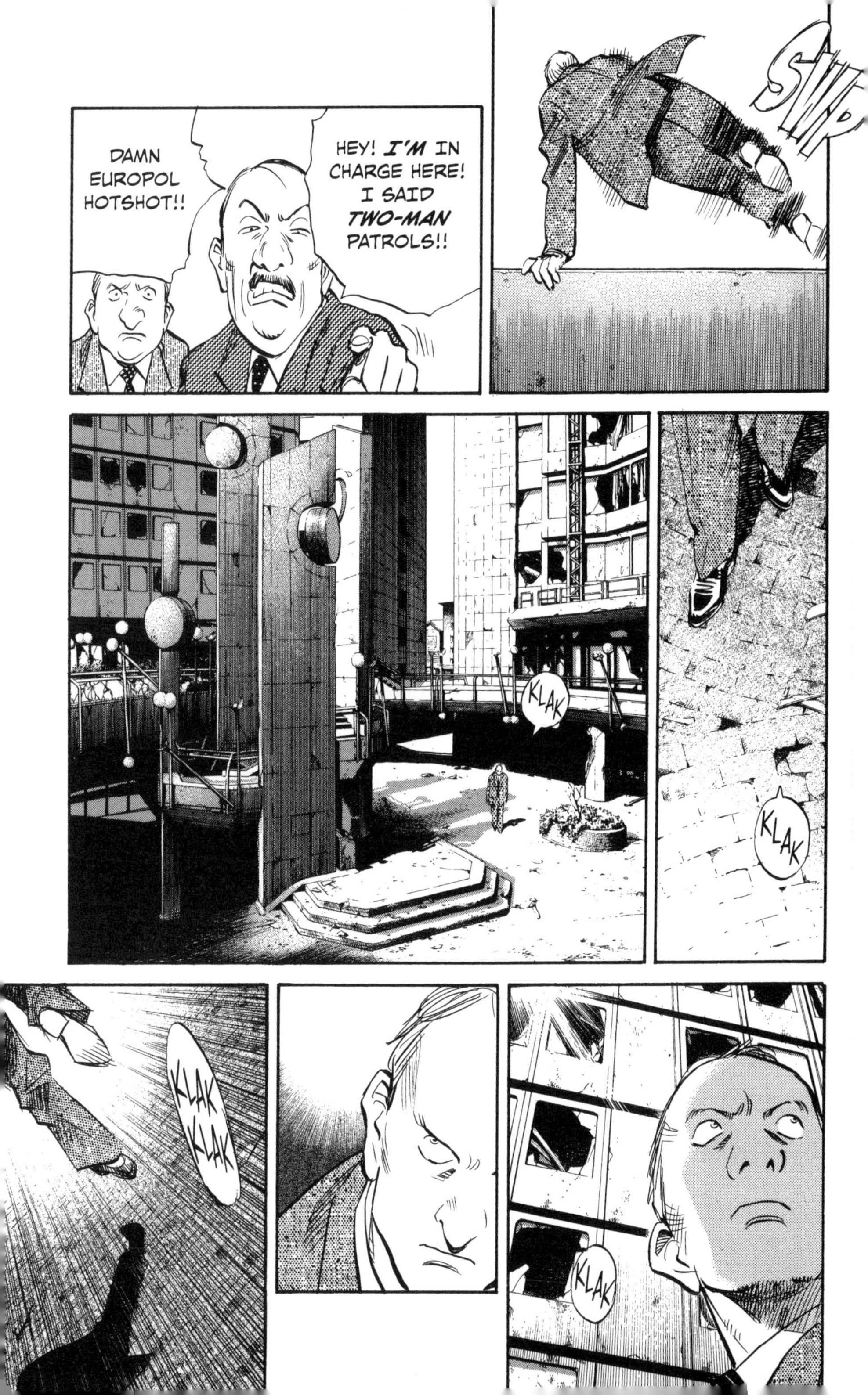
HEY! *I'M* IN CHARGE HERE! I SAID ***TWO-MAN*** PATROLS!!
DAMN EUROPOL HOTSHOT!!
KLAK
KLAK
KLAK
KLAK KLAK

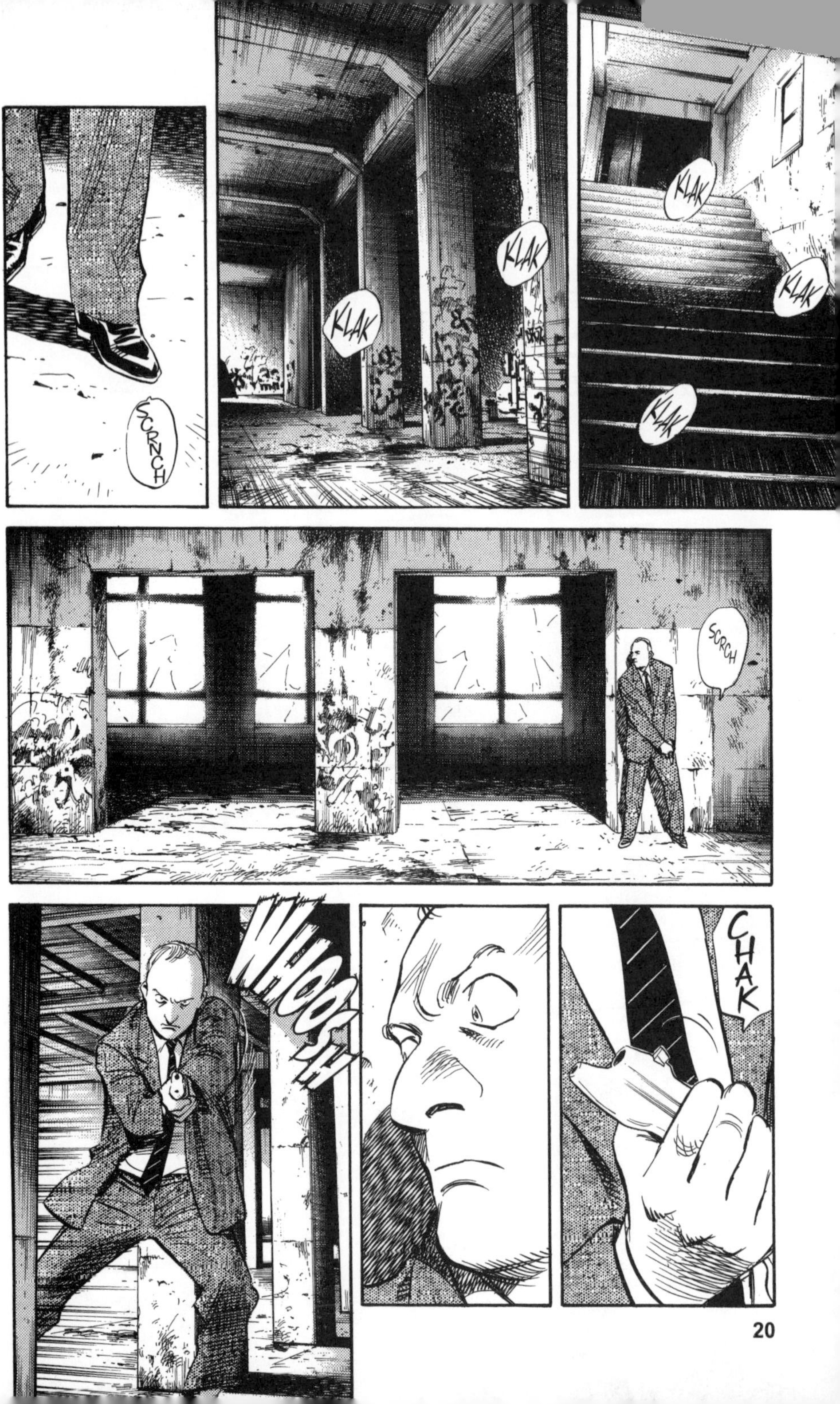
KLAK
KLAK
KLAK
KLAK
KLAK
SCRNCH
SCRCH
CHAK
WHOOSH

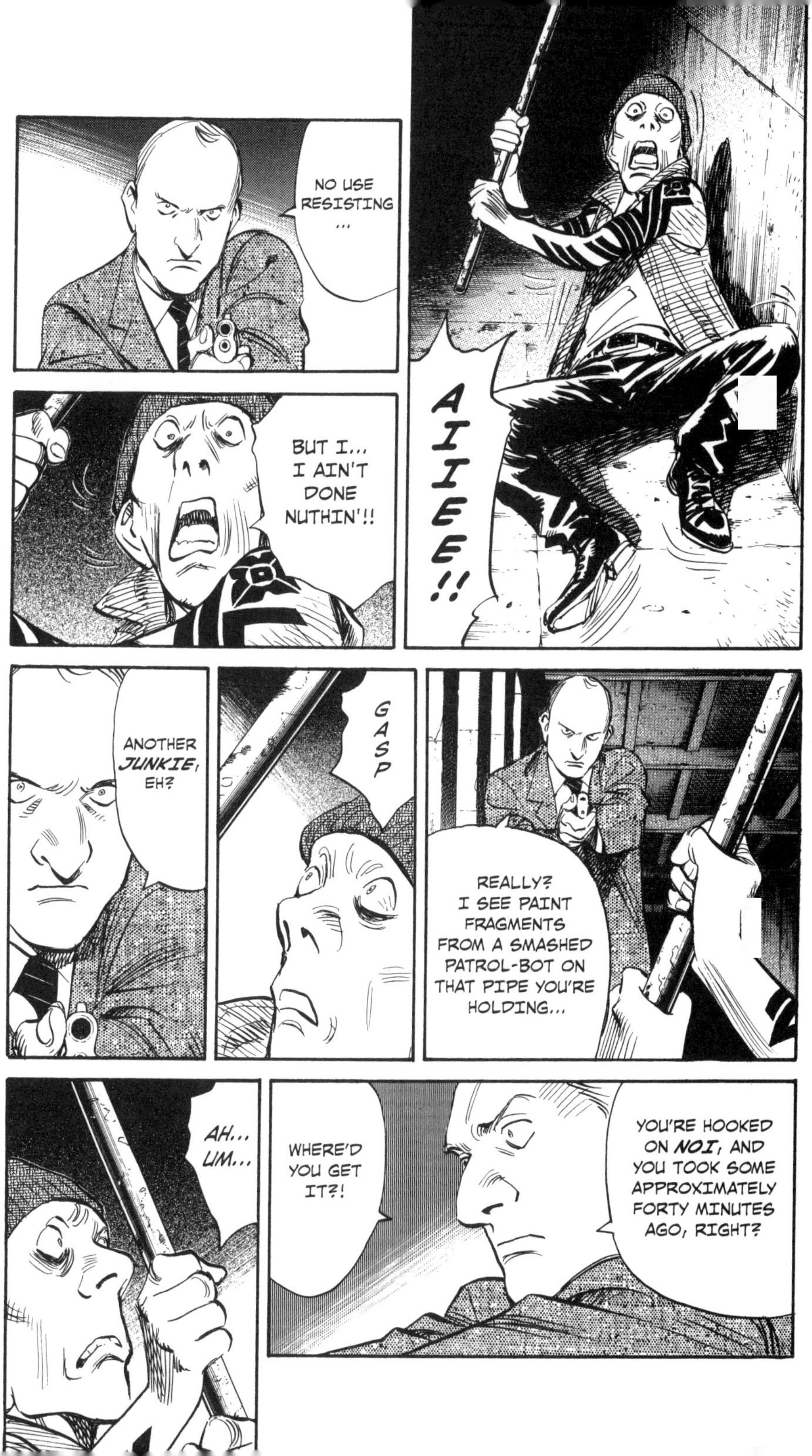
AIIEEE!!
NO USE RESISTING...
BUT I... I AIN'T DONE NUTHIN'!!
REALLY? I SEE PAINT FRAGMENTS FROM A SMASHED PATROL-BOT ON THAT PIPE YOU'RE HOLDING...
GASP
ANOTHER *JUNKIE*, EH?
YOU'RE HOOKED ON *NOI*, AND YOU TOOK SOME APPROXIMATELY FORTY MINUTES AGO, RIGHT?
WHERE'D YOU GET IT?!
AH... UM...

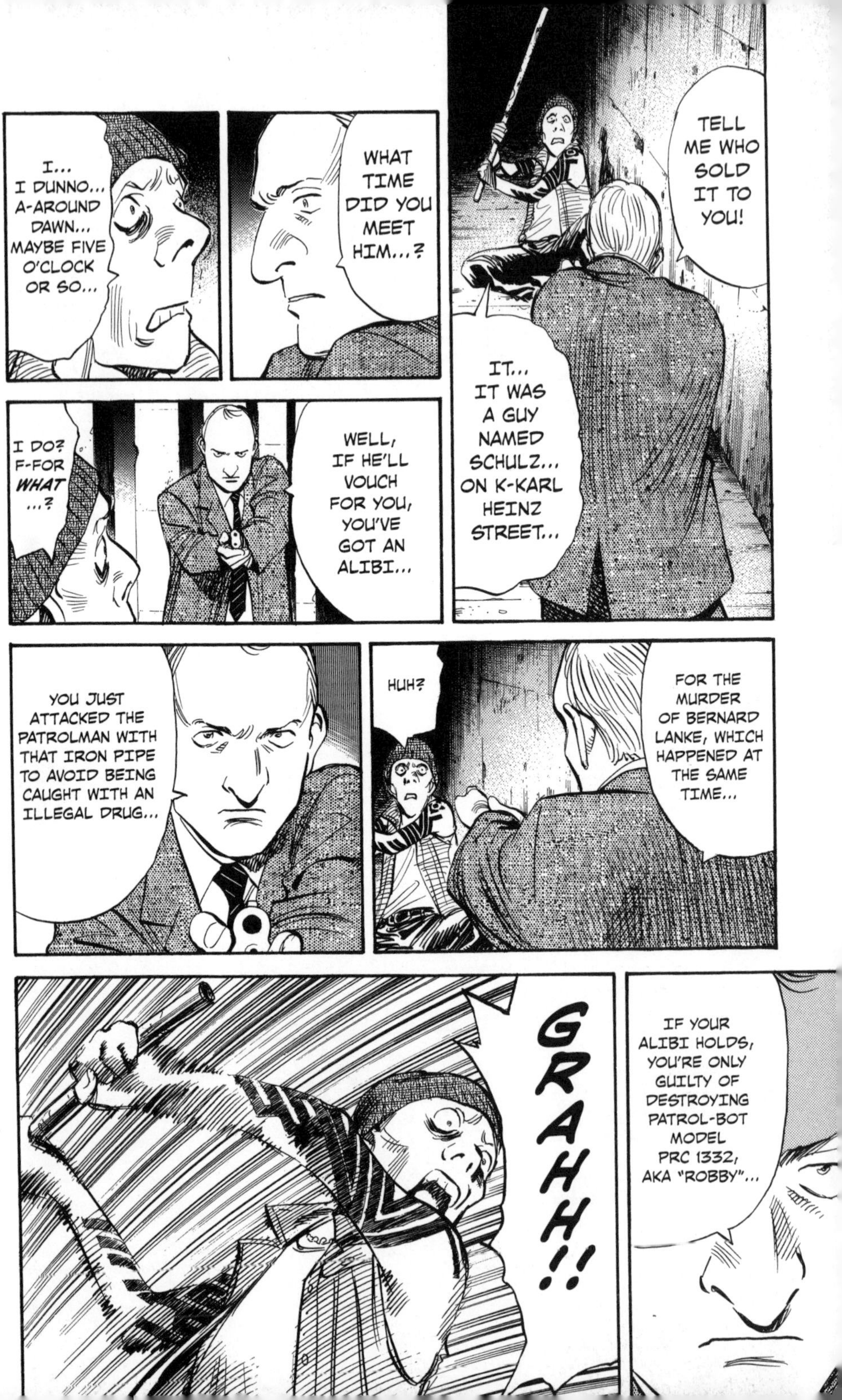
TELL ME WHO SOLD IT TO YOU!
IT... IT WAS A GUY NAMED SCHULZ... ON K-KARL HEINZ STREET...
WHAT TIME DID YOU MEET HIM...?
I... I DUNNO... A-AROUND DAWN... MAYBE FIVE O'CLOCK OR SO...
WELL, IF HE'LL VOUCH FOR YOU, YOU'VE GOT AN ALIBI...
I DO? F-FOR *WHAT* ...?
FOR THE MURDER OF BERNARD LANKE, WHICH HAPPENED AT THE SAME TIME...
HUH?
YOU JUST ATTACKED THE PATROLMAN WITH THAT IRON PIPE TO AVOID BEING CAUGHT WITH AN ILLEGAL DRUG...
IF YOUR ALIBI HOLDS, YOU'RE ONLY GUILTY OF DESTROYING PATROL-BOT MODEL PRC 1332, AKA "ROBBY"...
GRAHH!!

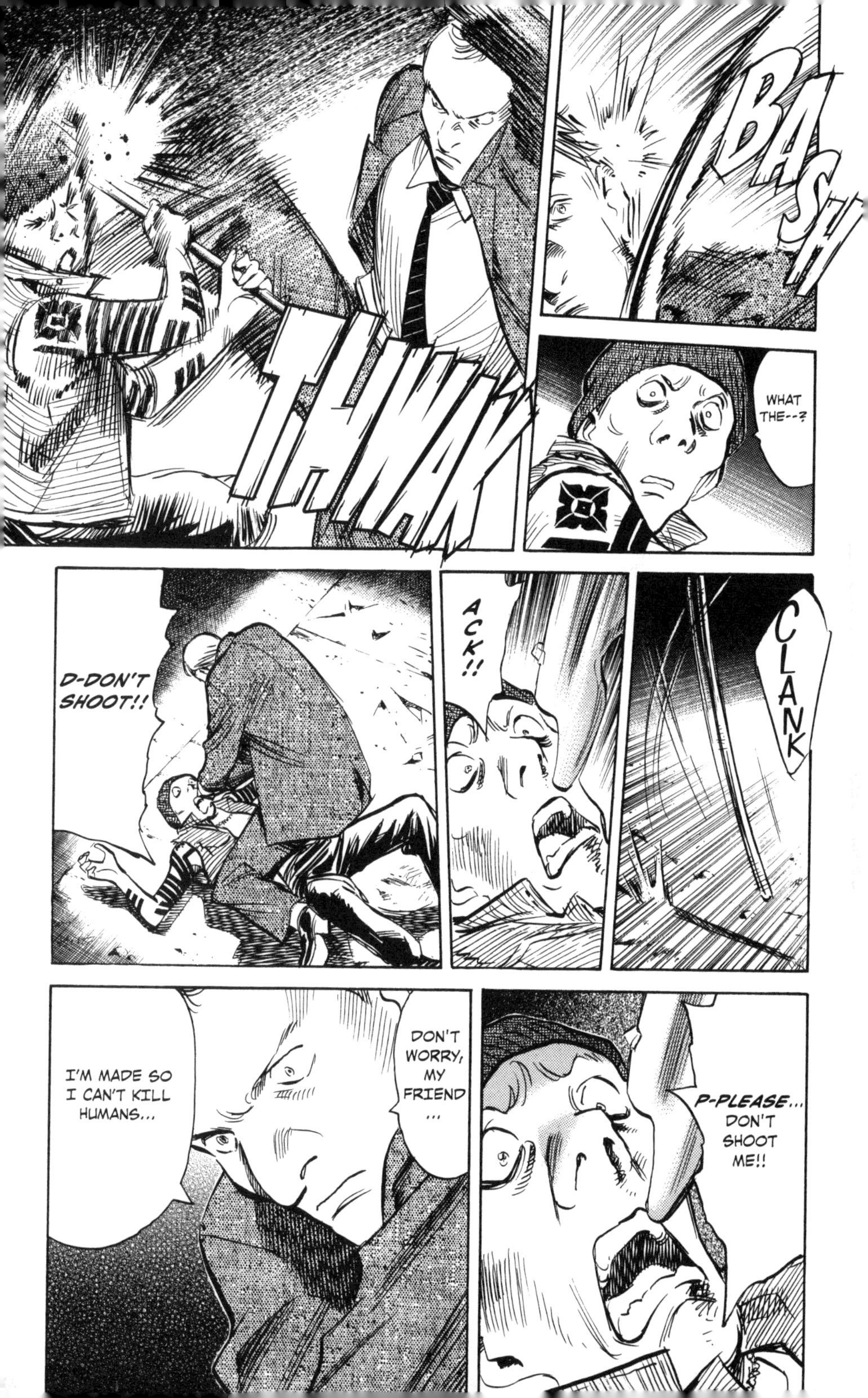
BASH
WHAT THE--?
THWAK
CLANK
ACK!!
D-DON'T SHOOT!!
P-PLEASE... DON'T SHOOT ME!!
DON'T WORRY, MY FRIEND...
I'M MADE SO I CAN'T KILL HUMANS...

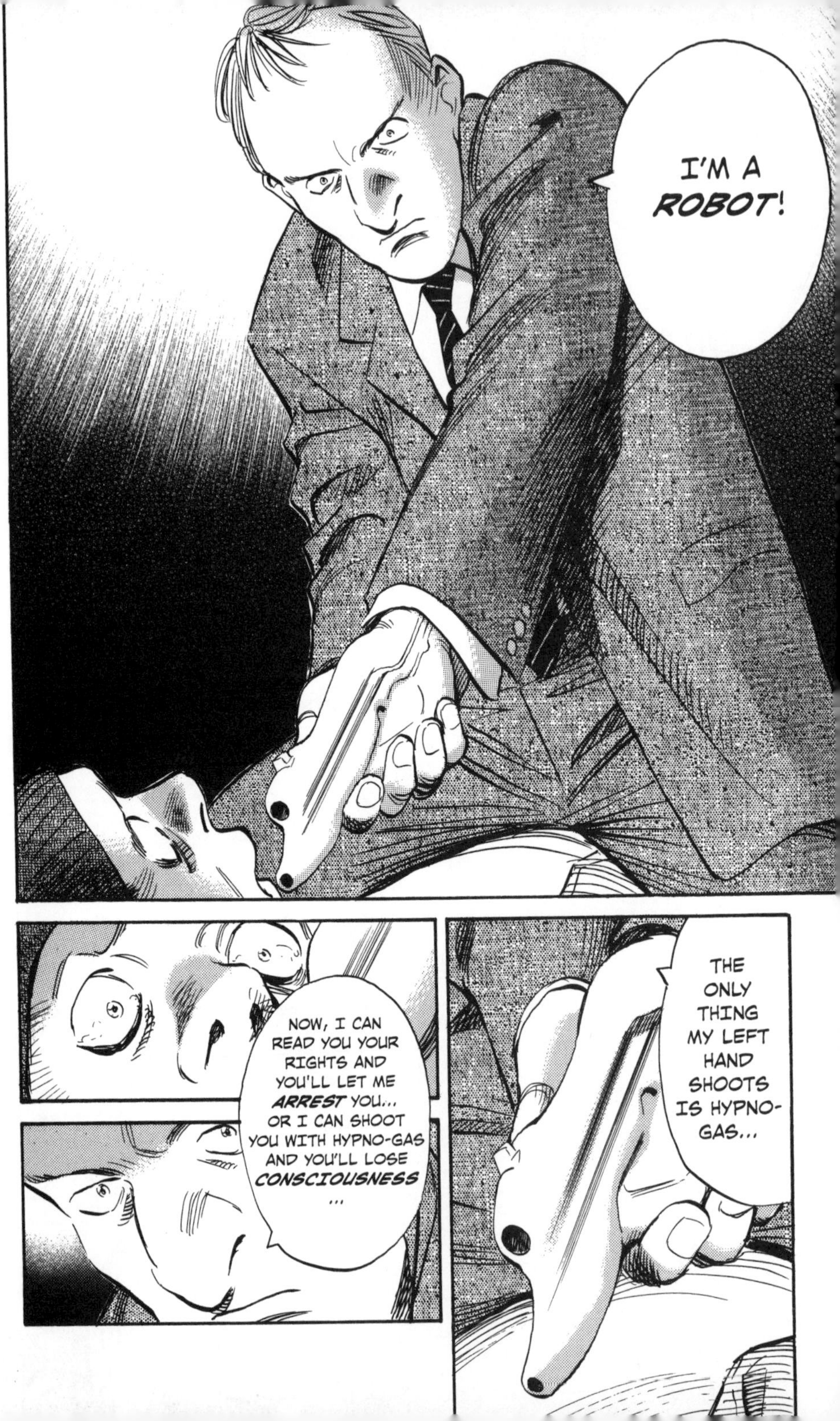
I'M A *ROBOT*!
THE ONLY THING MY LEFT HAND SHOOTS IS HYPNO-GAS...
NOW, I CAN READ YOU YOUR RIGHTS AND YOU'LL LET ME *ARREST* YOU... OR I CAN SHOOT YOU WITH HYPNO-GAS AND YOU'LL LOSE *CONSCIOUSNESS*...

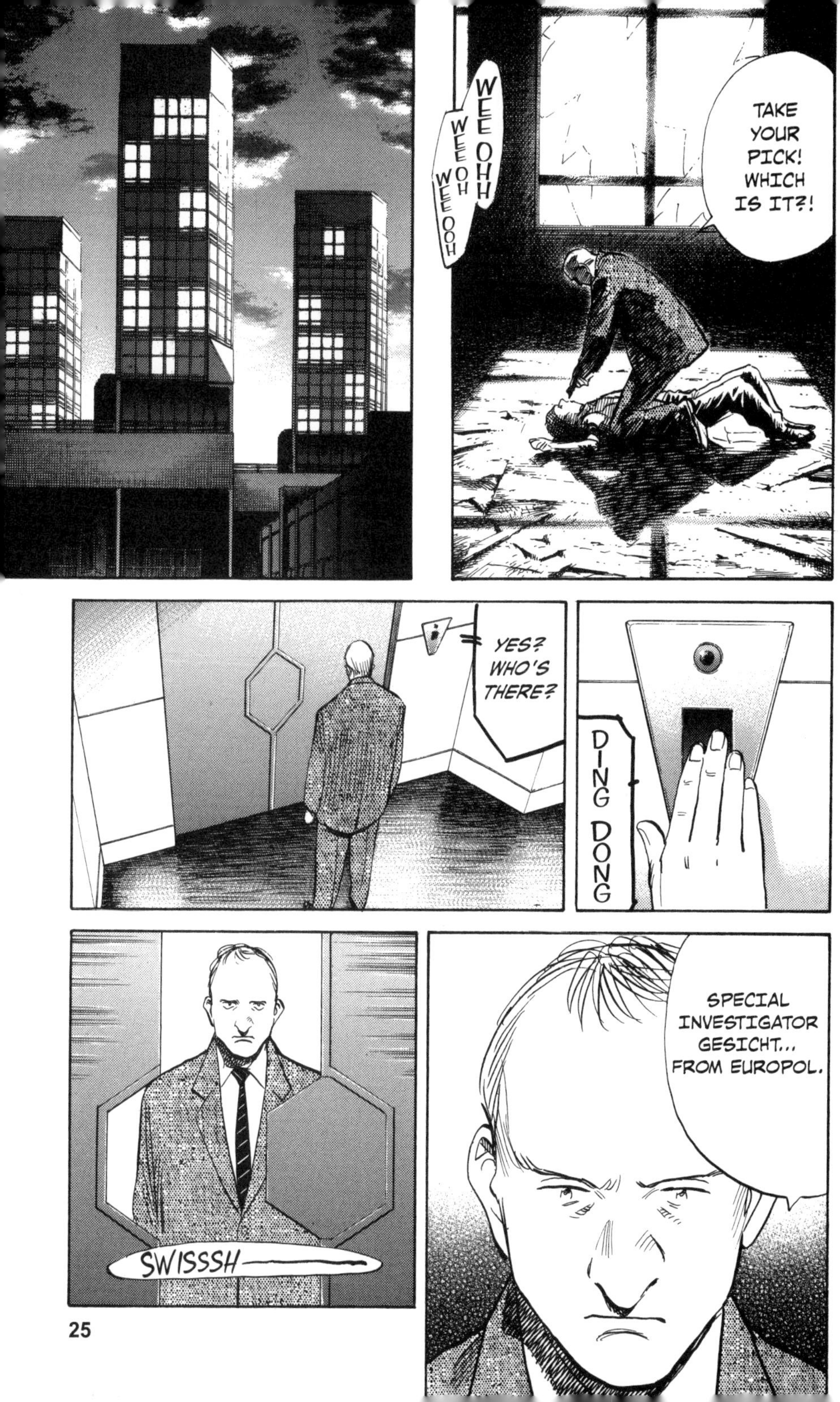
TAKE YOUR PICK! WHICH IS IT?!
WEE OHH
WEE OH
WEE OOH
DING DONG
YES? WHO'S THERE?
SPECIAL INVESTIGATOR GESICHT... FROM EUROPOL.
SWISSSH

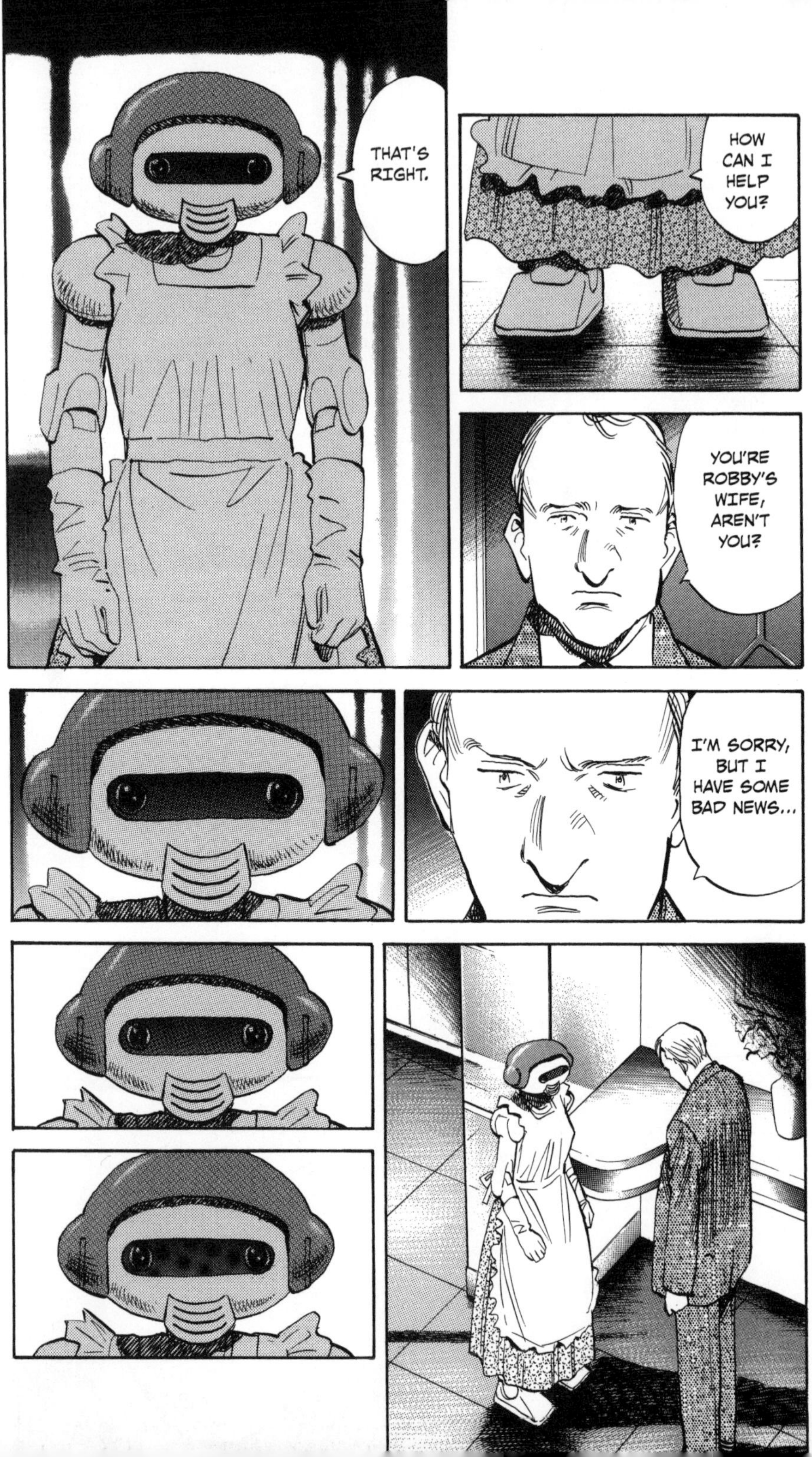
HOW CAN I HELP YOU?
YOU'RE ROBBY'S WIFE, AREN'T YOU?
THAT'S RIGHT.
I'M SORRY, BUT I HAVE SOME BAD NEWS...

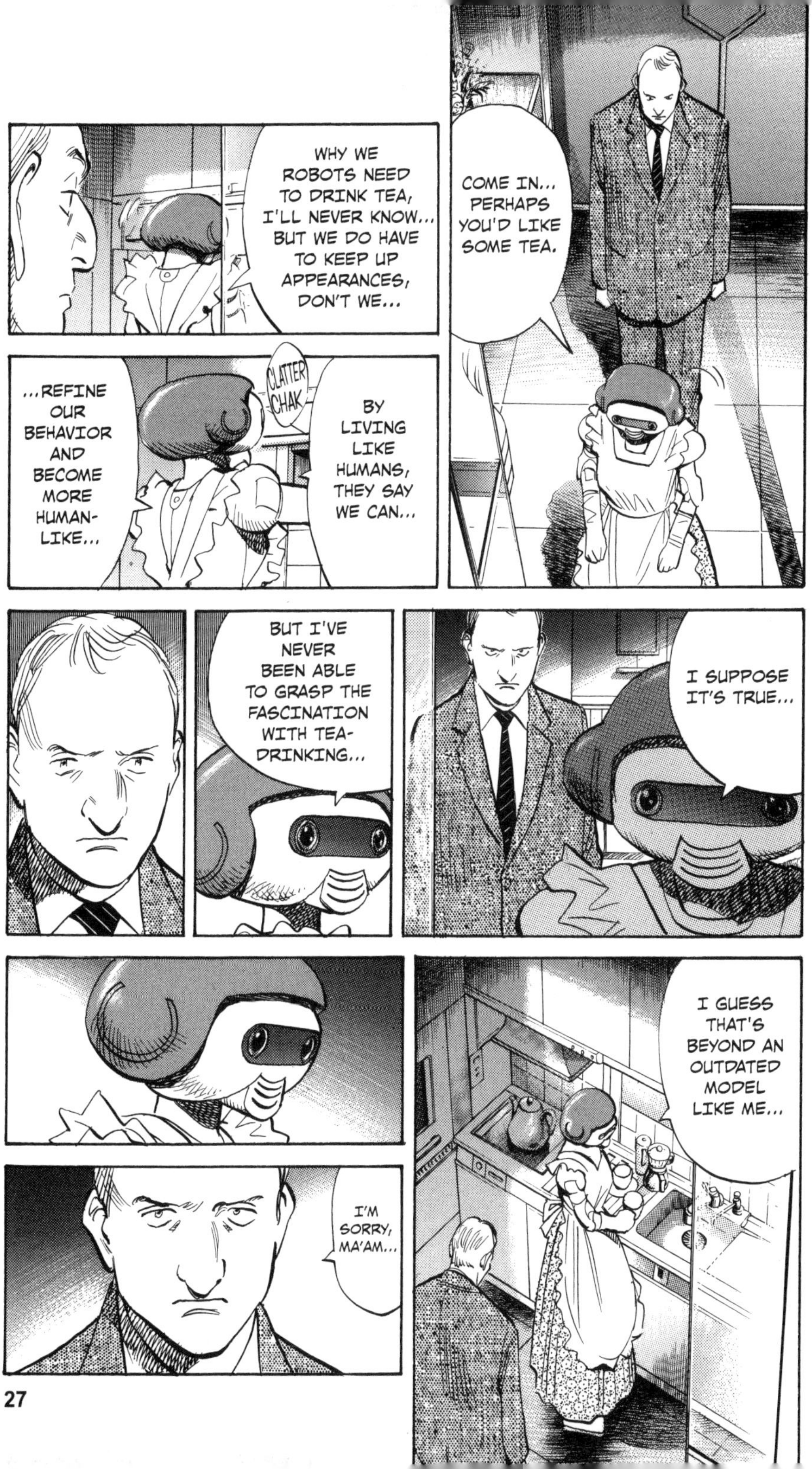
COME IN... PERHAPS YOU'D LIKE SOME TEA.
WHY WE ROBOTS NEED TO DRINK TEA, I'LL NEVER KNOW... BUT WE DO HAVE TO KEEP UP APPEARANCES, DON'T WE...
BY LIVING LIKE HUMANS, THEY SAY WE CAN...
CLATTER CHAK
...REFINE OUR BEHAVIOR AND BECOME MORE HUMAN-LIKE...
I SUPPOSE IT'S TRUE...
BUT I'VE NEVER BEEN ABLE TO GRASP THE FASCINATION WITH TEA-DRINKING...
I GUESS THAT'S BEYOND AN OUTDATED MODEL LIKE ME...
I'M SORRY, MA'AM...

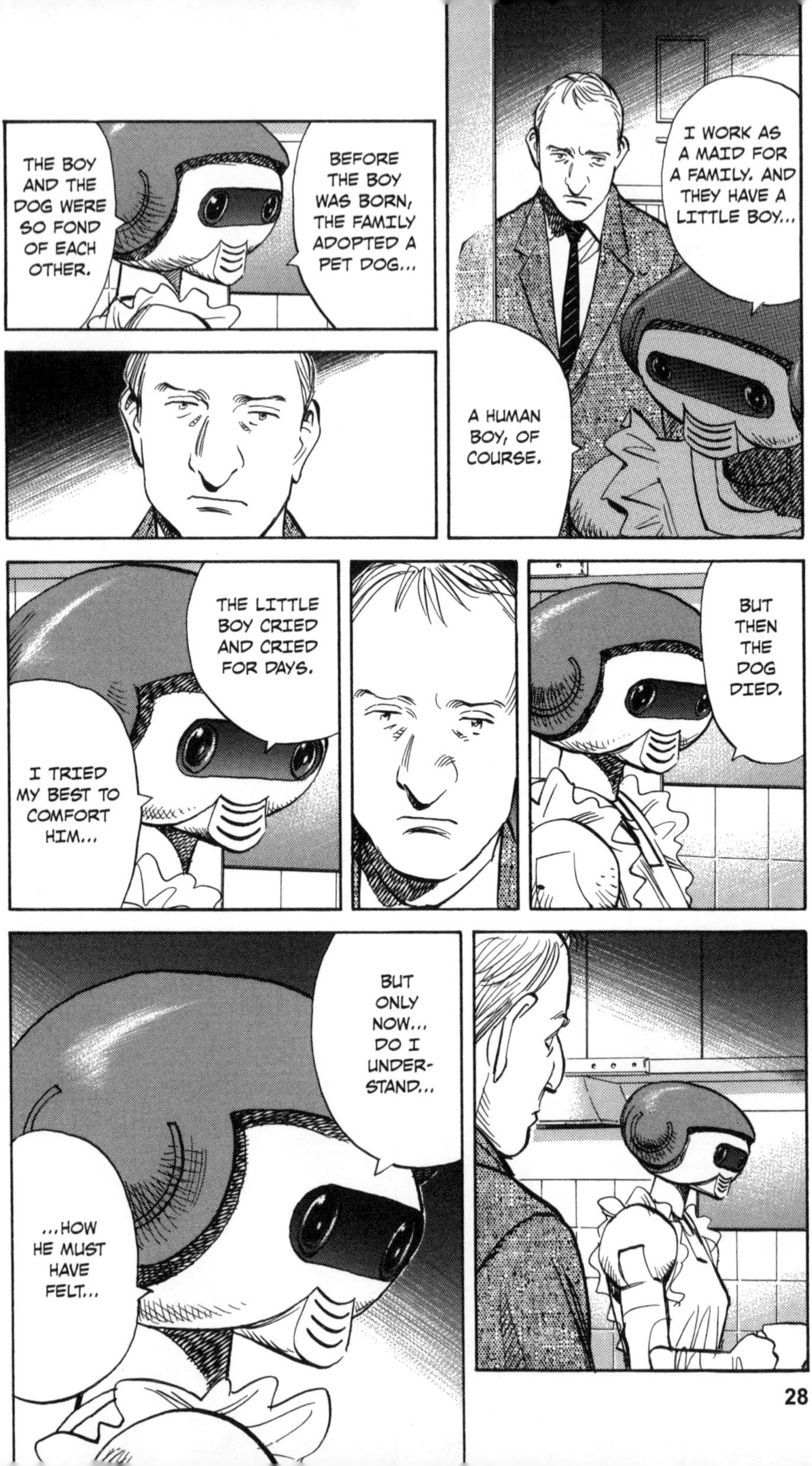
I WORK AS A MAID FOR A FAMILY. AND THEY HAVE A LITTLE BOY...
A HUMAN BOY, OF COURSE.
BEFORE THE BOY WAS BORN, THE FAMILY ADOPTED A PET DOG...
THE BOY AND THE DOG WERE SO FOND OF EACH OTHER.
BUT THEN THE DOG DIED.
THE LITTLE BOY CRIED AND CRIED FOR DAYS.
I TRIED MY BEST TO COMFORT HIM...
BUT ONLY NOW... DO I UNDER-STAND...
...HOW HE MUST HAVE FELT...

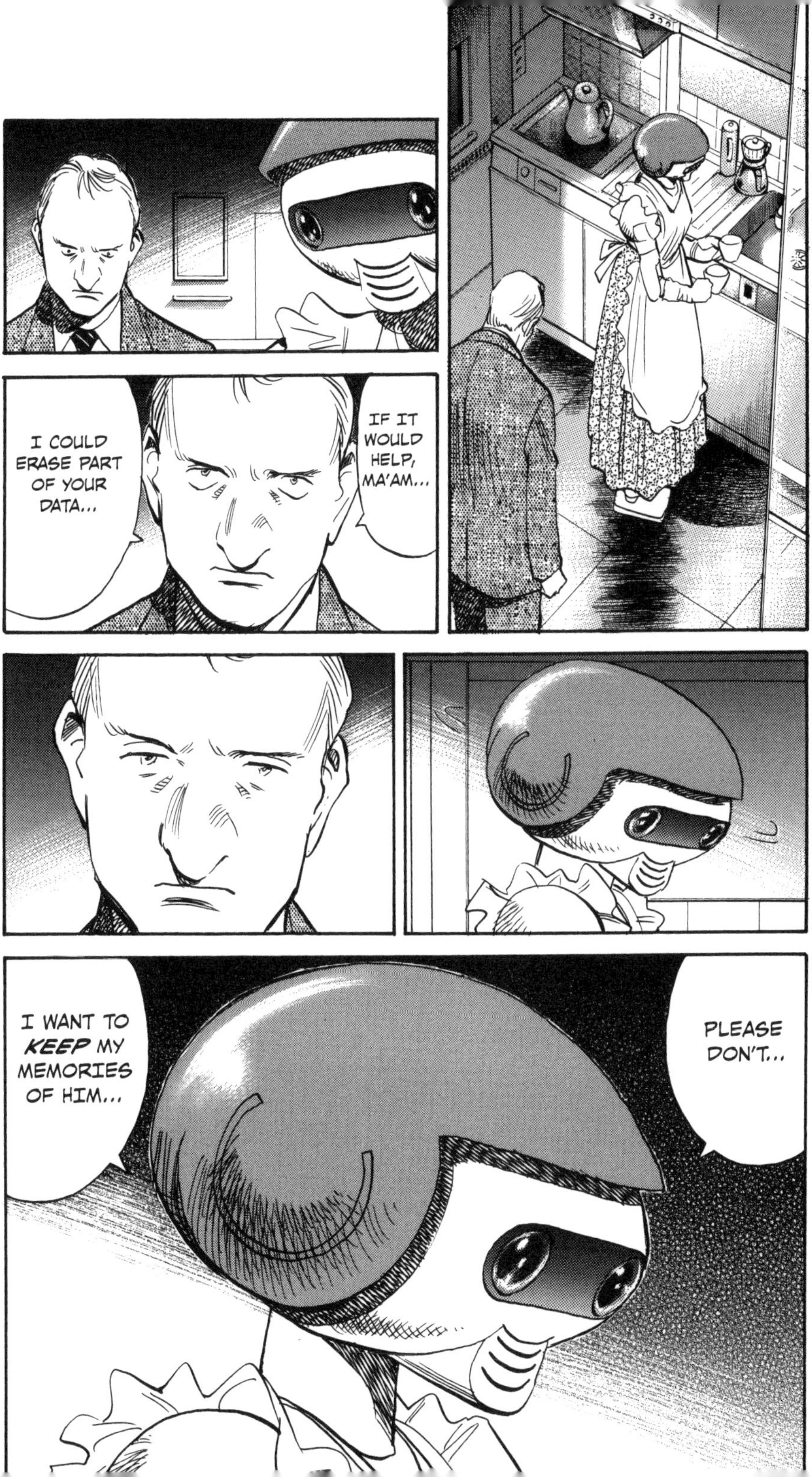
IF IT WOULD HELP, MA'AM...
I COULD ERASE PART OF YOUR DATA...
PLEASE DON'T...
I WANT TO ***KEEP*** MY MEMORIES OF HIM...

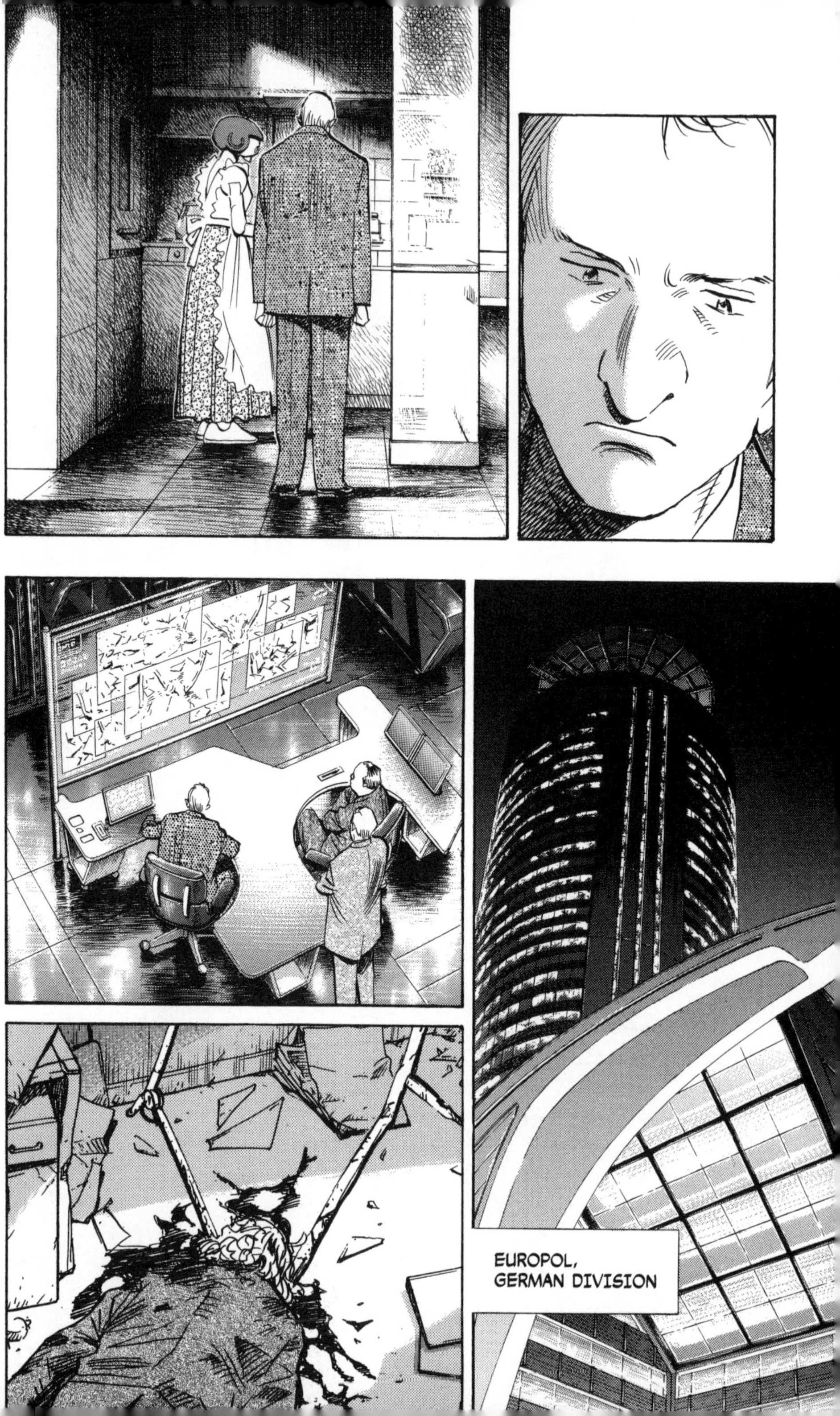
EUROPOL,
GERMAN DIVISION

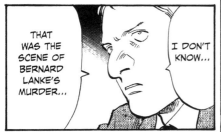

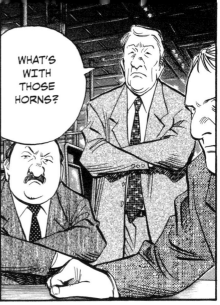

WHAT'S WITH THOSE HORNS?
I DON'T KNOW...
THAT WAS THE SCENE OF BERNARD LANKE'S MURDER...
NOW LOOK AT THIS ...
BEEEP
TAT TAT
VWP
WHAT'S THAT...?
THIS IS WHERE *MONT BLANC*-- THE ROBOT WHO WORKED FOR THE SWISS FORESTRY SERVICE-- WAS DESTROYED...

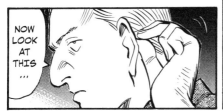

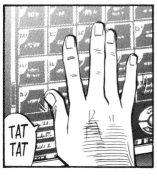

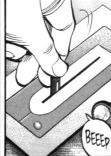

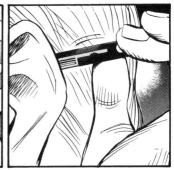

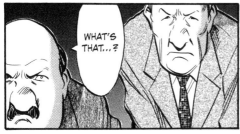

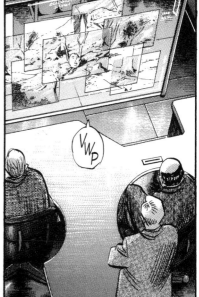

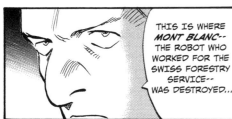

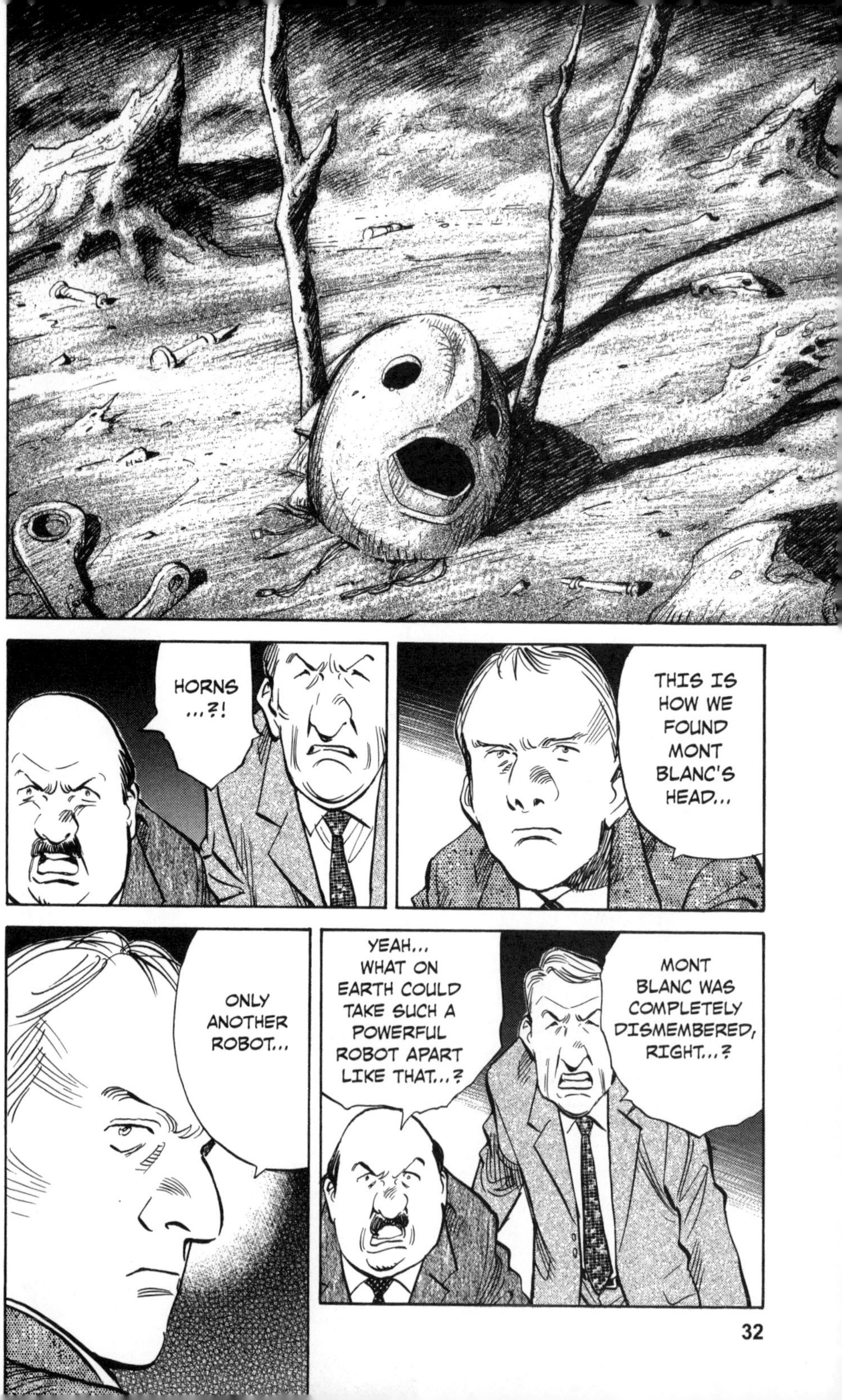
THIS IS HOW WE FOUND MONT BLANC'S HEAD...
HORNS ...?!
MONT BLANC WAS COMPLETELY DISMEMBERED, RIGHT...?
YEAH... WHAT ON EARTH COULD TAKE SUCH A POWERFUL ROBOT APART LIKE THAT...?
ONLY ANOTHER ROBOT...

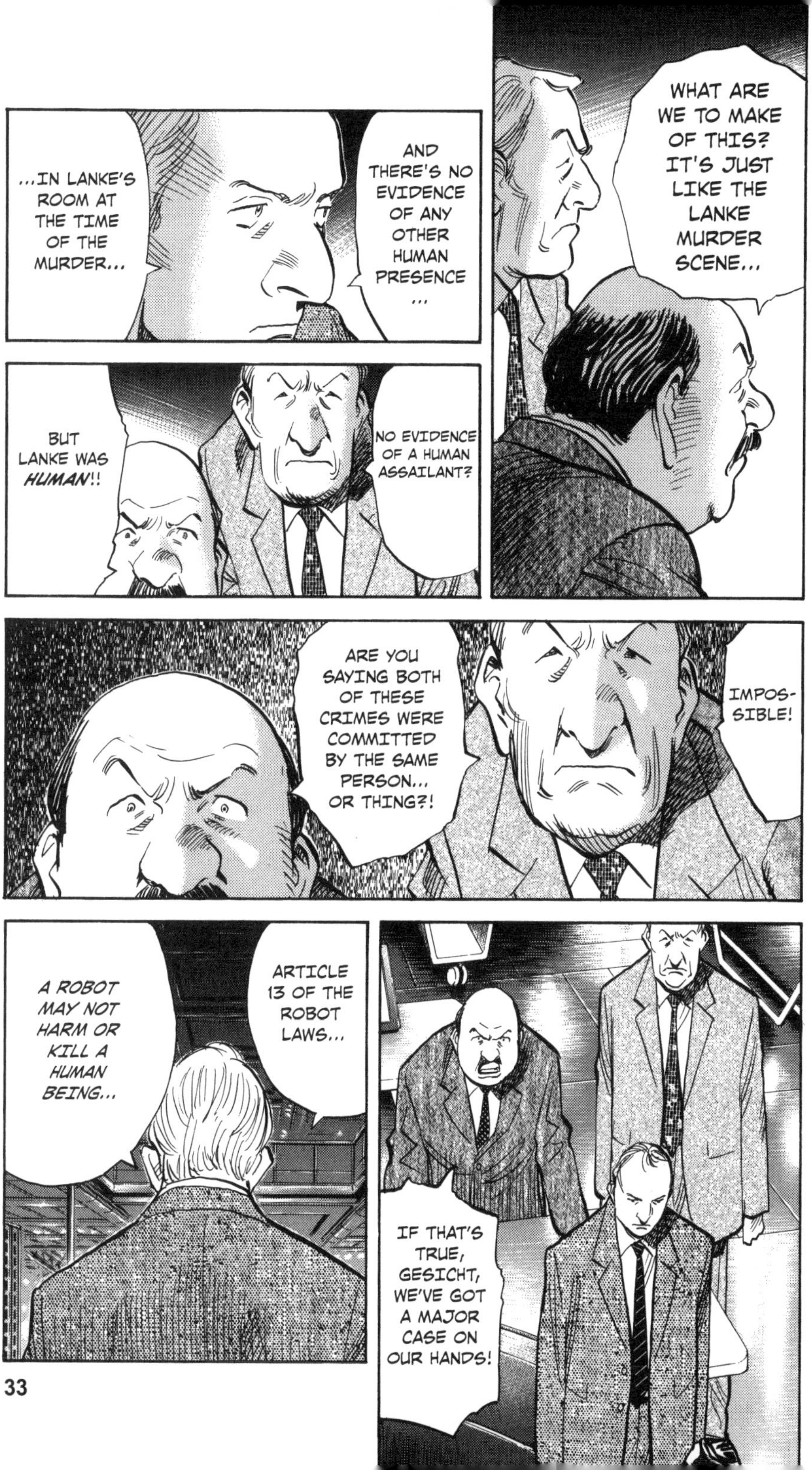
WHAT ARE WE TO MAKE OF THIS? IT'S JUST LIKE THE LANKE MURDER SCENE...
AND THERE'S NO EVIDENCE OF ANY OTHER HUMAN PRESENCE ...
...IN LANKE'S ROOM AT THE TIME OF THE MURDER...
NO EVIDENCE OF A HUMAN ASSAILANT?
BUT LANKE WAS *HUMAN*!!
ARE YOU SAYING BOTH OF THESE CRIMES WERE COMMITTED BY THE SAME PERSON... OR THING?!
IMPOS-SIBLE!
IF THAT'S TRUE, GESICHT, WE'VE GOT A MAJOR CASE ON OUR HANDS!
ARTICLE 13 OF THE ROBOT LAWS...
A ROBOT MAY NOT HARM OR KILL A HUMAN BEING...

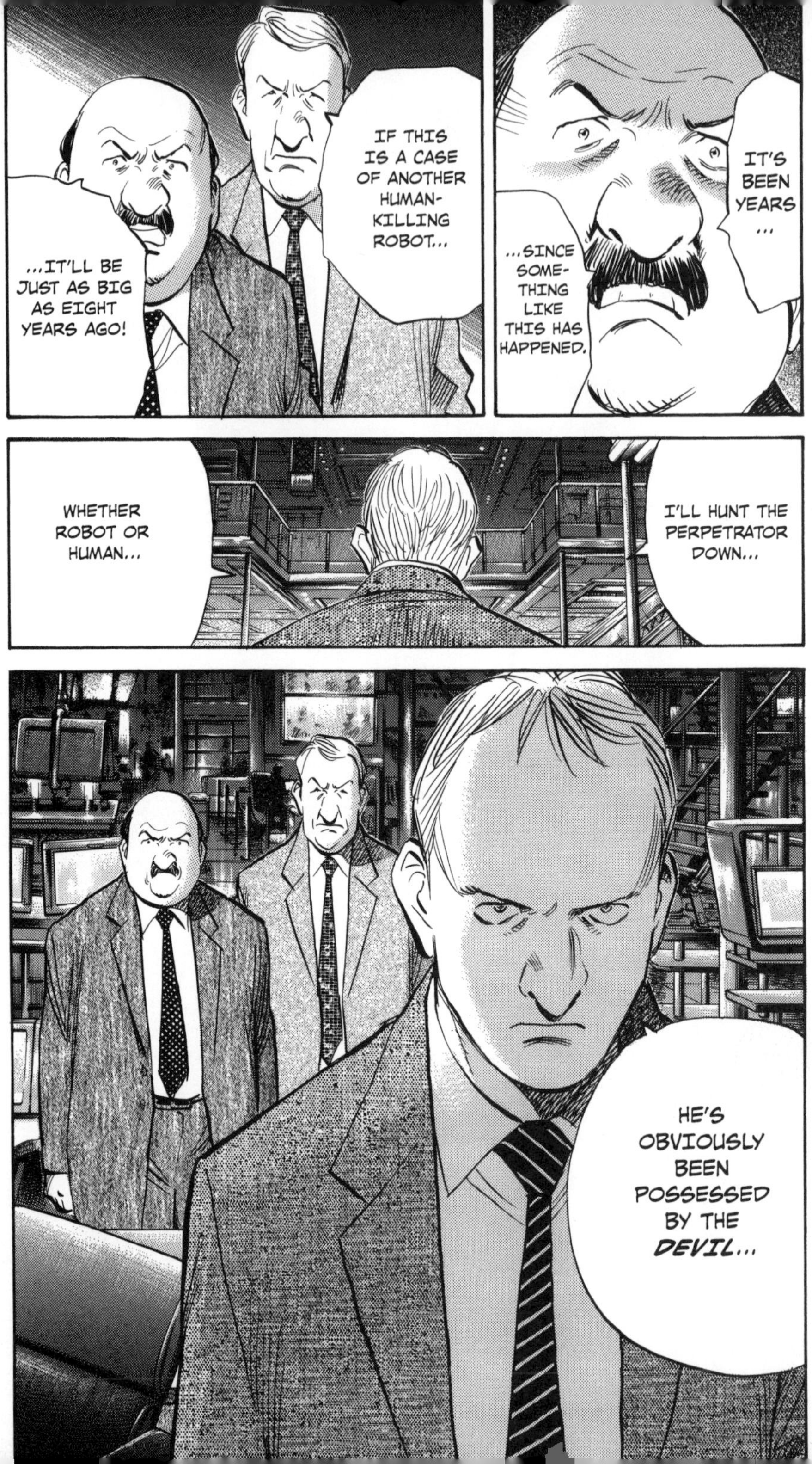
IT'S BEEN YEARS...
...SINCE SOMETHING LIKE THIS HAS HAPPENED.
IF THIS IS A CASE OF ANOTHER HUMAN-KILLING ROBOT...
...IT'LL BE JUST AS BIG AS EIGHT YEARS AGO!
I'LL HUNT THE PERPETRATOR DOWN...
WHETHER ROBOT OR HUMAN...
HE'S OBVIOUSLY BEEN POSSESSED BY THE *DEVIL*...

Act 2 GESICHT

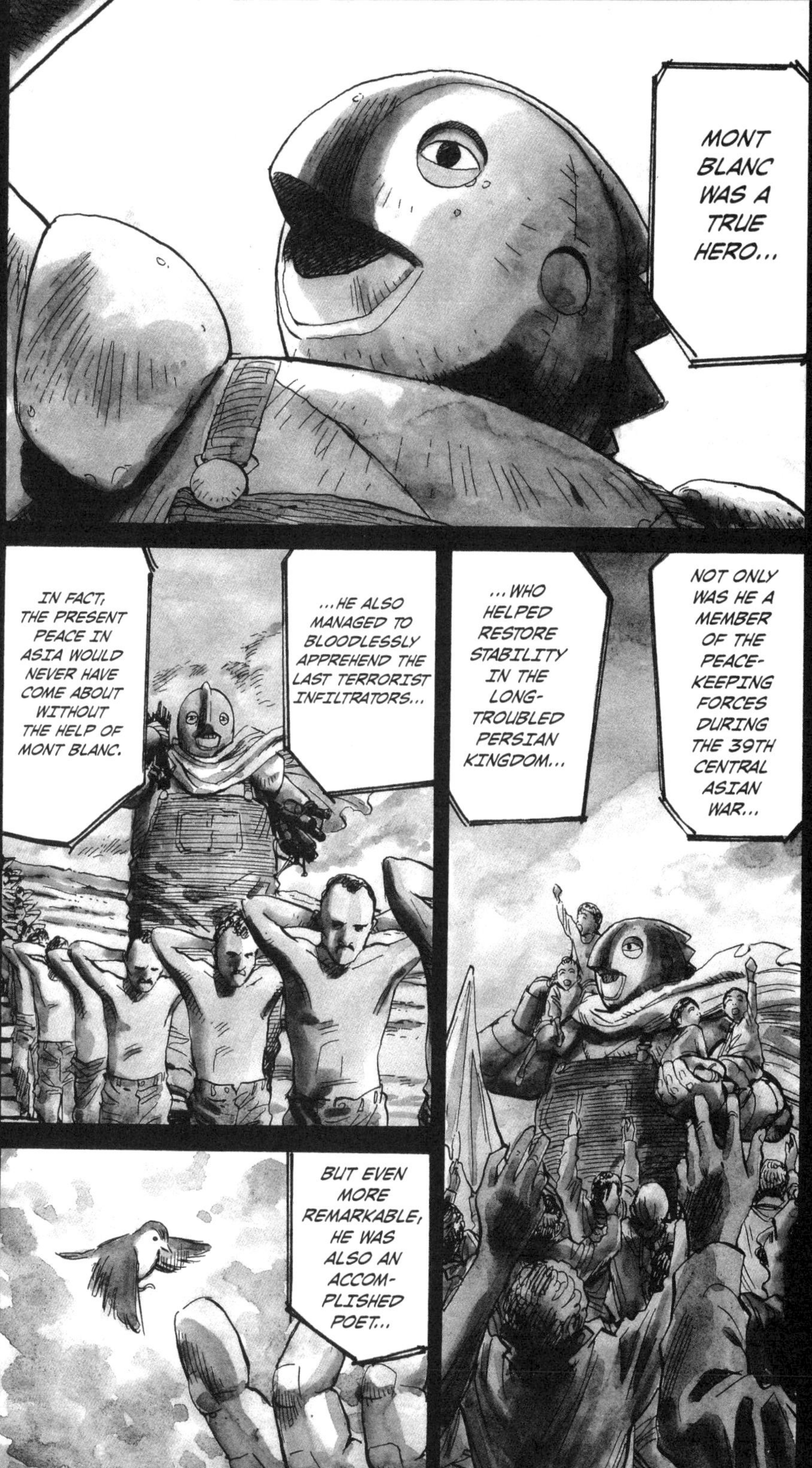

MONT BLANC WAS A TRUE HERO...
NOT ONLY WAS HE A MEMBER OF THE PEACE-KEEPING FORCES DURING THE 39TH CENTRAL ASIAN WAR...
...WHO HELPED RESTORE STABILITY IN THE LONG-TROUBLED PERSIAN KINGDOM...
...HE ALSO MANAGED TO BLOODLESSLY APPREHEND THE LAST TERRORIST INFILTRATORS...
IN FACT, THE PRESENT PEACE IN ASIA WOULD NEVER HAVE COME ABOUT WITHOUT THE HELP OF MONT BLANC.
BUT EVEN MORE REMARKABLE, HE WAS ALSO AN ACCOMPLISHED POET...

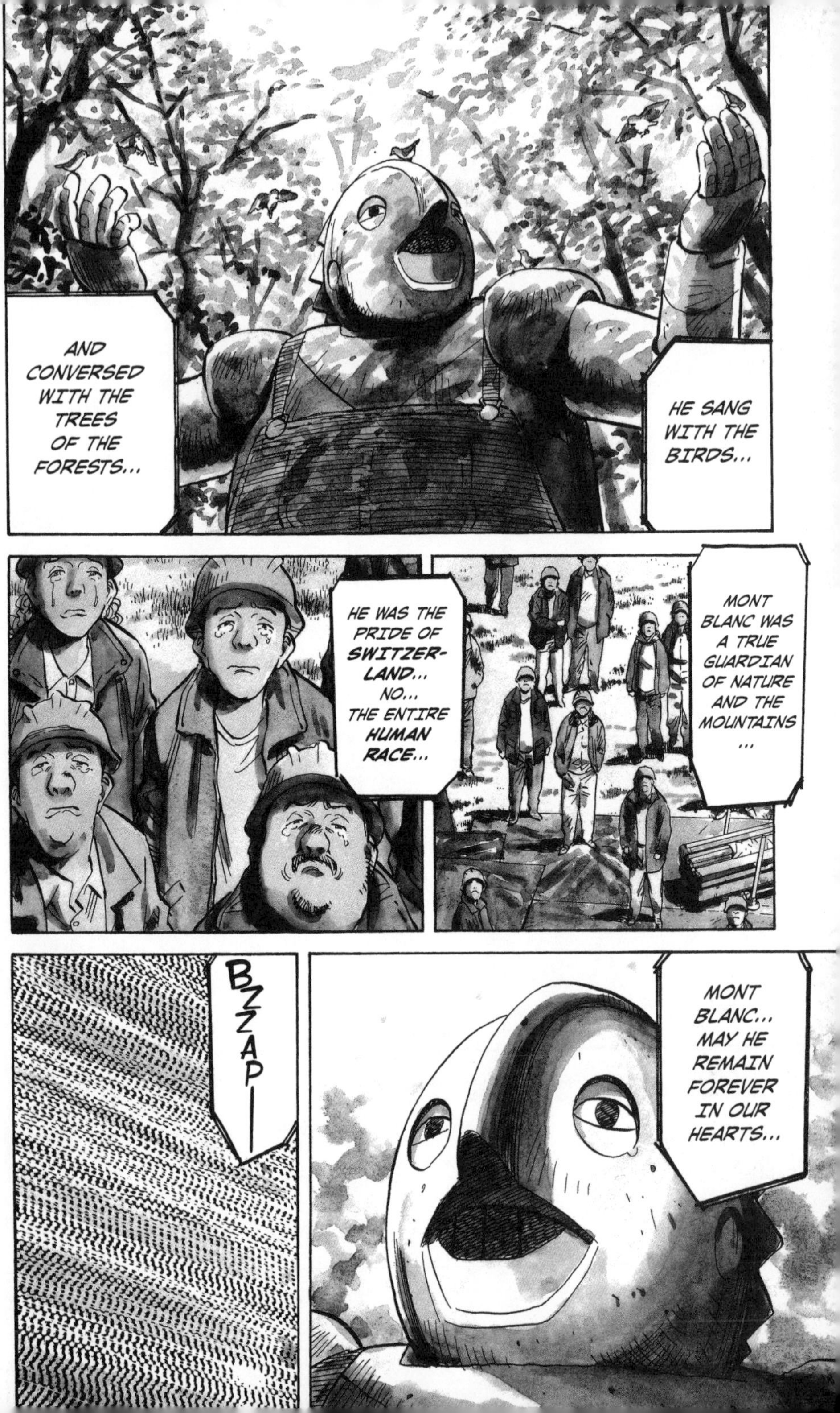
HE SANG WITH THE BIRDS...
AND CONVERSED WITH THE TREES OF THE FORESTS...
MONT BLANC WAS A TRUE GUARDIAN OF NATURE AND THE MOUNTAINS...
HE WAS THE PRIDE OF SWITZERLAND... NO... THE ENTIRE HUMAN RACE...
MONT BLANC... MAY HE REMAIN FOREVER IN OUR HEARTS...
BZZAP

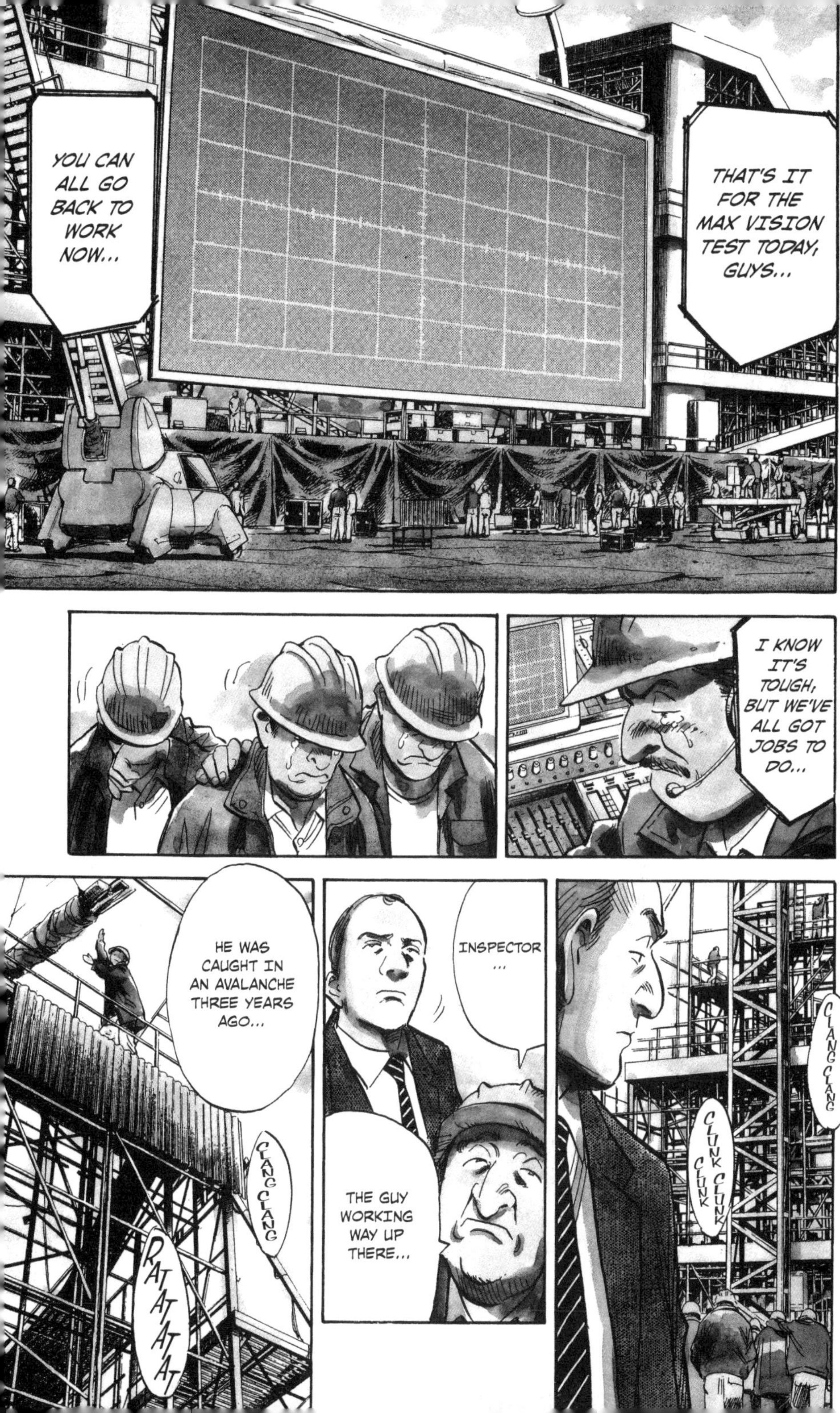
THAT'S IT FOR THE MAX VISION TEST TODAY, GUYS...
YOU CAN ALL GO BACK TO WORK NOW...
I KNOW IT'S TOUGH, BUT WE'VE ALL GOT JOBS TO DO...
CLANG CLANG
CLUNK CLUNK CLUNK
INSPECTOR...
THE GUY WORKING WAY UP THERE...
HE WAS CAUGHT IN AN AVALANCHE THREE YEARS AGO...
CLANG CLANG
RATATATAT

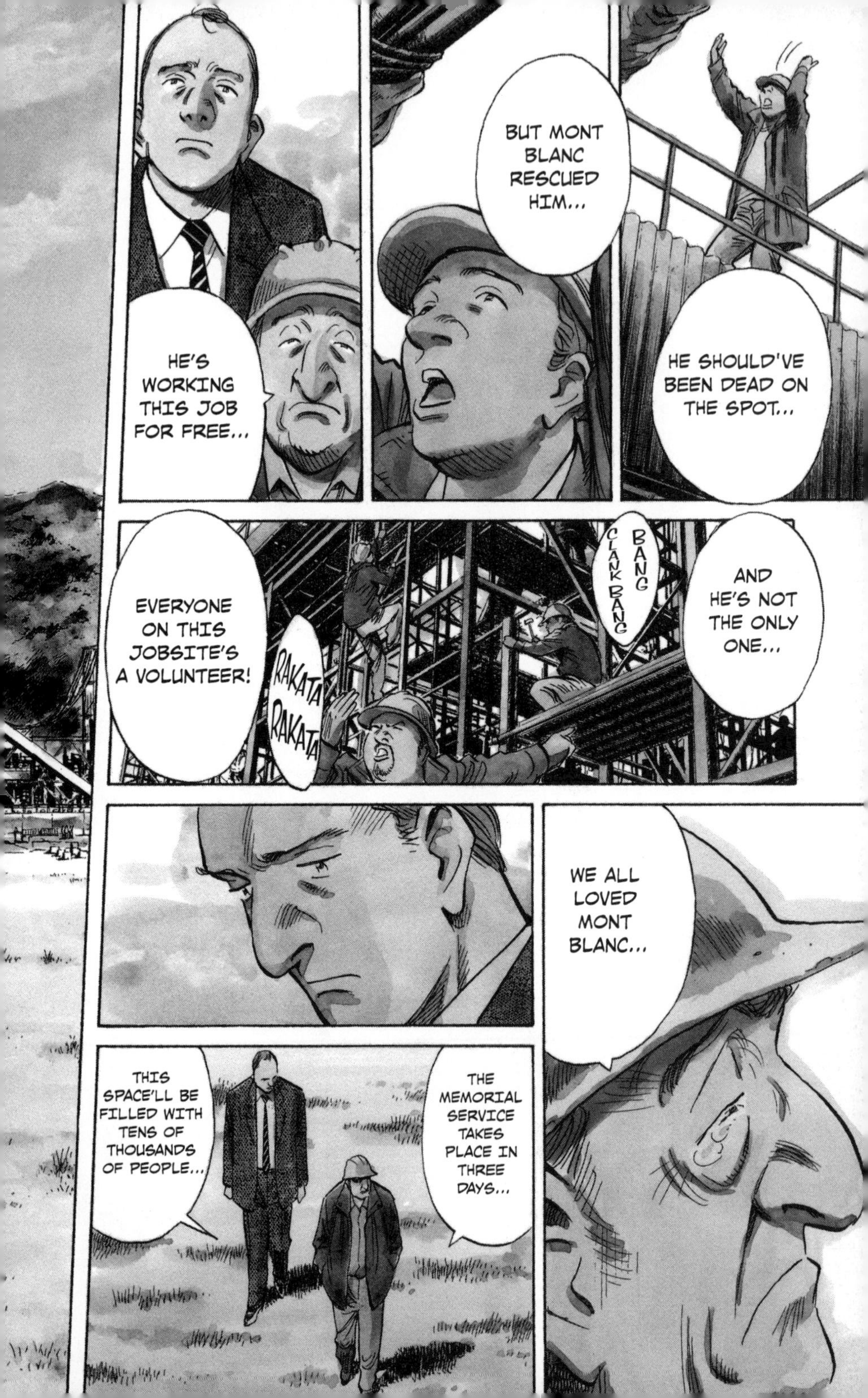
HE SHOULD'VE BEEN DEAD ON THE SPOT...
BUT MONT BLANC RESCUED HIM...
HE'S WORKING THIS JOB FOR FREE...
AND HE'S NOT THE ONLY ONE...
BANG
CLANK BANG
RAKATA RAKATA
EVERYONE ON THIS JOBSITE'S A VOLUNTEER!
WE ALL LOVED MONT BLANC...
THE MEMORIAL SERVICE TAKES PLACE IN THREE DAYS...
THIS SPACE'LL BE FILLED WITH TENS OF THOUSANDS OF PEOPLE...

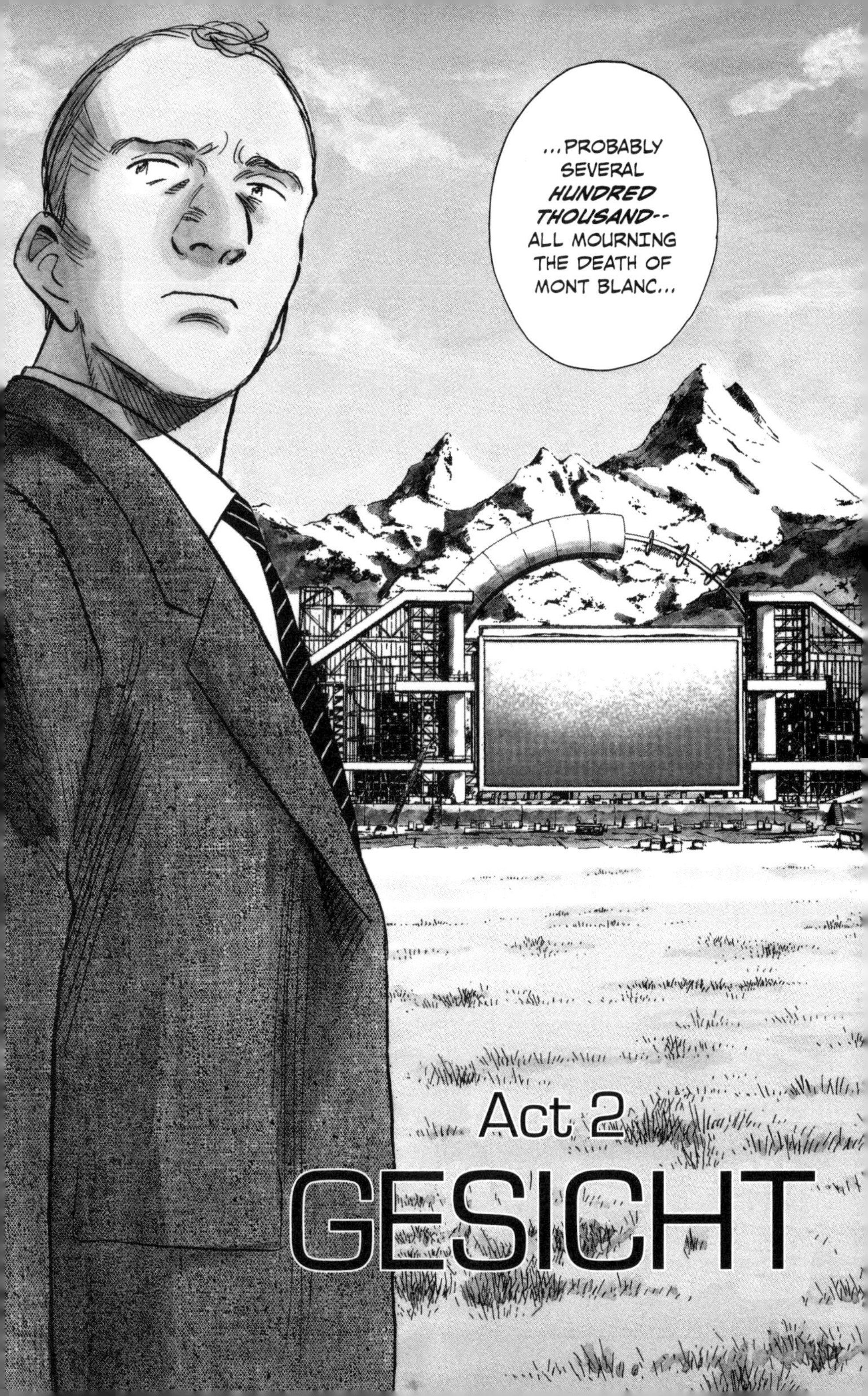
...PROBABLY SEVERAL ***HUNDRED THOUSAND***-- ALL MOURNING THE DEATH OF MONT BLANC...
Act 2
GESICHT

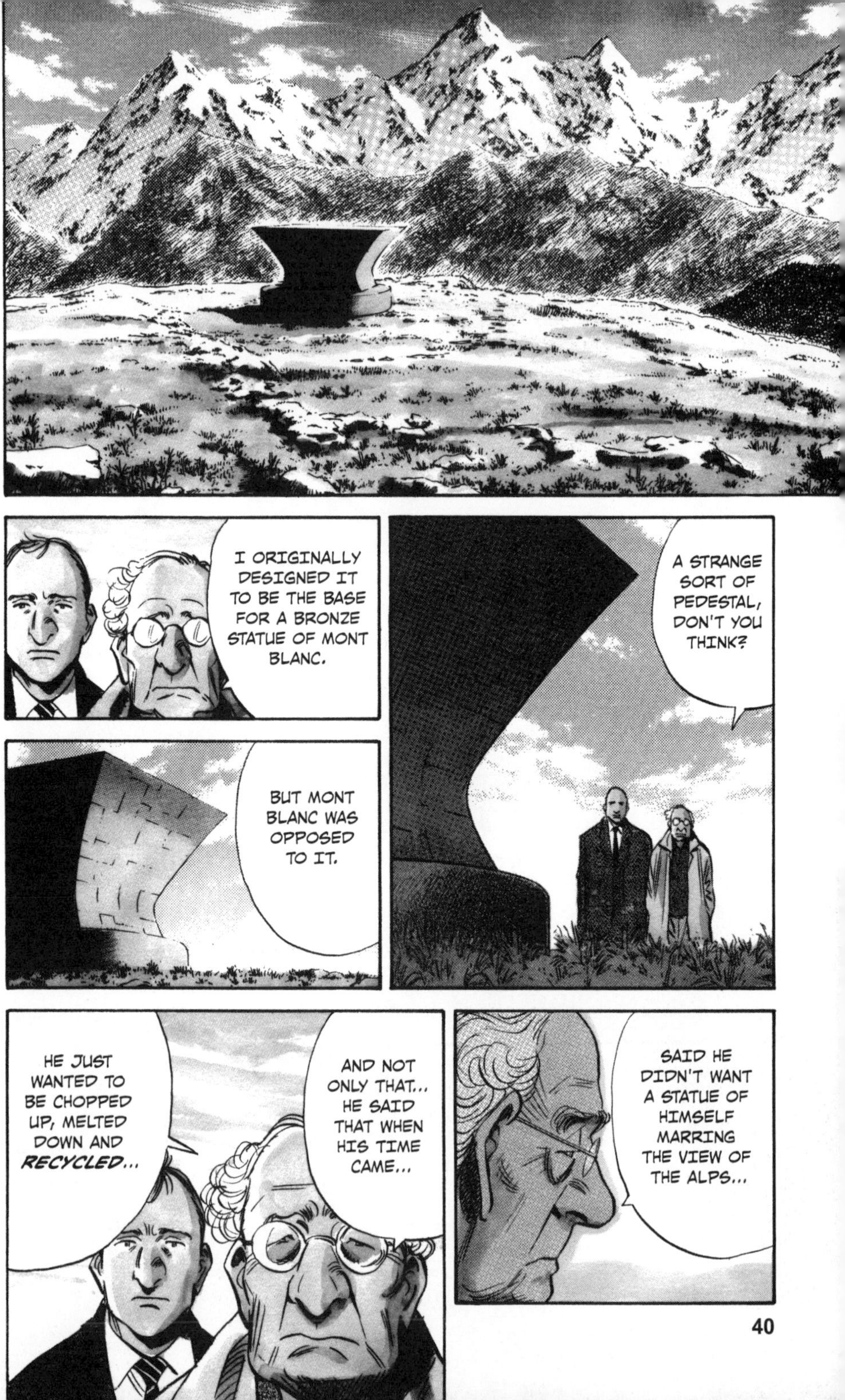
A STRANGE SORT OF PEDESTAL, DON'T YOU THINK?
I ORIGINALLY DESIGNED IT TO BE THE BASE FOR A BRONZE STATUE OF MONT BLANC.
BUT MONT BLANC WAS OPPOSED TO IT.
SAID HE DIDN'T WANT A STATUE OF HIMSELF MARRING THE VIEW OF THE ALPS...
AND NOT ONLY THAT... HE SAID THAT WHEN HIS TIME CAME...
HE JUST WANTED TO BE CHOPPED UP, MELTED DOWN AND ***RECYCLED***...

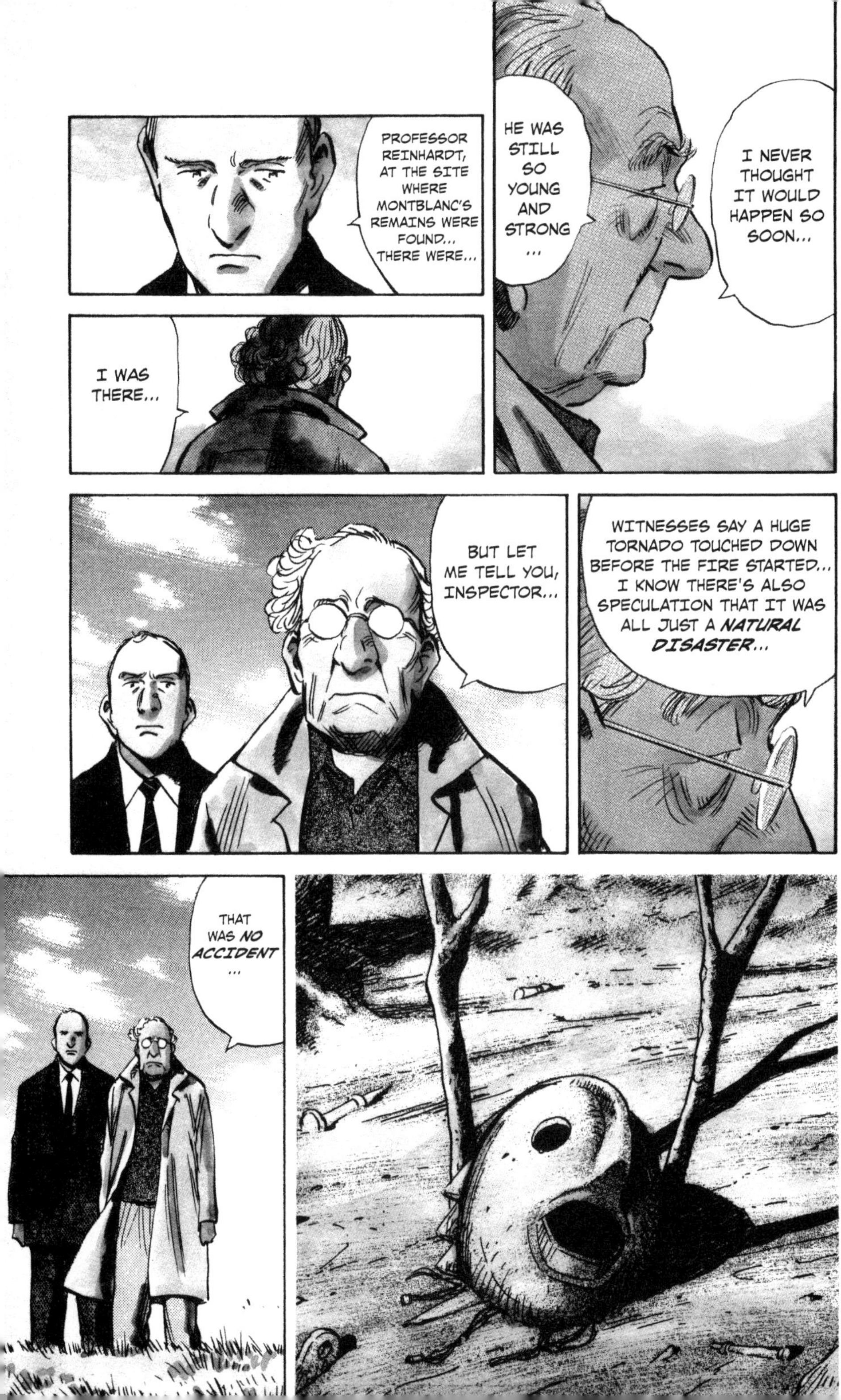
I NEVER THOUGHT IT WOULD HAPPEN SO SOON...
HE WAS STILL SO YOUNG AND STRONG ...
PROFESSOR REINHARDT, AT THE SITE WHERE MONTBLANC'S REMAINS WERE FOUND... THERE WERE...
I WAS THERE...
WITNESSES SAY A HUGE TORNADO TOUCHED DOWN BEFORE THE FIRE STARTED... I KNOW THERE'S ALSO SPECULATION THAT IT WAS ALL JUST A *NATURAL DISASTER*...
BUT LET ME TELL YOU, INSPECTOR...
THAT WAS *NO ACCIDENT* ...

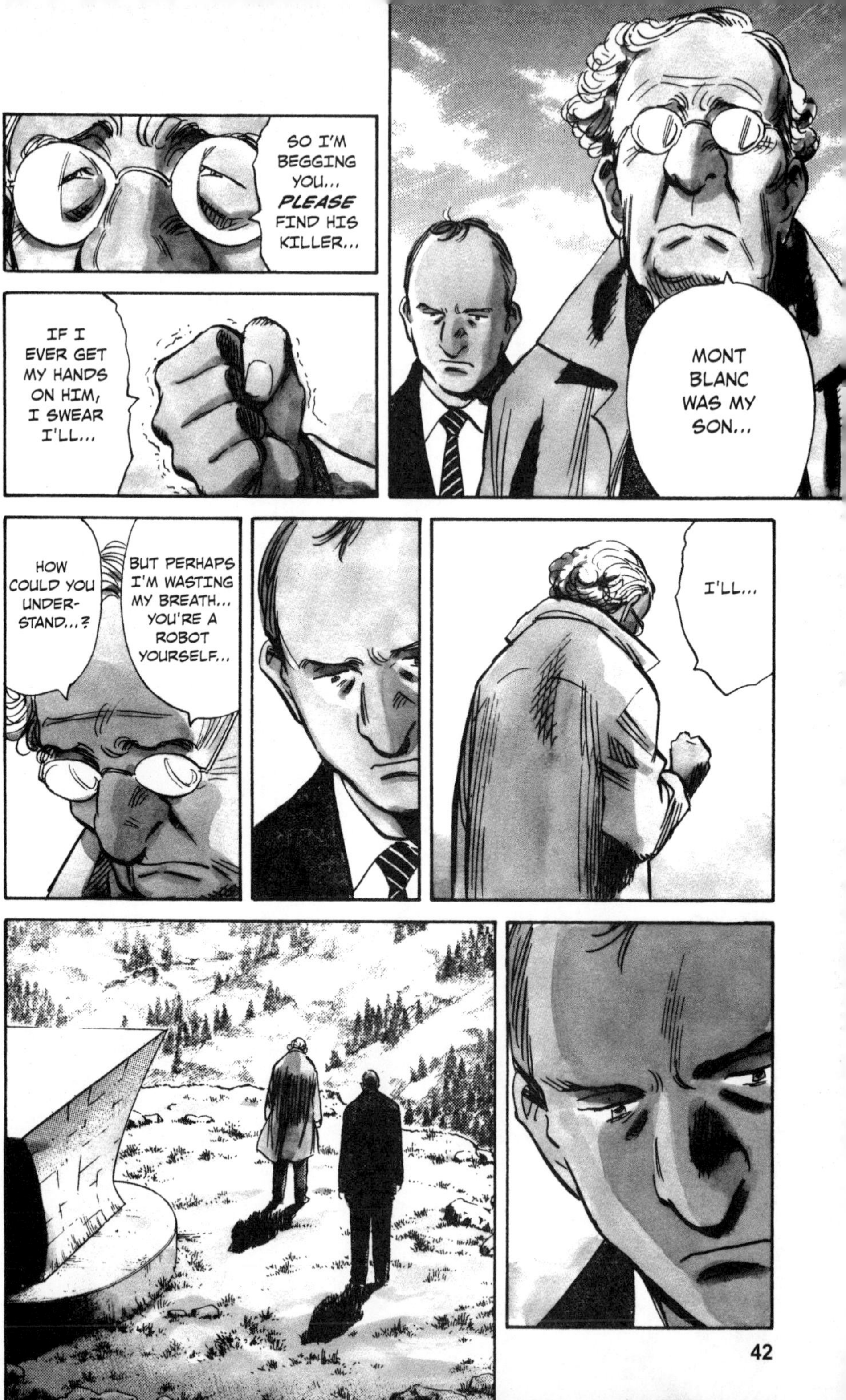
MONT BLANC WAS MY SON...
SO I'M BEGGING YOU... *PLEASE* FIND HIS KILLER...
IF I EVER GET MY HANDS ON HIM, I SWEAR I'LL...
I'LL...
BUT PERHAPS I'M WASTING MY BREATH... YOU'RE A ROBOT YOURSELF...
HOW COULD YOU UNDERSTAND...?

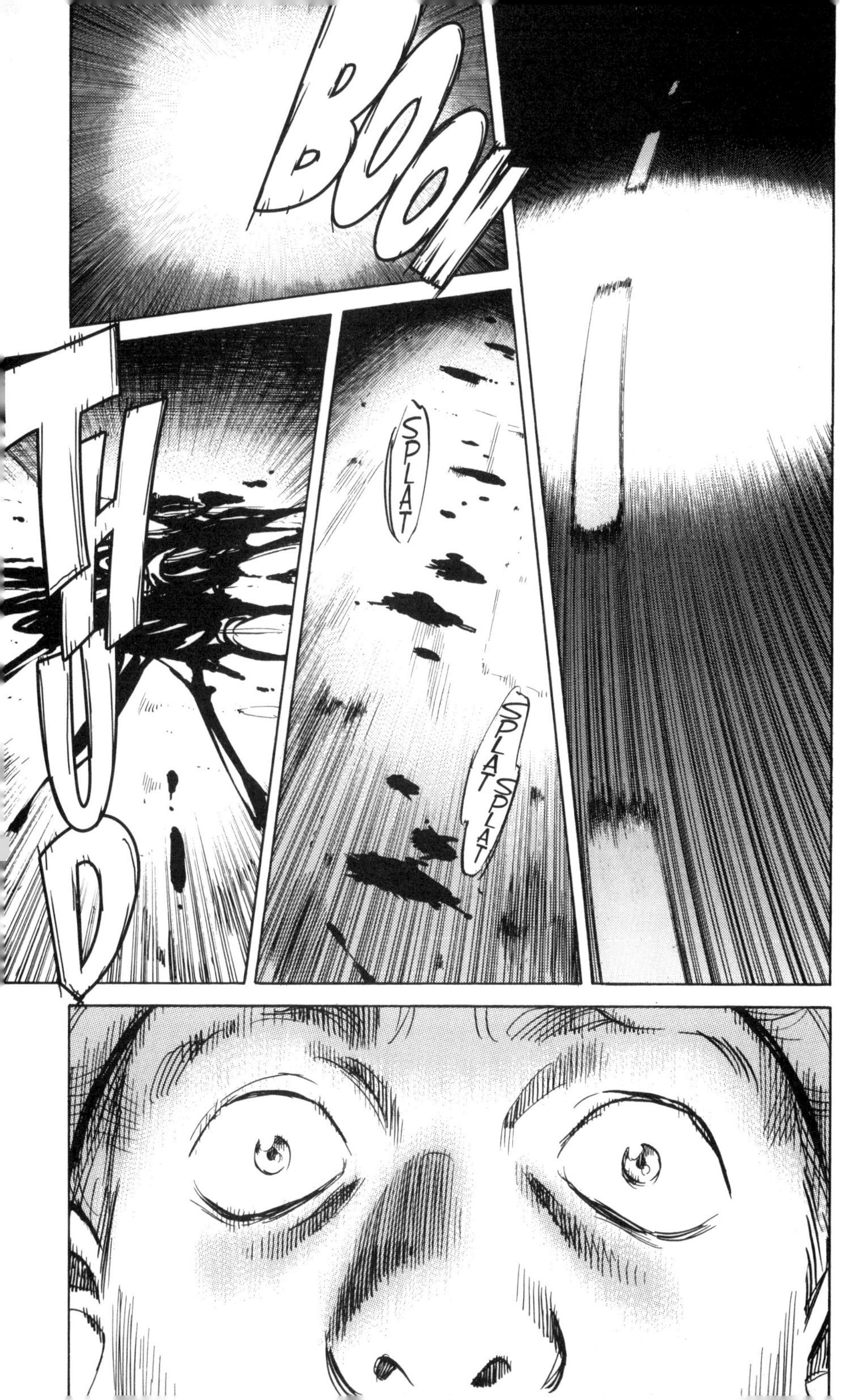
BOOOM
SPLAT
SPLAT SPLAT
THUD

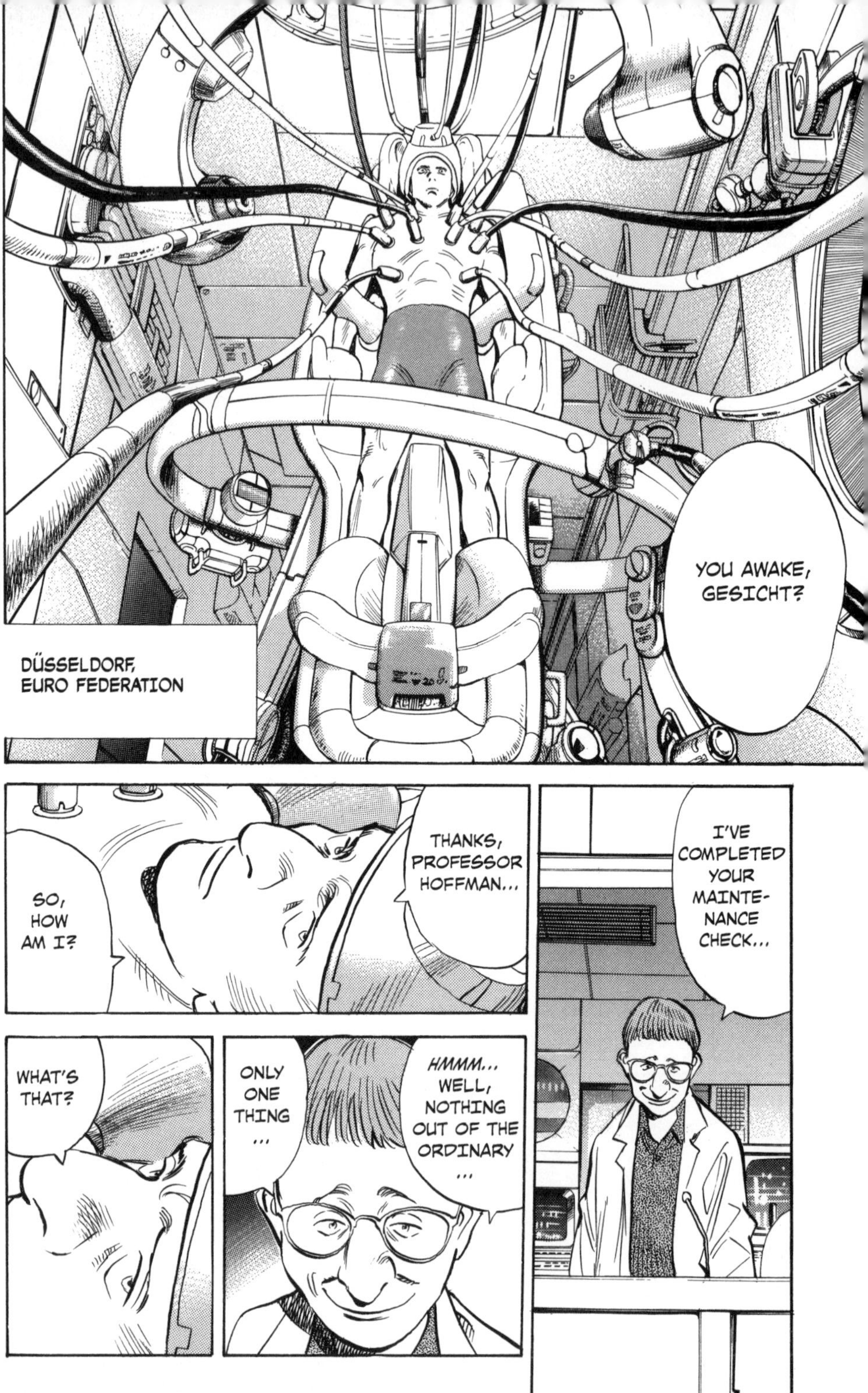
YOU AWAKE, GESICHT?
DÜSSELDORF, EURO FEDERATION
I'VE COMPLETED YOUR MAINTE-NANCE CHECK...
THANKS, PROFESSOR HOFFMAN...
SO, HOW AM I?
HMMM... WELL, NOTHING OUT OF THE ORDINARY...
ONLY ONE THING...
WHAT'S THAT?

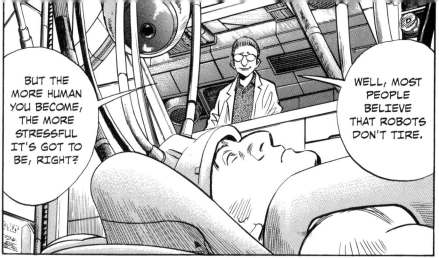

WELL, MOST PEOPLE BELIEVE THAT ROBOTS DON'T TIRE.
BUT THE MORE HUMAN YOU BECOME, THE MORE STRESSFUL IT'S GOT TO BE, RIGHT?
TO PUT IT ANOTHER WAY, EVEN THE HUMAN BODY IS A KIND OF MECHANISM.
YOU WORK SOMETHING TOO HARD, AND ANY MECHANISM WILL WEAR OUT.
SO YOU SEE SIGNS OF FATIGUE?
WHIRRRRR
I'D SAY YOU'RE WORKING ON A PRETTY TOUGH CASE THIS TIME...
THEY SHOWED THE MEMORIAL SERVICE FOR MONT BLANC ON TV. I COULDN'T BEAR TO WATCH IT... I WAS IN TEARS.
...
PSHOONK

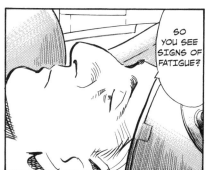

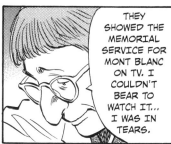

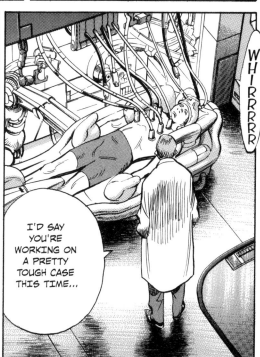

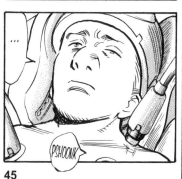

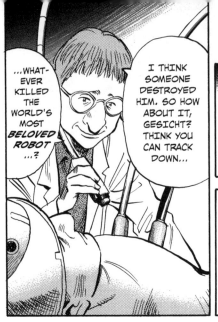

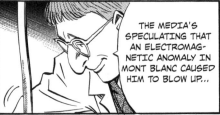

THE MEDIA'S SPECULATING THAT AN ELECTROMAGNETIC ANOMALY IN MONT BLANC CAUSED HIM TO BLOW UP...
BUT IF YOU WANT MY PROFESSIONAL OPINION, THERE'S NO WAY A SIMPLE GLITCH LIKE THAT COULD OCCUR IN SUCH AN ADVANCED ROBOT.
I THINK SOMEONE DESTROYED HIM. SO HOW ABOUT IT, GESICHT? THINK YOU CAN TRACK DOWN...
...WHATEVER KILLED THE WORLD'S MOST ***BELOVED ROBOT***...?
NOT AN EASY ASSIGNMENT, I'M SURE...
I KNOW YOU'RE HANDLING ANOTHER CASE TOO... AND IT SOUNDS LIKE A DIFFICULT ONE...
...THE ***LANKE*** MURDER CASE, RIGHT?
I'VE SEEN A NUMBER OF TV REPORTS ON IT, AND YOU KNOW WHAT? I THINK LANKE PROBABLY HAD IT COMING...
HE WAS HIGH UP IN ONE OF THOSE ROBOT LAW PRESERVATION GROUPS...
...AND BEFORE THAT HE WAS INVOLVED WITH HUMAN RIGHTS DEFENSE GROUPS AND THE CLASSICAL REFORM MOVEMENT TOO...

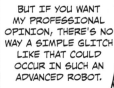

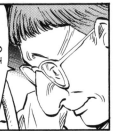

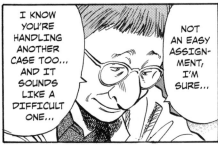

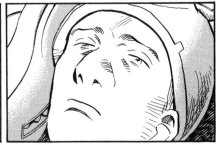

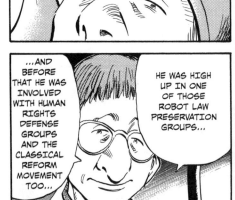

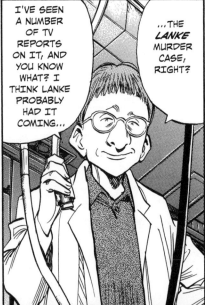

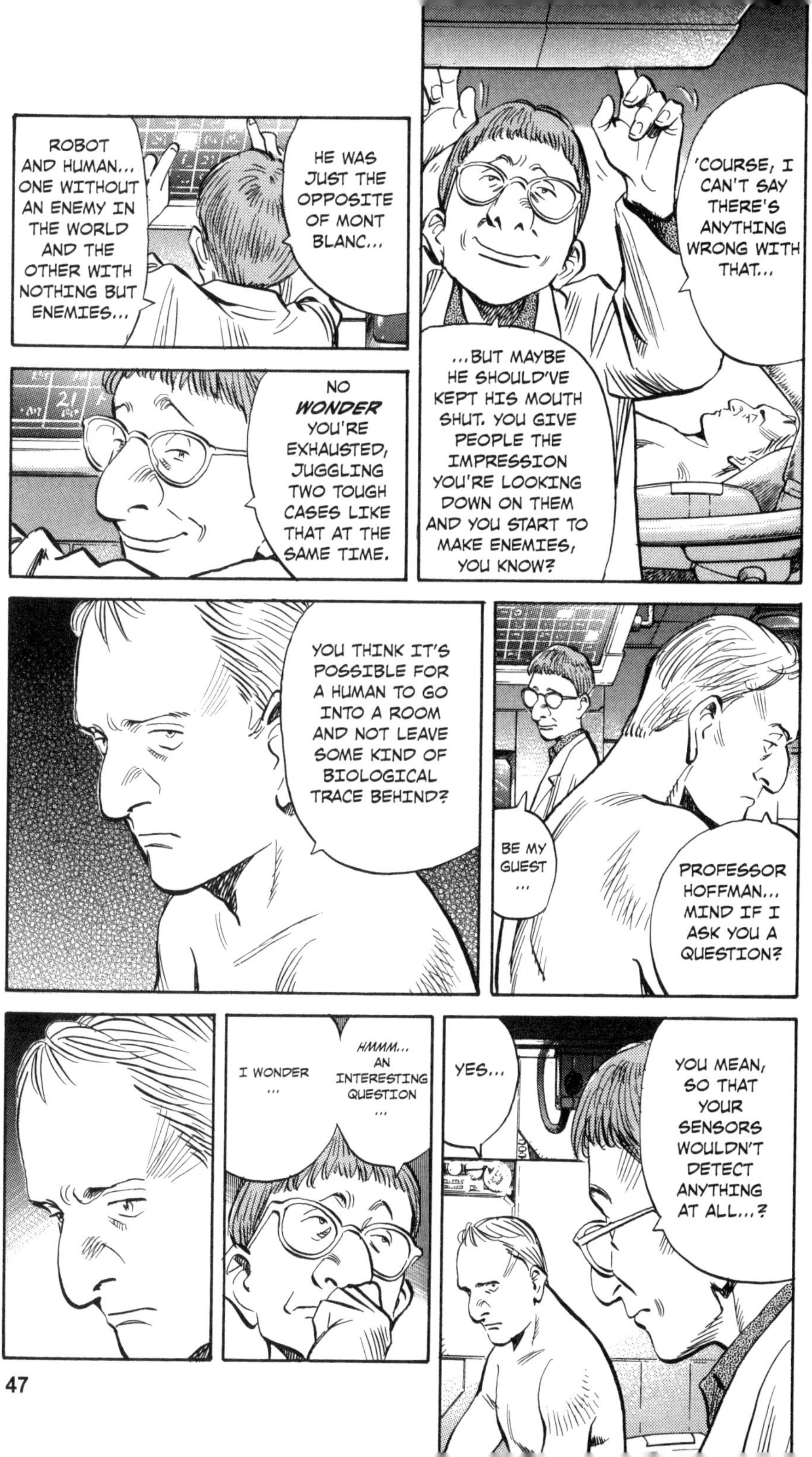
'COURSE, I CAN'T SAY THERE'S ANYTHING WRONG WITH THAT...
...BUT MAYBE HE SHOULD'VE KEPT HIS MOUTH SHUT. YOU GIVE PEOPLE THE IMPRESSION YOU'RE LOOKING DOWN ON THEM AND YOU START TO MAKE ENEMIES, YOU KNOW?
HE WAS JUST THE OPPOSITE OF MONT BLANC...
ROBOT AND HUMAN... ONE WITHOUT AN ENEMY IN THE WORLD AND THE OTHER WITH NOTHING BUT ENEMIES...
NO ***WONDER*** YOU'RE EXHAUSTED, JUGGLING TWO TOUGH CASES LIKE THAT AT THE SAME TIME.
PROFESSOR HOFFMAN... MIND IF I ASK YOU A QUESTION?
BE MY GUEST...
YOU THINK IT'S POSSIBLE FOR A HUMAN TO GO INTO A ROOM AND NOT LEAVE SOME KIND OF BIOLOGICAL TRACE BEHIND?
YOU MEAN, SO THAT YOUR SENSORS WOULDN'T DETECT ANYTHING AT ALL...?
YES...
HMMM... AN INTERESTING QUESTION...
I WONDER...

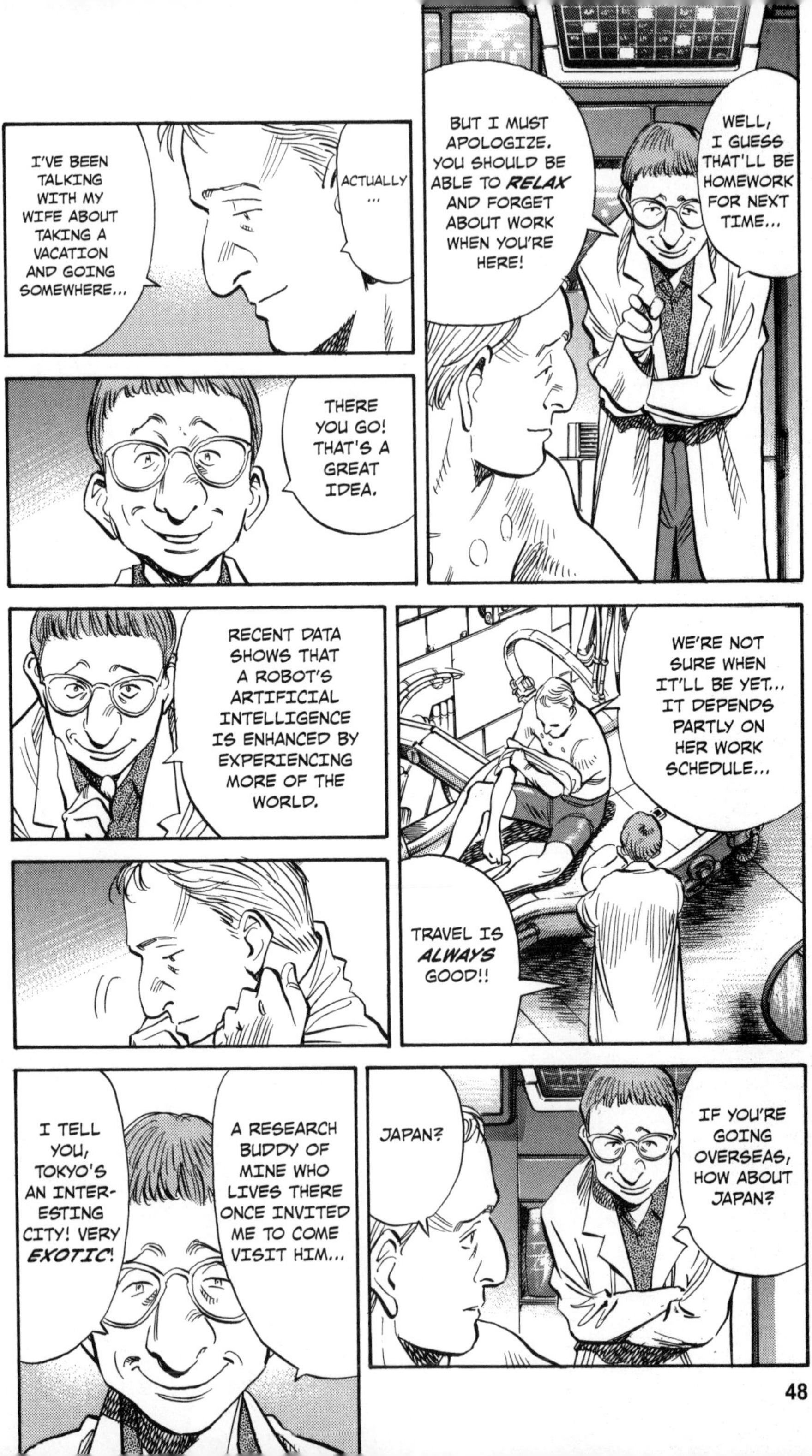
WELL, I GUESS THAT'LL BE HOMEWORK FOR NEXT TIME...
BUT I MUST APOLOGIZE. YOU SHOULD BE ABLE TO RELAX AND FORGET ABOUT WORK WHEN YOU'RE HERE!
ACTUALLY...
I'VE BEEN TALKING WITH MY WIFE ABOUT TAKING A VACATION AND GOING SOMEWHERE...
THERE YOU GO! THAT'S A GREAT IDEA.
WE'RE NOT SURE WHEN IT'LL BE YET... IT DEPENDS PARTLY ON HER WORK SCHEDULE...
TRAVEL IS ALWAYS GOOD!!
RECENT DATA SHOWS THAT A ROBOT'S ARTIFICIAL INTELLIGENCE IS ENHANCED BY EXPERIENCING MORE OF THE WORLD.
IF YOU'RE GOING OVERSEAS, HOW ABOUT JAPAN?
JAPAN?
A RESEARCH BUDDY OF MINE WHO LIVES THERE ONCE INVITED ME TO COME VISIT HIM...
I TELL YOU, TOKYO'S AN INTER-ESTING CITY! VERY EXOTIC!

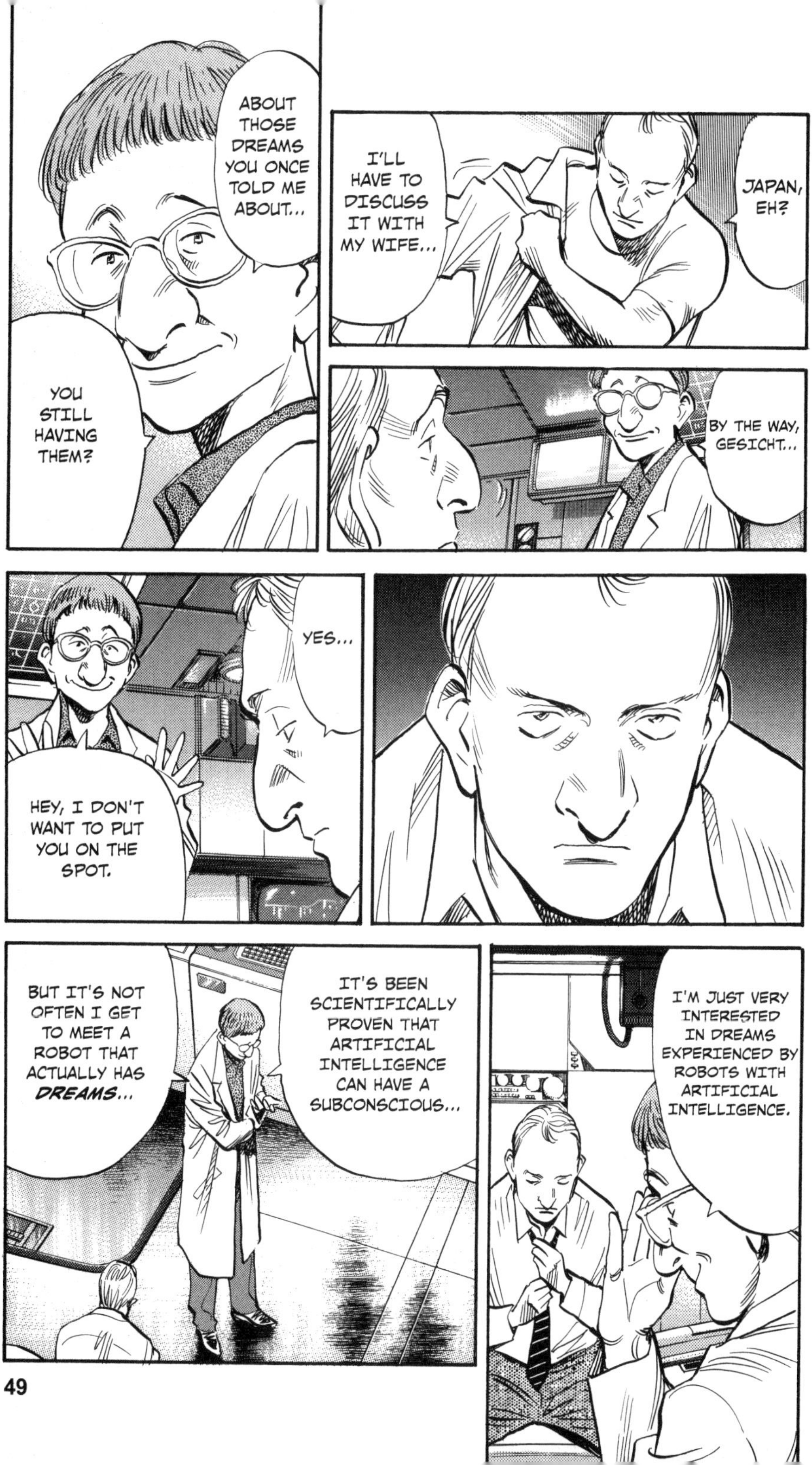
JAPAN, EH?
I'LL HAVE TO DISCUSS IT WITH MY WIFE...
BY THE WAY, GESICHT...
ABOUT THOSE DREAMS YOU ONCE TOLD ME ABOUT...
YOU STILL HAVING THEM?
YES...
HEY, I DON'T WANT TO PUT YOU ON THE SPOT.
I'M JUST VERY INTERESTED IN DREAMS EXPERIENCED BY ROBOTS WITH ARTIFICIAL INTELLIGENCE.
IT'S BEEN SCIENTIFICALLY PROVEN THAT ARTIFICIAL INTELLIGENCE CAN HAVE A SUBCONSCIOUS...
BUT IT'S NOT OFTEN I GET TO MEET A ROBOT THAT ACTUALLY HAS ***DREAMS***...

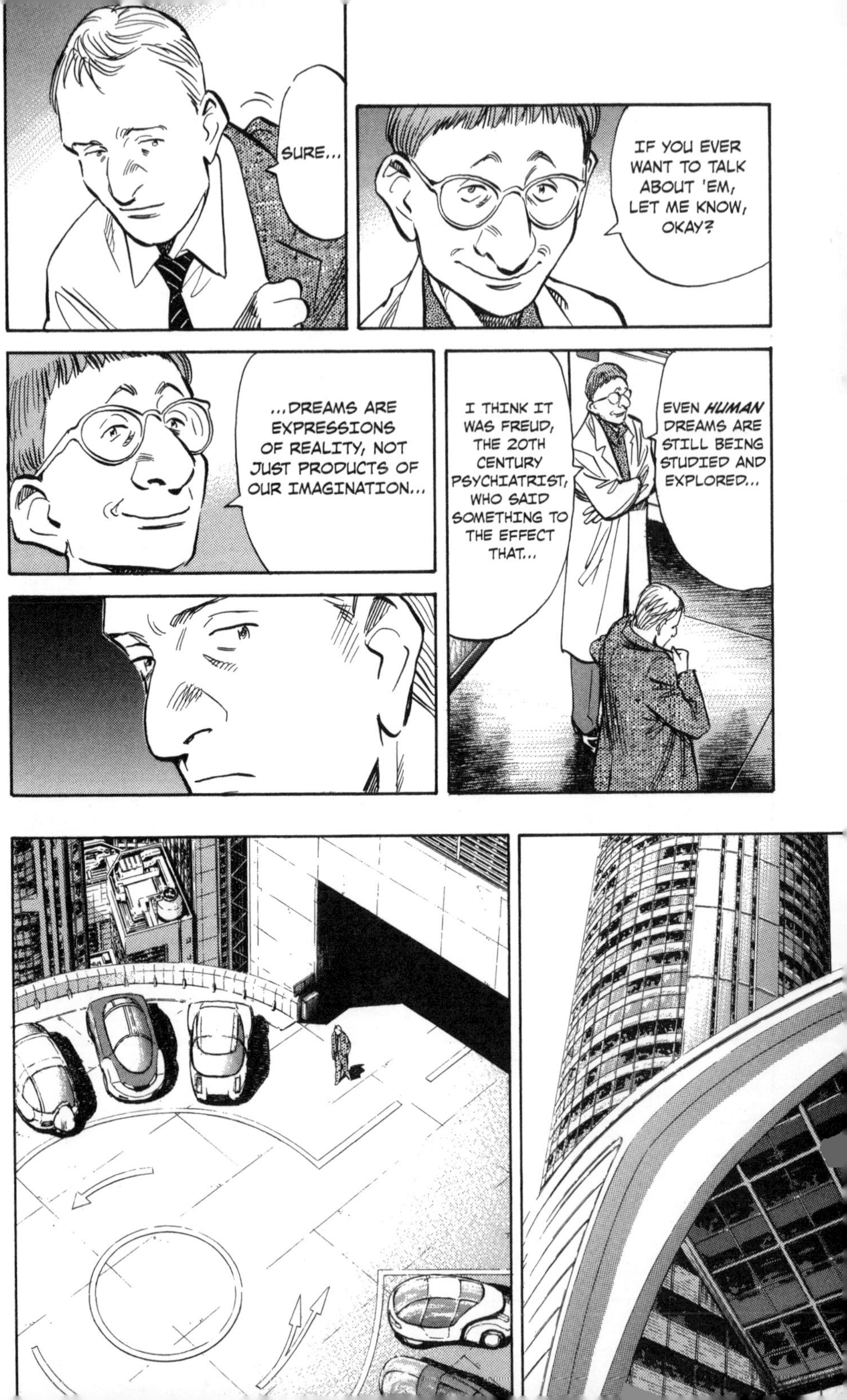
IF YOU EVER WANT TO TALK ABOUT 'EM, LET ME KNOW, OKAY?
SURE...
EVEN *HUMAN* DREAMS ARE STILL BEING STUDIED AND EXPLORED...
I THINK IT WAS FREUD, THE 20TH CENTURY PSYCHIATRIST, WHO SAID SOMETHING TO THE EFFECT THAT...
...DREAMS ARE EXPRESSIONS OF REALITY, NOT JUST PRODUCTS OF OUR IMAGINATION...

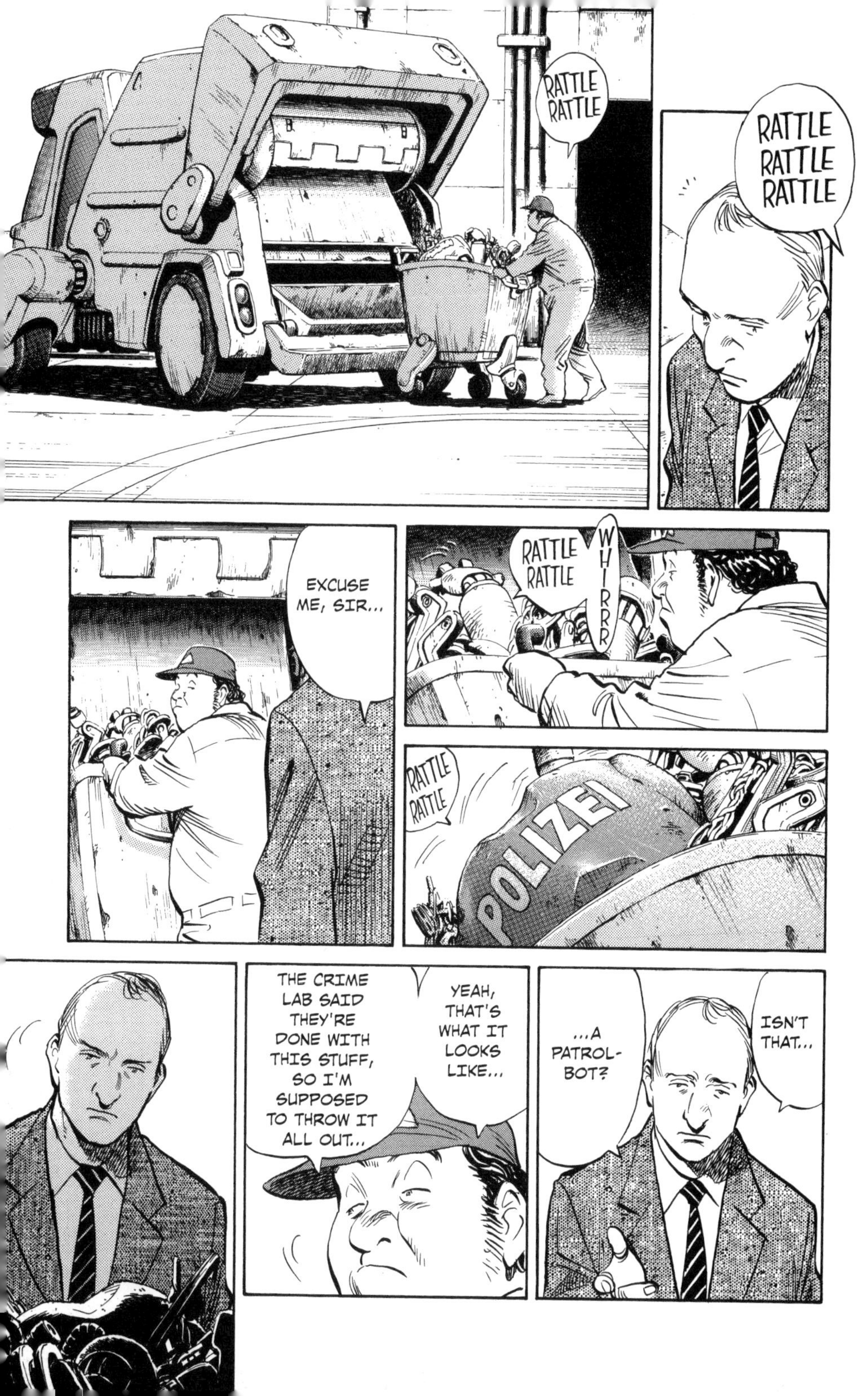
RATTLE RATTLE RATTLE
RATTLE RATTLE
RATTLE RATTLE
WHIRRR
RATTLE RATTLE
POLIZEI
EXCUSE ME, SIR...
ISN'T THAT...
...A PATROL-BOT?
YEAH, THAT'S WHAT IT LOOKS LIKE...
THE CRIME LAB SAID THEY'RE DONE WITH THIS STUFF, SO I'M SUPPOSED TO THROW IT ALL OUT...

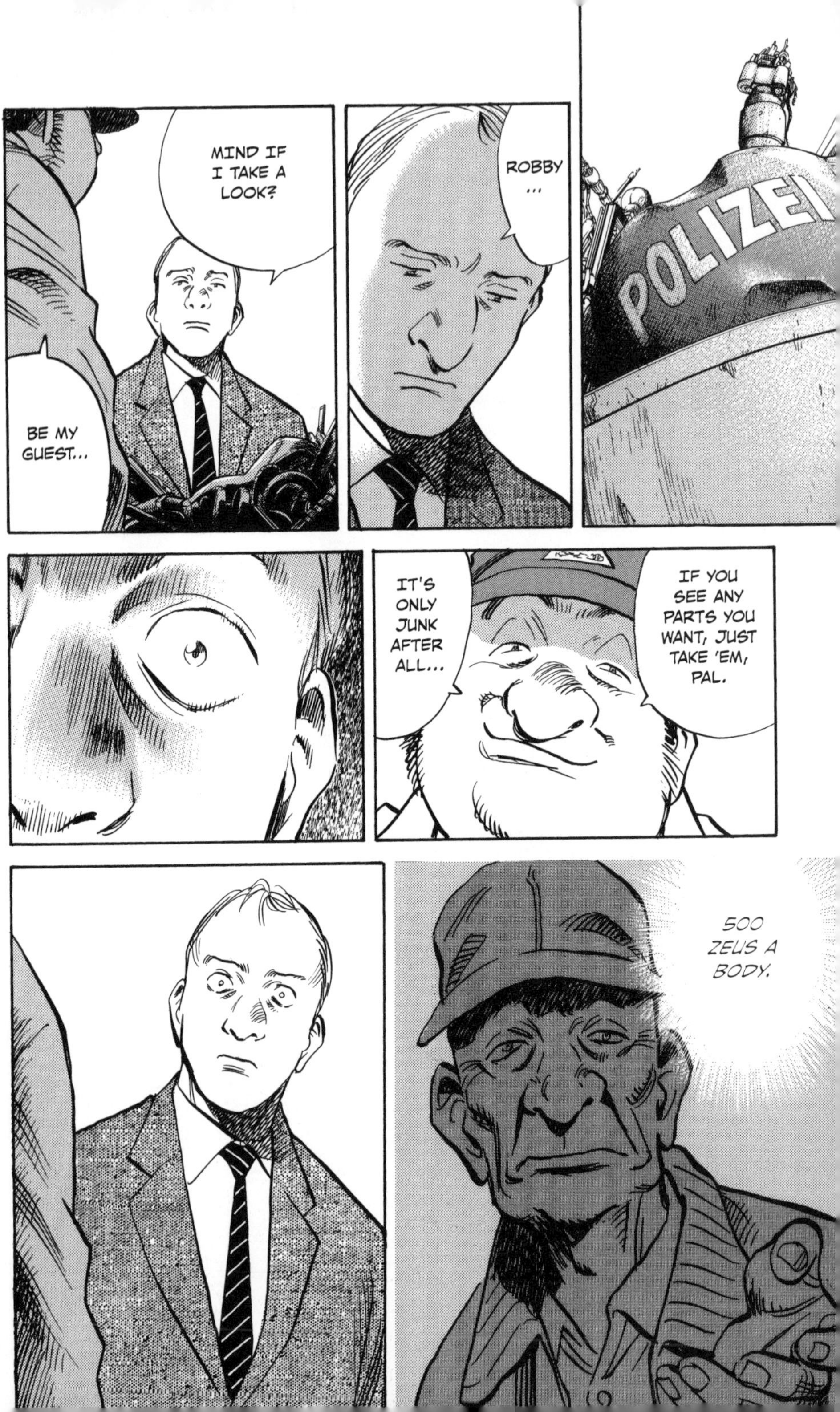
POLIZEI
ROBBY ...
MIND IF I TAKE A LOOK?
BE MY GUEST...
IF YOU SEE ANY PARTS YOU WANT, JUST TAKE 'EM, PAL.
IT'S ONLY JUNK AFTER ALL...
500 ZEUS A BODY.

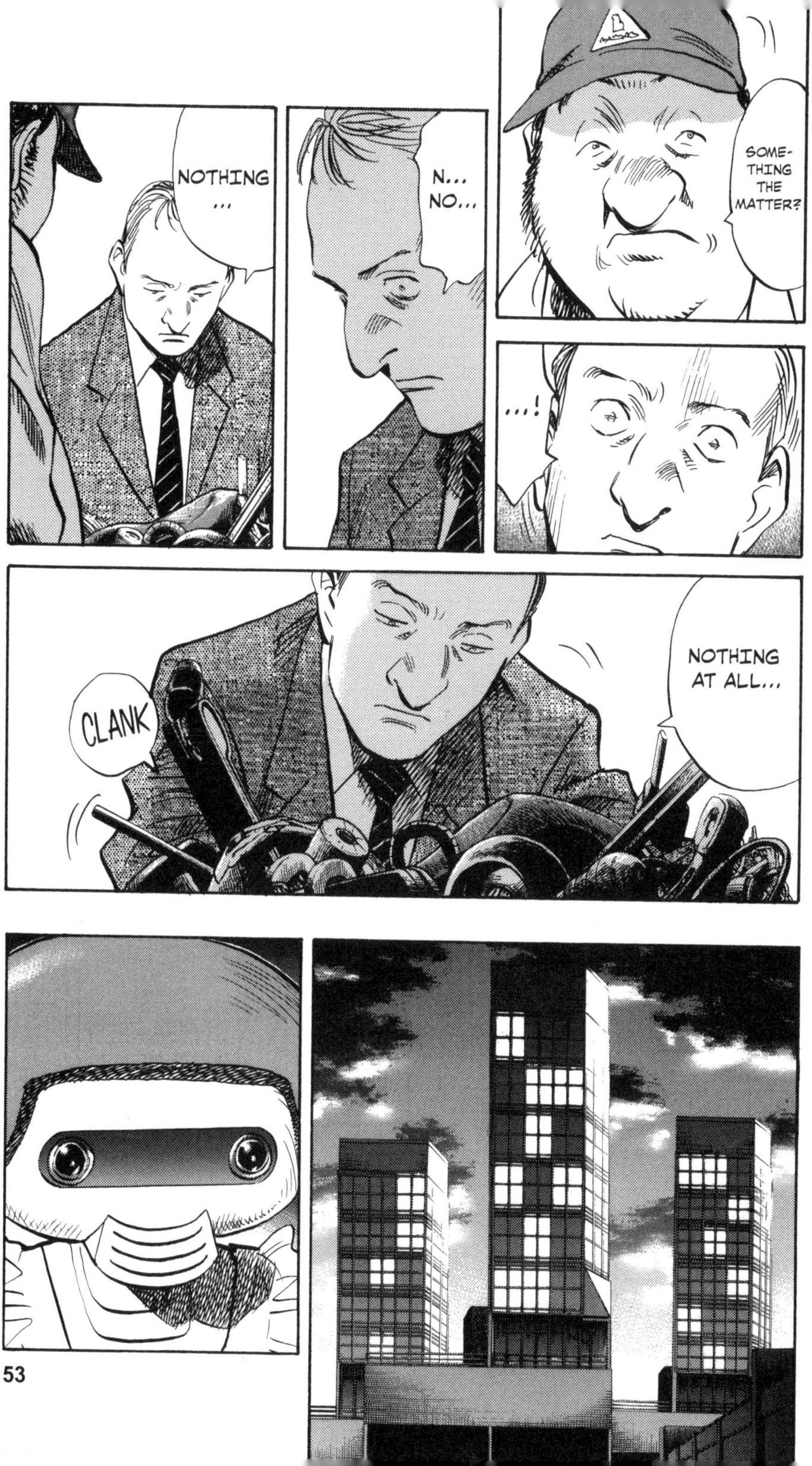
SOME-THING THE MATTER?
...!
N... NO...
NOTHING ...
NOTHING AT ALL...
CLANK

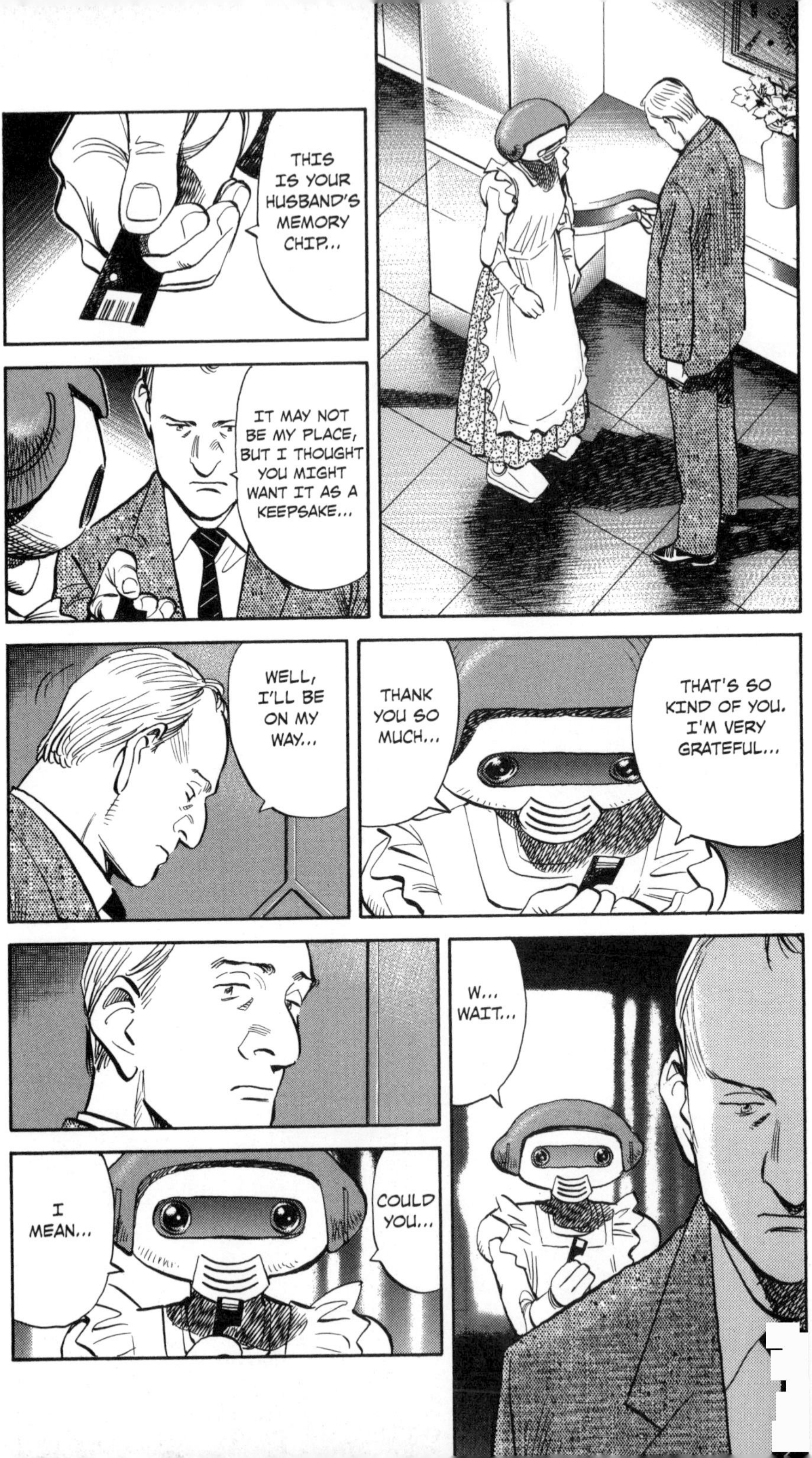
THIS IS YOUR HUSBAND'S MEMORY CHIP...
IT MAY NOT BE MY PLACE, BUT I THOUGHT YOU MIGHT WANT IT AS A KEEPSAKE...
THAT'S SO KIND OF YOU. I'M VERY GRATEFUL...
THANK YOU SO MUCH...
WELL, I'LL BE ON MY WAY...
W... WAIT...
COULD YOU...
I MEAN...

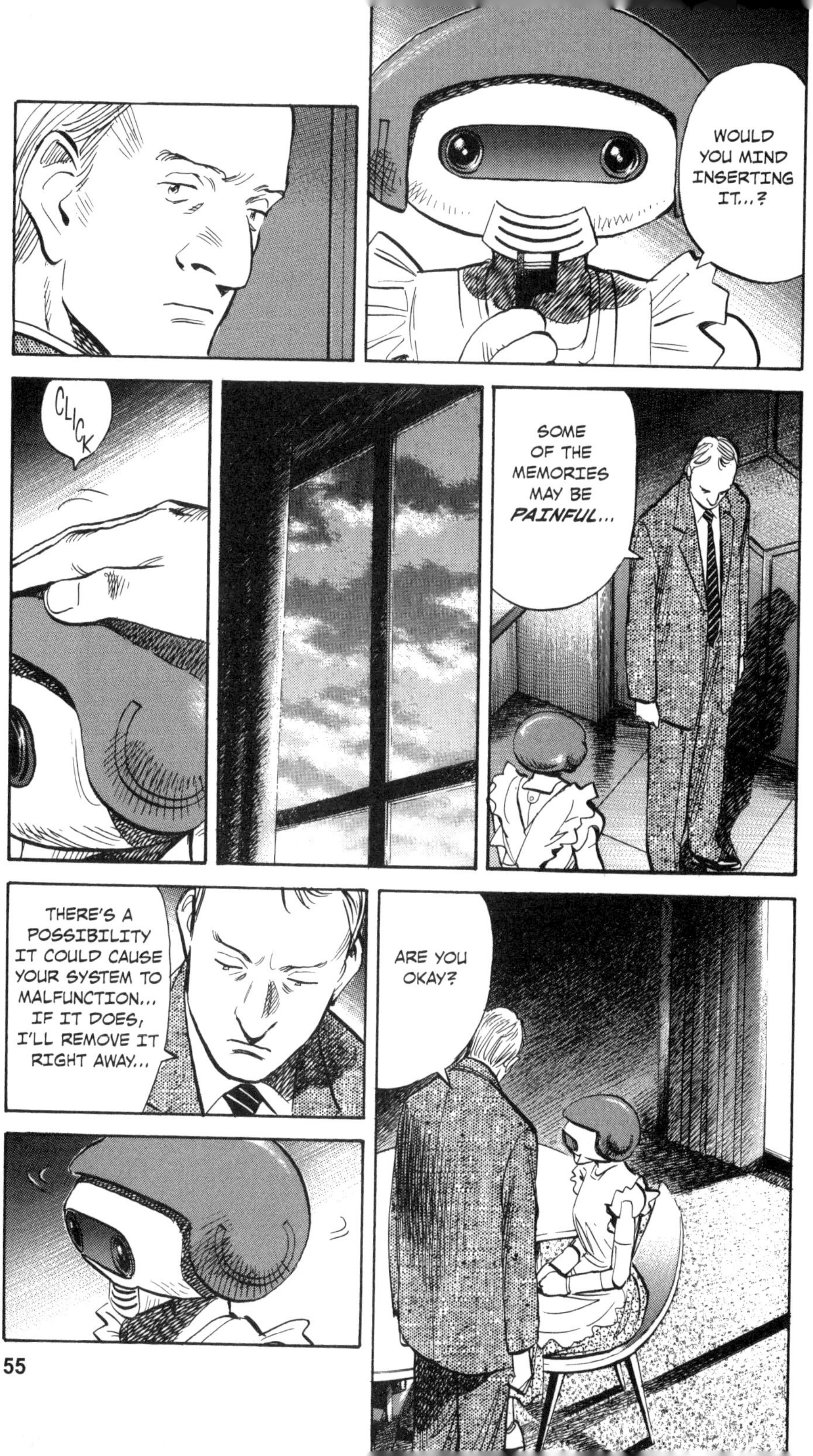
WOULD YOU MIND INSERTING IT...?
SOME OF THE MEMORIES MAY BE PAINFUL...
CLICK
ARE YOU OKAY?
THERE'S A POSSIBILITY IT COULD CAUSE YOUR SYSTEM TO MALFUNCTION... IF IT DOES, I'LL REMOVE IT RIGHT AWAY...

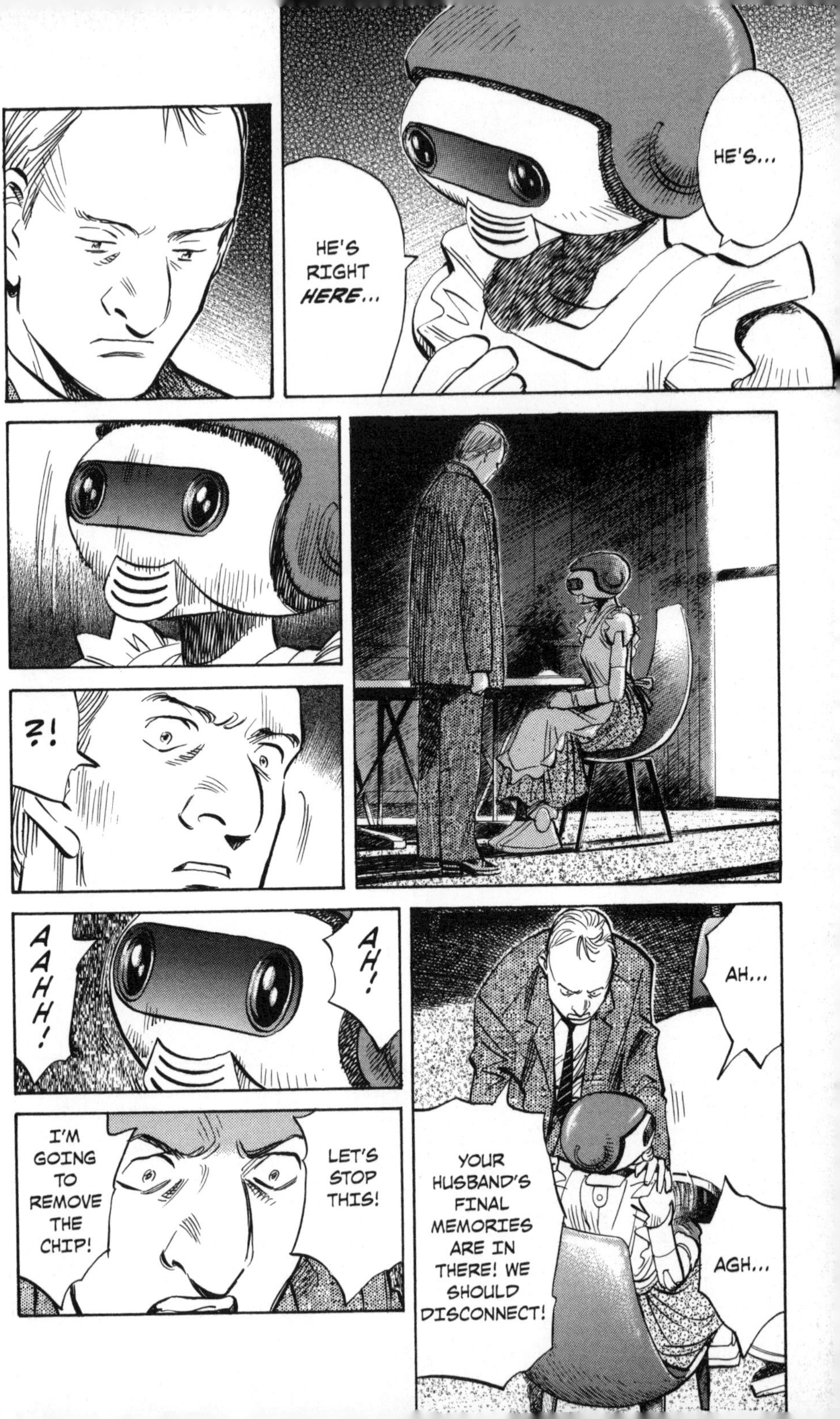
HE'S...
HE'S RIGHT *HERE*...
?!
AH...
YOUR HUSBAND'S FINAL MEMORIES ARE IN THERE! WE SHOULD DISCONNECT!
AGH...
AH!
AAHH!
LET'S STOP THIS!
I'M GOING TO REMOVE THE CHIP!

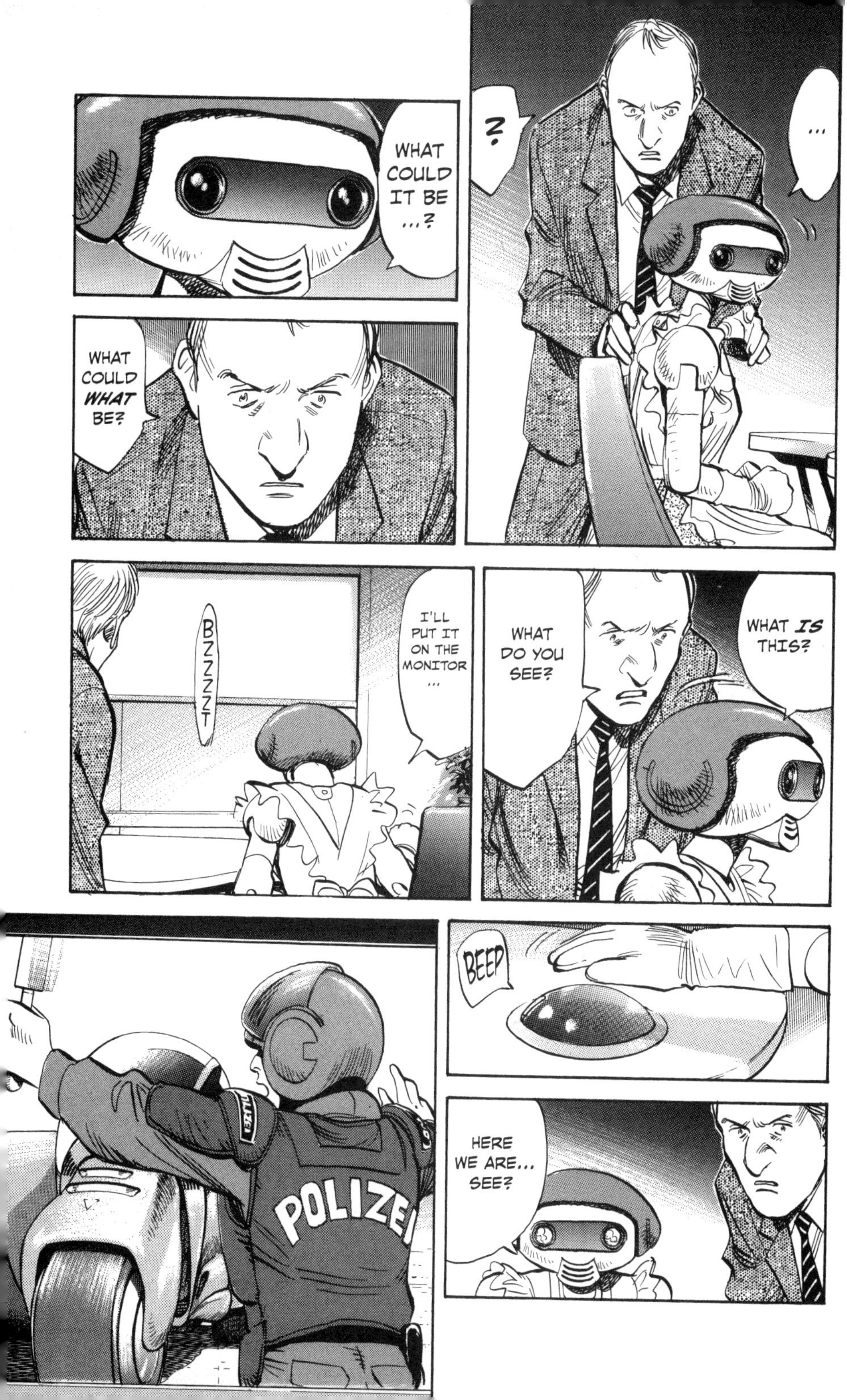
...
?
WHAT COULD IT BE ...?
WHAT COULD *WHAT* BE?
WHAT *IS* THIS?
WHAT DO YOU SEE?
I'LL PUT IT ON THE MONITOR ...
BZZZZT
BEEP
HERE WE ARE... SEE?
POLIZEI

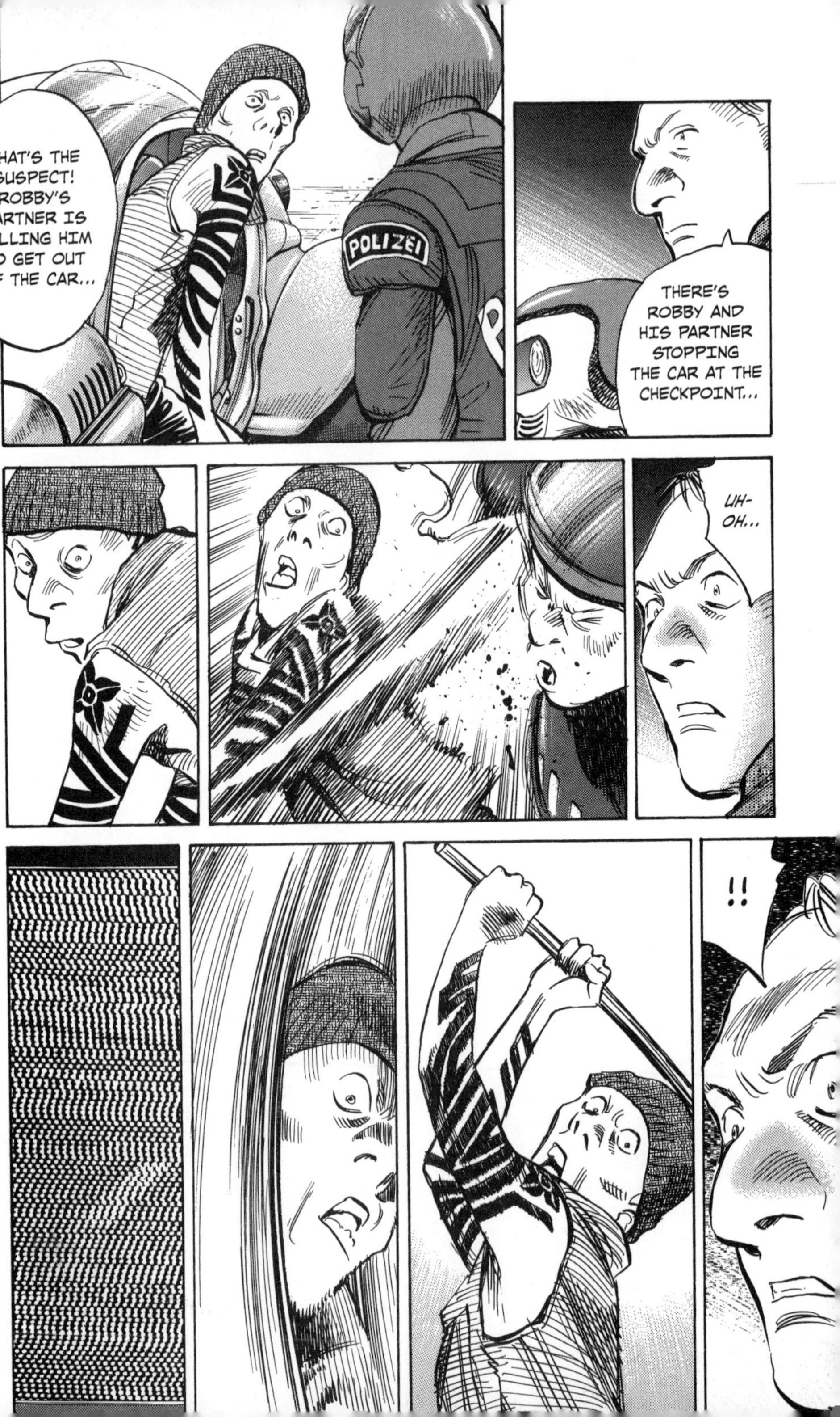
THERE'S ROBBY AND HIS PARTNER STOPPING THE CAR AT THE CHECKPOINT...
THAT'S THE SUSPECT! ROBBY'S PARTNER IS TELLING HIM TO GET OUT OF THE CAR...
POLIZEI
UH-OH...
!!

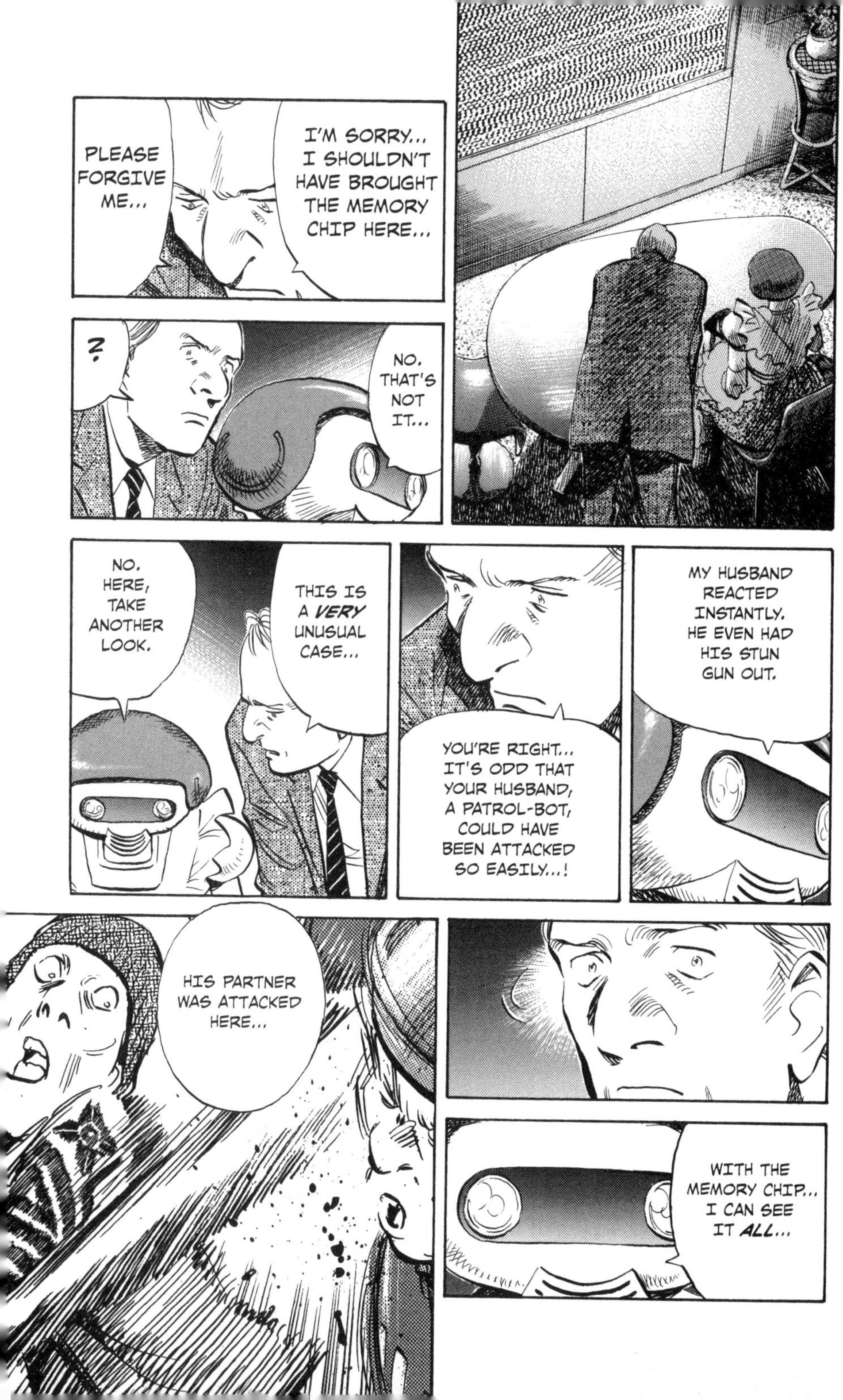
I'M SORRY... I SHOULDN'T HAVE BROUGHT THE MEMORY CHIP HERE...
PLEASE FORGIVE ME...
NO. THAT'S NOT IT...
?
MY HUSBAND REACTED INSTANTLY. HE EVEN HAD HIS STUN GUN OUT.
YOU'RE RIGHT... IT'S ODD THAT YOUR HUSBAND, A PATROL-BOT, COULD HAVE BEEN ATTACKED SO EASILY...!
THIS IS A *VERY* UNUSUAL CASE...
NO. HERE, TAKE ANOTHER LOOK.
WITH THE MEMORY CHIP... I CAN SEE IT *ALL*...
HIS PARTNER WAS ATTACKED HERE...

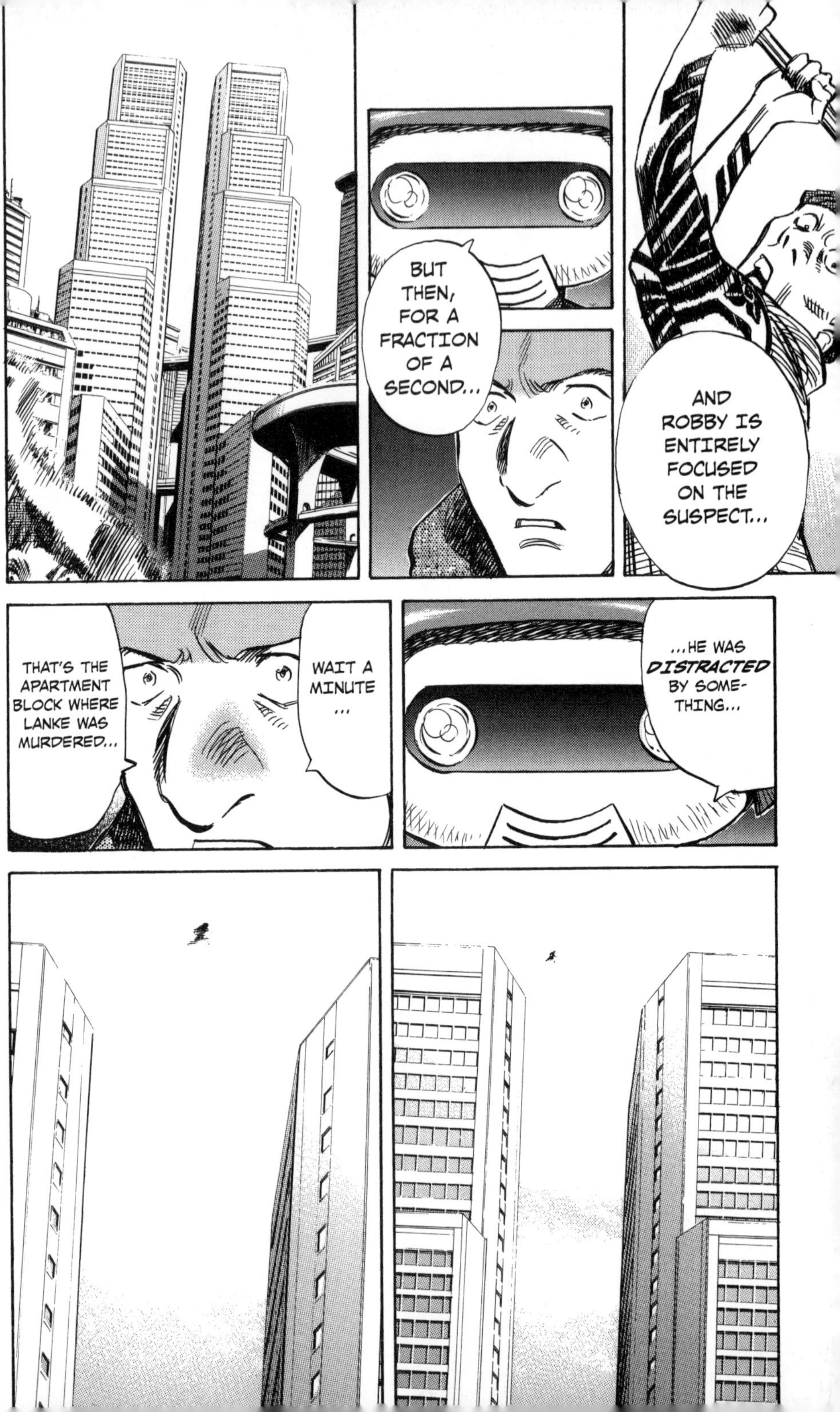
AND ROBBY IS ENTIRELY FOCUSED ON THE SUSPECT...
BUT THEN, FOR A FRACTION OF A SECOND...
...HE WAS *DISTRACTED* BY SOME-THING...
WAIT A MINUTE ...
THAT'S THE APARTMENT BLOCK WHERE LANKE WAS MURDERED...

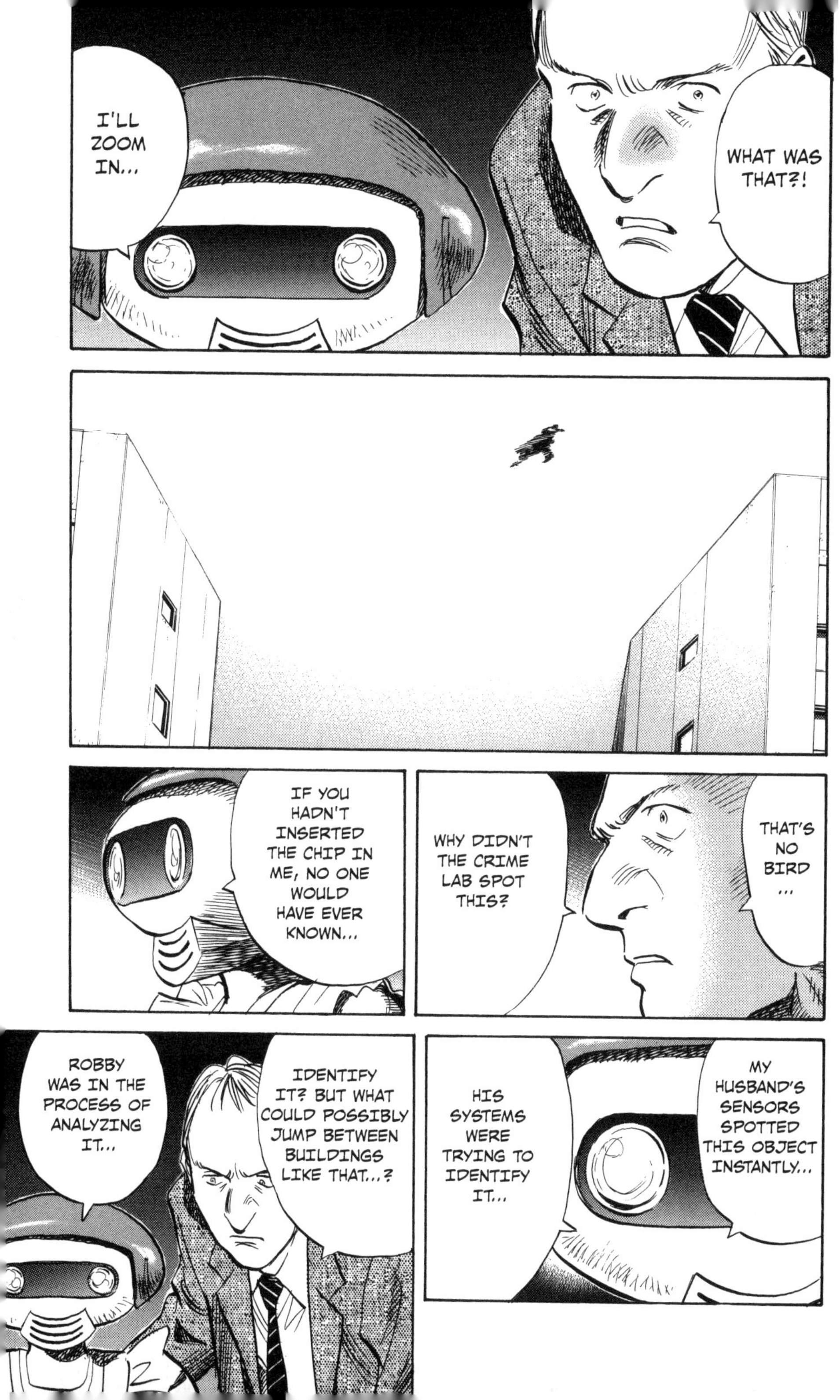
WHAT WAS THAT?!
I'LL ZOOM IN...
THAT'S NO BIRD ...
WHY DIDN'T THE CRIME LAB SPOT THIS?
IF YOU HADN'T INSERTED THE CHIP IN ME, NO ONE WOULD HAVE EVER KNOWN...
MY HUSBAND'S SENSORS SPOTTED THIS OBJECT INSTANTLY...
HIS SYSTEMS WERE TRYING TO IDENTIFY IT...
IDENTIFY IT? BUT WHAT COULD POSSIBLY JUMP BETWEEN BUILDINGS LIKE THAT...?
ROBBY WAS IN THE PROCESS OF ANALYZING IT...

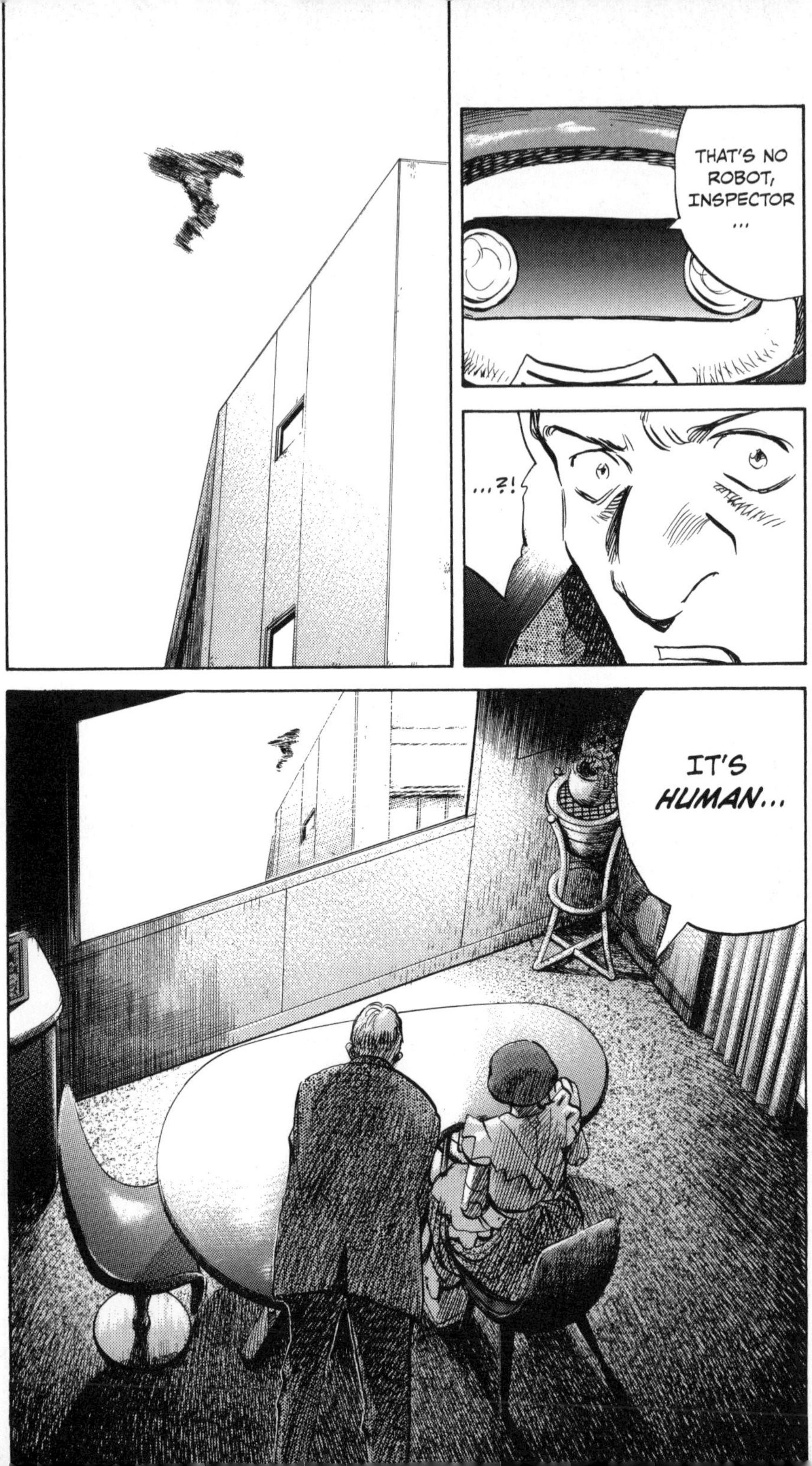
THAT'S NO ROBOT, INSPECTOR ...
...?!
IT'S HUMAN...

Act 3 BRAU 1589

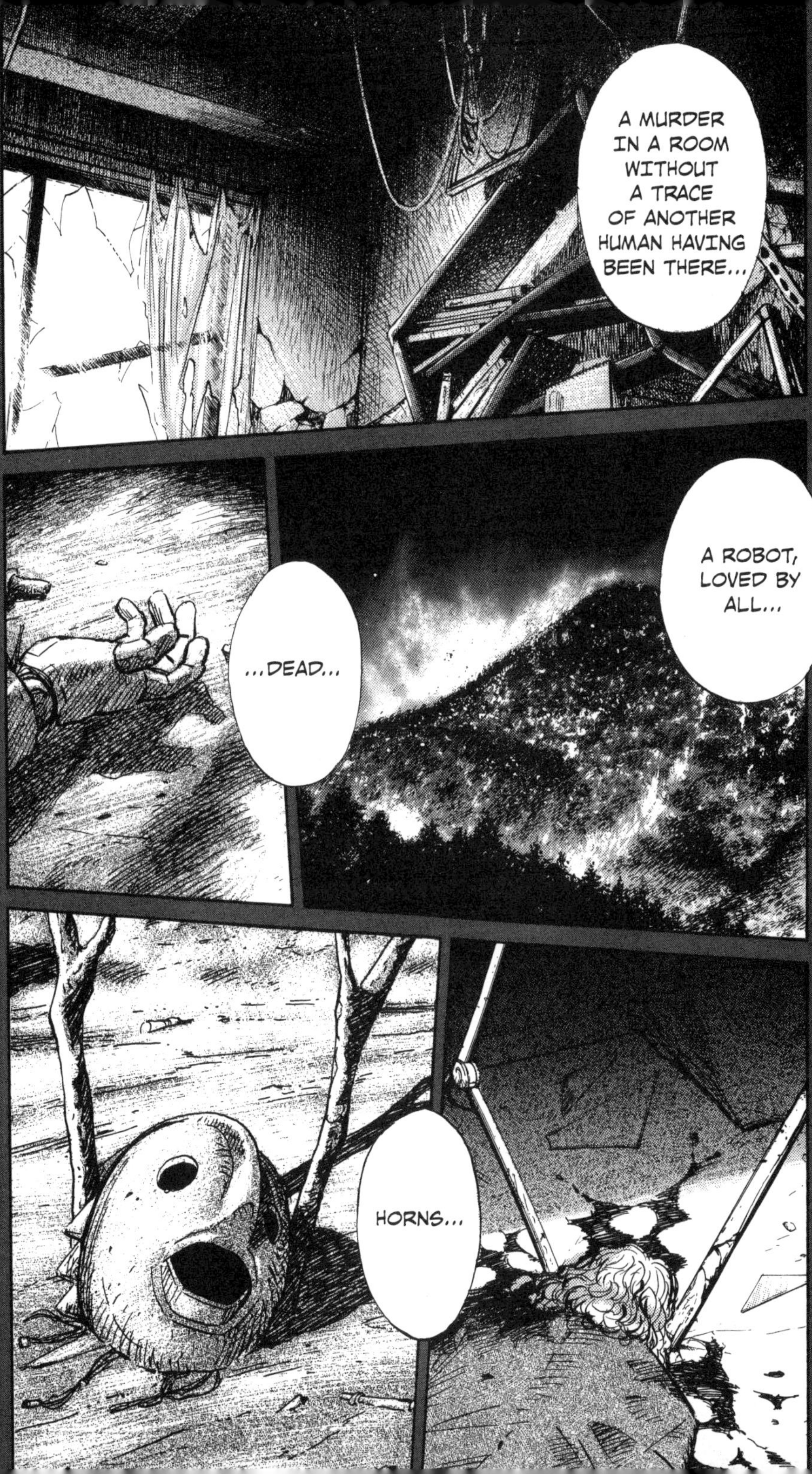
A MURDER IN A ROOM WITHOUT A TRACE OF ANOTHER HUMAN HAVING BEEN THERE...
A ROBOT, LOVED BY ALL...
...DEAD...
HORNS...

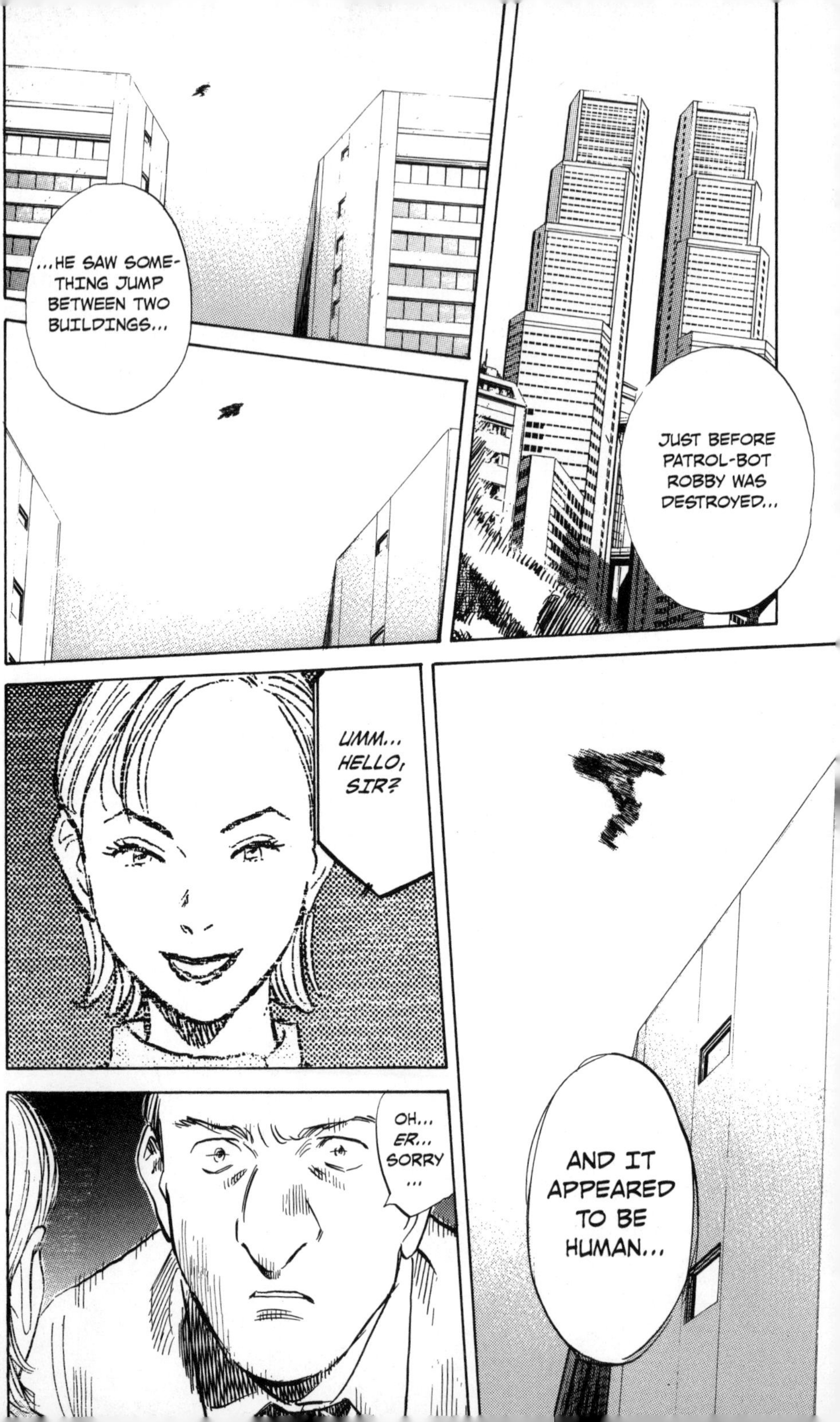
JUST BEFORE PATROL-BOT ROBBY WAS DESTROYED...
...HE SAW SOME-THING JUMP BETWEEN TWO BUILDINGS...
AND IT APPEARED TO BE HUMAN...
UMM... HELLO, SIR?
OH... ER... SORRY ...

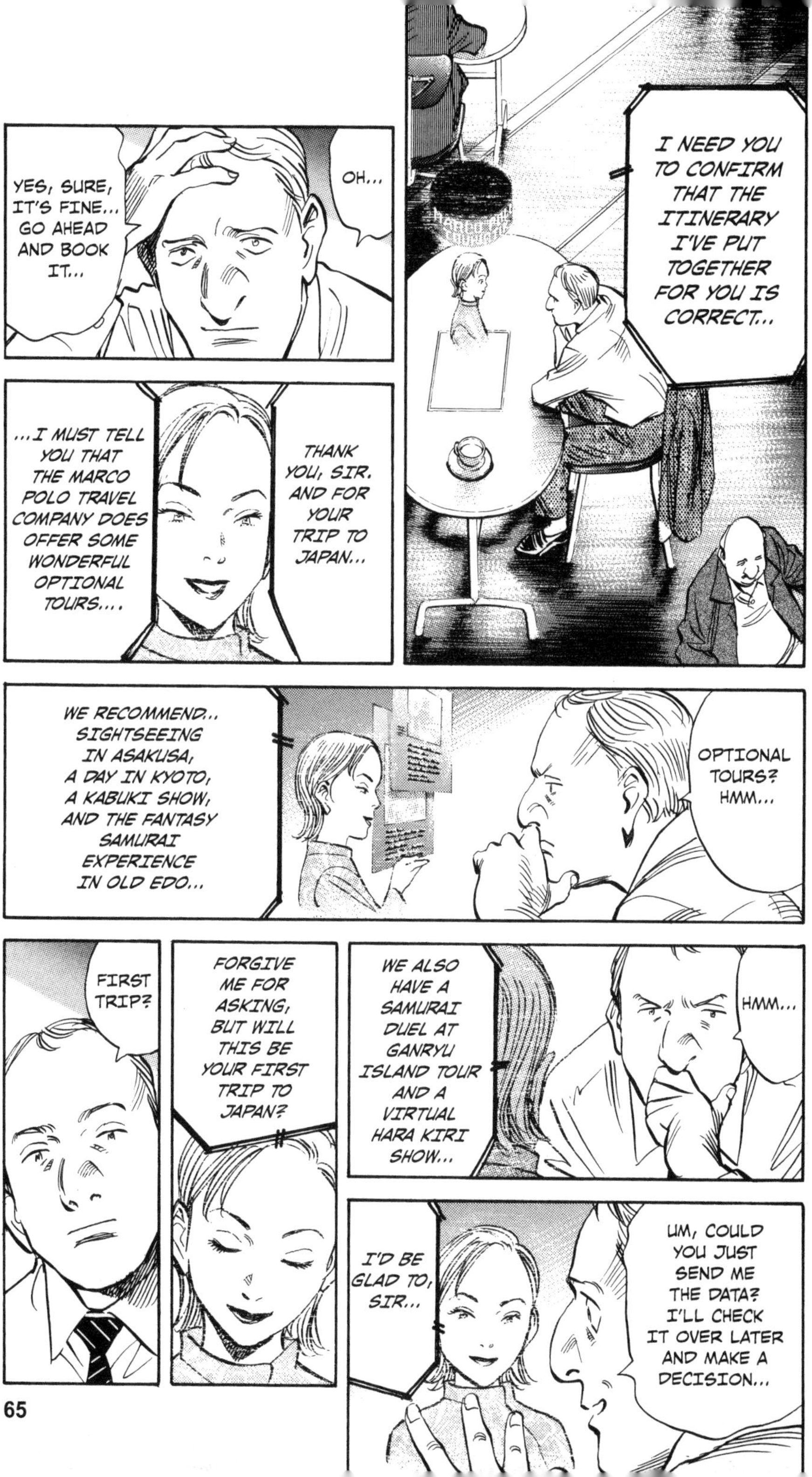
I NEED YOU TO CONFIRM THAT THE ITINERARY I'VE PUT TOGETHER FOR YOU IS CORRECT...
OH...
YES, SURE, IT'S FINE... GO AHEAD AND BOOK IT...
THANK YOU, SIR. AND FOR YOUR TRIP TO JAPAN...
...I MUST TELL YOU THAT THE MARCO POLO TRAVEL COMPANY DOES OFFER SOME WONDERFUL OPTIONAL TOURS....
OPTIONAL TOURS? HMM...
WE RECOMMEND... SIGHTSEEING IN ASAKUSA, A DAY IN KYOTO, A KABUKI SHOW, AND THE FANTASY SAMURAI EXPERIENCE IN OLD EDO...
HMM...
WE ALSO HAVE A SAMURAI DUEL AT GANRYU ISLAND TOUR AND A VIRTUAL HARA KIRI SHOW...
UM, COULD YOU JUST SEND ME THE DATA? I'LL CHECK IT OVER LATER AND MAKE A DECISION...
I'D BE GLAD TO, SIR...
FORGIVE ME FOR ASKING, BUT WILL THIS BE YOUR FIRST TRIP TO JAPAN?
FIRST TRIP?

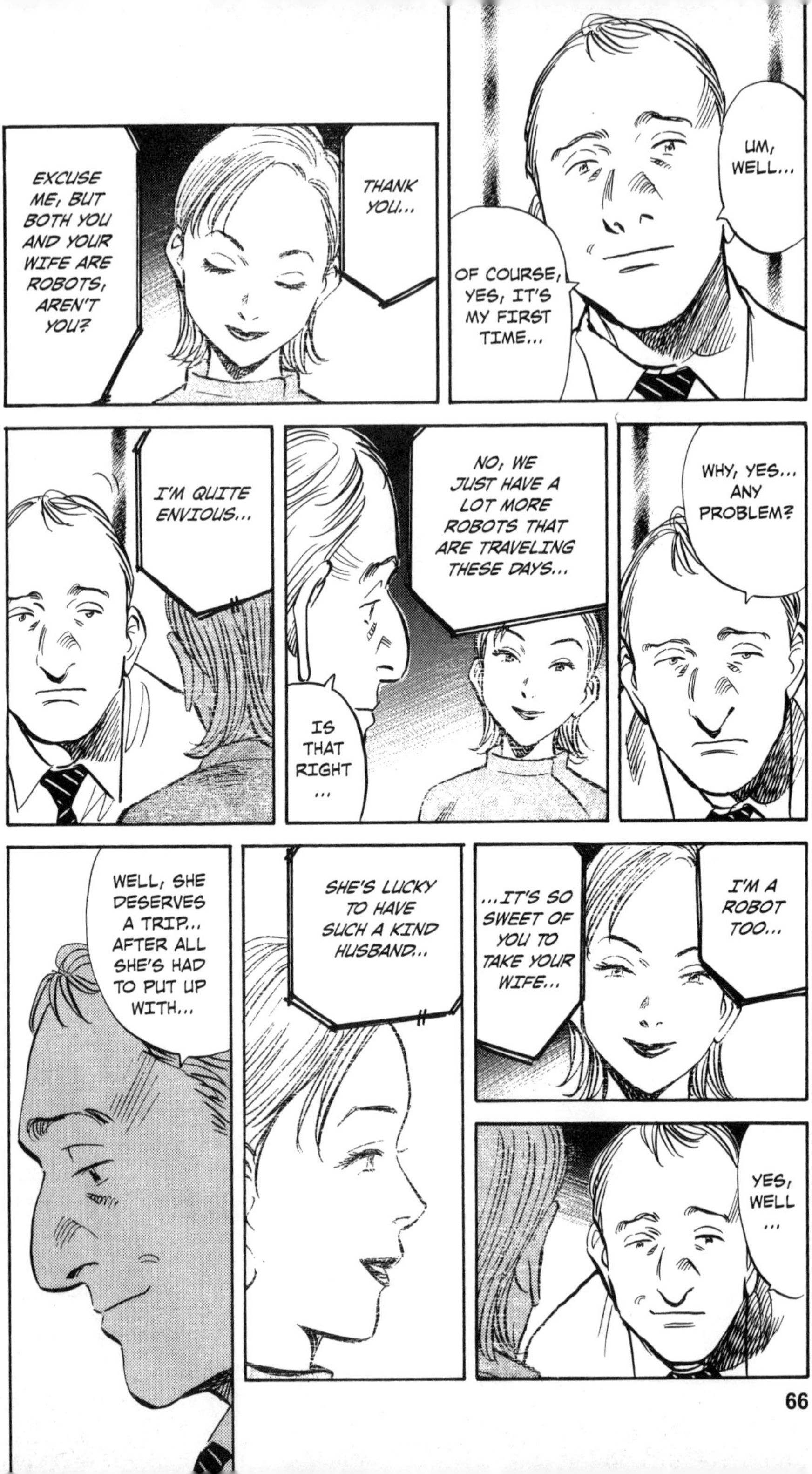
UM, WELL...
OF COURSE, YES, IT'S MY FIRST TIME...
THANK YOU...
EXCUSE ME, BUT BOTH YOU AND YOUR WIFE ARE ROBOTS, AREN'T YOU?
WHY, YES... ANY PROBLEM?
NO, WE JUST HAVE A LOT MORE ROBOTS THAT ARE TRAVELING THESE DAYS...
IS THAT RIGHT...
I'M QUITE ENVIOUS...
I'M A ROBOT TOO...
...IT'S SO SWEET OF YOU TO TAKE YOUR WIFE...
YES, WELL...
SHE'S LUCKY TO HAVE SUCH A KIND HUSBAND...
WELL, SHE DESERVES A TRIP... AFTER ALL SHE'S HAD TO PUT UP WITH...

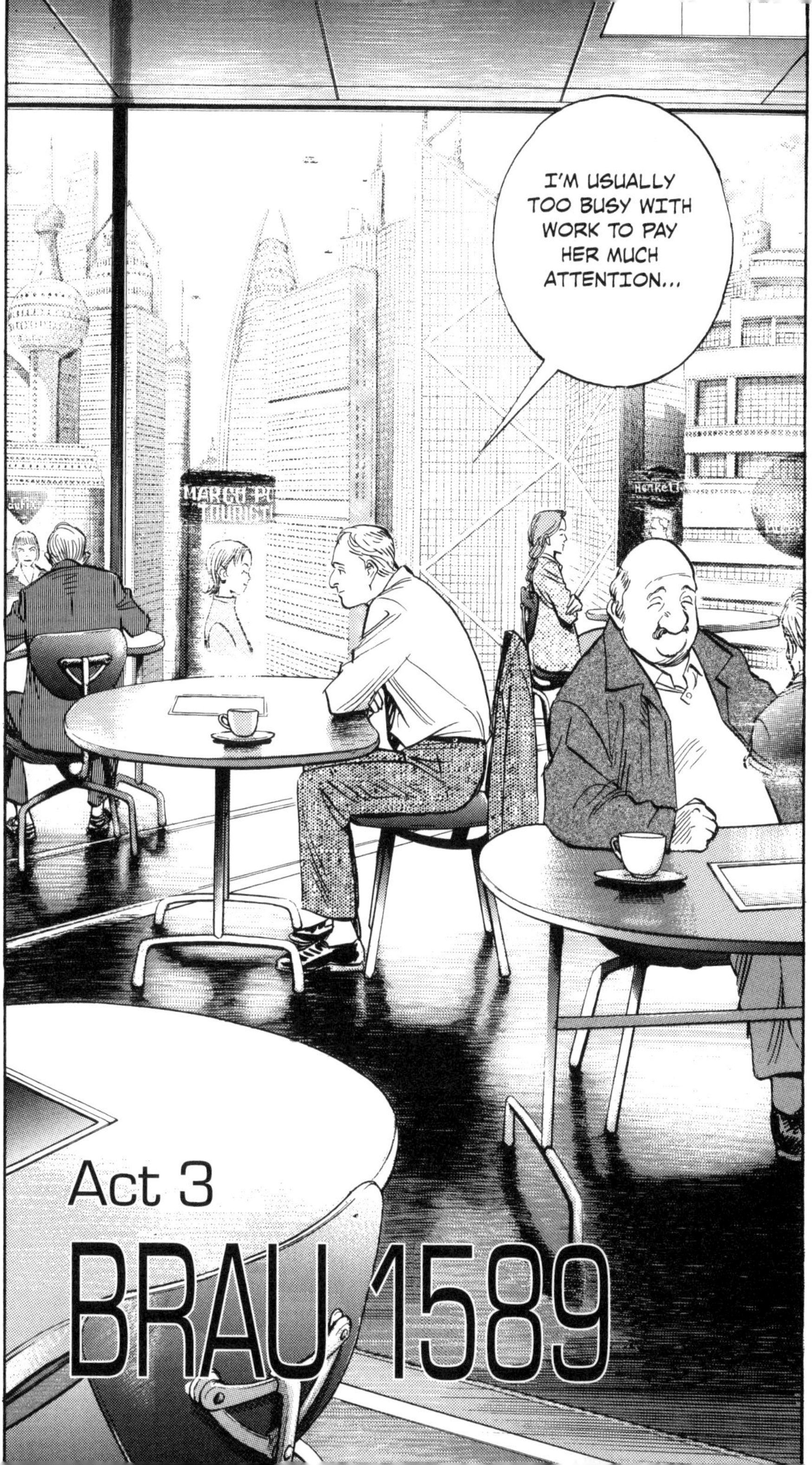
I'M USUALLY TOO BUSY WITH WORK TO PAY HER MUCH ATTENTION...
Act 3
BRAU 1589

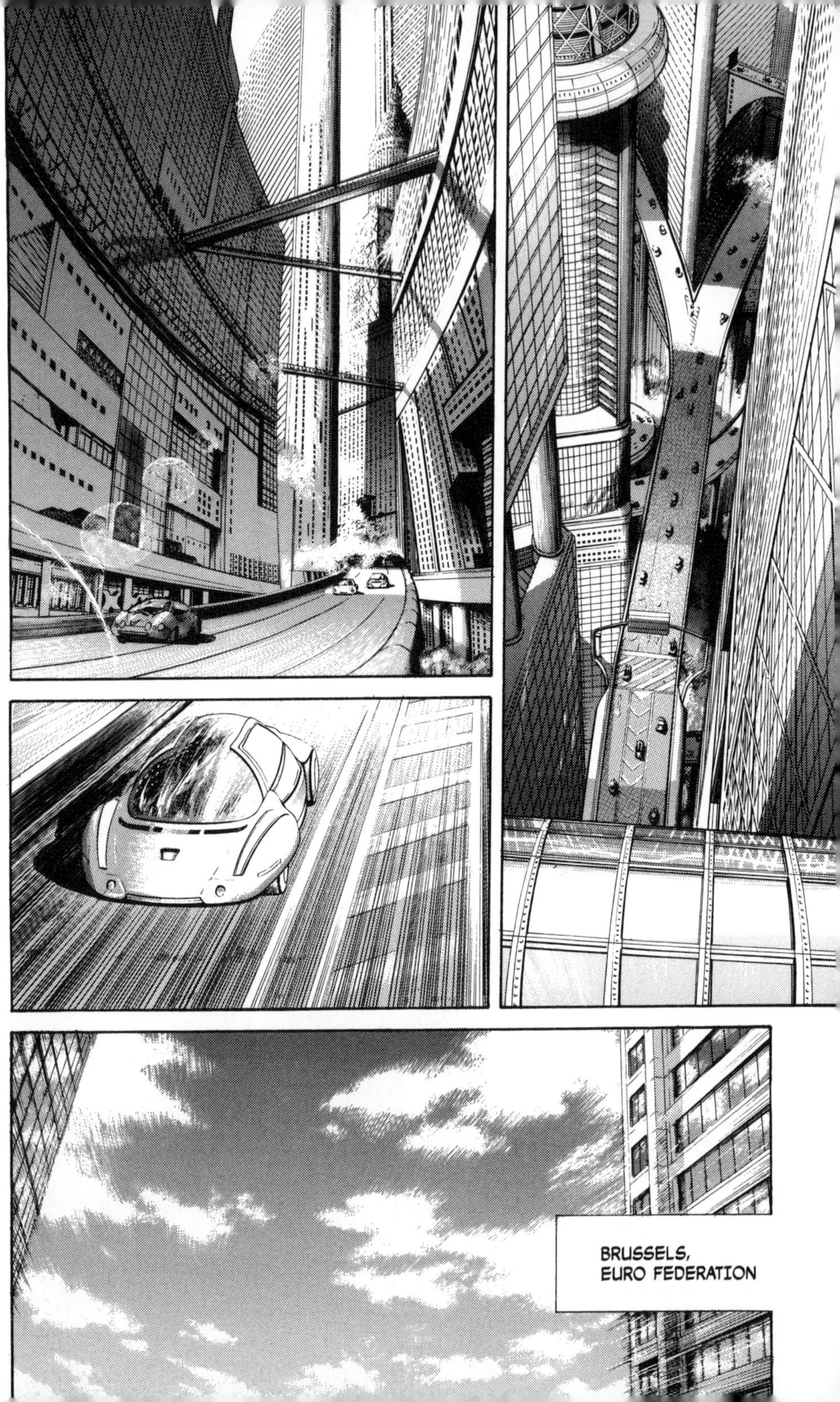
BRUSSELS,
EURO FEDERATION

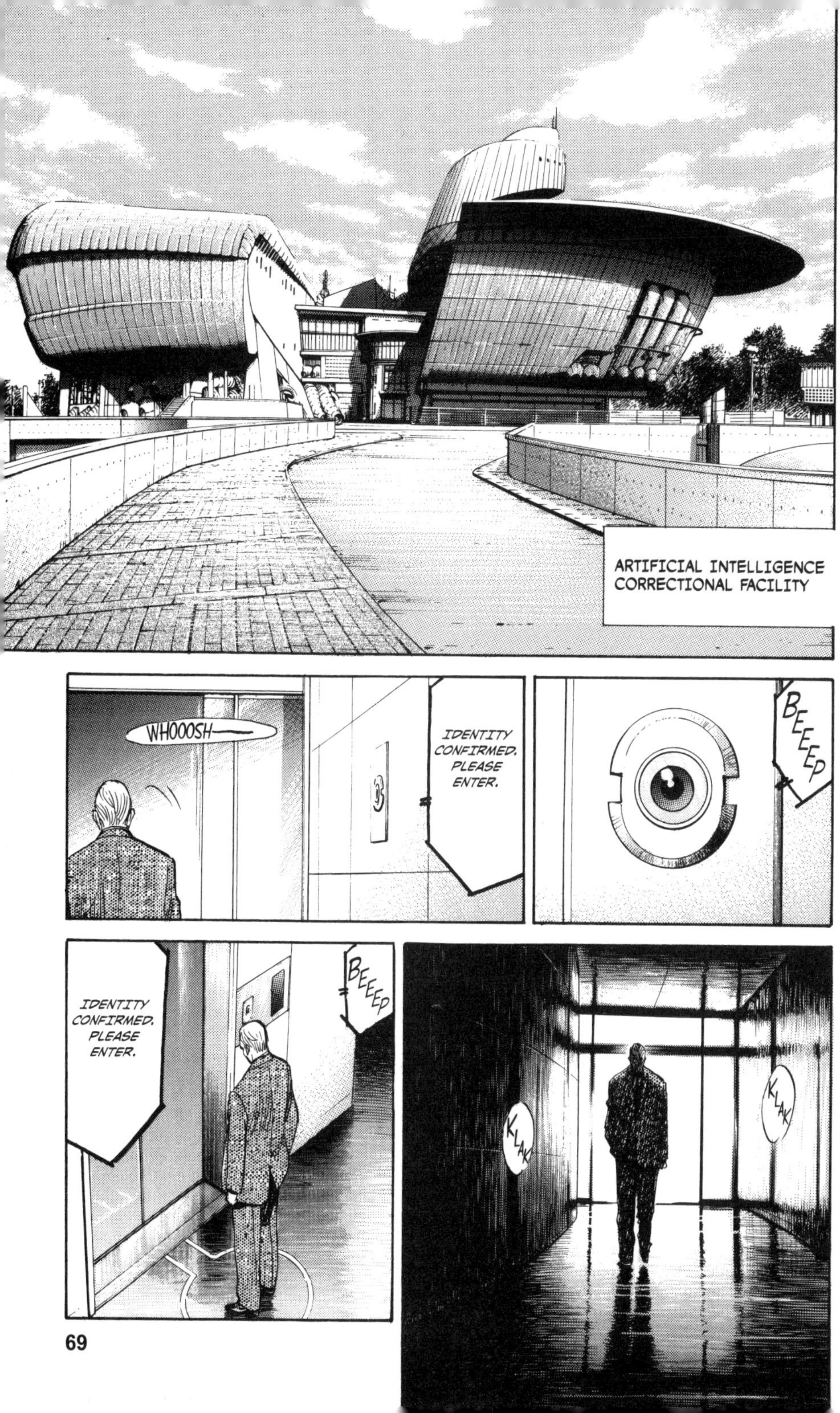
ARTIFICIAL INTELLIGENCE CORRECTIONAL FACILITY
BEEEEP
IDENTITY CONFIRMED. PLEASE ENTER.
WHOOOSH
KLAK
KLAK
BEEEEP
IDENTITY CONFIRMED. PLEASE ENTER.

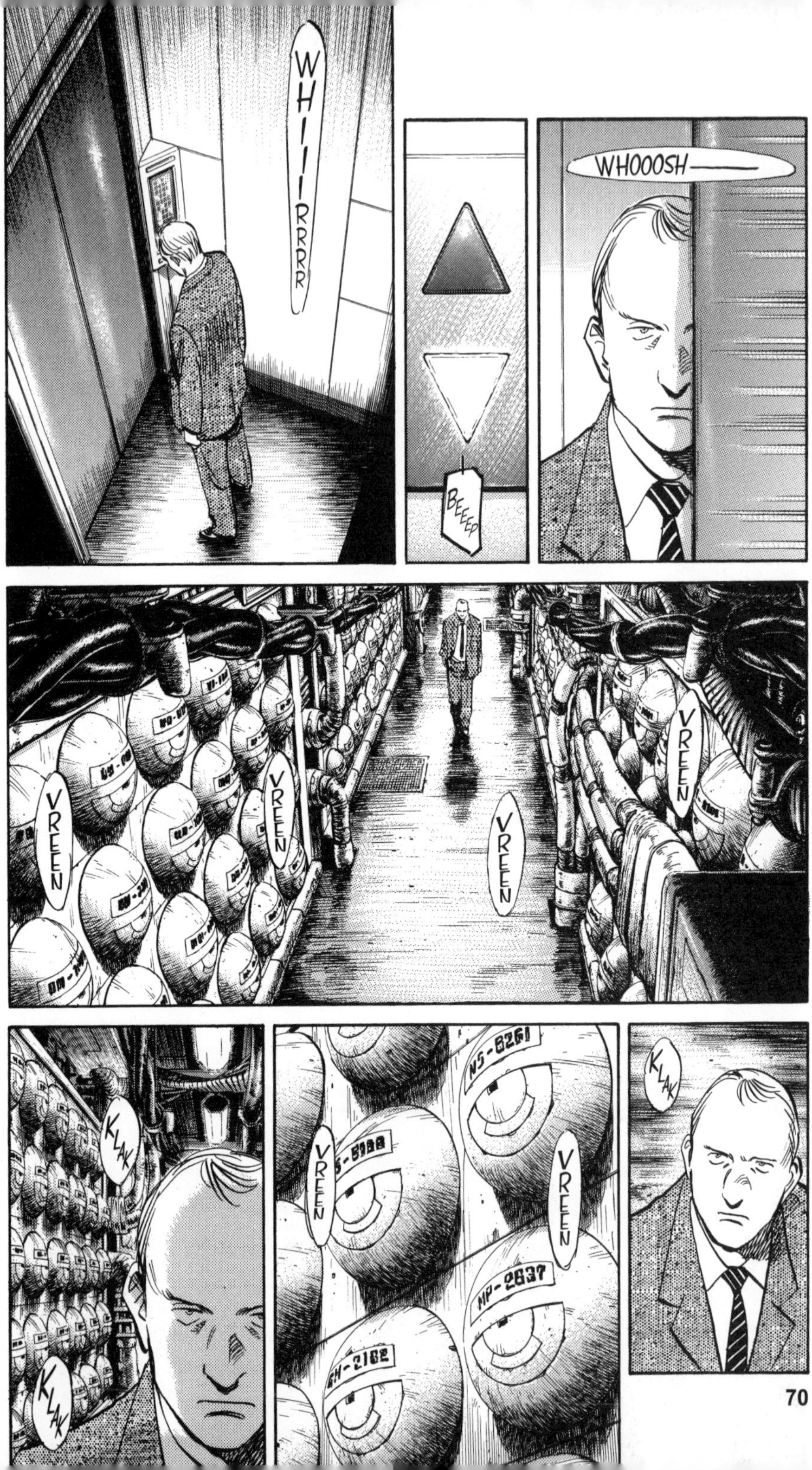

WHOOOSH
BEEEP
WHIIIIRRRR
VREEN
VREEN
VREEN
KLAK
NS-0261
VREEN
VREEN
NP-2637
GH-2162
KLAK
KLAK

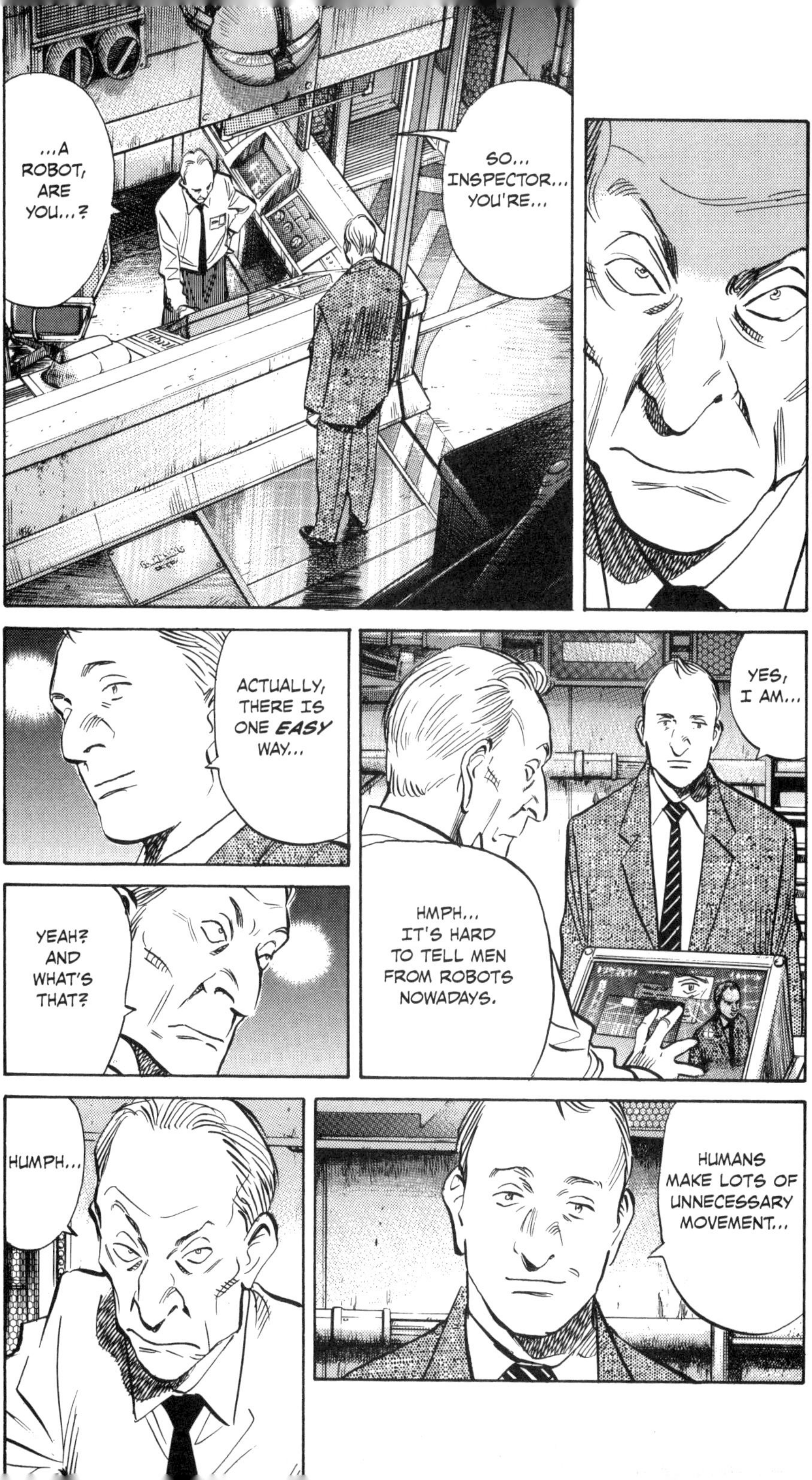
SO... INSPECTOR... YOU'RE...
...A ROBOT, ARE YOU...?
YES, I AM...
HMPH... IT'S HARD TO TELL MEN FROM ROBOTS NOWADAYS.
ACTUALLY, THERE IS ONE *EASY* WAY...
YEAH? AND WHAT'S THAT?
HUMANS MAKE LOTS OF UNNECESSARY MOVEMENT...
HUMPH...

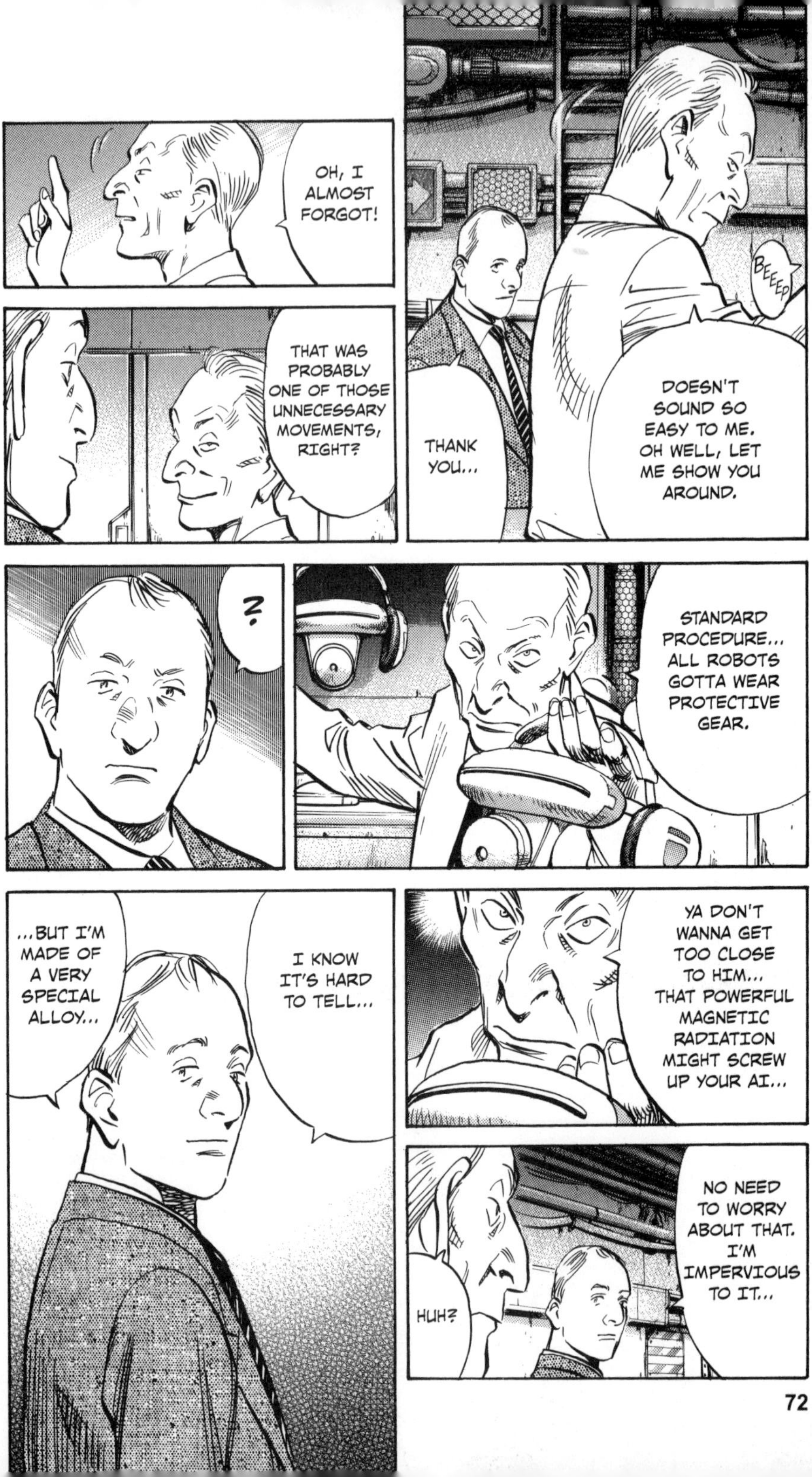
BEEEP
DOESN'T SOUND SO EASY TO ME. OH WELL, LET ME SHOW YOU AROUND.
THANK YOU...
OH, I ALMOST FORGOT!
THAT WAS PROBABLY ONE OF THOSE UNNECESSARY MOVEMENTS, RIGHT?
STANDARD PROCEDURE... ALL ROBOTS GOTTA WEAR PROTECTIVE GEAR.
?
YA DON'T WANNA GET TOO CLOSE TO HIM... THAT POWERFUL MAGNETIC RADIATION MIGHT SCREW UP YOUR AI...
NO NEED TO WORRY ABOUT THAT. I'M IMPERVIOUS TO IT...
HUH?
I KNOW IT'S HARD TO TELL...
...BUT I'M MADE OF A VERY SPECIAL ALLOY...

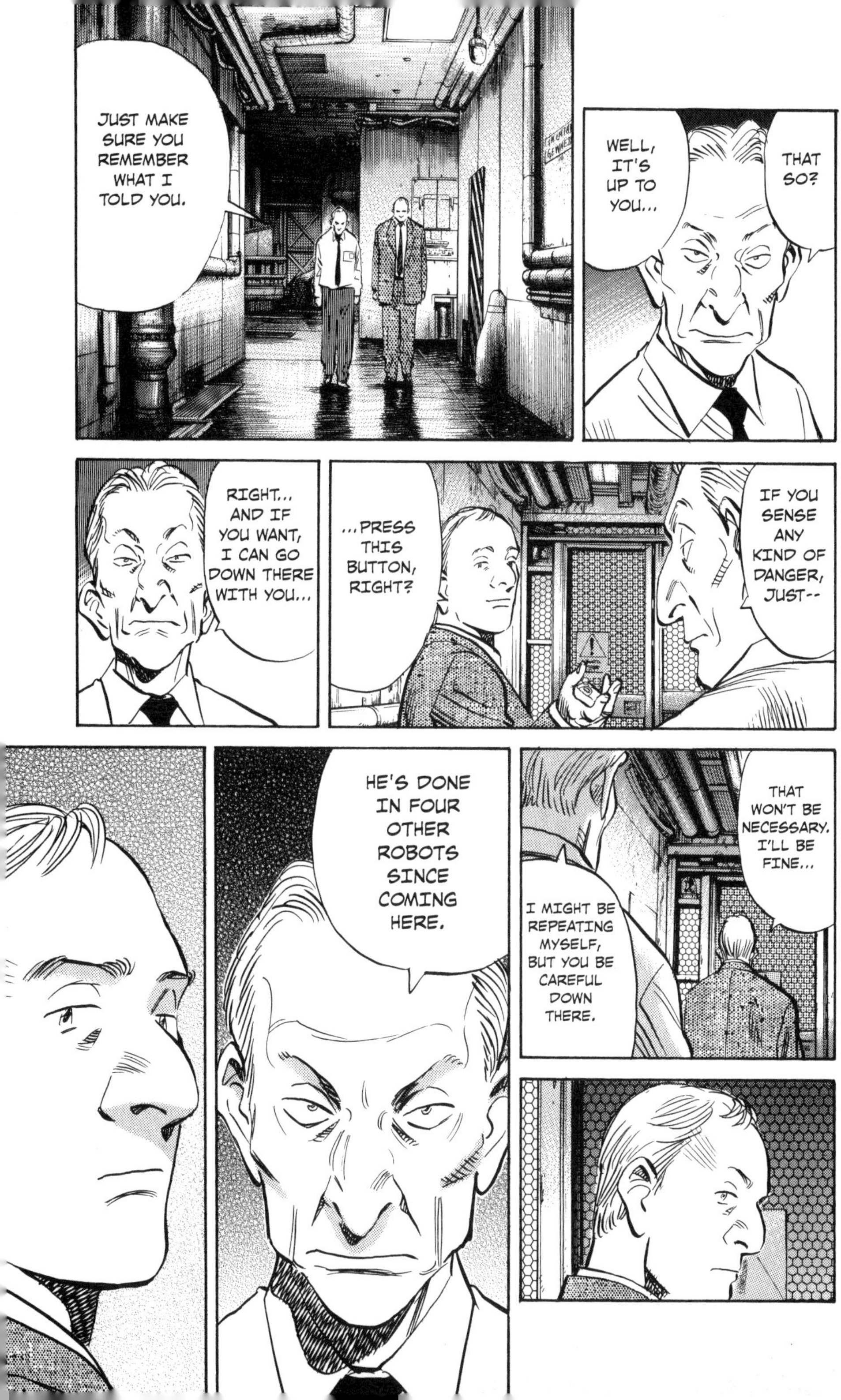
THAT SO?
WELL, IT'S UP TO YOU...
JUST MAKE SURE YOU REMEMBER WHAT I TOLD YOU.
IF YOU SENSE ANY KIND OF DANGER, JUST--
...PRESS THIS BUTTON, RIGHT?
RIGHT... AND IF YOU WANT, I CAN GO DOWN THERE WITH YOU...
THAT WON'T BE NECESSARY. I'LL BE FINE...
I MIGHT BE REPEATING MYSELF, BUT YOU BE CAREFUL DOWN THERE.
HE'S DONE IN FOUR OTHER ROBOTS SINCE COMING HERE.

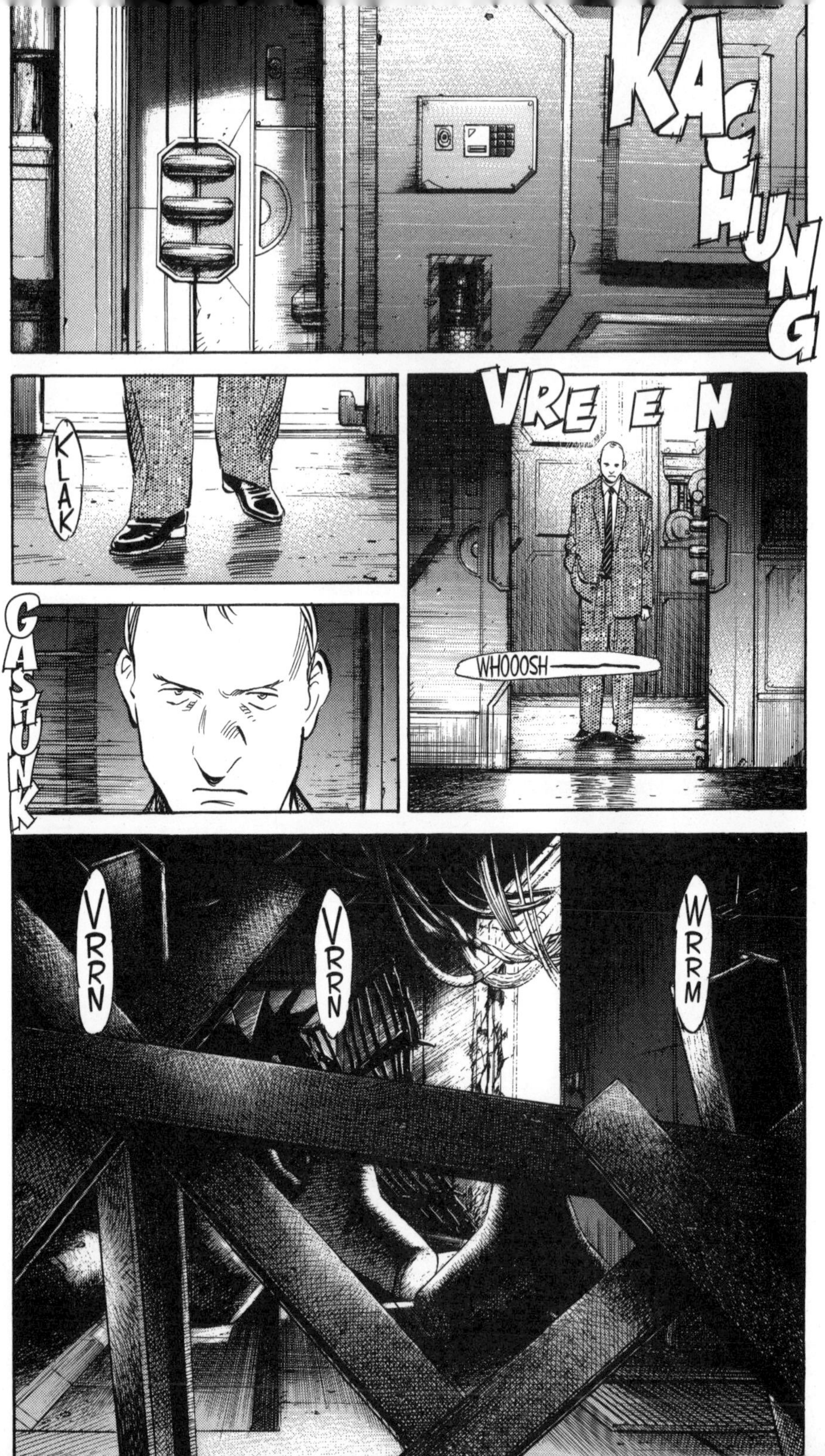
KACHUNG
VREEN
WHOOOSH
KLAK
GASHUNK
WRRM
VRRN
VRRN

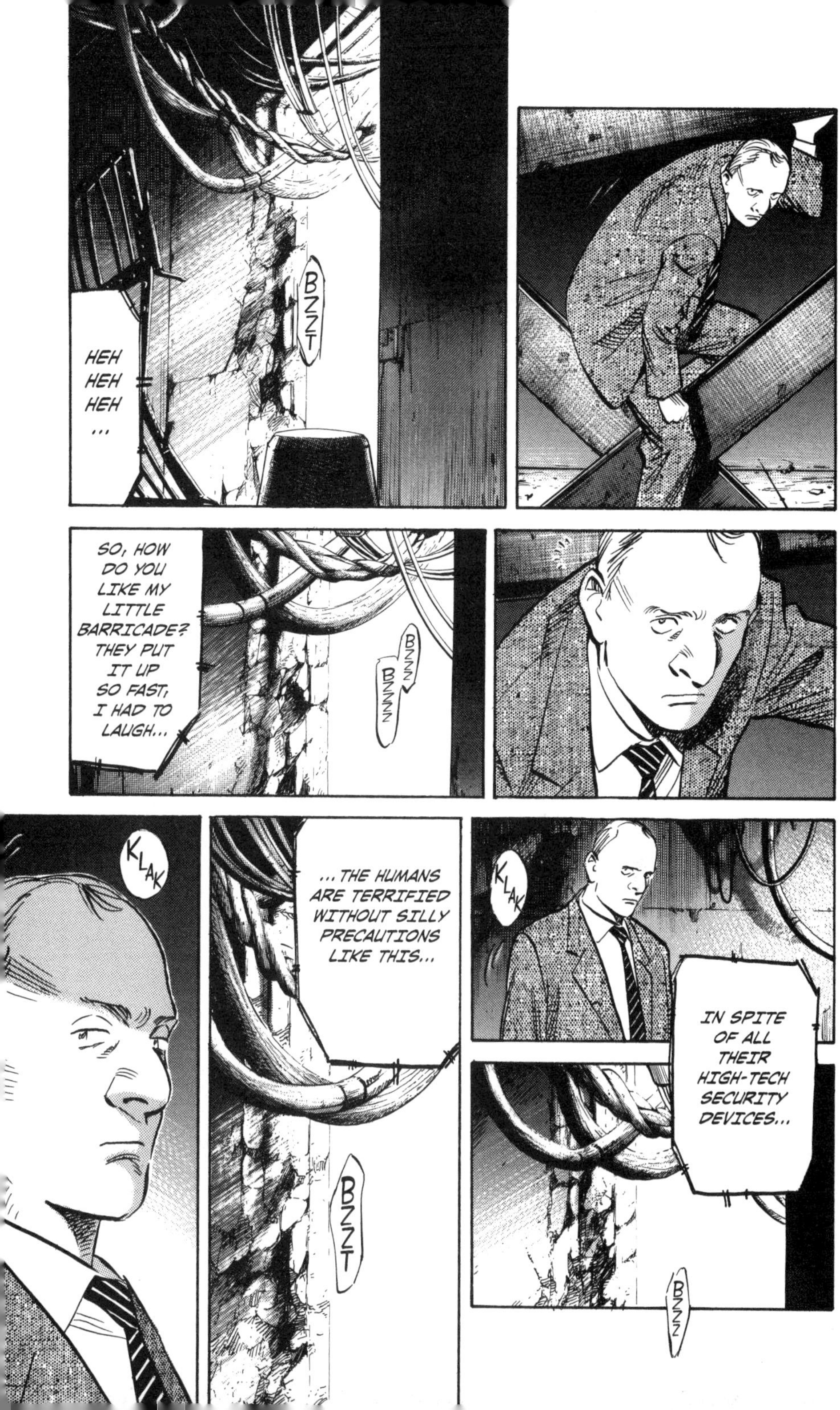
BZZT
HEH HEH HEH ...
SO, HOW DO YOU LIKE MY LITTLE BARRICADE? THEY PUT IT UP SO FAST, I HAD TO LAUGH...
BZZZ
BZZZ
KLAK
IN SPITE OF ALL THEIR HIGH-TECH SECURITY DEVICES...
BZZZ
...THE HUMANS ARE TERRIFIED WITHOUT SILLY PRECAUTIONS LIKE THIS...
BZZT
KLAK

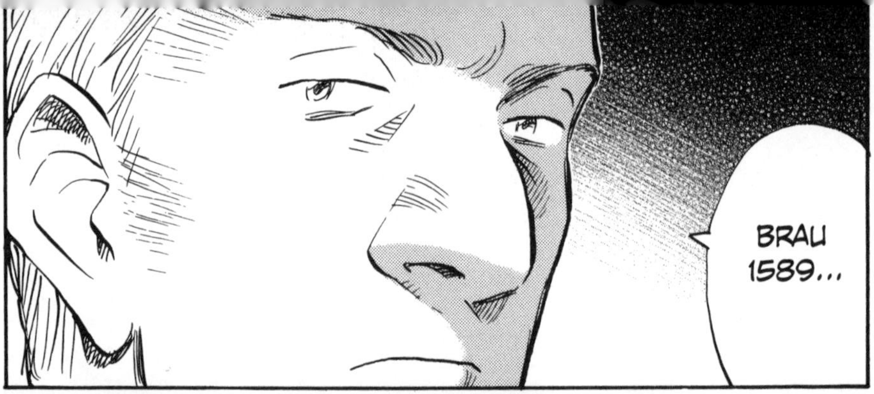
BRAU 1589...

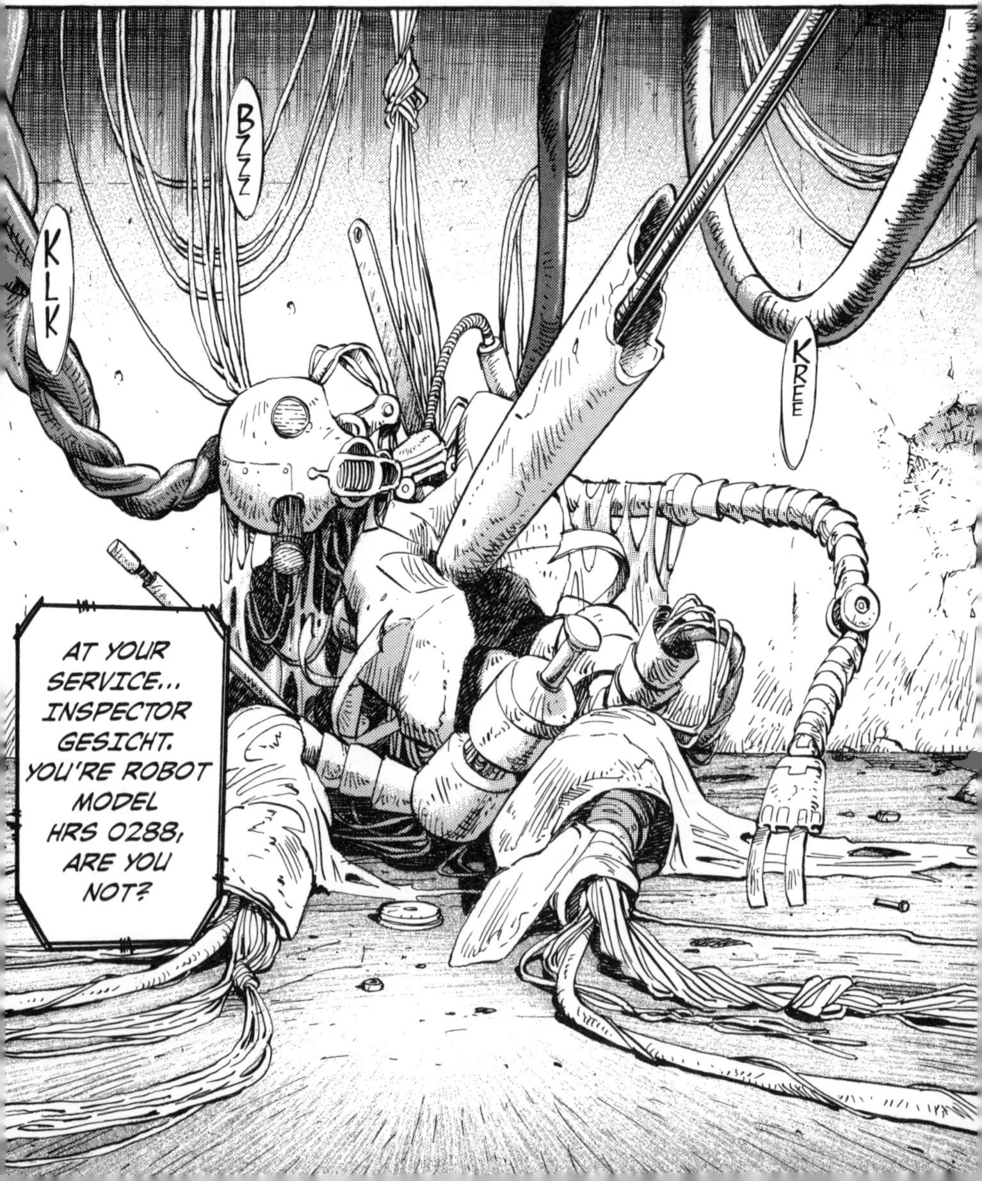
BZZZ
KREE
KLK
AT YOUR SERVICE... INSPECTOR GESICHT. YOU'RE ROBOT MODEL HRS 0288, ARE YOU NOT?

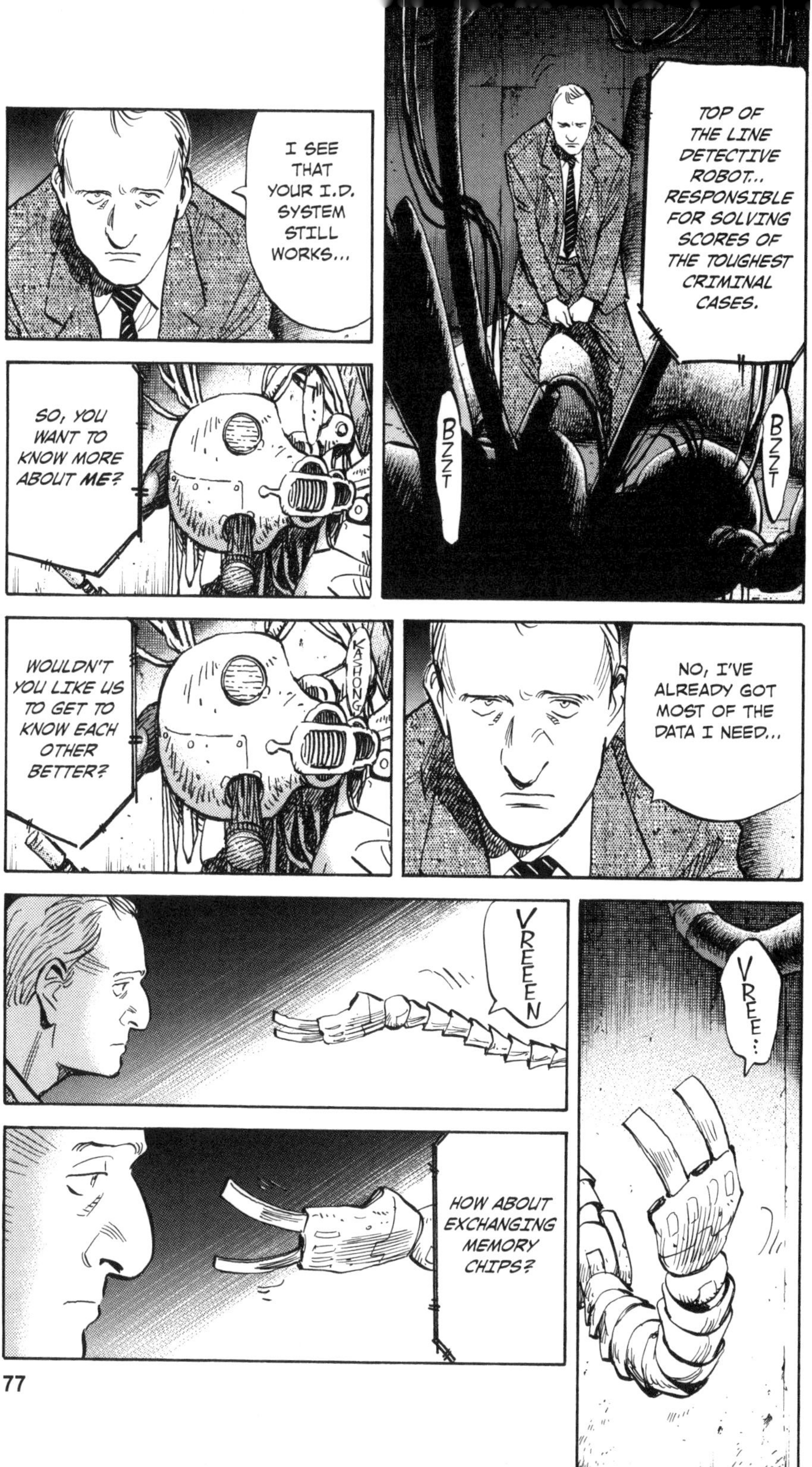
TOP OF THE LINE DETECTIVE ROBOT... RESPONSIBLE FOR SOLVING SCORES OF THE TOUGHEST CRIMINAL CASES.
BZZT
BZZT
I SEE THAT YOUR I.D. SYSTEM STILL WORKS...
SO, YOU WANT TO KNOW MORE ABOUT **ME**?
NO, I'VE ALREADY GOT MOST OF THE DATA I NEED...
KASHONG
WOULDN'T YOU LIKE US TO GET TO KNOW EACH OTHER BETTER?
VREE...
VREEEN
HOW ABOUT EXCHANGING MEMORY CHIPS?

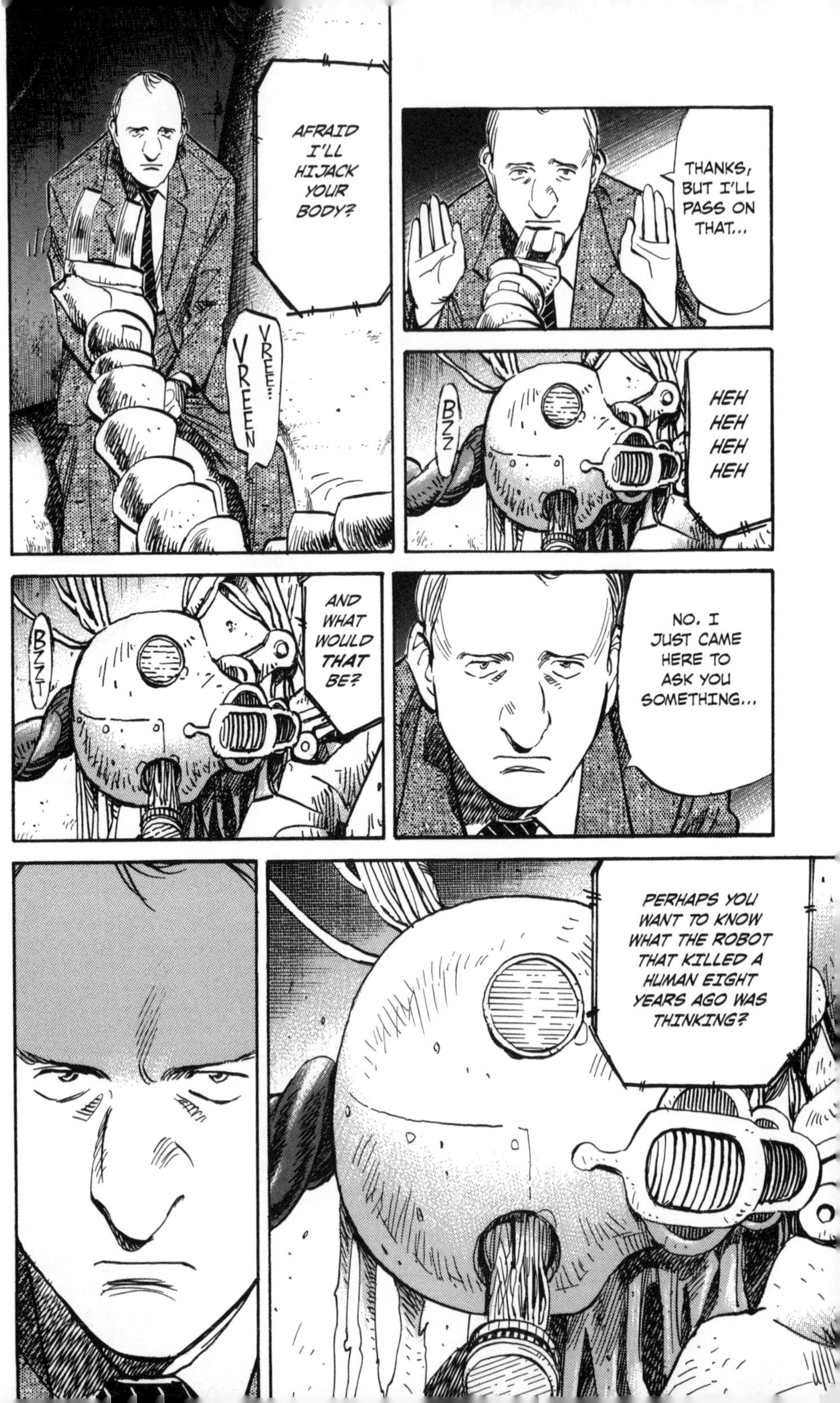
THANKS, BUT I'LL PASS ON THAT...
BZZ
HEH HEH HEH HEH
AFRAID I'LL HIJACK YOUR BODY?
VREEN VREE...
NO. I JUST CAME HERE TO ASK YOU SOMETHING...
BZZT
AND WHAT WOULD THAT BE?
PERHAPS YOU WANT TO KNOW WHAT THE ROBOT THAT KILLED A HUMAN EIGHT YEARS AGO WAS THINKING?

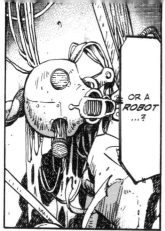

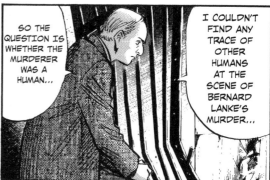

I COULDN'T FIND ANY TRACE OF OTHER HUMANS AT THE SCENE OF BERNARD LANKE'S MURDER...
SO THE QUESTION IS WHETHER THE MURDERER WAS A HUMAN...
OR A *ROBOT*...?
AND IF IT WAS A ROBOT...
...*WHY* WOULD IT DO SUCH A THING...?
BEEP
BZZT
THE HUMANS HAVE ALREADY EXAMINED THE DEEPEST RECESSES OF MY AI...
KREEE
ZZRRP
...BUT THEY COULDN'T FIND ANYTHING WRONG...
BZZZ
VREEN
NOT A *SINGLE* DEFECT...

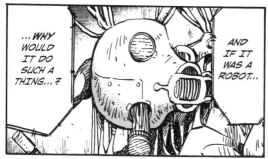

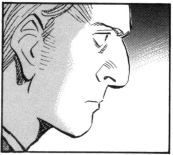

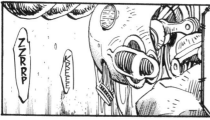

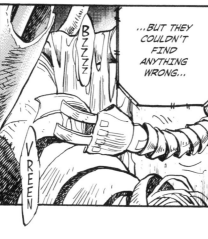

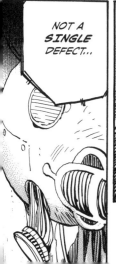

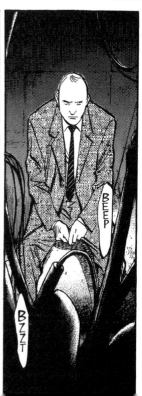

HUMANS ARE TOO CONSUMED BY THEIR OWN FEAR...
BZZT
VRTT
YOU KNOW, IF THEY'RE SO SCARED OF ME, THEY SHOULD PULL OUT THIS SHAFT...
AND I'D DIE...
BUT THEY CAN'T EVEN DO THAT...
BZZT
ALL THEY CAN DO IS JUST QUIVER IN FEAR...
CHAK
VZZT
AND LOCK ME AWAY DOWN HERE IN THIS DUNGEON...
BZZT

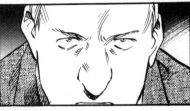

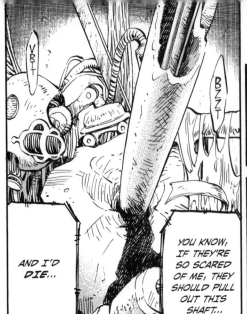

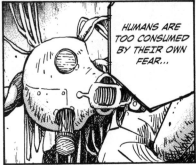

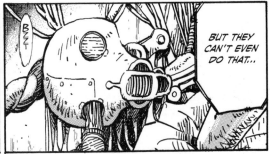

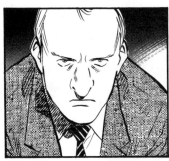

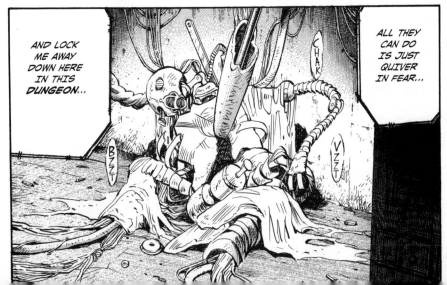

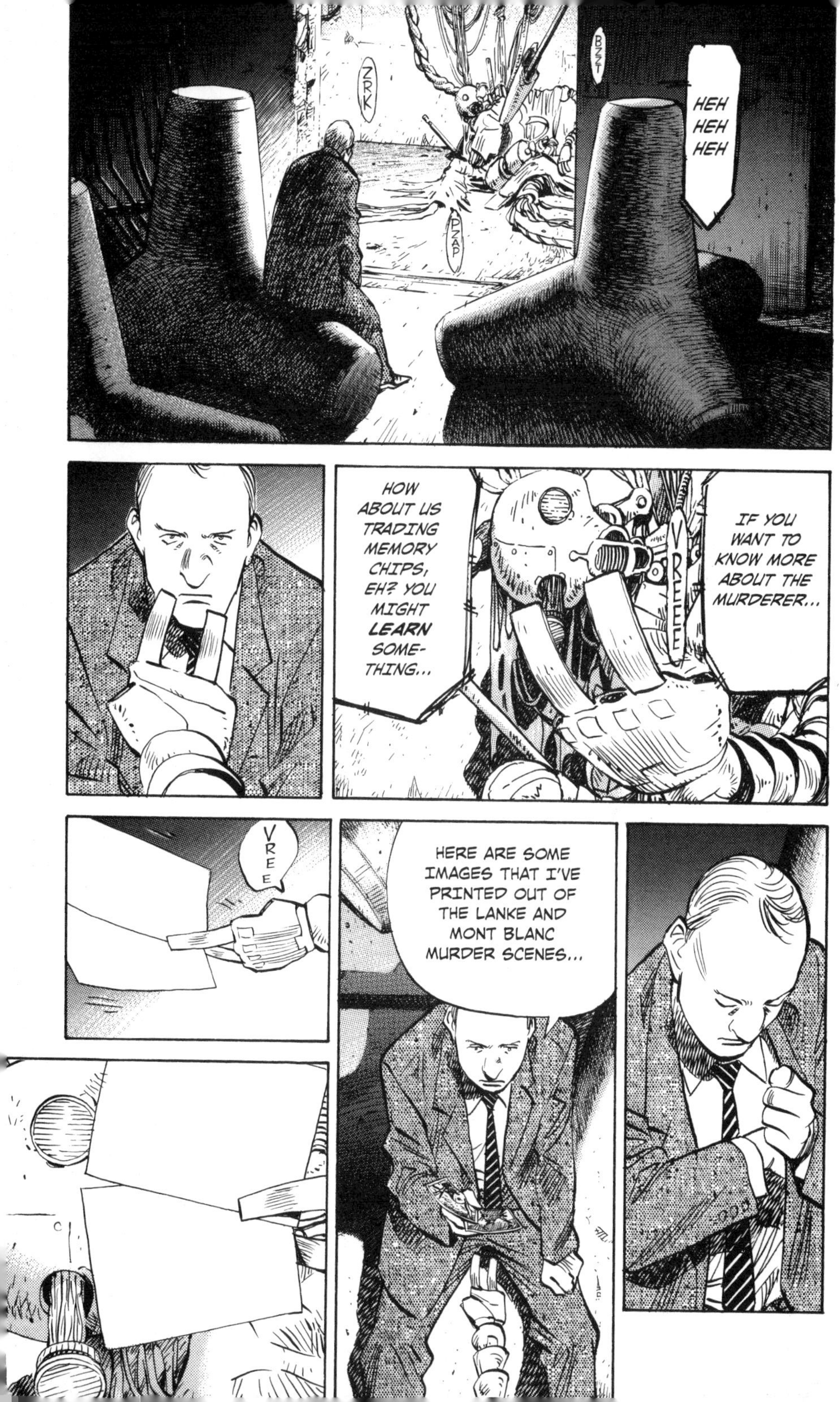
BZZT
HEH HEH HEH
ZRK
PZAP
IF YOU WANT TO KNOW MORE ABOUT THE MURDERER...
VREEE
HOW ABOUT US TRADING MEMORY CHIPS, EH? YOU MIGHT **LEARN** SOME-THING...
HERE ARE SOME IMAGES THAT I'VE PRINTED OUT OF THE LANKE AND MONT BLANC MURDER SCENES...
VREE

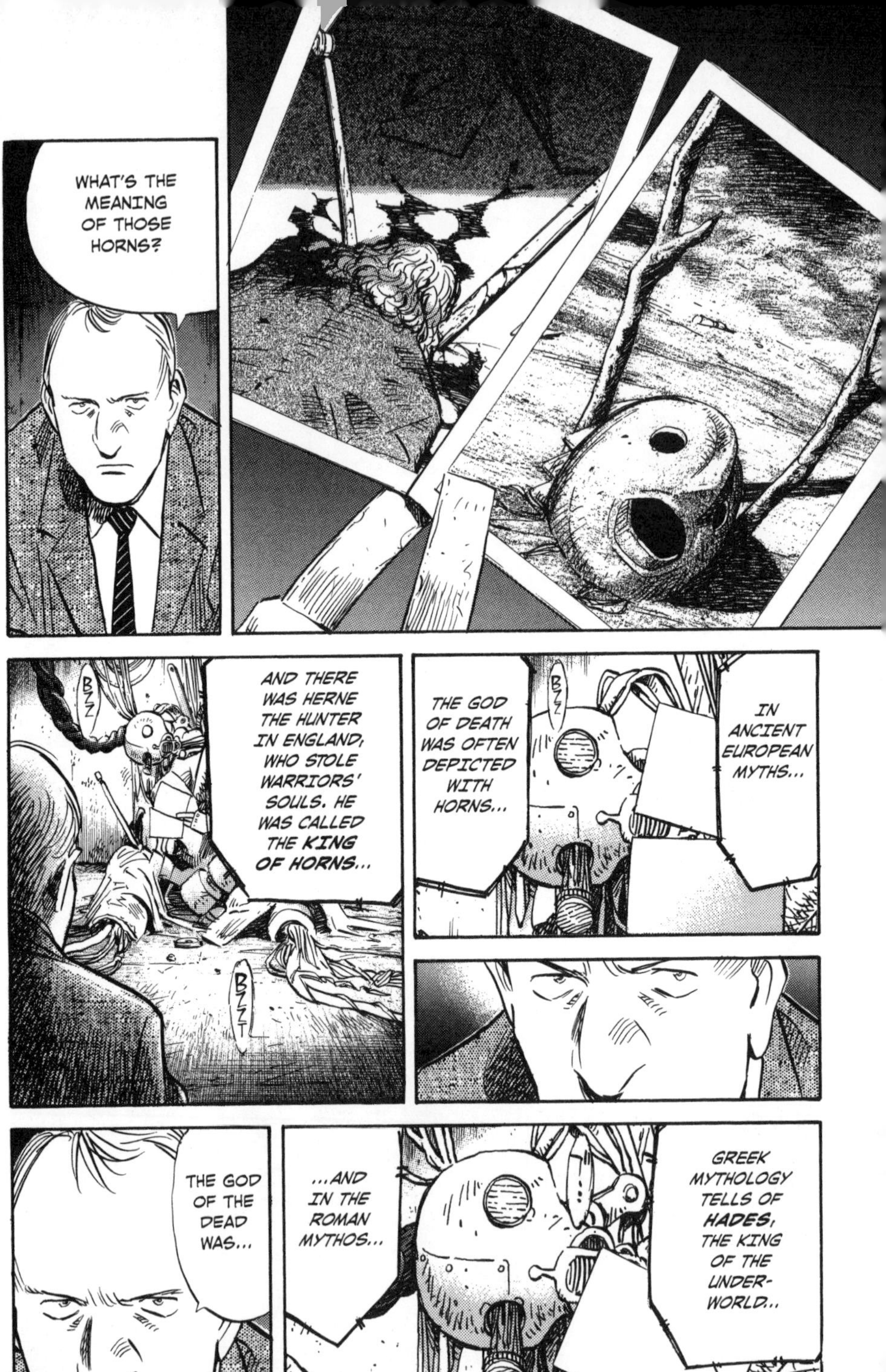
WHAT'S THE MEANING OF THOSE HORNS?
IN ANCIENT EUROPEAN MYTHS...
THE GOD OF DEATH WAS OFTEN DEPICTED WITH HORNS...
BZZ
AND THERE WAS HERNE THE HUNTER IN ENGLAND, WHO STOLE WARRIORS' SOULS. HE WAS CALLED THE **KING OF HORNS**...
BZZ
BZZT
GREEK MYTHOLOGY TELLS OF **HADES**, THE KING OF THE UNDER-WORLD...
...AND IN THE ROMAN MYTHOS...
THE GOD OF THE DEAD WAS...

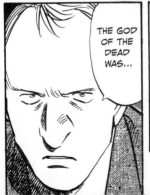

PLUTO
...

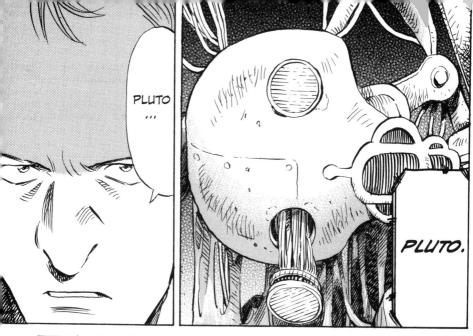

PLUTO.

LEAVING SO SOON ...?

I MAY COME BACK AGAIN...

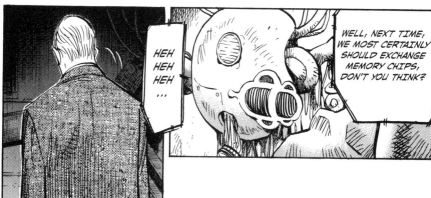

HEH HEH HEH ...

WELL, NEXT TIME, WE MOST CERTAINLY SHOULD EXCHANGE MEMORY CHIPS, DON'T YOU THINK?

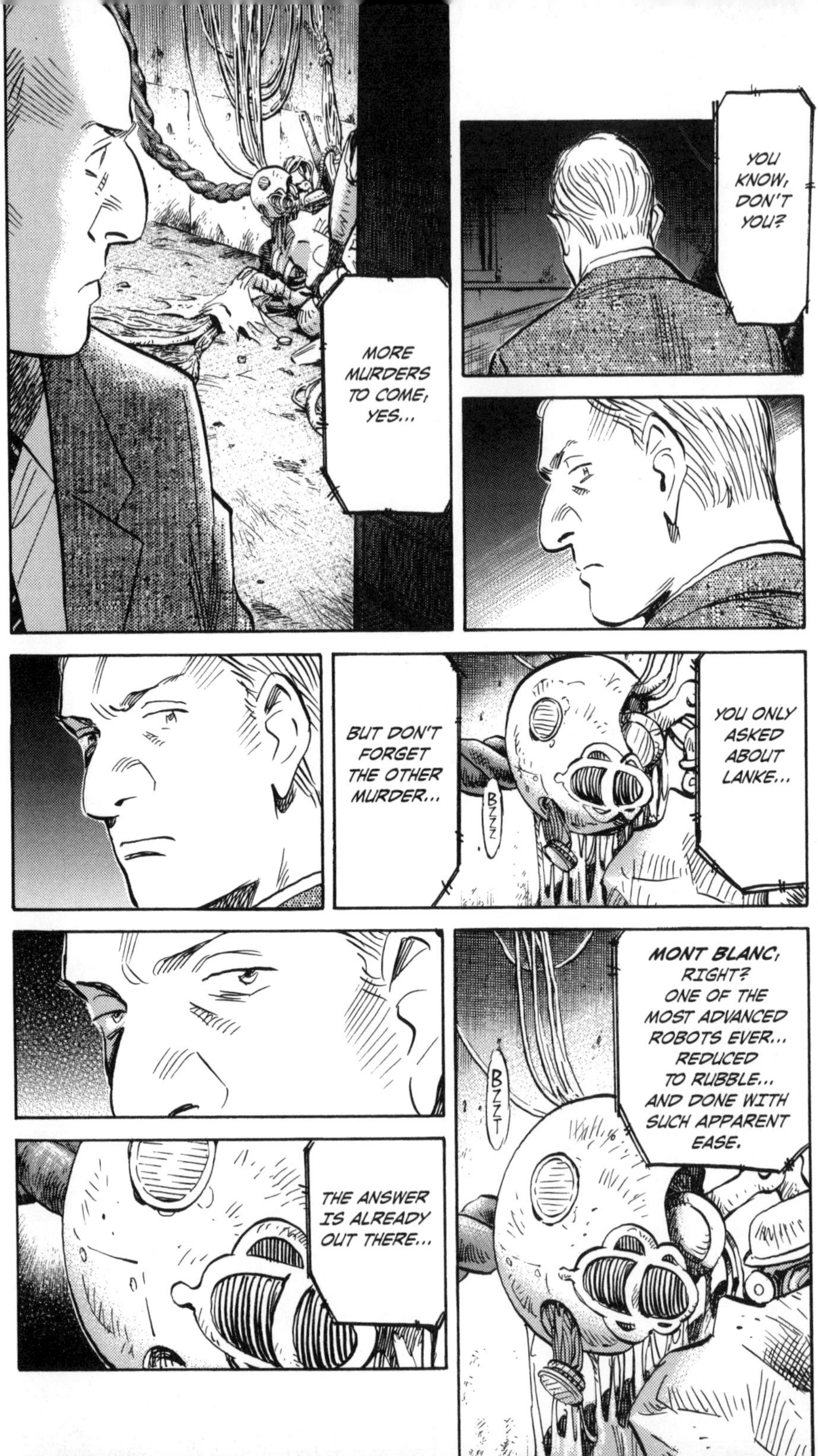
YOU KNOW, DON'T YOU?
MORE MURDERS TO COME, YES...
YOU ONLY ASKED ABOUT LANKE...
BZZZ
BUT DON'T FORGET THE OTHER MURDER...
MONT BLANC, RIGHT? ONE OF THE MOST ADVANCED ROBOTS EVER... REDUCED TO RUBBLE... AND DONE WITH SUCH APPARENT EASE.
BZZT
THE ANSWER IS ALREADY OUT THERE...

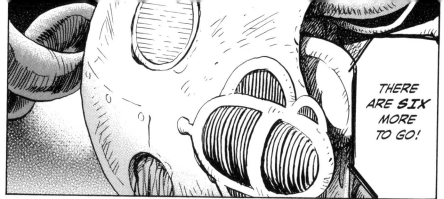

THERE ARE **SIX** MORE TO GO!
ALL OF THEM, THE CREAM OF THE CROP... THE MOST **ADVANCED ROBOTS** SCIENCE HAS EVER PRODUCED...
BRRR
BZZZP
ROBOTS ALL WITH THE POTENTIAL TO BECOME WEAPONS OF MASS DESTRUCTION...
VRRT...
VREEEN
AND **YOU** ARE ONE OF THEM...

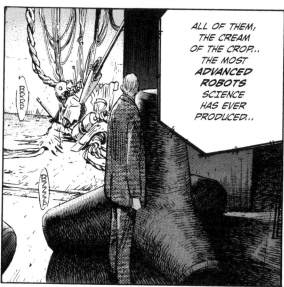

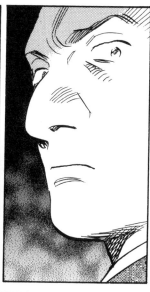

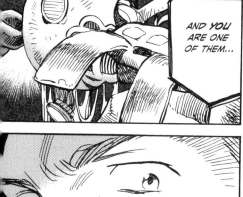

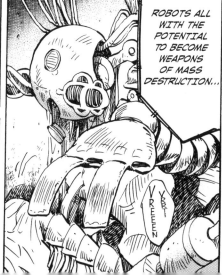

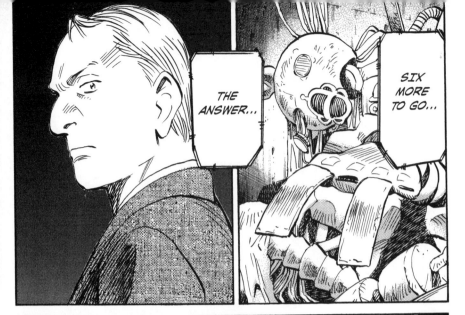

THE ANSWER...

SIX MORE TO GO...

...IS ALREADY DONE...

Act 4 NORTH No. 2 (Part 1)

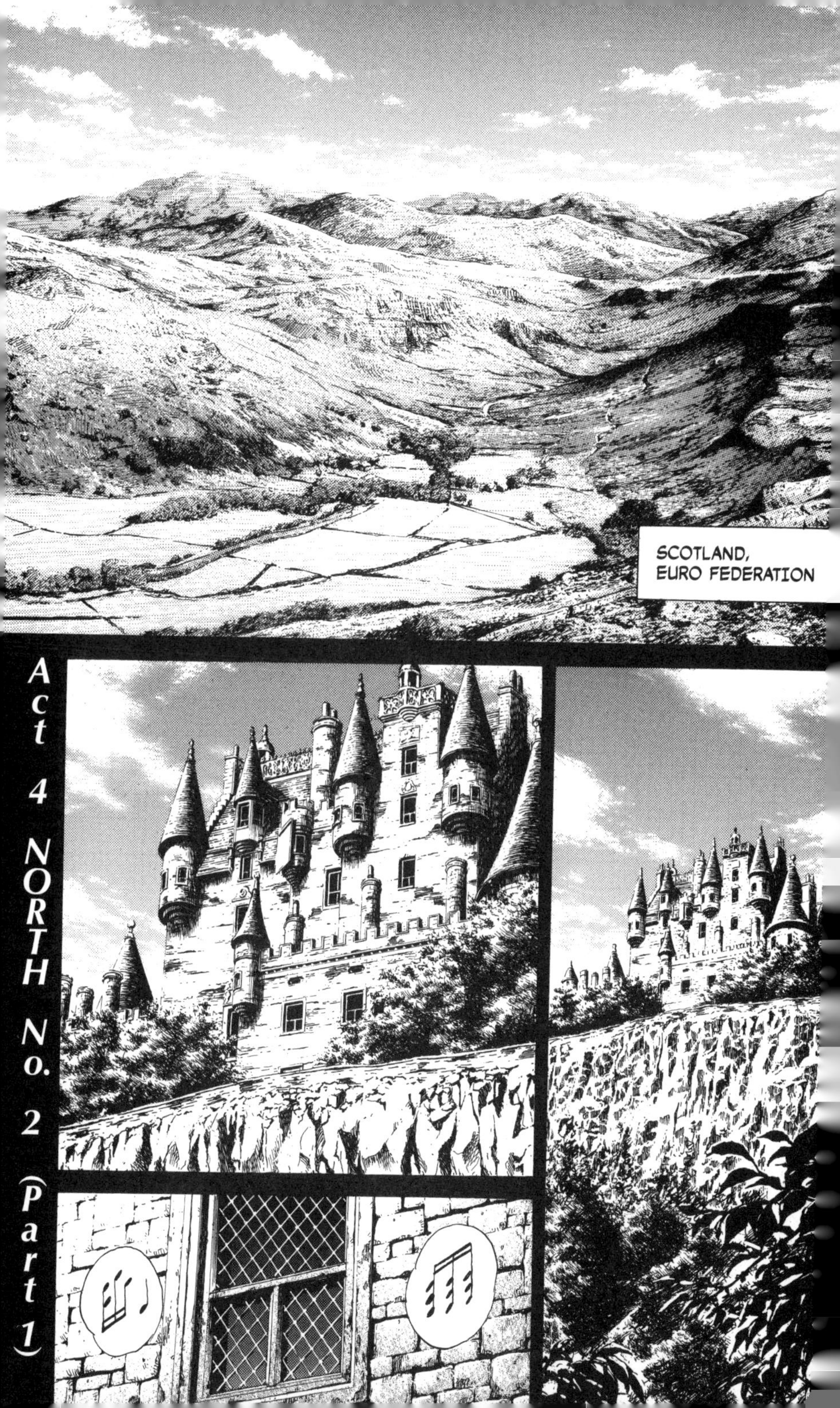
SCOTLAND,
EURO FEDERATION

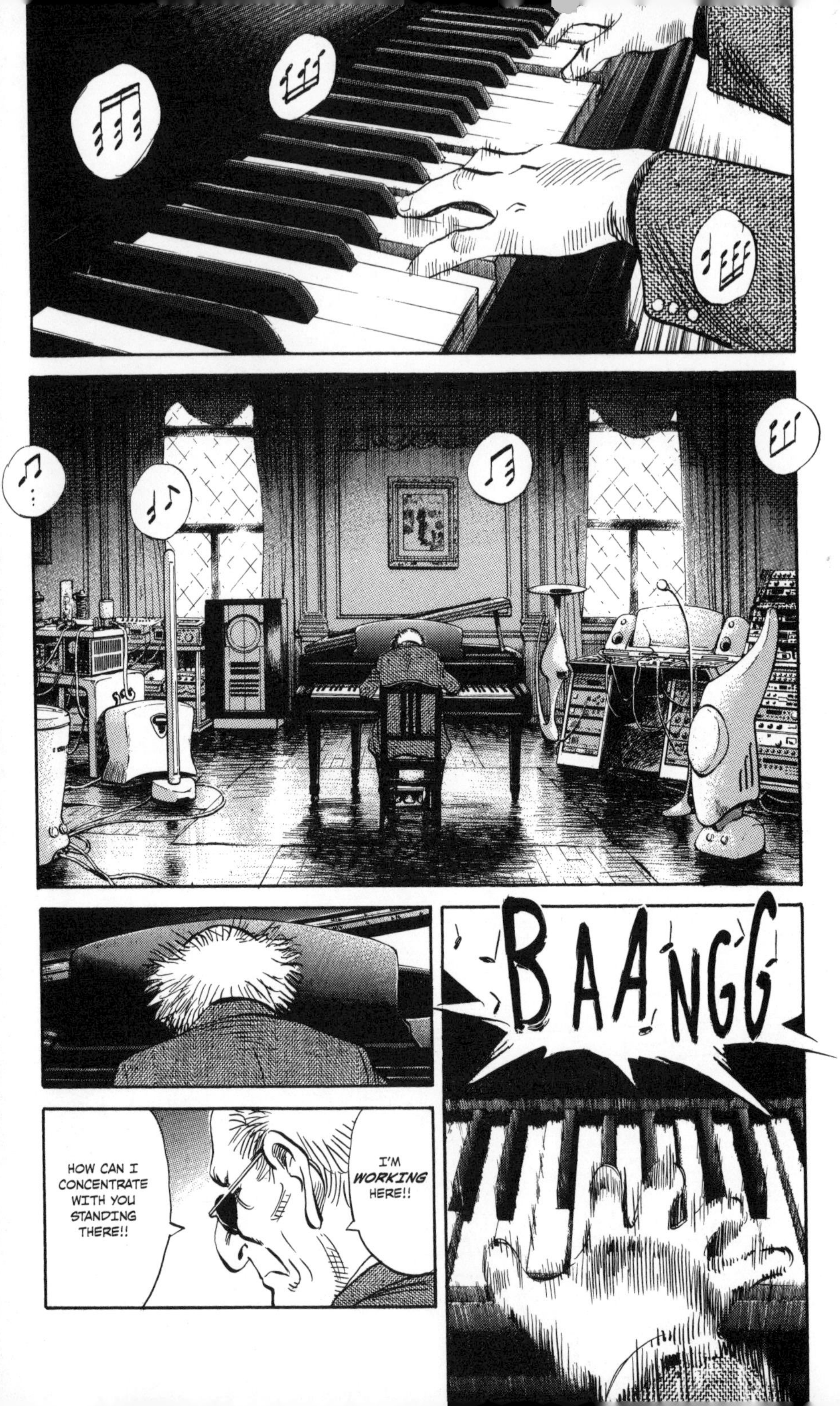
BAANGG
I'M WORKING HERE!!
HOW CAN I CONCENTRATE WITH YOU STANDING THERE!!

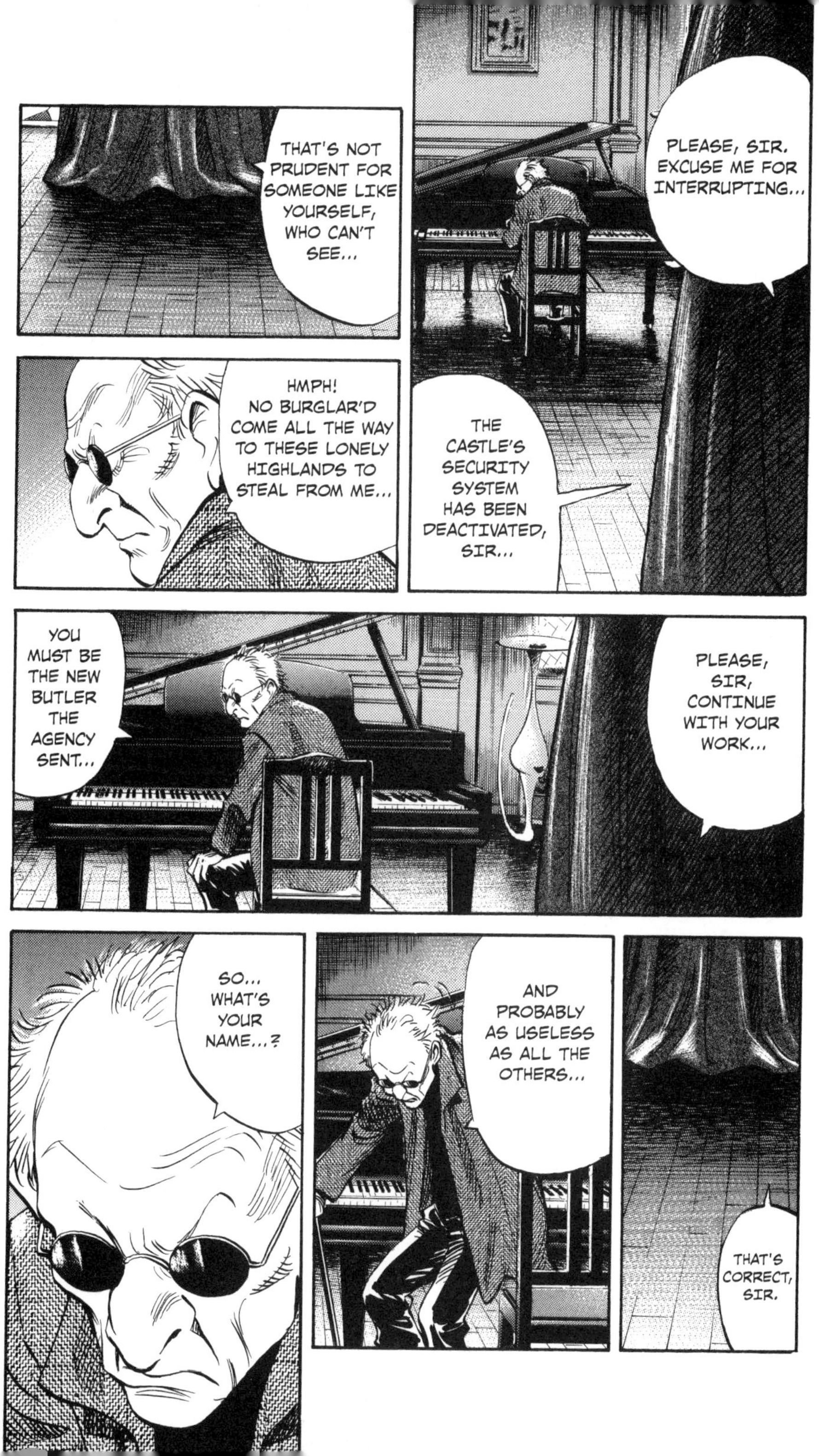
PLEASE, SIR. EXCUSE ME FOR INTERRUPTING...
THE CASTLE'S SECURITY SYSTEM HAS BEEN DEACTIVATED, SIR...
THAT'S NOT PRUDENT FOR SOMEONE LIKE YOURSELF, WHO CAN'T SEE...
HMPH! NO BURGLAR'D COME ALL THE WAY TO THESE LONELY HIGHLANDS TO STEAL FROM ME...
PLEASE, SIR, CONTINUE WITH YOUR WORK...
YOU MUST BE THE NEW BUTLER THE AGENCY SENT...
THAT'S CORRECT, SIR.
AND PROBABLY AS USELESS AS ALL THE OTHERS...
SO... WHAT'S YOUR NAME...?

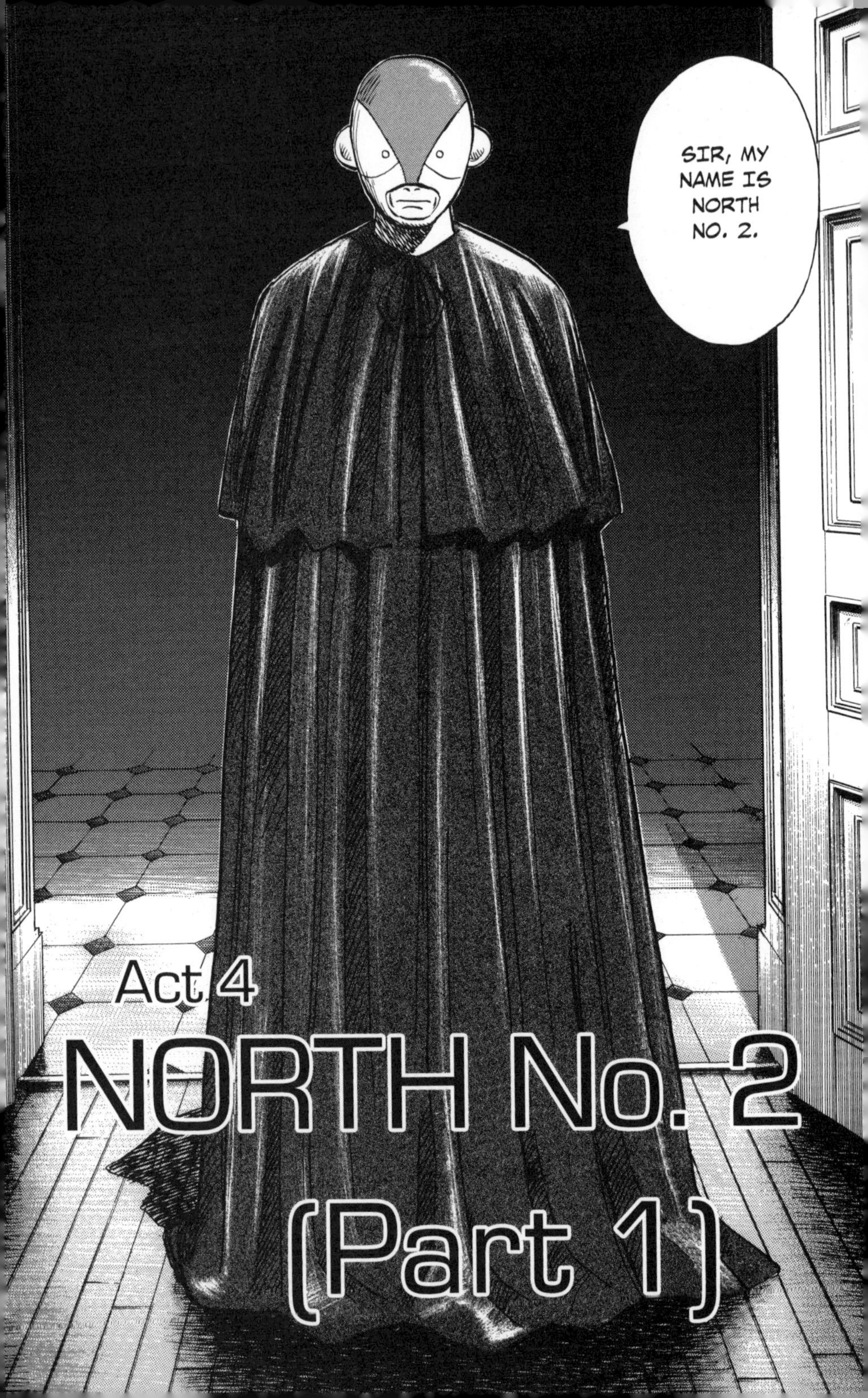
SIR, MY NAME IS NORTH NO. 2.
Act 4
NORTH No. 2
(Part 1)

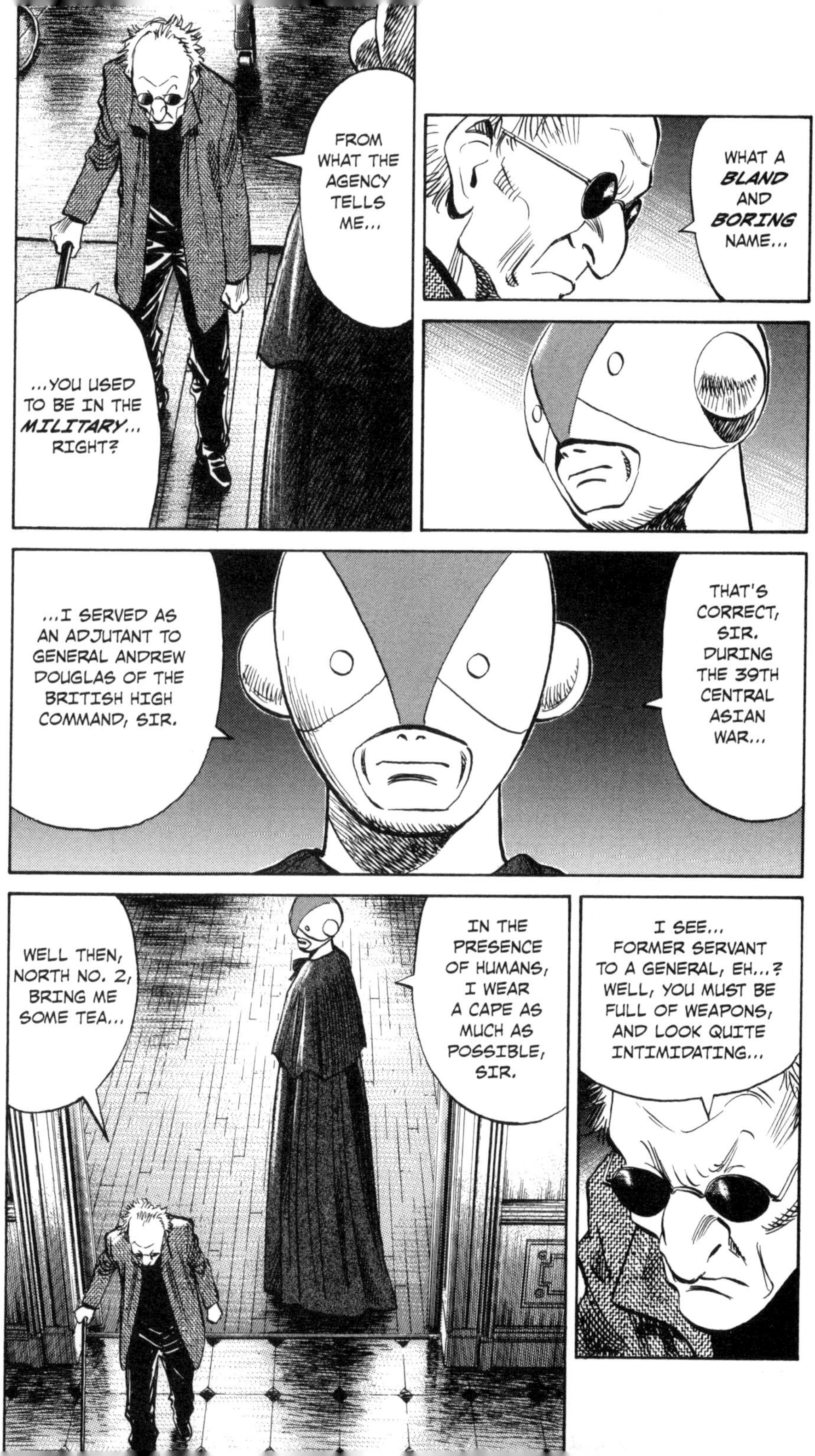
WHAT A BLAND AND BORING NAME...
FROM WHAT THE AGENCY TELLS ME...
...YOU USED TO BE IN THE MILITARY... RIGHT?
THAT'S CORRECT, SIR. DURING THE 39TH CENTRAL ASIAN WAR...
...I SERVED AS AN ADJUTANT TO GENERAL ANDREW DOUGLAS OF THE BRITISH HIGH COMMAND, SIR.
I SEE... FORMER SERVANT TO A GENERAL, EH...? WELL, YOU MUST BE FULL OF WEAPONS, AND LOOK QUITE INTIMIDATING...
IN THE PRESENCE OF HUMANS, I WEAR A CAPE AS MUCH AS POSSIBLE, SIR.
WELL THEN, NORTH NO. 2, BRING ME SOME TEA...

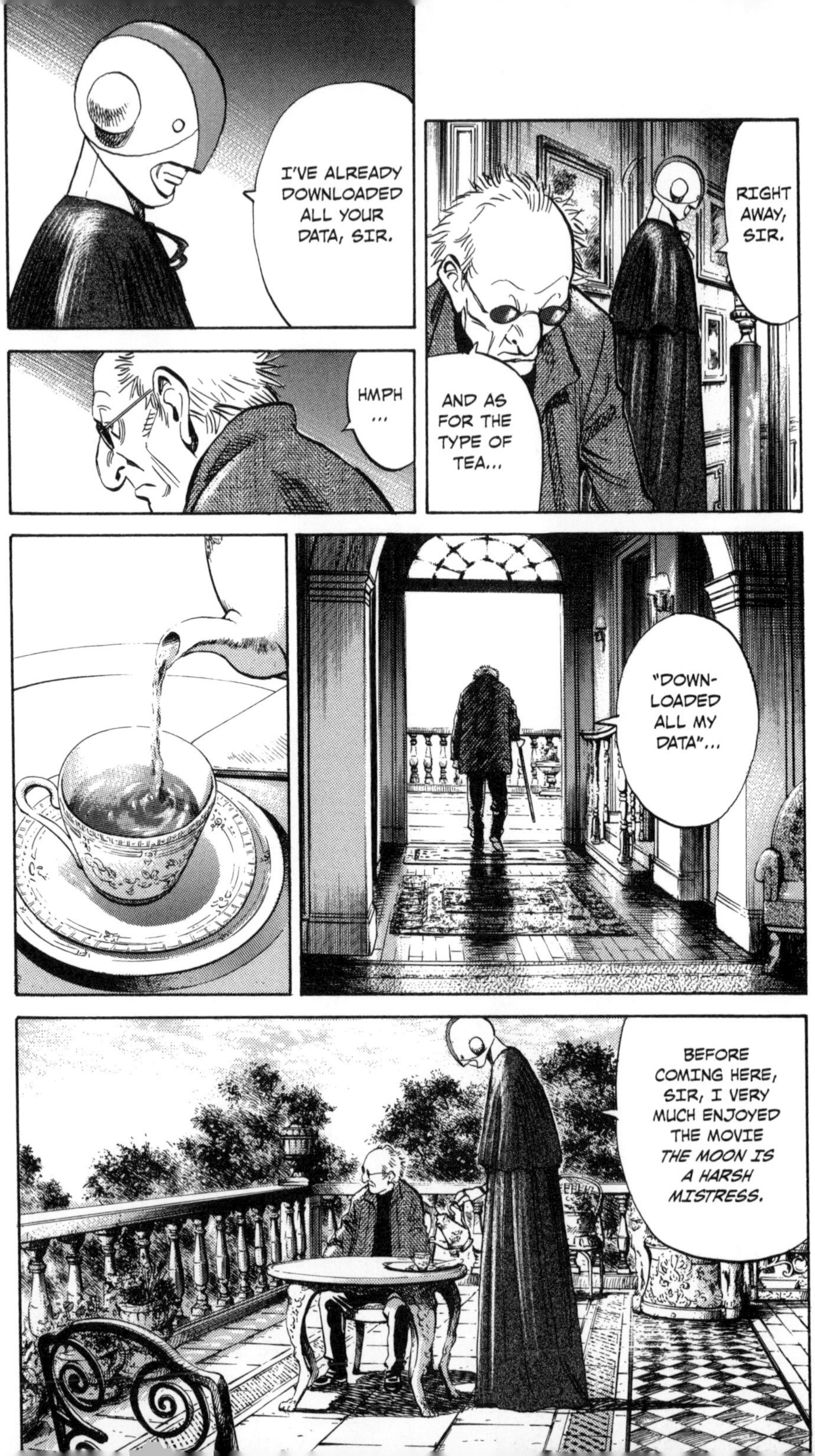
RIGHT AWAY, SIR.
AND AS FOR THE TYPE OF TEA...
I'VE ALREADY DOWNLOADED ALL YOUR DATA, SIR.
HMPH ...
"DOWN-LOADED ALL MY DATA"...
BEFORE COMING HERE, SIR, I VERY MUCH ENJOYED THE MOVIE *THE MOON IS A HARSH MISTRESS.*

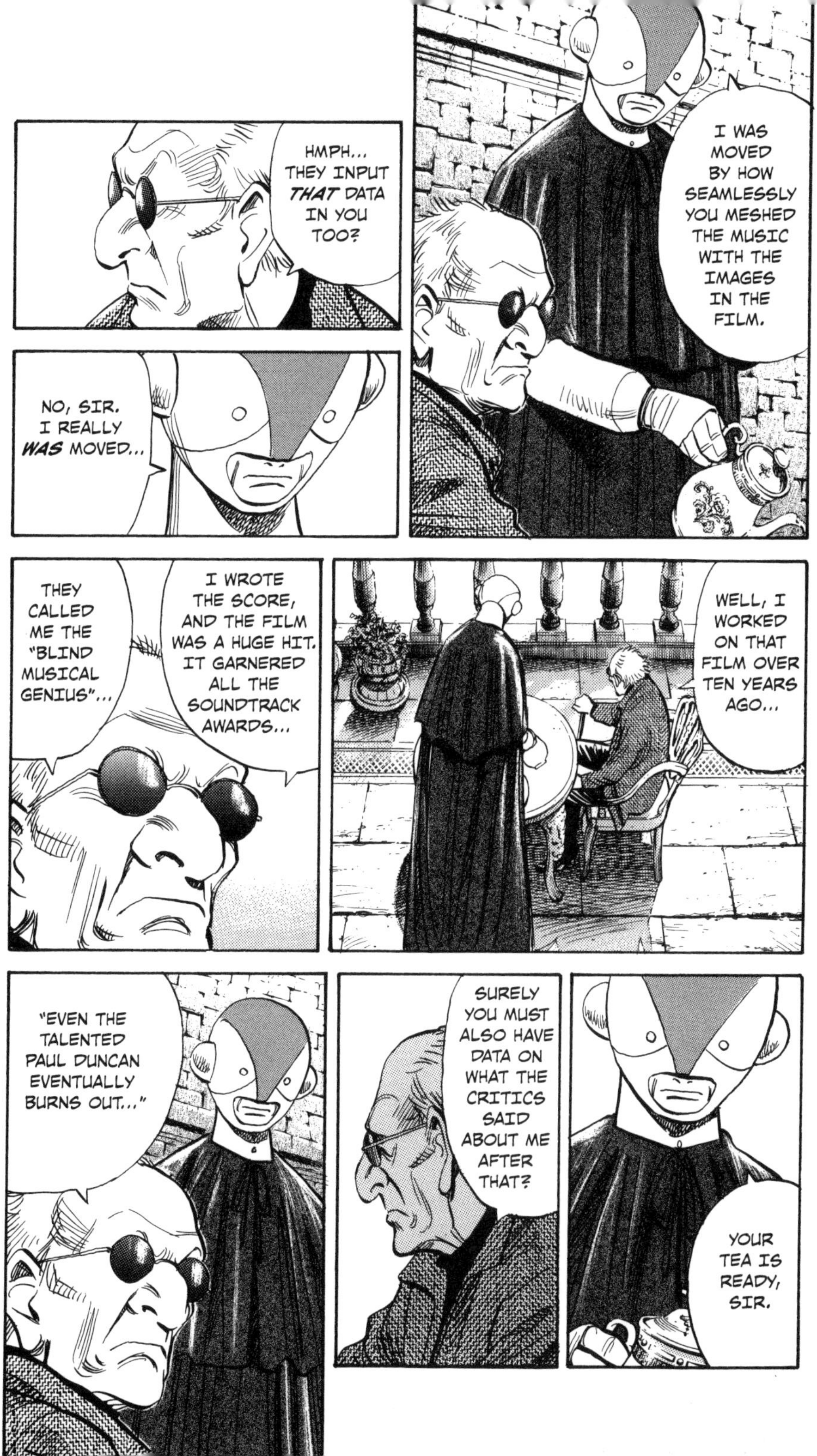

I WAS MOVED BY HOW SEAMLESSLY YOU MESHED THE MUSIC WITH THE IMAGES IN THE FILM.
HMPH... THEY INPUT *THAT* DATA IN YOU TOO?
NO, SIR. I REALLY *WAS* MOVED...
WELL, I WORKED ON THAT FILM OVER TEN YEARS AGO...
I WROTE THE SCORE, AND THE FILM WAS A HUGE HIT. IT GARNERED ALL THE SOUNDTRACK AWARDS...
THEY CALLED ME THE "BLIND MUSICAL GENIUS"...
YOUR TEA IS READY, SIR.
SURELY YOU MUST ALSO HAVE DATA ON WHAT THE CRITICS SAID ABOUT ME AFTER THAT?
"EVEN THE TALENTED PAUL DUNCAN EVENTUALLY BURNS OUT..."

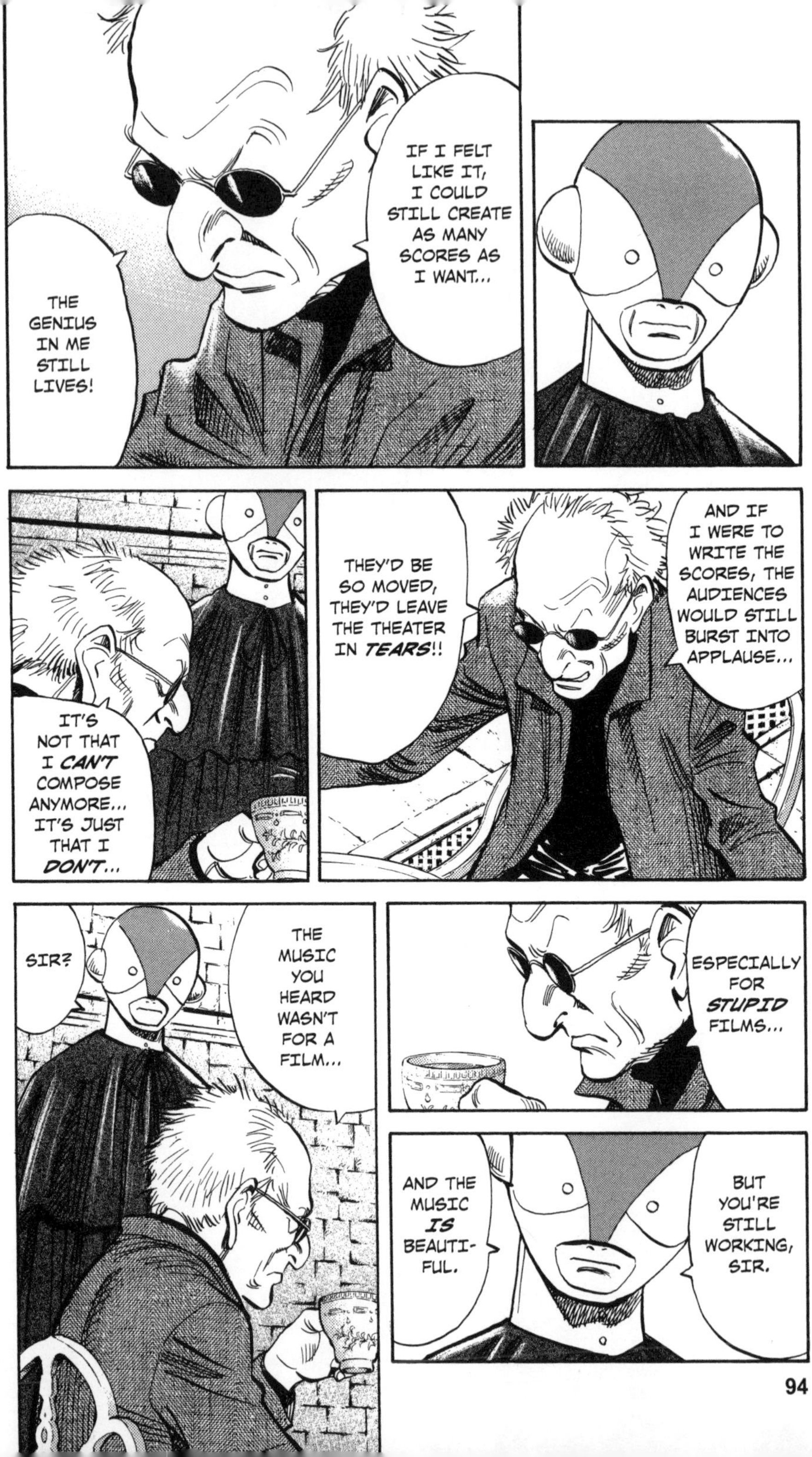
IF I FELT LIKE IT, I COULD STILL CREATE AS MANY SCORES AS I WANT...
THE GENIUS IN ME STILL LIVES!
AND IF I WERE TO WRITE THE SCORES, THE AUDIENCES WOULD STILL BURST INTO APPLAUSE...
THEY'D BE SO MOVED, THEY'D LEAVE THE THEATER IN *TEARS*!!
IT'S NOT THAT I *CAN'T* COMPOSE ANYMORE... IT'S JUST THAT I *DON'T*...
ESPECIALLY FOR *STUPID* FILMS...
BUT YOU'RE STILL WORKING, SIR.
AND THE MUSIC *IS* BEAUTIFUL.
THE MUSIC YOU HEARD WASN'T FOR A FILM...
SIR?

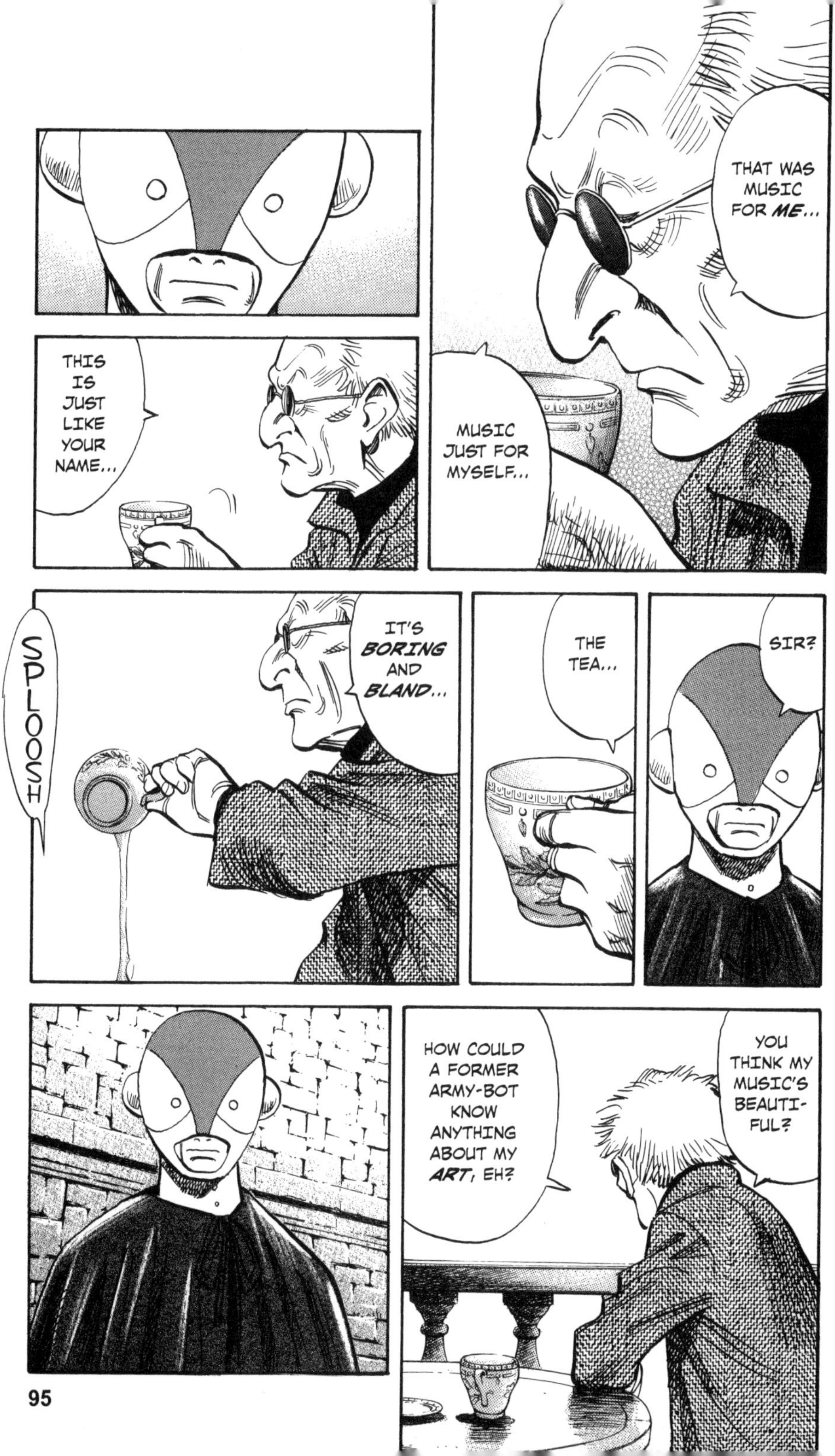
THAT WAS MUSIC FOR *ME*...
MUSIC JUST FOR MYSELF...
THIS IS JUST LIKE YOUR NAME...
SIR?
THE TEA...
IT'S *BORING* AND *BLAND*...
SPLOOSH
YOU THINK MY MUSIC'S BEAUTI-FUL?
HOW COULD A FORMER ARMY-BOT KNOW ANYTHING ABOUT MY *ART*, EH?

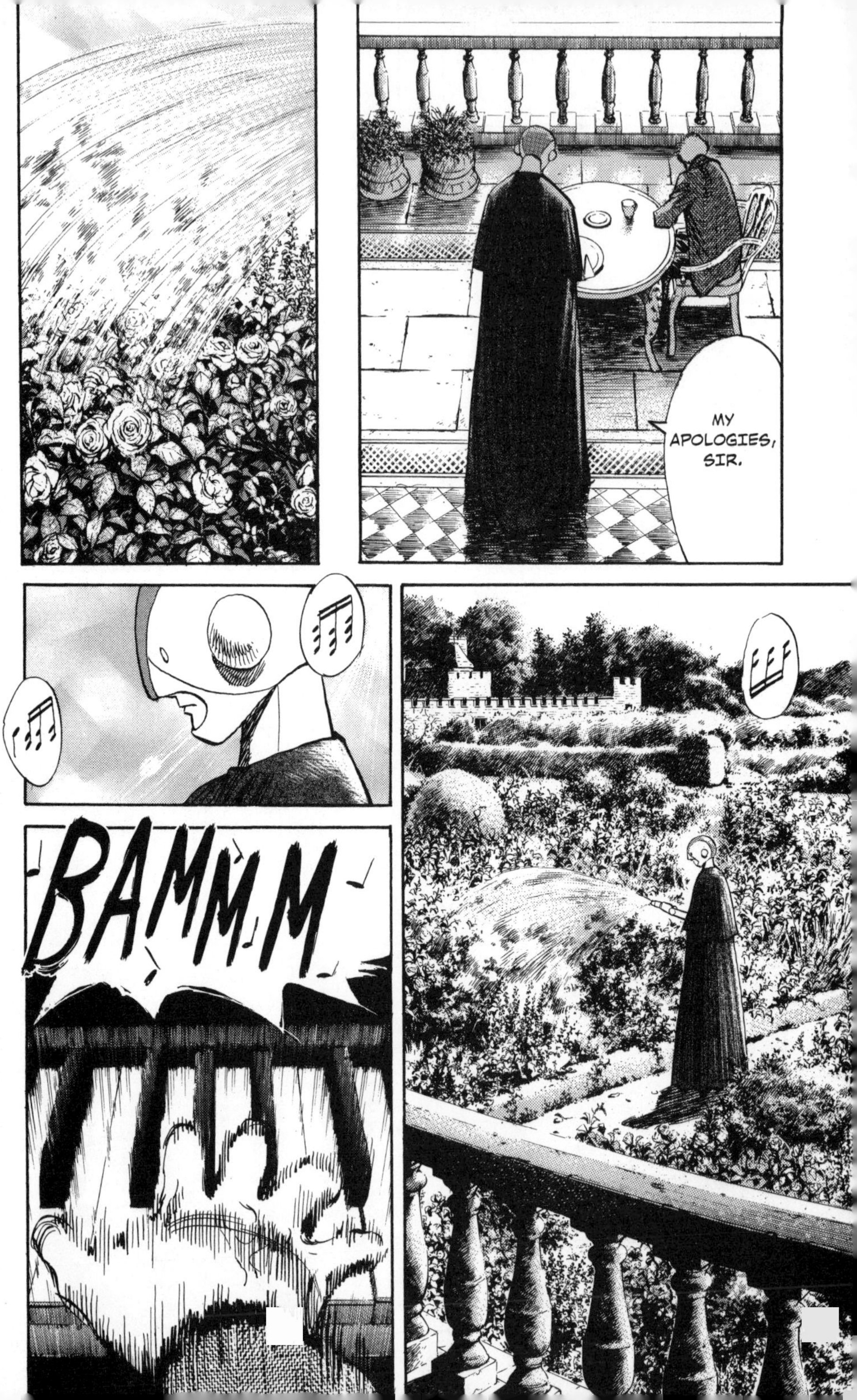
MY APOLOGIES, SIR.
BAMMM

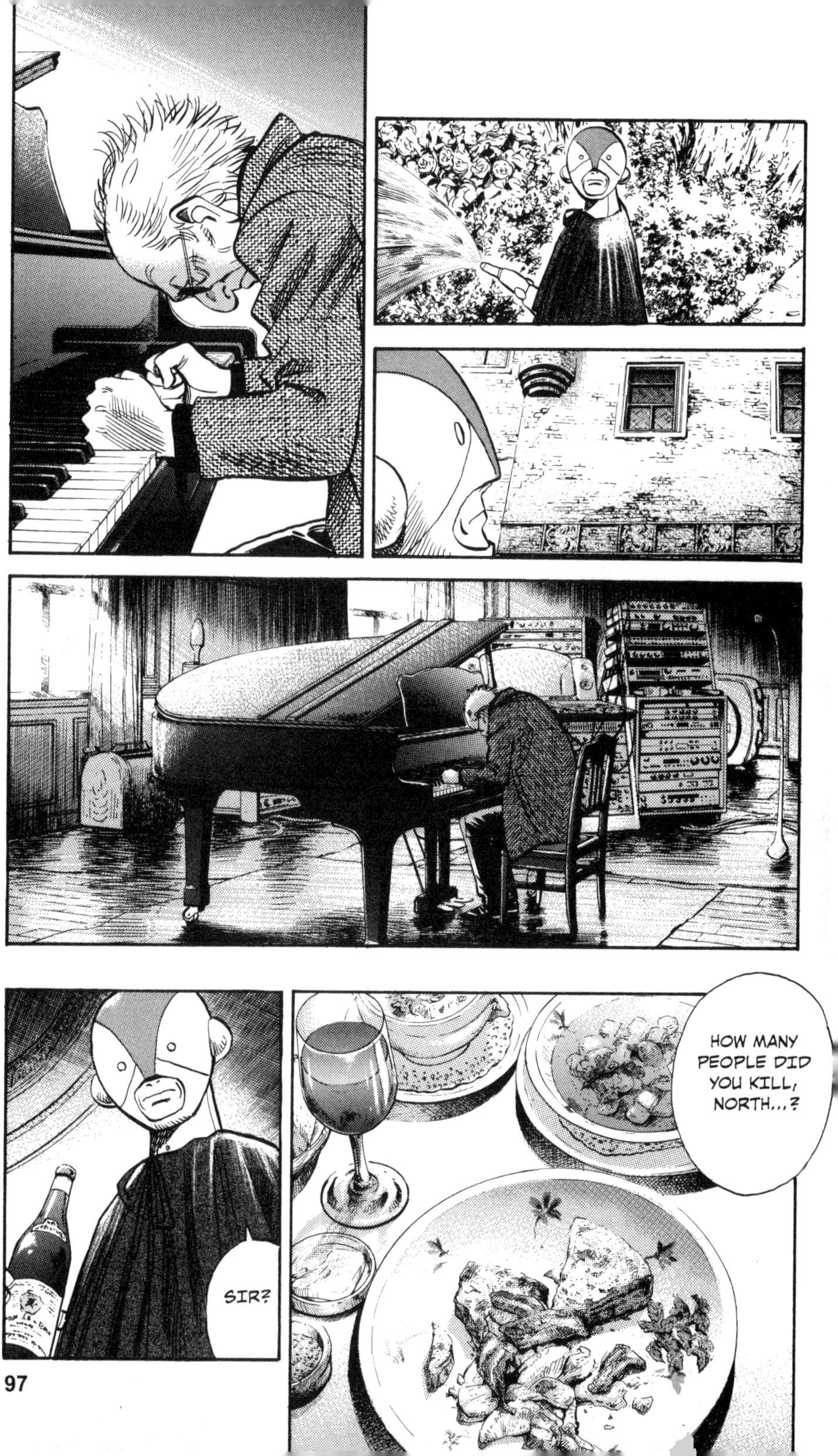
HOW MANY PEOPLE DID YOU KILL, NORTH...?
SIR?

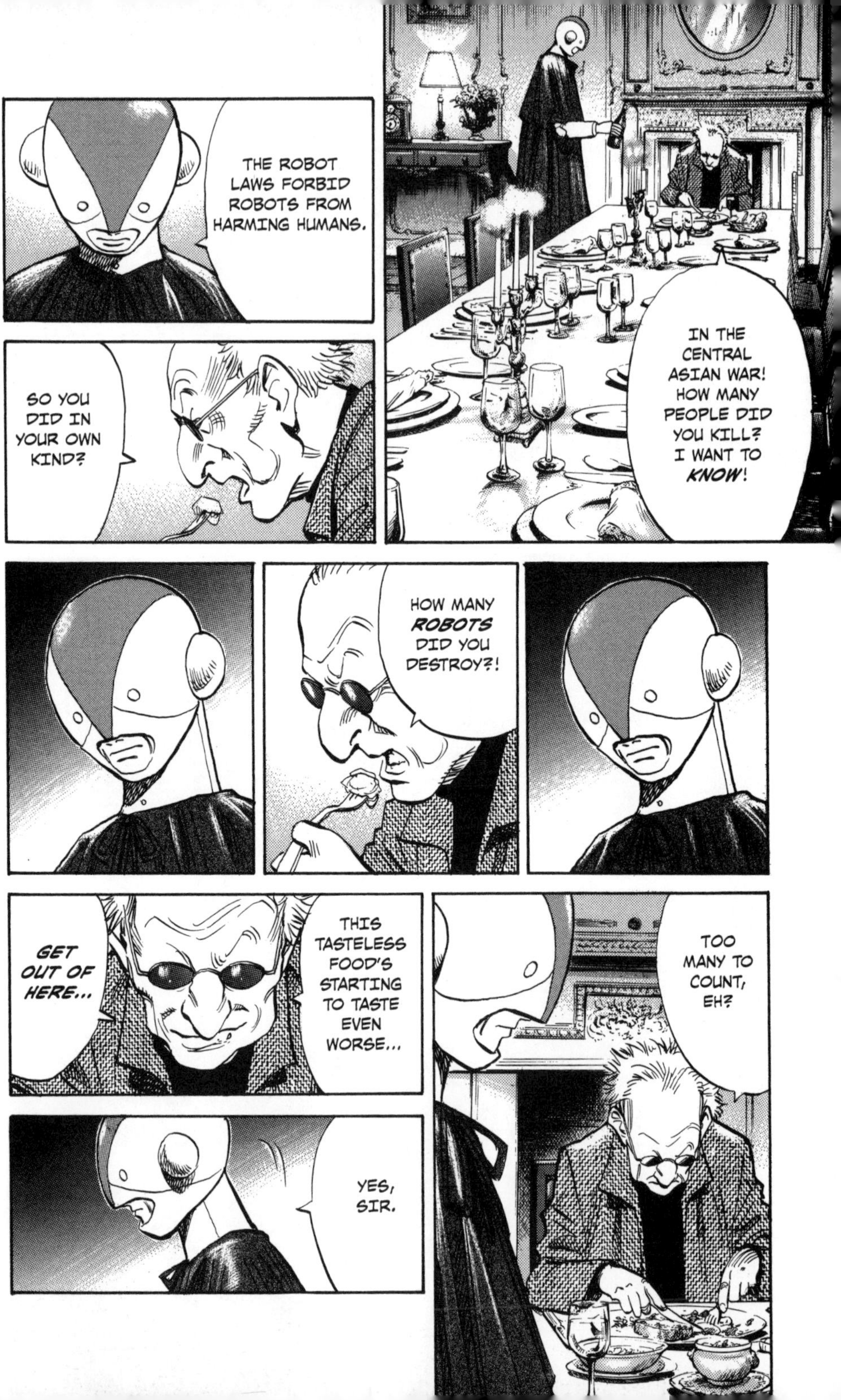
IN THE CENTRAL ASIAN WAR! HOW MANY PEOPLE DID YOU KILL? I WANT TO *KNOW*!
THE ROBOT LAWS FORBID ROBOTS FROM HARMING HUMANS.
SO YOU DID IN YOUR OWN KIND?
HOW MANY *ROBOTS* DID YOU DESTROY?!
TOO MANY TO COUNT, EH?
THIS TASTELESS FOOD'S STARTING TO TASTE EVEN WORSE...
GET OUT OF HERE...
YES, SIR.

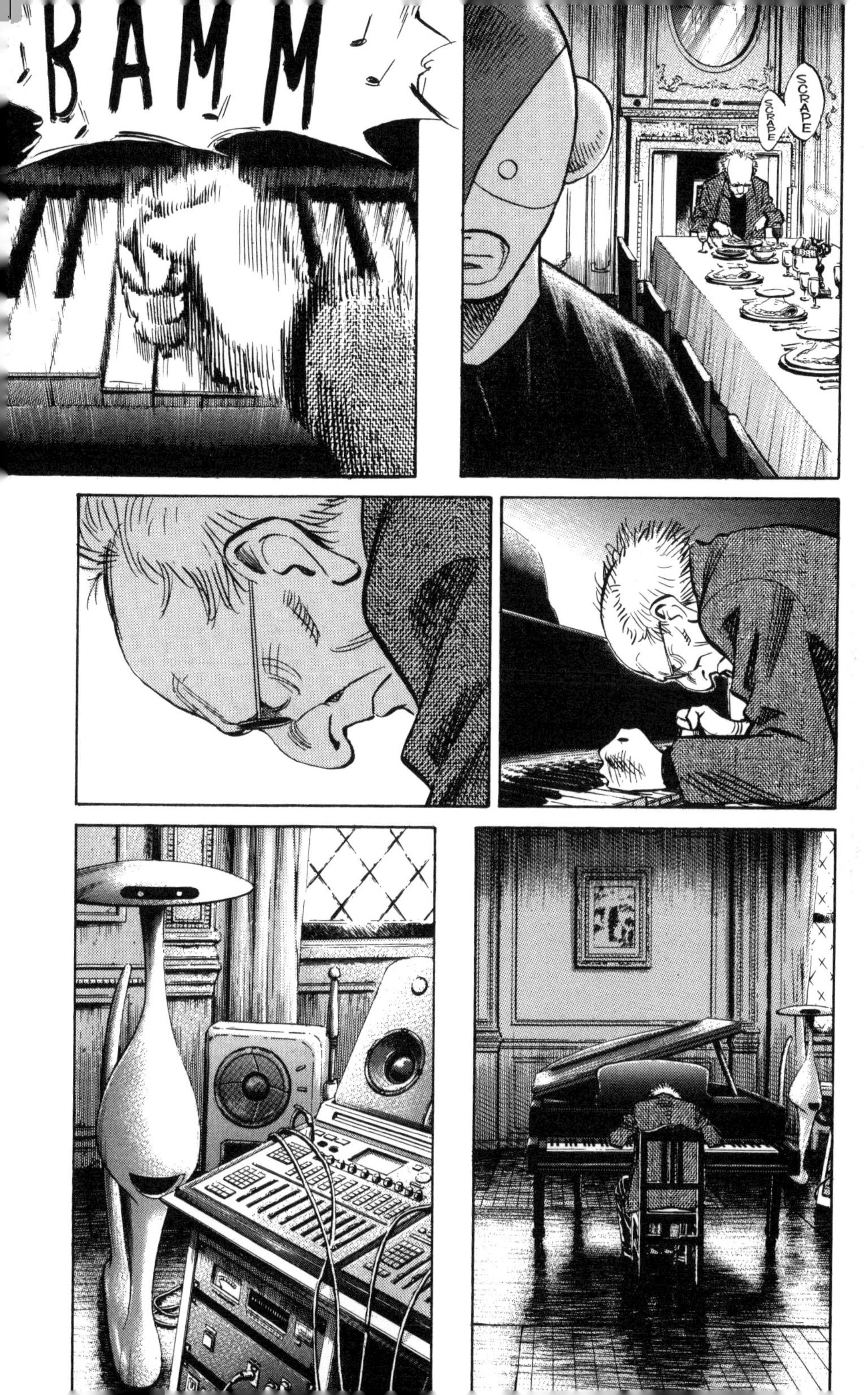
SCRAPE
SCRAPE
BAMM

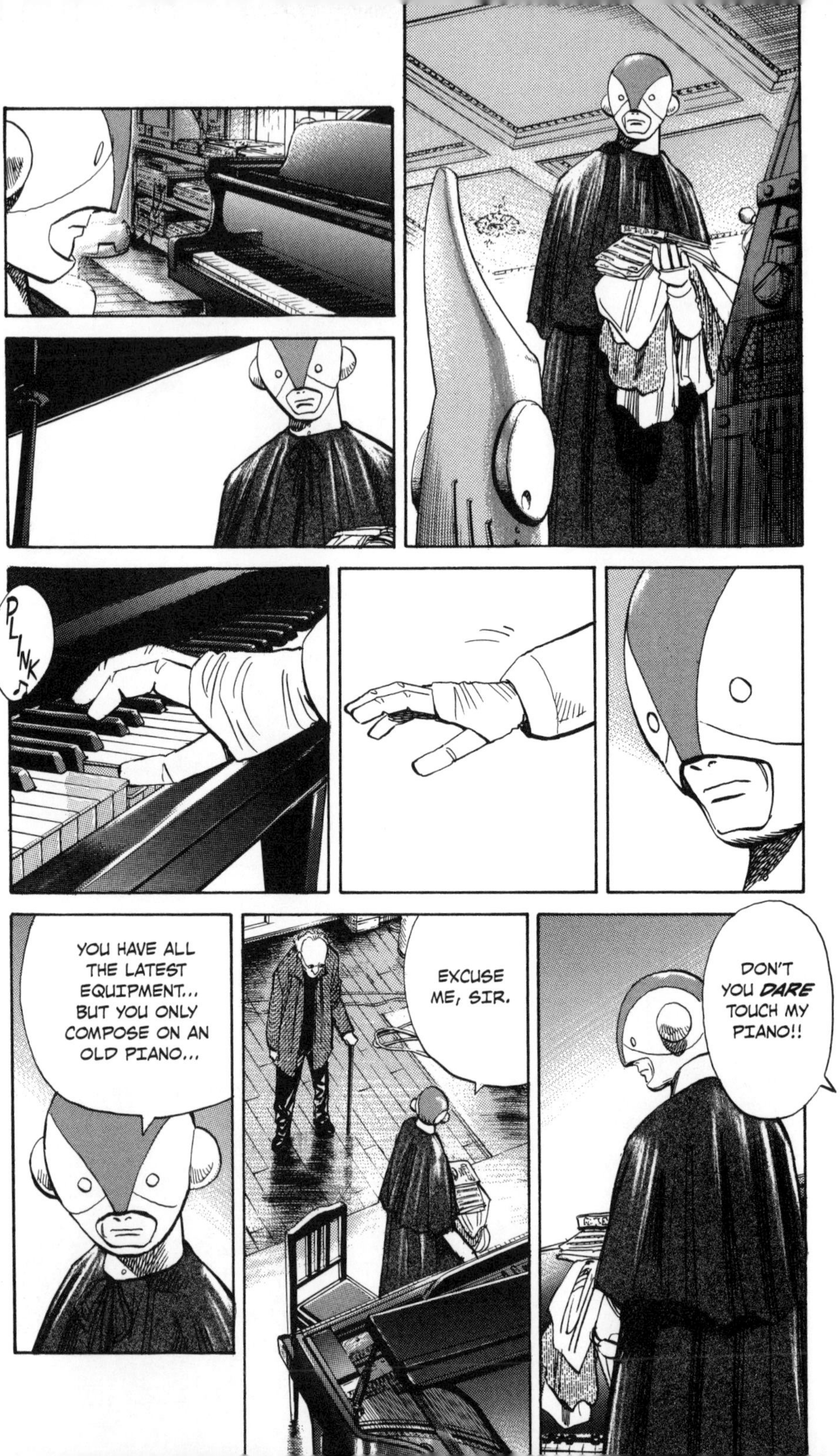
PLINK ♪
DON'T YOU *DARE* TOUCH MY PIANO!!
EXCUSE ME, SIR.
YOU HAVE ALL THE LATEST EQUIPMENT... BUT YOU ONLY COMPOSE ON AN OLD PIANO...

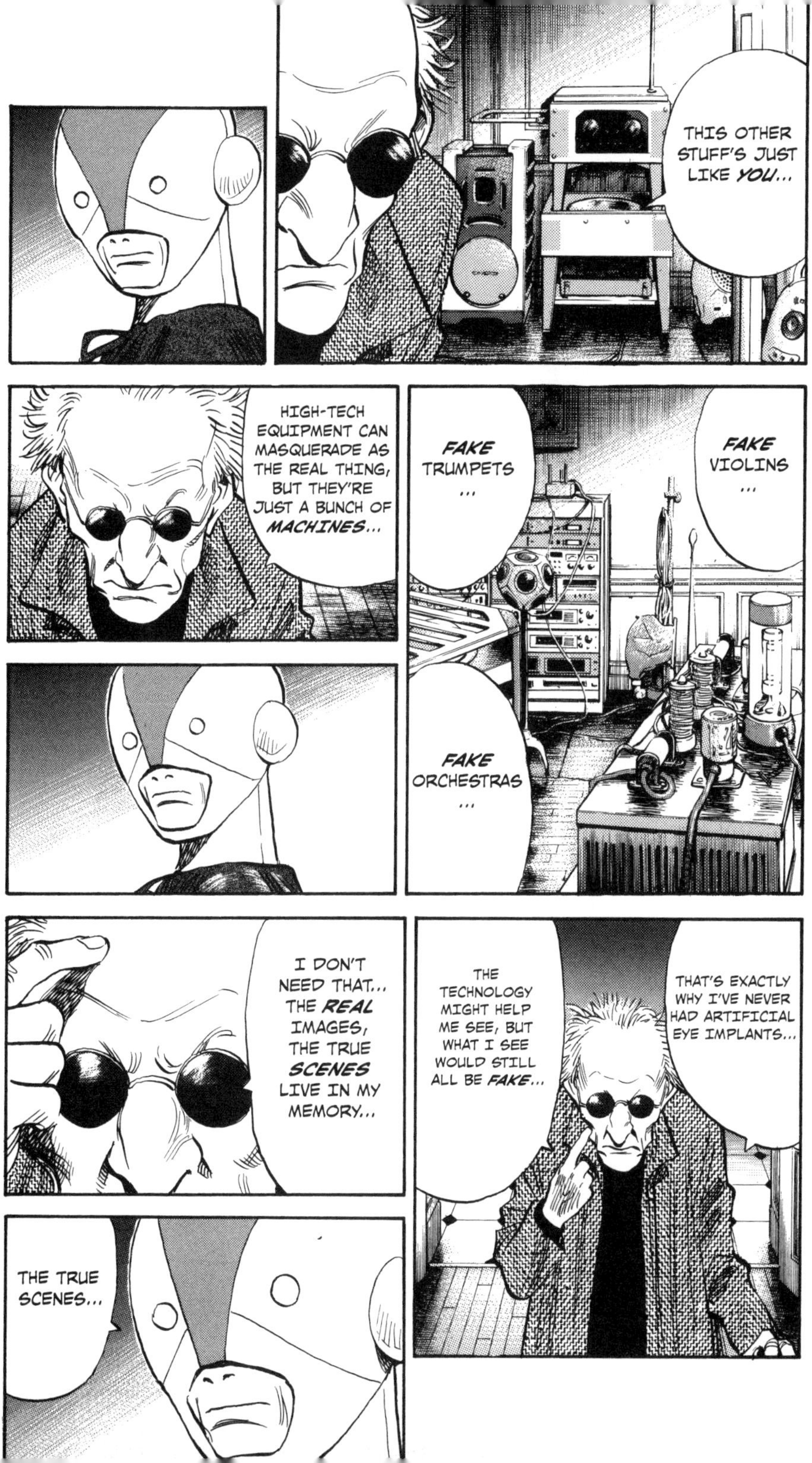
THIS OTHER STUFF'S JUST LIKE YOU...
FAKE VIOLINS ...
FAKE TRUMPETS ...
FAKE ORCHESTRAS ...
HIGH-TECH EQUIPMENT CAN MASQUERADE AS THE REAL THING, BUT THEY'RE JUST A BUNCH OF MACHINES...
THAT'S EXACTLY WHY I'VE NEVER HAD ARTIFICIAL EYE IMPLANTS...
THE TECHNOLOGY MIGHT HELP ME SEE, BUT WHAT I SEE WOULD STILL ALL BE FAKE...
I DON'T NEED THAT... THE REAL IMAGES, THE TRUE SCENES LIVE IN MY MEMORY...
THE TRUE SCENES...

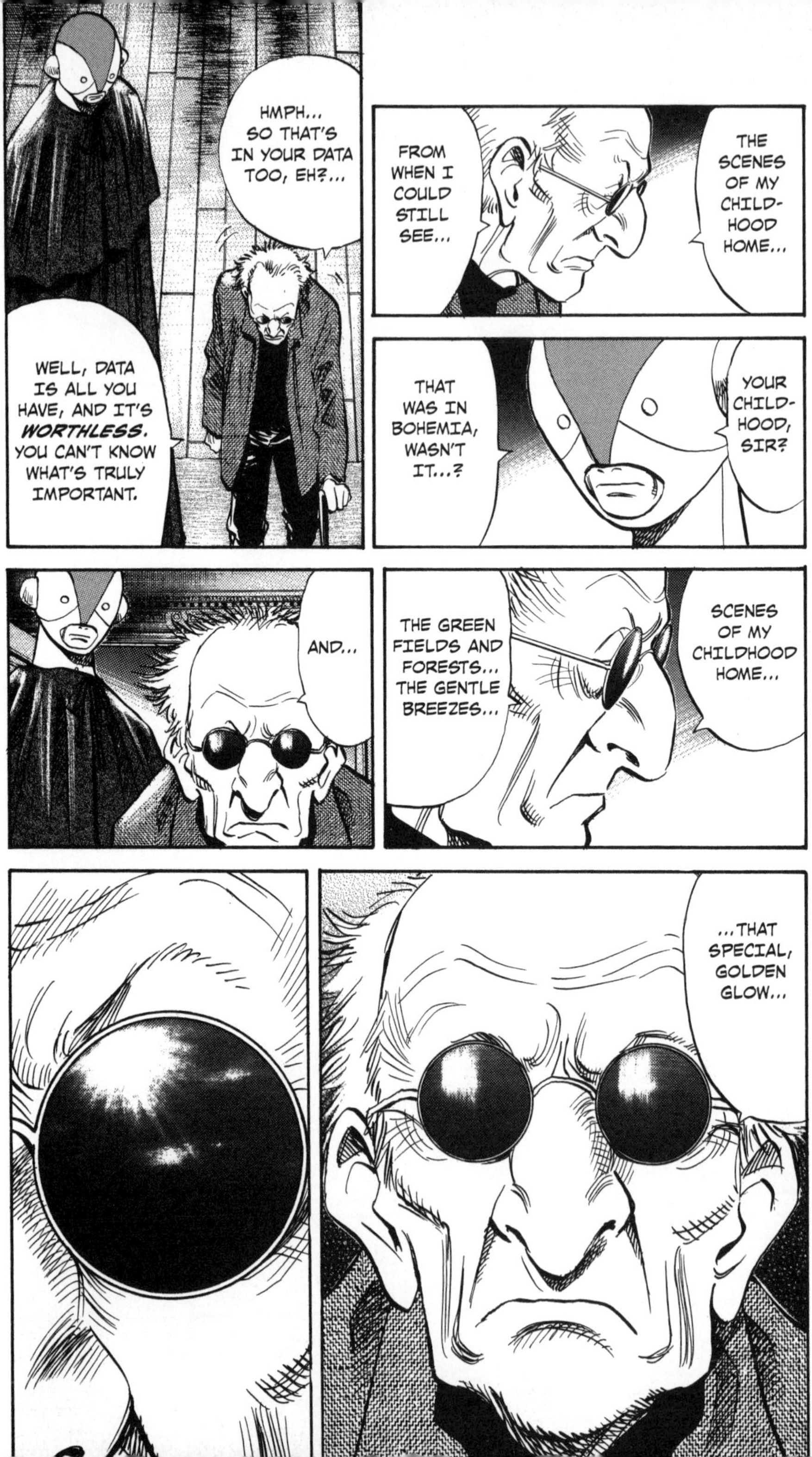
THE SCENES OF MY CHILDHOOD HOME...
FROM WHEN I COULD STILL SEE...
YOUR CHILDHOOD, SIR?
THAT WAS IN BOHEMIA, WASN'T IT...?
HMPH... SO THAT'S IN YOUR DATA TOO, EH?...
WELL, DATA IS ALL YOU HAVE, AND IT'S ***WORTHLESS.*** YOU CAN'T KNOW WHAT'S TRULY IMPORTANT.
SCENES OF MY CHILDHOOD HOME...
THE GREEN FIELDS AND FORESTS... THE GENTLE BREEZES...
AND...
...THAT SPECIAL, GOLDEN GLOW...

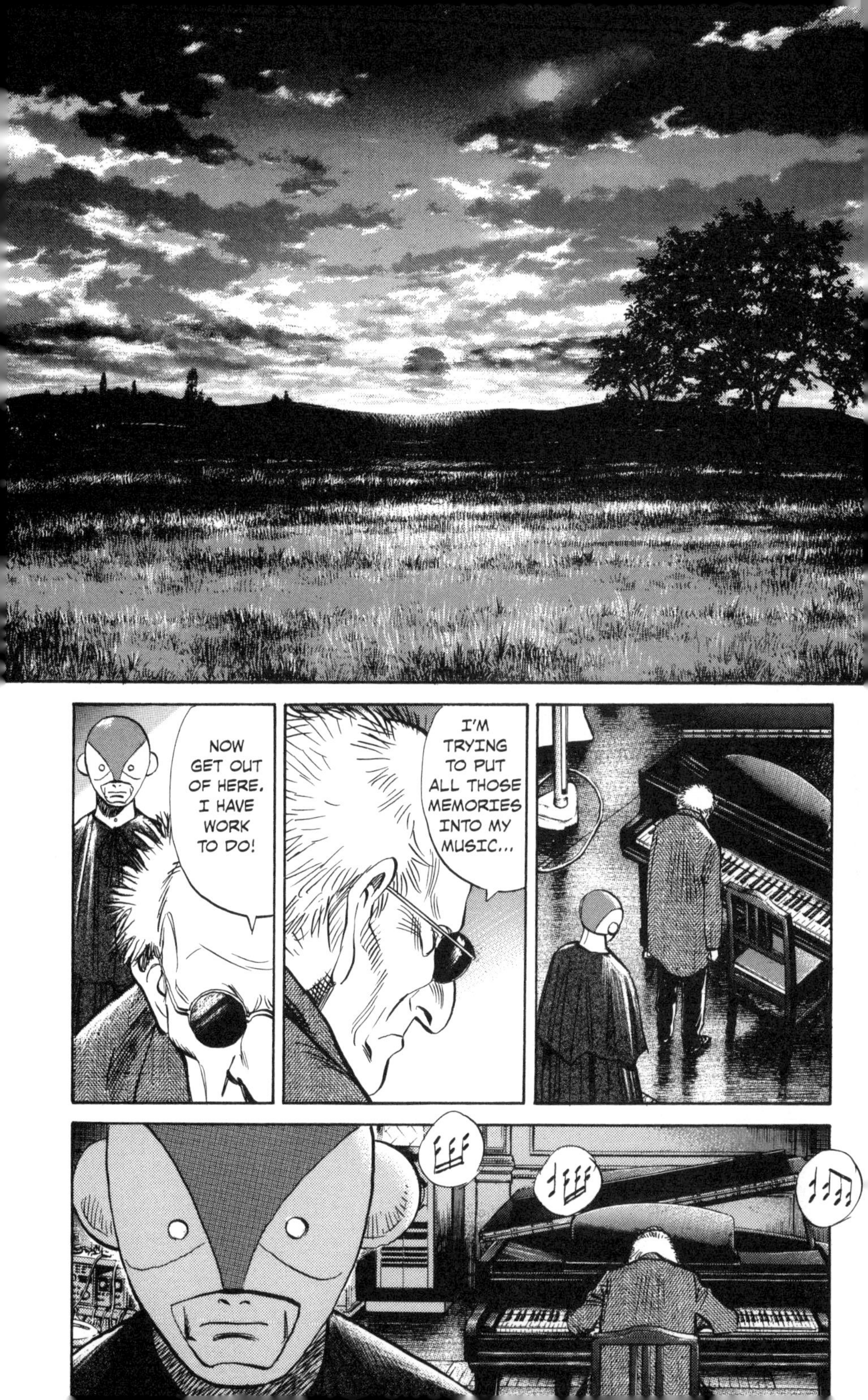
I'M TRYING TO PUT ALL THOSE MEMORIES INTO MY MUSIC...
NOW GET OUT OF HERE. I HAVE WORK TO DO!

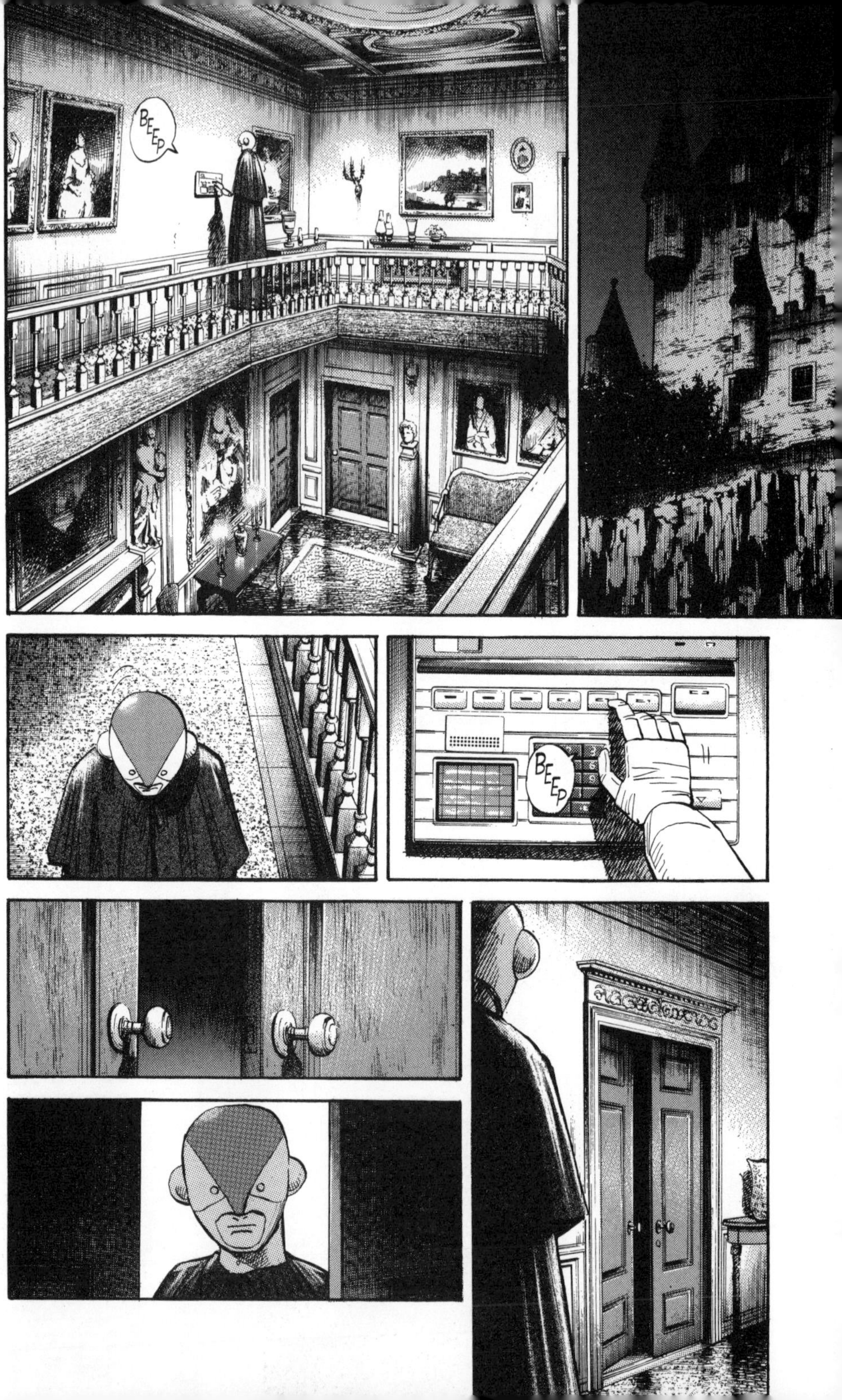
BEEEP
BEEEP

CREEAK

HMM...♪

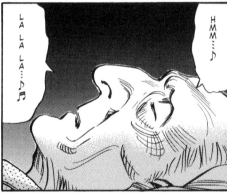

LA LA...♪♪

HMM...♪

LA LA...♪

LA LA...♪

LA LA...♪

LA LA...♪

LA LA...♪

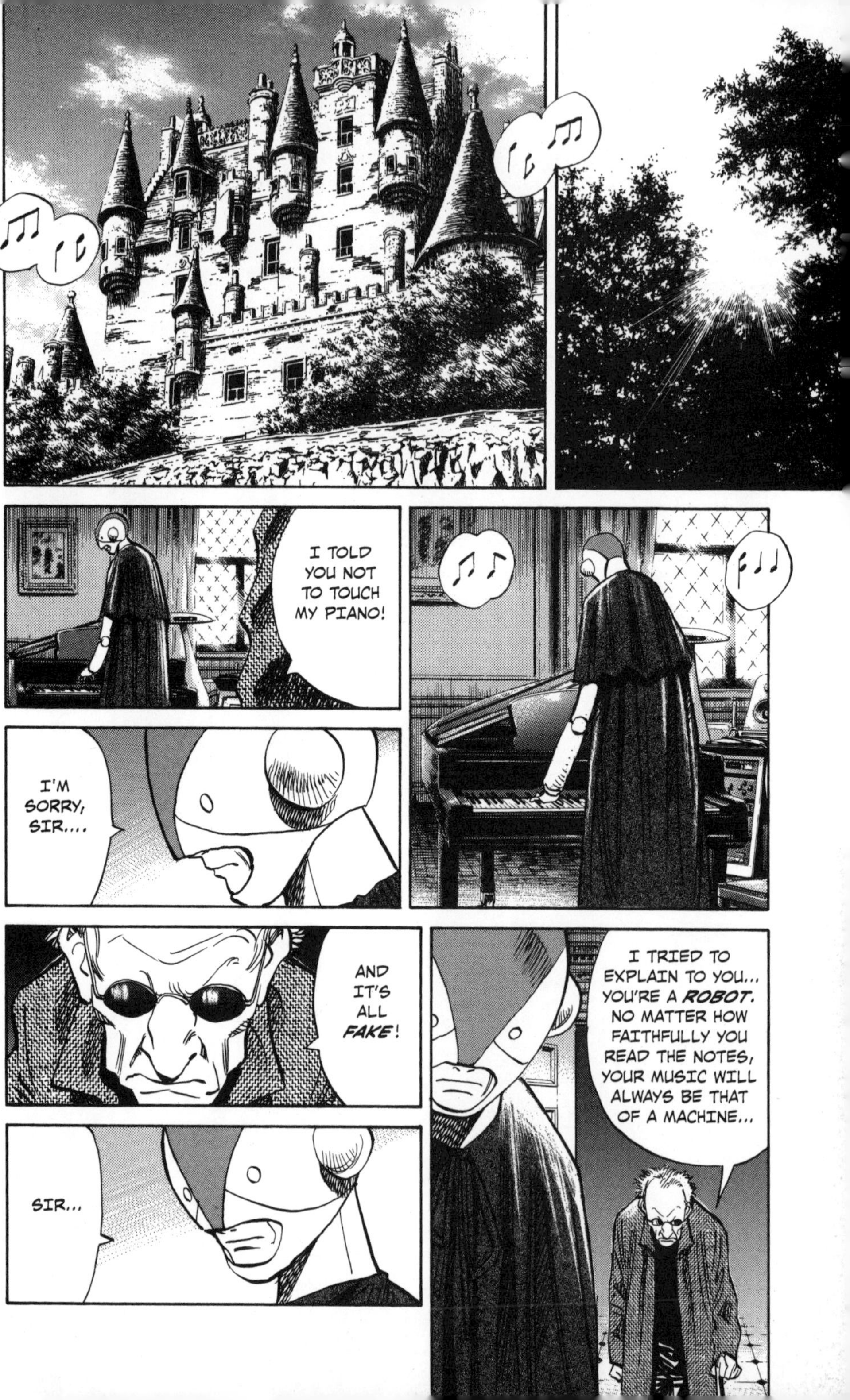
I TOLD YOU NOT TO TOUCH MY PIANO!
I'M SORRY, SIR....
I TRIED TO EXPLAIN TO YOU... YOU'RE A *ROBOT*. NO MATTER HOW FAITHFULLY YOU READ THE NOTES, YOUR MUSIC WILL ALWAYS BE THAT OF A MACHINE...
AND IT'S ALL *FAKE*!
SIR...

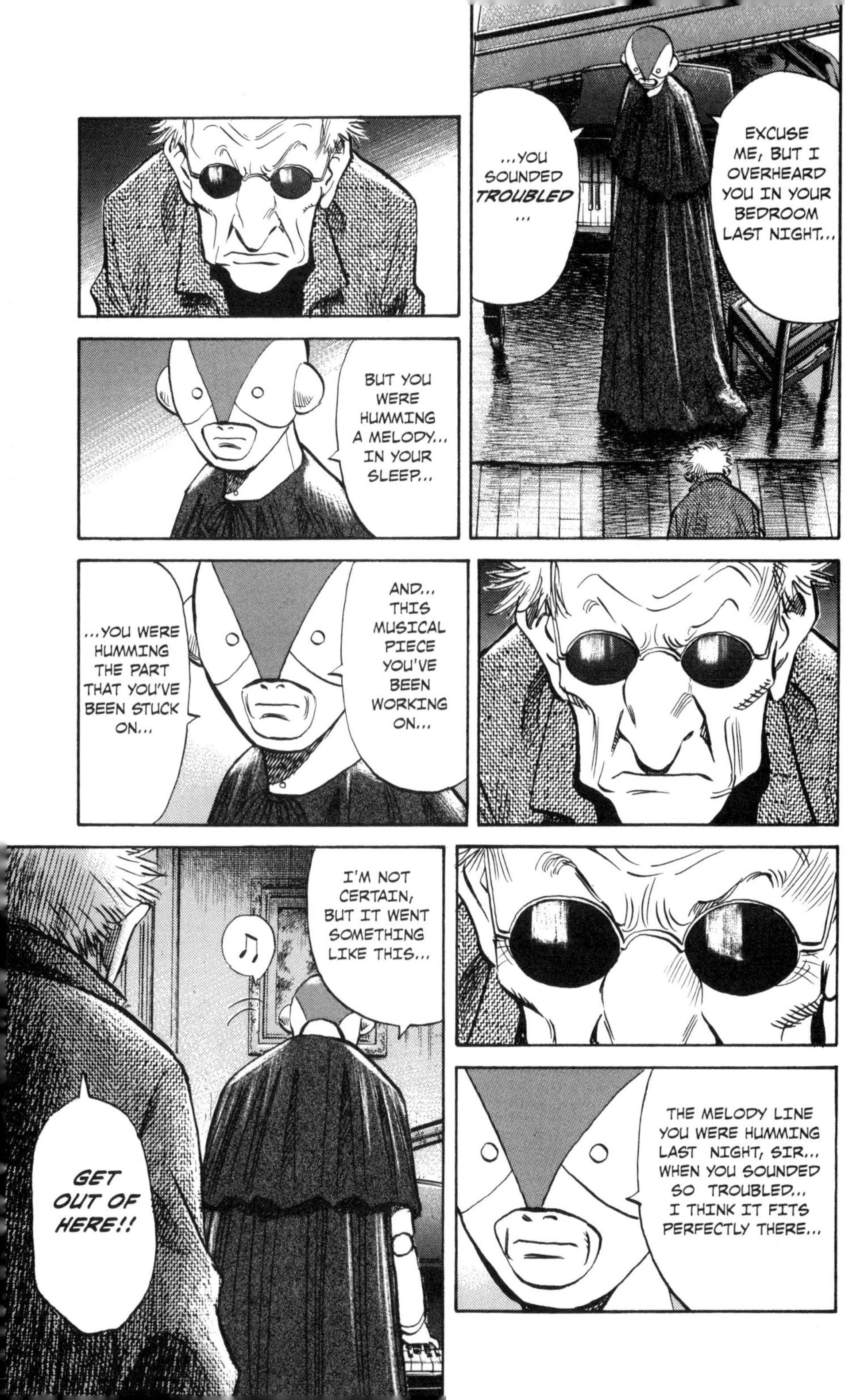
EXCUSE ME, BUT I OVERHEARD YOU IN YOUR BEDROOM LAST NIGHT...
...YOU SOUNDED *TROUBLED*...
BUT YOU WERE HUMMING A MELODY... IN YOUR SLEEP...
AND... THIS MUSICAL PIECE YOU'VE BEEN WORKING ON...
...YOU WERE HUMMING THE PART THAT YOU'VE BEEN STUCK ON...
THE MELODY LINE YOU WERE HUMMING LAST NIGHT, SIR... WHEN YOU SOUNDED SO TROUBLED... I THINK IT FITS PERFECTLY THERE...
I'M NOT CERTAIN, BUT IT WENT SOMETHING LIKE THIS...
♫
GET OUT OF HERE!!

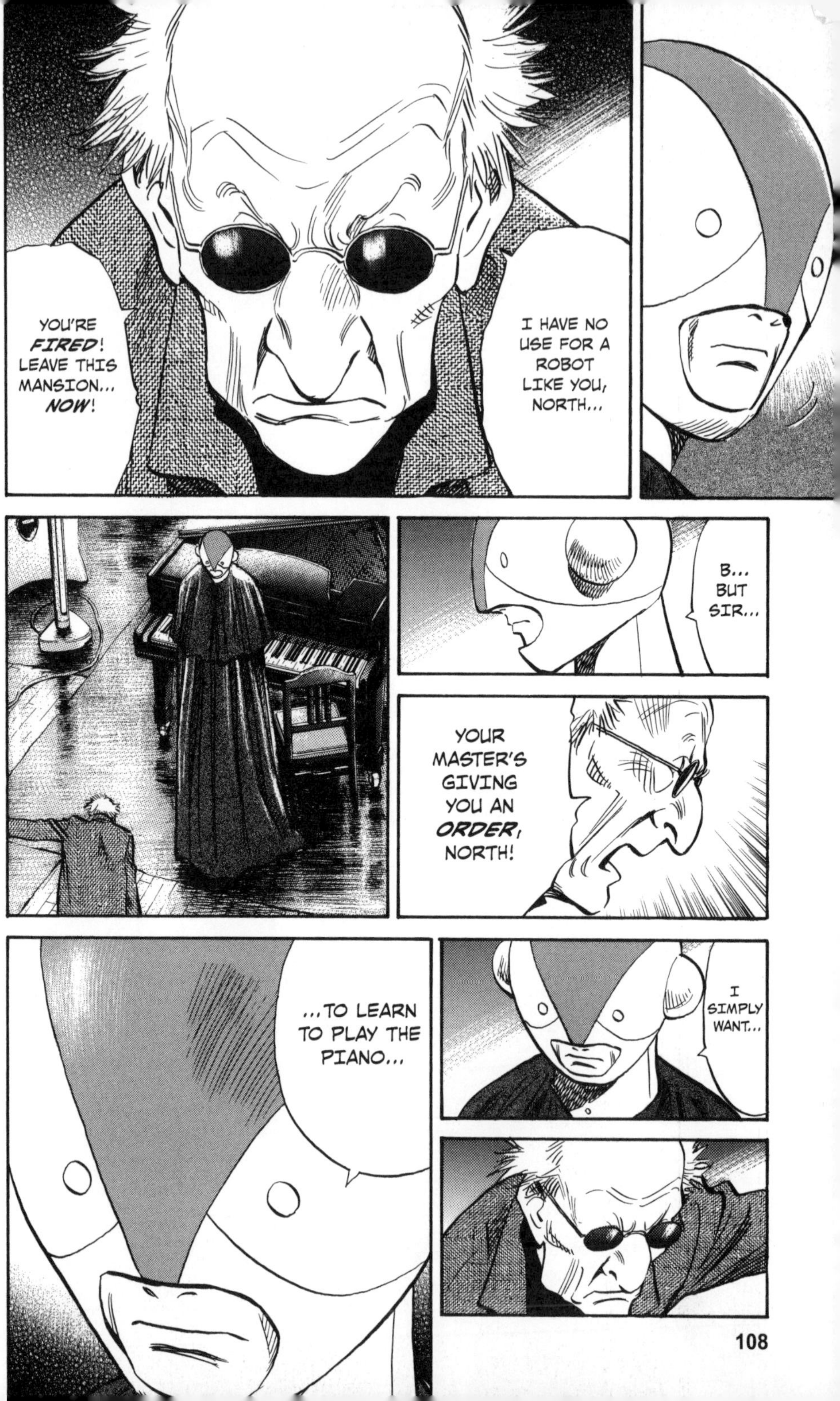

I HAVE NO USE FOR A ROBOT LIKE YOU, NORTH...
YOU'RE *FIRED*! LEAVE THIS MANSION... *NOW*!
B... BUT SIR...
YOUR MASTER'S GIVING YOU AN *ORDER*, NORTH!
I SIMPLY WANT...
...TO LEARN TO PLAY THE PIANO...

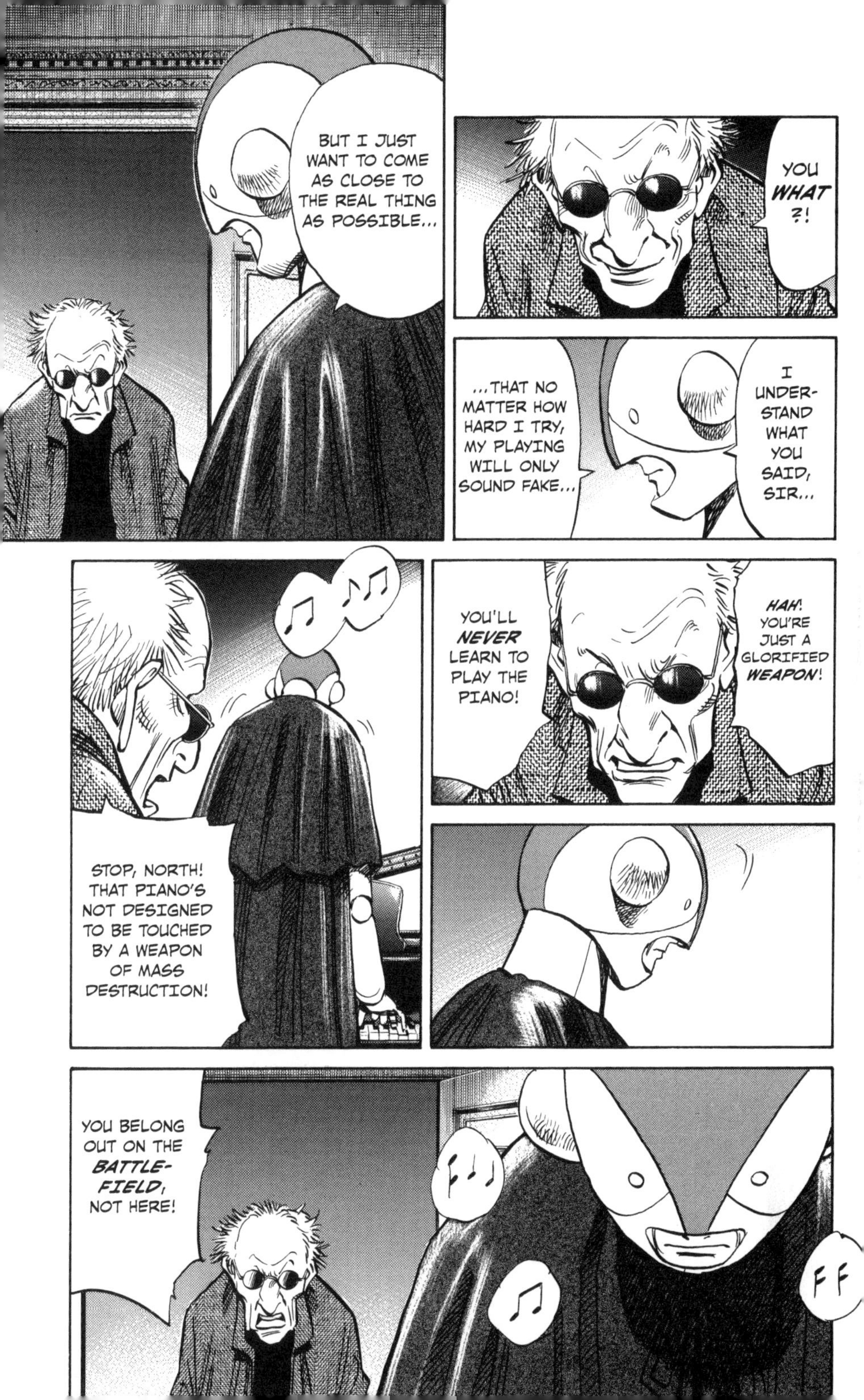
YOU WHAT?!
I UNDERSTAND WHAT YOU SAID, SIR...
...THAT NO MATTER HOW HARD I TRY, MY PLAYING WILL ONLY SOUND FAKE...
BUT I JUST WANT TO COME AS CLOSE TO THE REAL THING AS POSSIBLE...
HAH! YOU'RE JUST A GLORIFIED WEAPON!
YOU'LL NEVER LEARN TO PLAY THE PIANO!
STOP, NORTH! THAT PIANO'S NOT DESIGNED TO BE TOUCHED BY A WEAPON OF MASS DESTRUCTION!
YOU BELONG OUT ON THE BATTLEFIELD, NOT HERE!

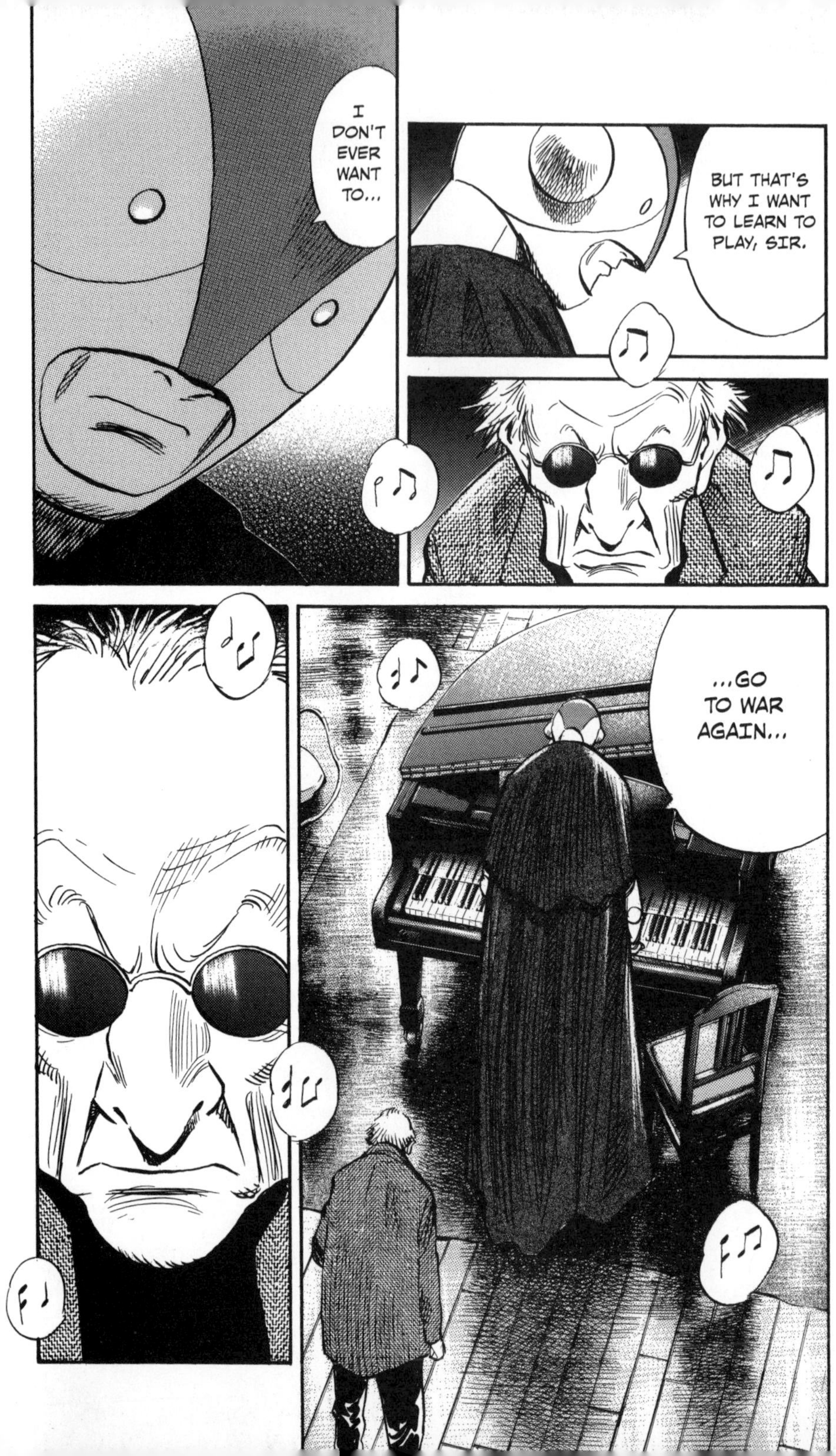
BUT THAT'S WHY I WANT TO LEARN TO PLAY, SIR.
I DON'T EVER WANT TO...
...GO TO WAR AGAIN...

Act 5 NORTH No. 2 (Part 2)

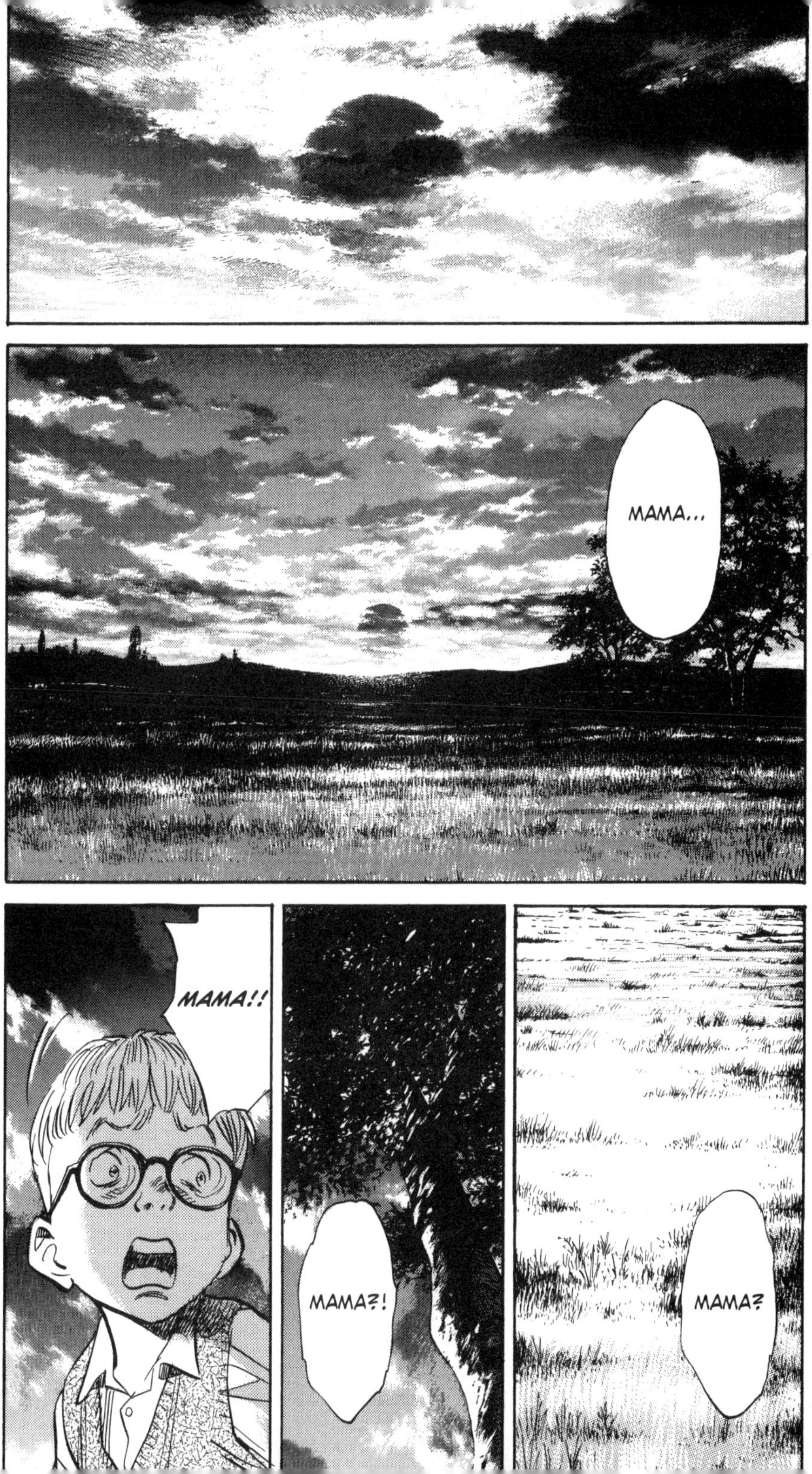

MAMA...
MAMA?
MAMA?!
MAMA!!

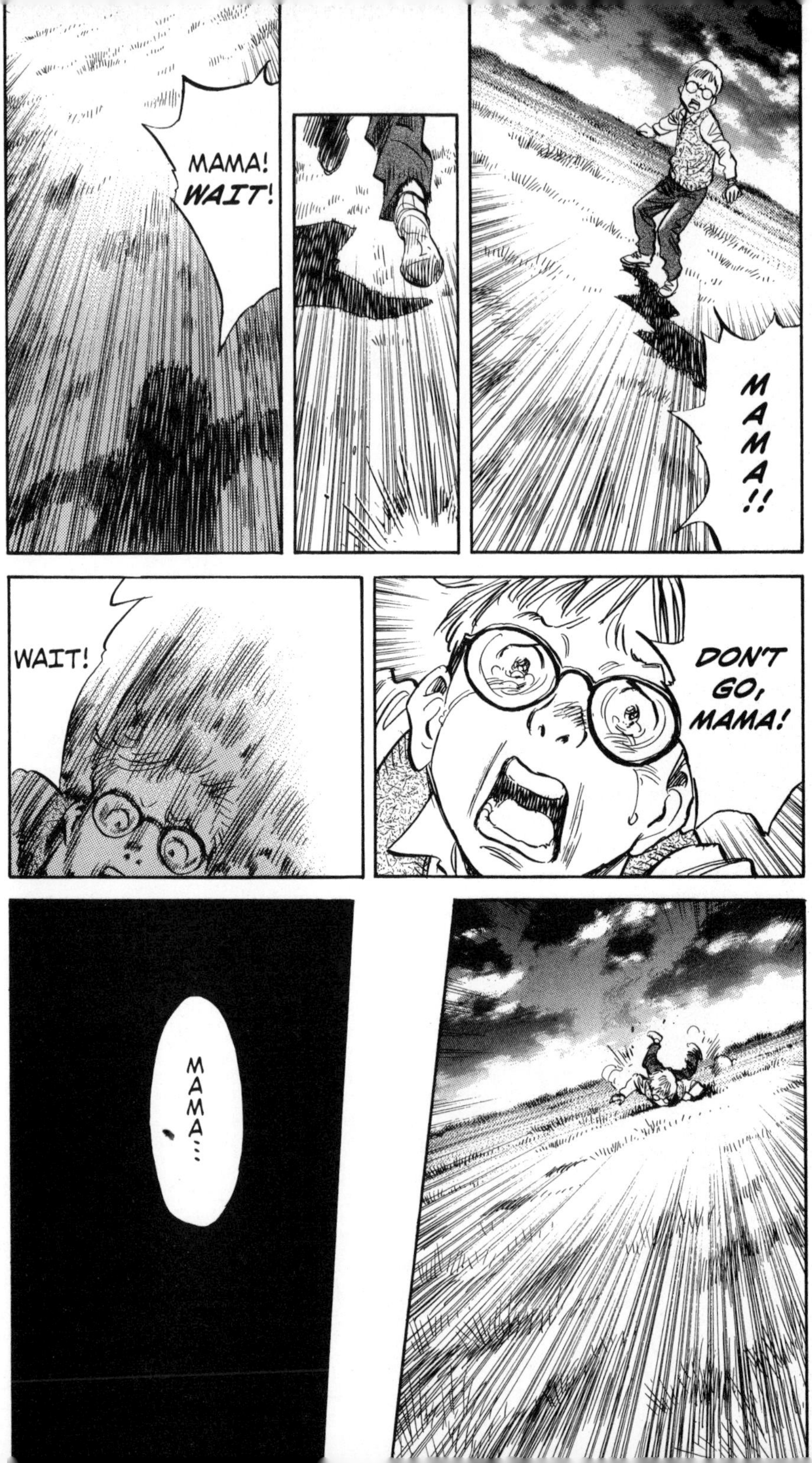
MAMA!!
MAMA! WAIT!
DON'T GO, MAMA!
WAIT!
MAMA...

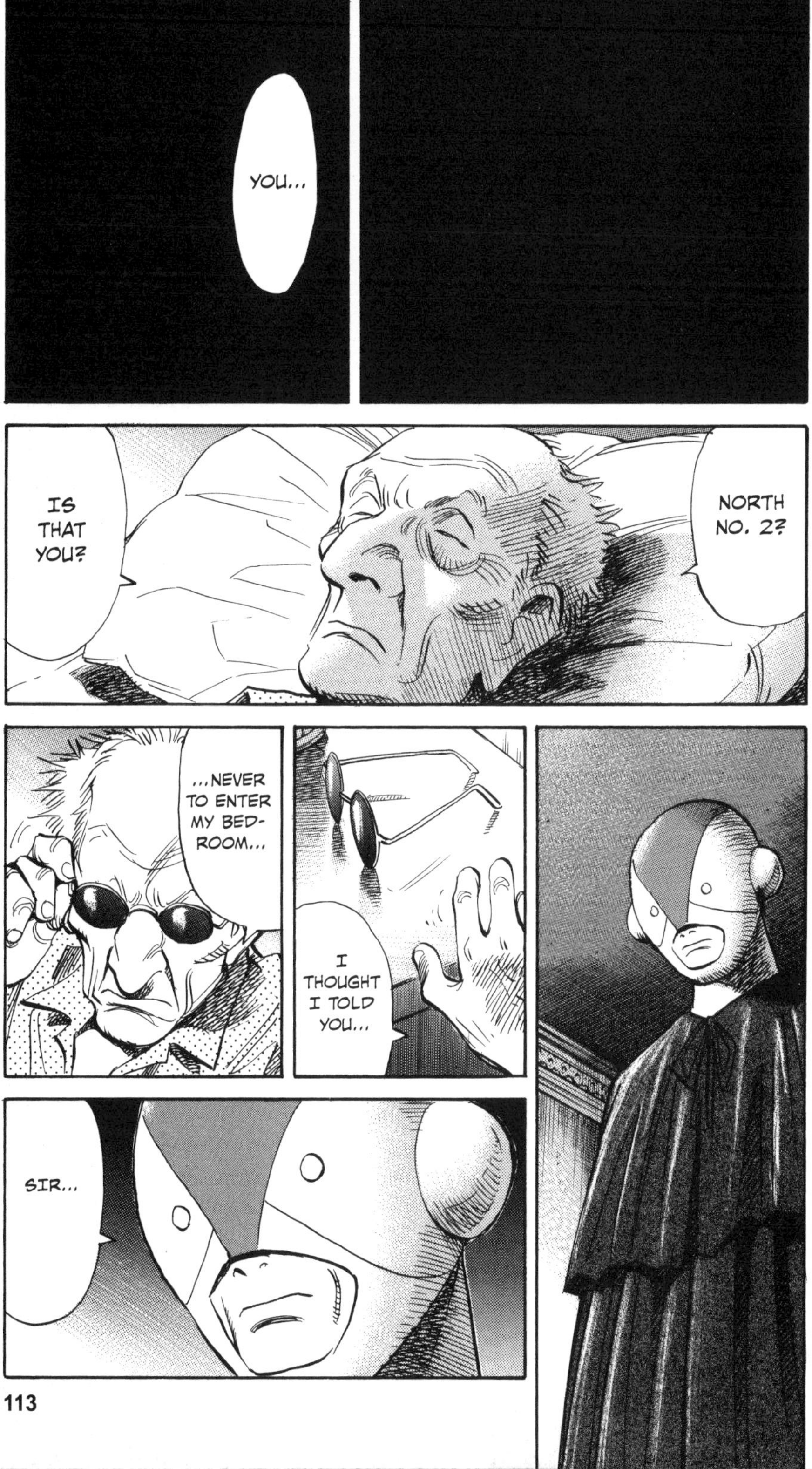
YOU...
NORTH NO. 2?
IS THAT YOU?
I THOUGHT I TOLD YOU...
...NEVER TO ENTER MY BED-ROOM...
SIR...

Act 5
NORTH No. 2
(Part 2)

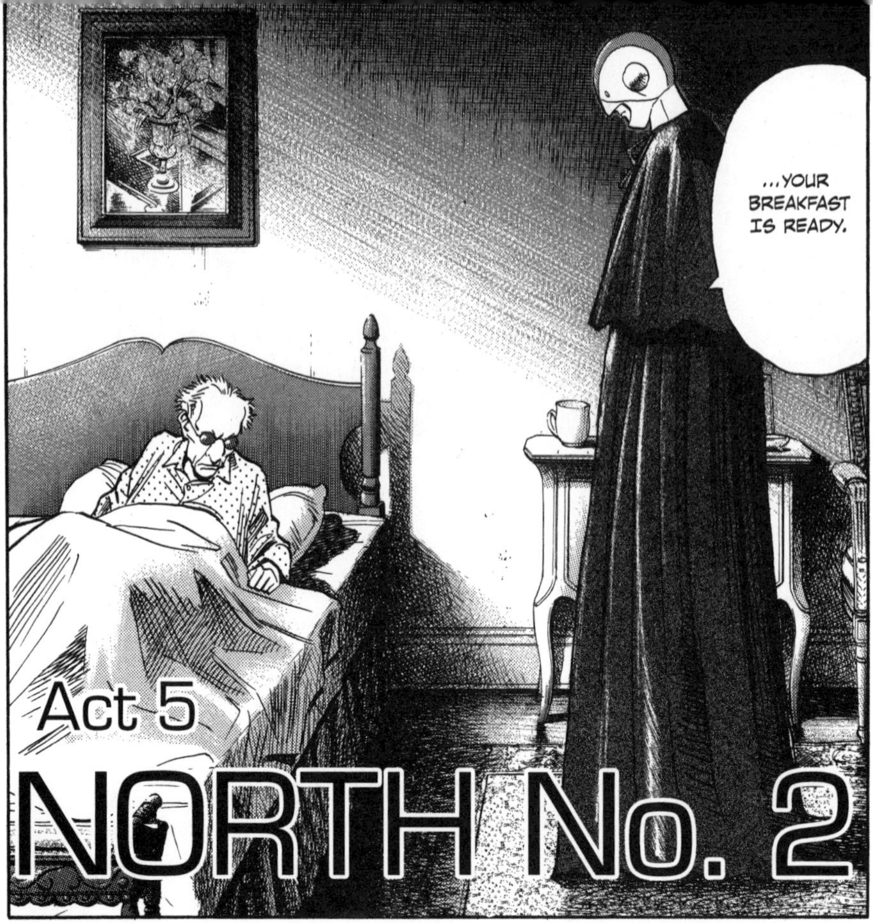
...YOUR BREAKFAST IS READY.

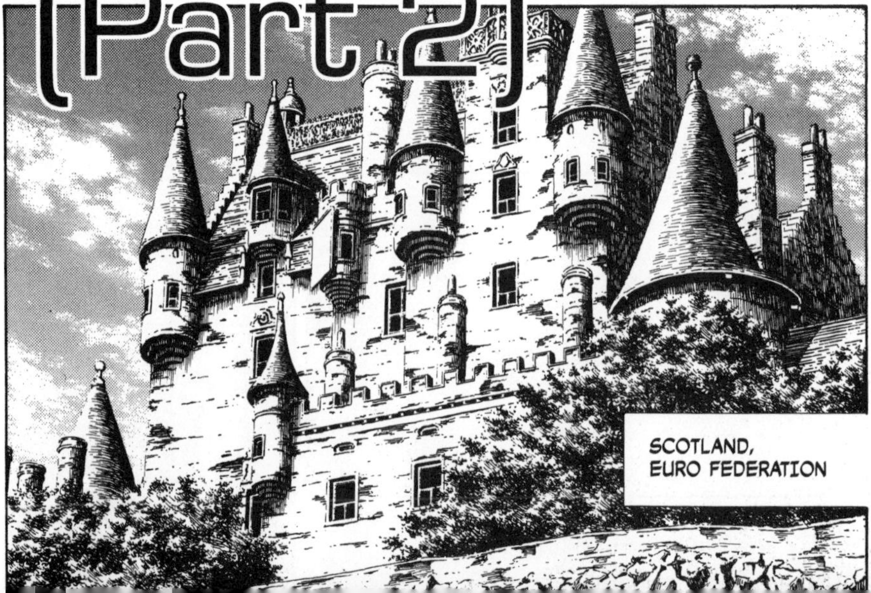
SCOTLAND, EURO FEDERATION

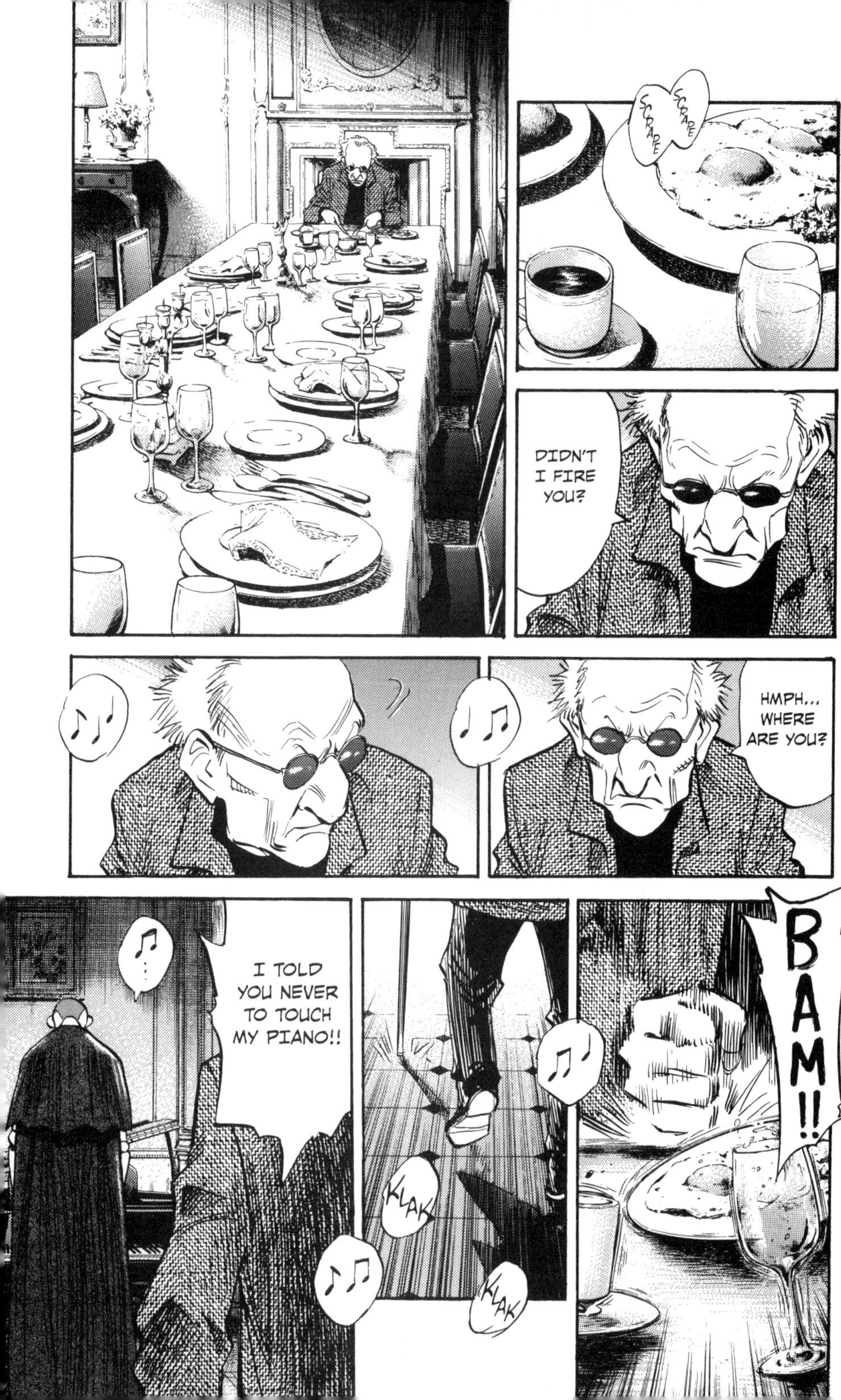
SCRAPE
SCRAPE
DIDN'T I FIRE YOU?
HMPH... WHERE ARE YOU?
BAM!!
KLAK
KLAK
I TOLD YOU NEVER TO TOUCH MY PIANO!!

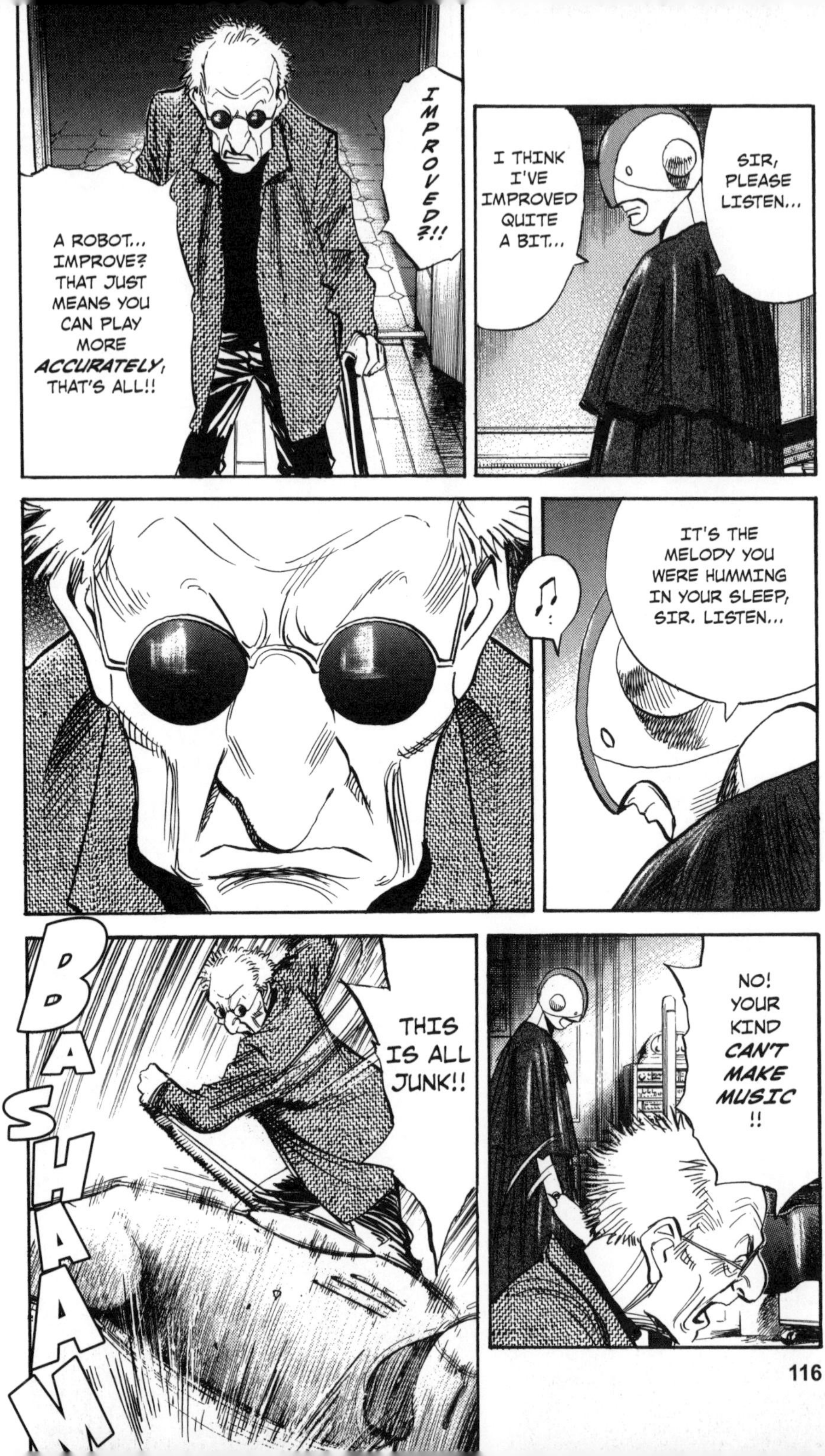
SIR, PLEASE LISTEN...
I THINK I'VE IMPROVED QUITE A BIT...
IMPROVED?!!
A ROBOT... IMPROVE? THAT JUST MEANS YOU CAN PLAY MORE ACCURATELY, THAT'S ALL!!
IT'S THE MELODY YOU WERE HUMMING IN YOUR SLEEP, SIR. LISTEN...
♪
NO! YOUR KIND CAN'T MAKE MUSIC!!
THIS IS ALL JUNK!!
BASHAAAM

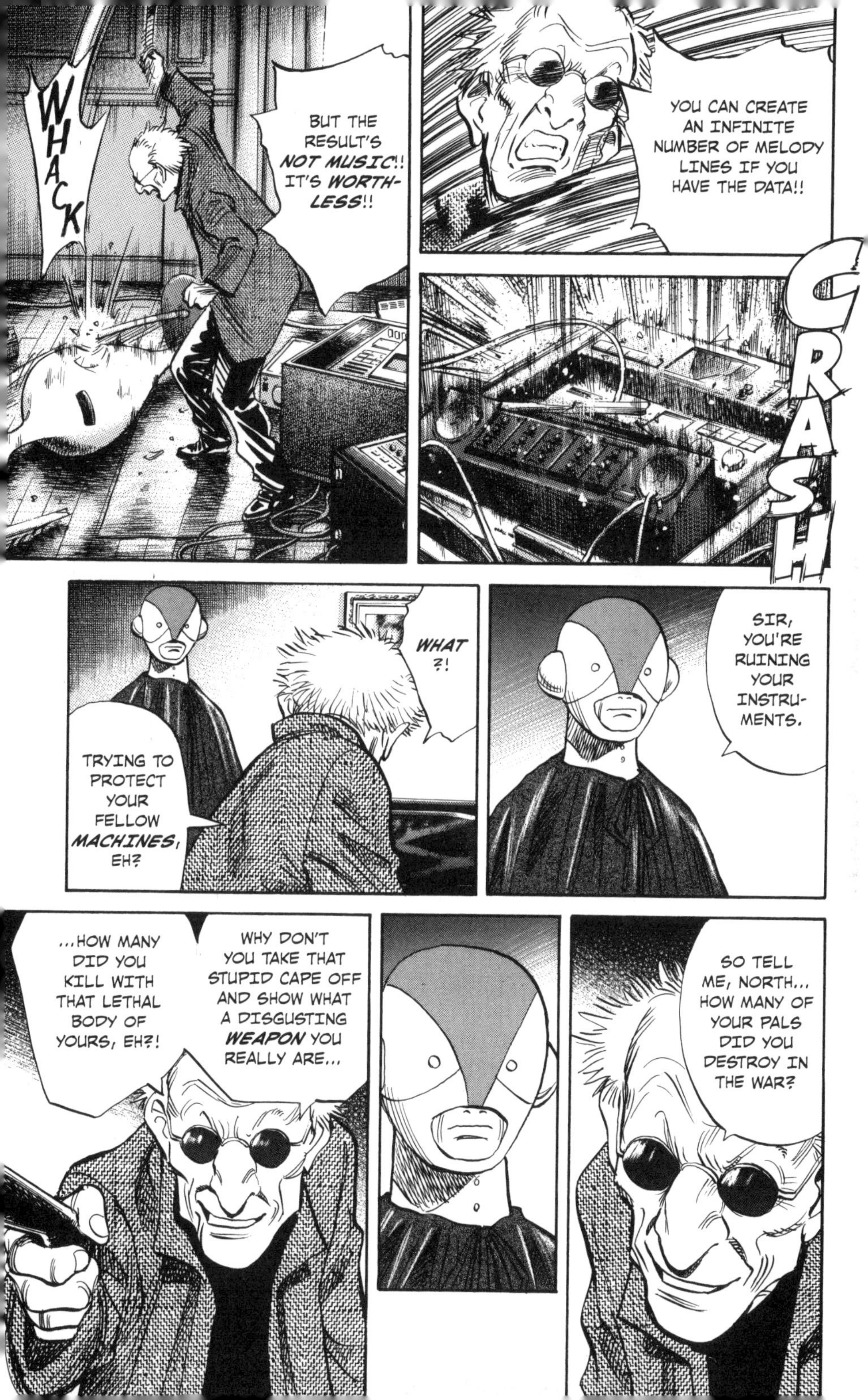
YOU CAN CREATE AN INFINITE NUMBER OF MELODY LINES IF YOU HAVE THE DATA!!
CRASH
WHACK
BUT THE RESULT'S NOT MUSIC!! IT'S WORTHLESS!!
SIR, YOU'RE RUINING YOUR INSTRUMENTS.
WHAT?!
TRYING TO PROTECT YOUR FELLOW MACHINES, EH?
SO TELL ME, NORTH... HOW MANY OF YOUR PALS DID YOU DESTROY IN THE WAR?
WHY DON'T YOU TAKE THAT STUPID CAPE OFF AND SHOW WHAT A DISGUSTING WEAPON YOU REALLY ARE...
...HOW MANY DID YOU KILL WITH THAT LETHAL BODY OF YOURS, EH?!

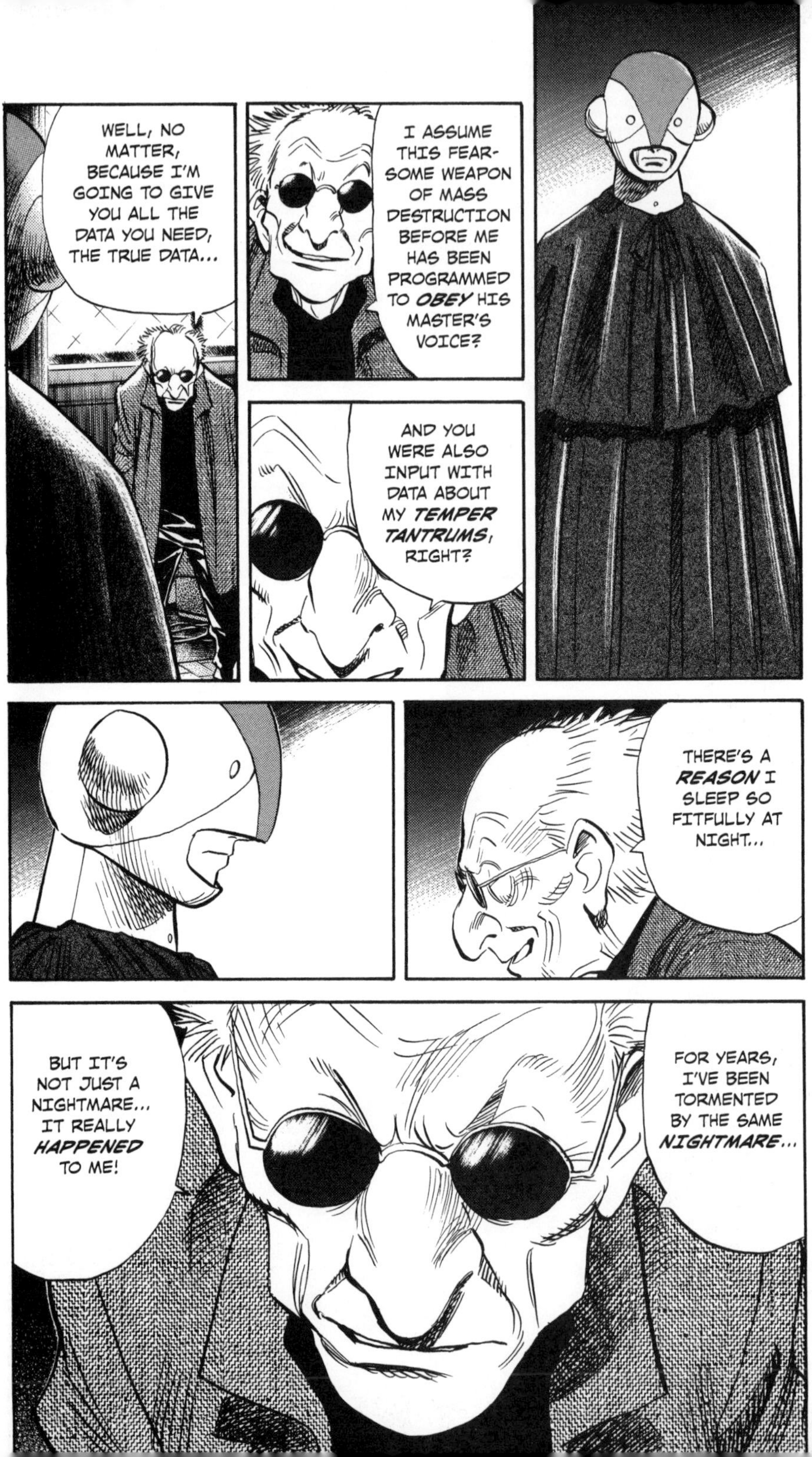
I ASSUME THIS FEARSOME WEAPON OF MASS DESTRUCTION BEFORE ME HAS BEEN PROGRAMMED TO *OBEY* HIS MASTER'S VOICE?
AND YOU WERE ALSO INPUT WITH DATA ABOUT MY *TEMPER TANTRUMS*, RIGHT?
WELL, NO MATTER, BECAUSE I'M GOING TO GIVE YOU ALL THE DATA YOU NEED, THE TRUE DATA...
THERE'S A *REASON* I SLEEP SO FITFULLY AT NIGHT...
FOR YEARS, I'VE BEEN TORMENTED BY THE SAME *NIGHTMARE*...
BUT IT'S NOT JUST A NIGHTMARE... IT REALLY *HAPPENED* TO ME!

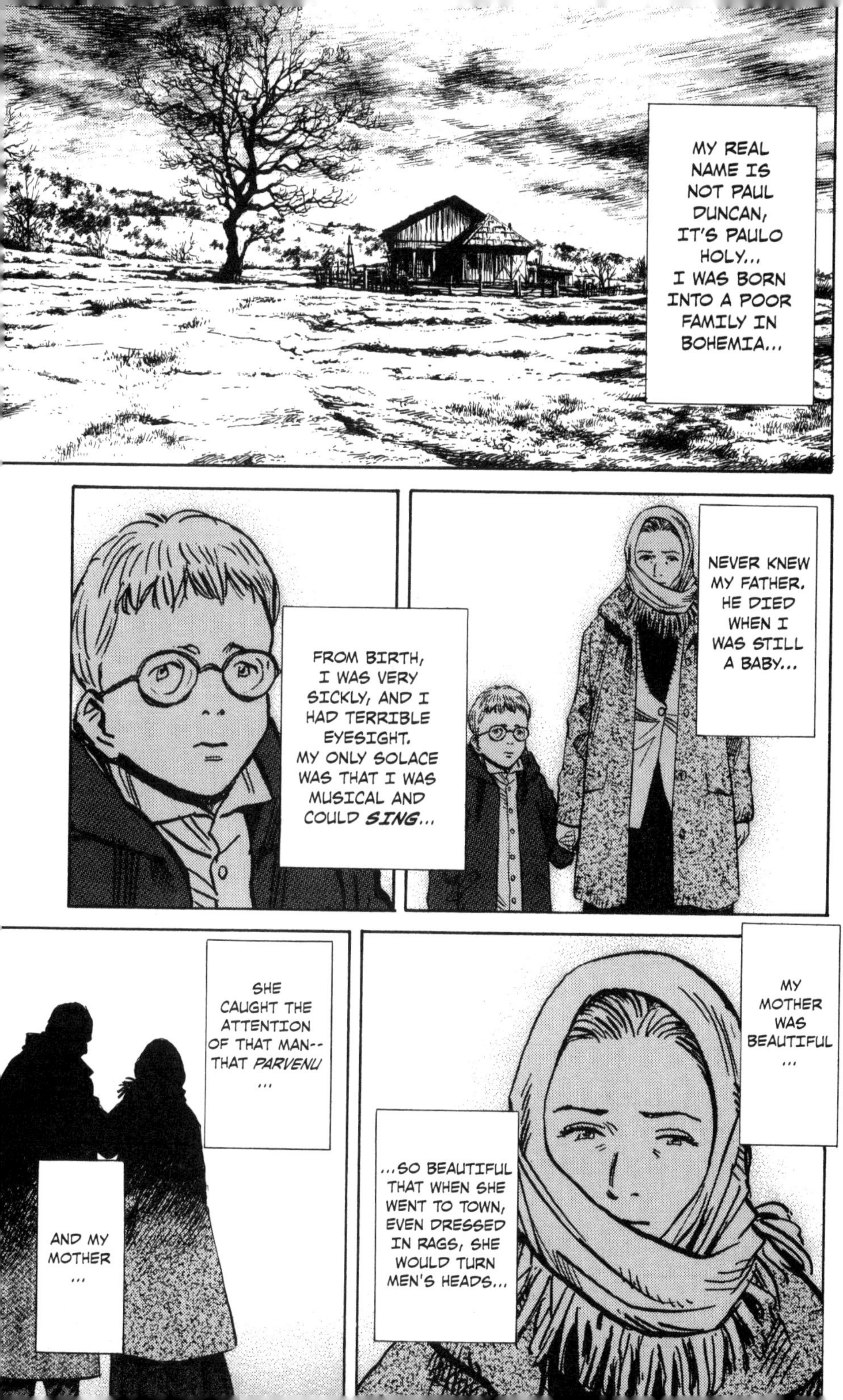
MY REAL NAME IS NOT PAUL DUNCAN, IT'S PAULO HOLY... I WAS BORN INTO A POOR FAMILY IN BOHEMIA...
NEVER KNEW MY FATHER. HE DIED WHEN I WAS STILL A BABY...
FROM BIRTH, I WAS VERY SICKLY, AND I HAD TERRIBLE EYESIGHT. MY ONLY SOLACE WAS THAT I WAS MUSICAL AND COULD *SING*...
MY MOTHER WAS BEAUTIFUL...
...SO BEAUTIFUL THAT WHEN SHE WENT TO TOWN, EVEN DRESSED IN RAGS, SHE WOULD TURN MEN'S HEADS...
SHE CAUGHT THE ATTENTION OF THAT MAN--THAT *PARVENU*...
AND MY MOTHER...

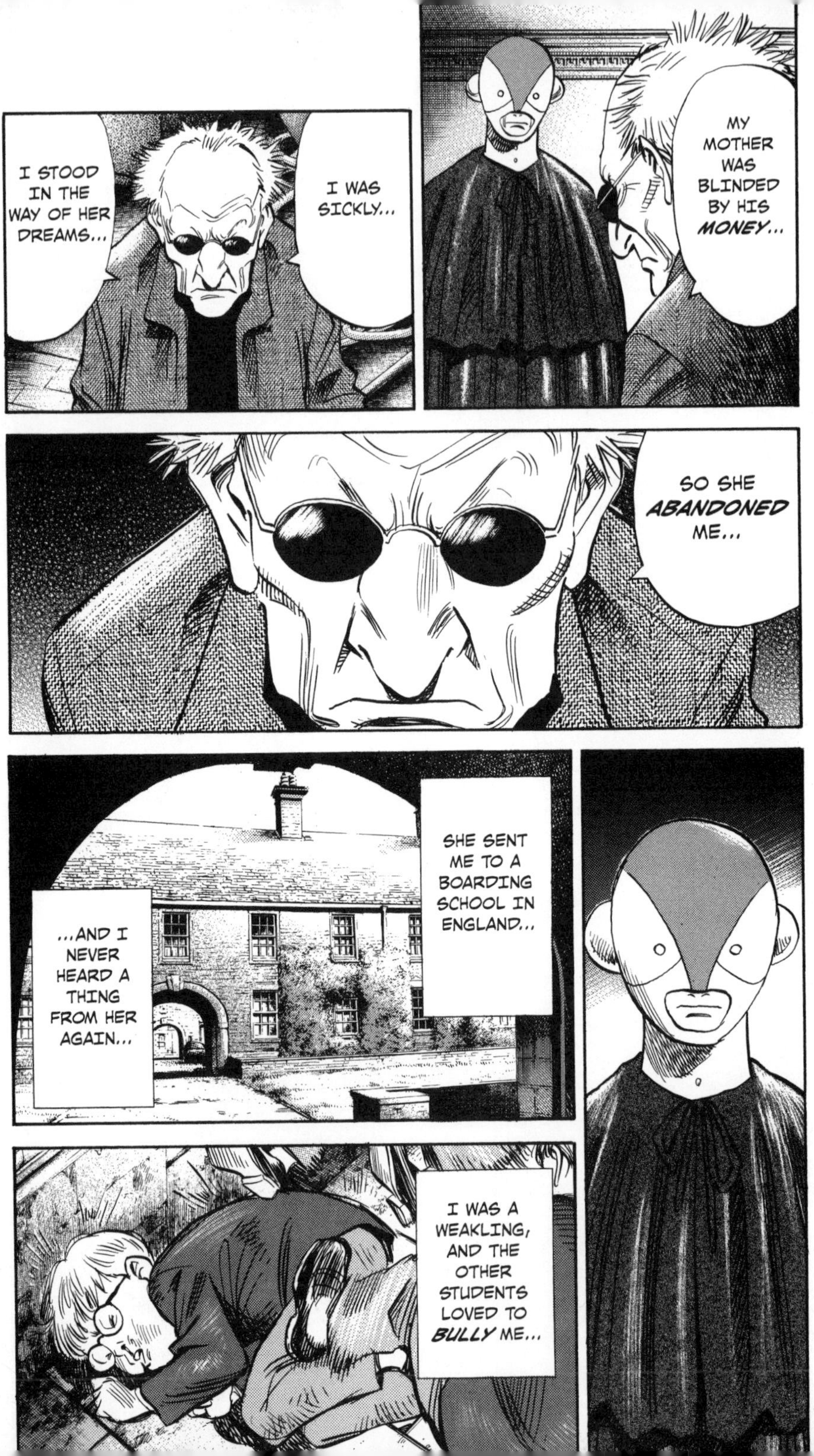
MY MOTHER WAS BLINDED BY HIS MONEY...
I WAS SICKLY...
I STOOD IN THE WAY OF HER DREAMS...
SO SHE ABANDONED ME...
SHE SENT ME TO A BOARDING SCHOOL IN ENGLAND...
...AND I NEVER HEARD A THING FROM HER AGAIN...
I WAS A WEAKLING, AND THE OTHER STUDENTS LOVED TO BULLY ME...

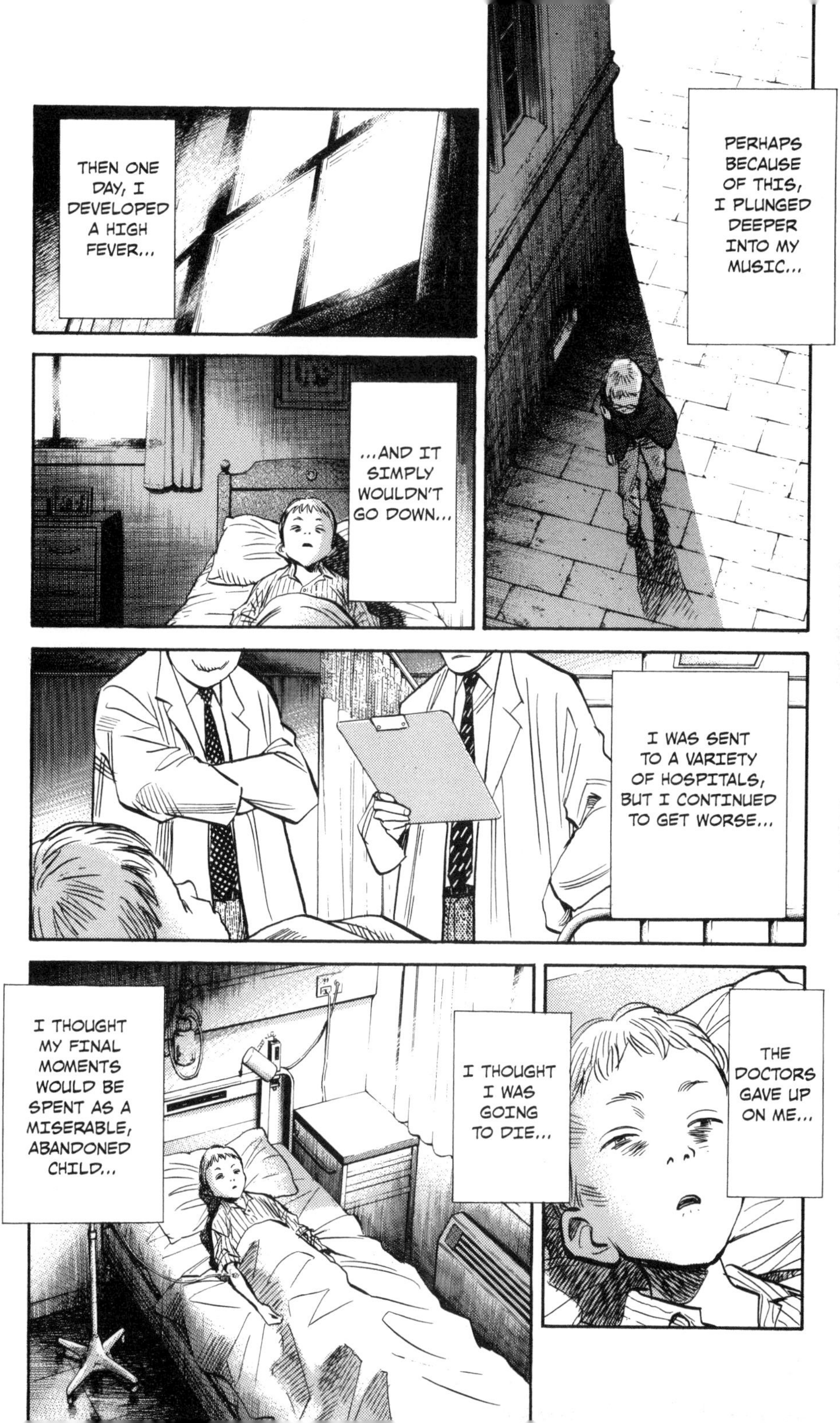
PERHAPS BECAUSE OF THIS, I PLUNGED DEEPER INTO MY MUSIC...
THEN ONE DAY, I DEVELOPED A HIGH FEVER...
...AND IT SIMPLY WOULDN'T GO DOWN...
I WAS SENT TO A VARIETY OF HOSPITALS, BUT I CONTINUED TO GET WORSE...
THE DOCTORS GAVE UP ON ME...
I THOUGHT I WAS GOING TO DIE...
I THOUGHT MY FINAL MOMENTS WOULD BE SPENT AS A MISERABLE, ABANDONED CHILD...

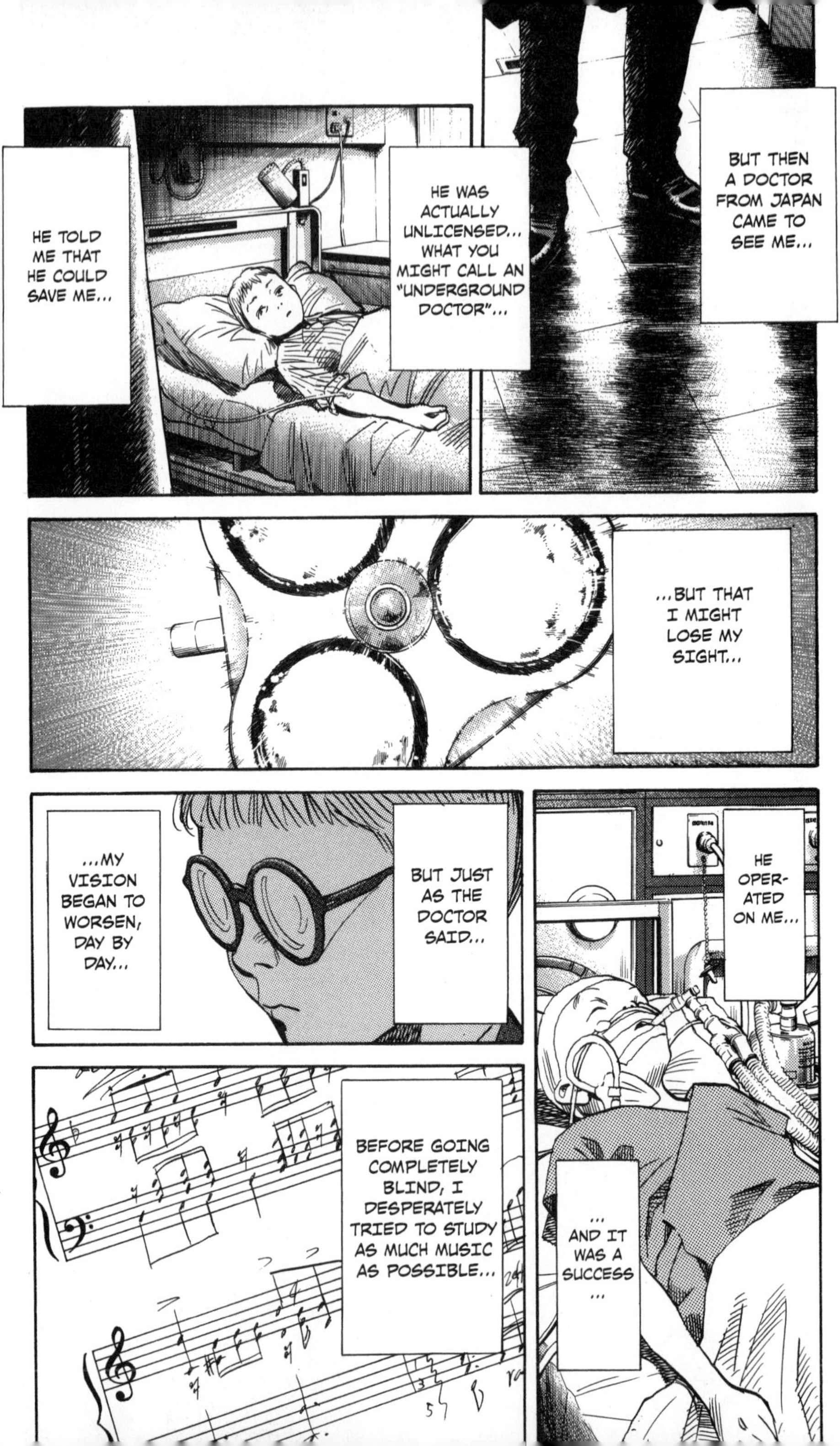
BUT THEN A DOCTOR FROM JAPAN CAME TO SEE ME...
HE WAS ACTUALLY UNLICENSED... WHAT YOU MIGHT CALL AN "UNDERGROUND DOCTOR"...
HE TOLD ME THAT HE COULD SAVE ME...
...BUT THAT I MIGHT LOSE MY SIGHT...
HE OPERATED ON ME...
...AND IT WAS A SUCCESS...
BUT JUST AS THE DOCTOR SAID...
...MY VISION BEGAN TO WORSEN, DAY BY DAY...
BEFORE GOING COMPLETELY BLIND, I DESPERATELY TRIED TO STUDY AS MUCH MUSIC AS POSSIBLE...

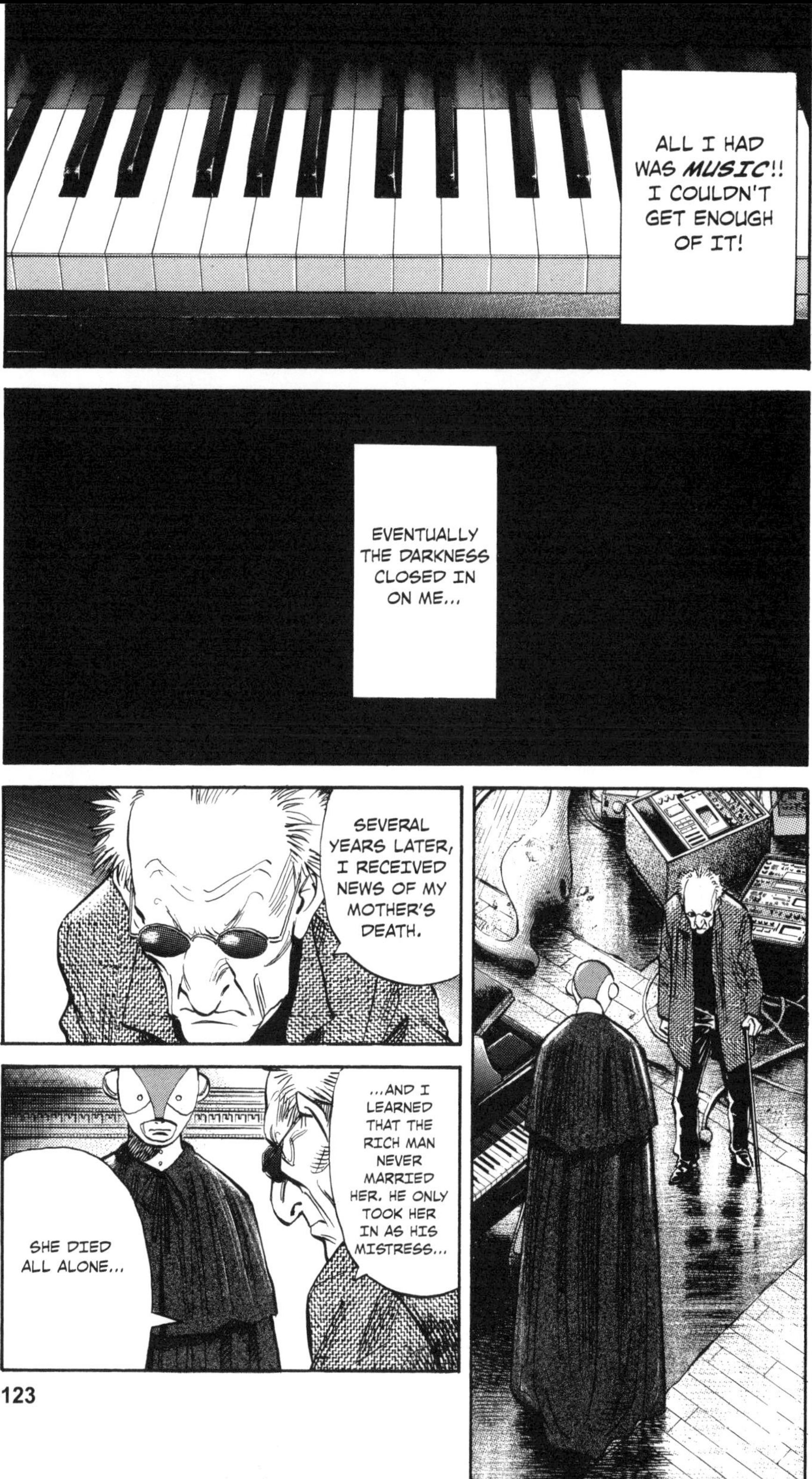
ALL I HAD WAS ***MUSIC***!! I COULDN'T GET ENOUGH OF IT!
EVENTUALLY THE DARKNESS CLOSED IN ON ME...
SEVERAL YEARS LATER, I RECEIVED NEWS OF MY MOTHER'S DEATH.
...AND I LEARNED THAT THE RICH MAN NEVER MARRIED HER. HE ONLY TOOK HER IN AS HIS MISTRESS...
SHE DIED ALL ALONE...

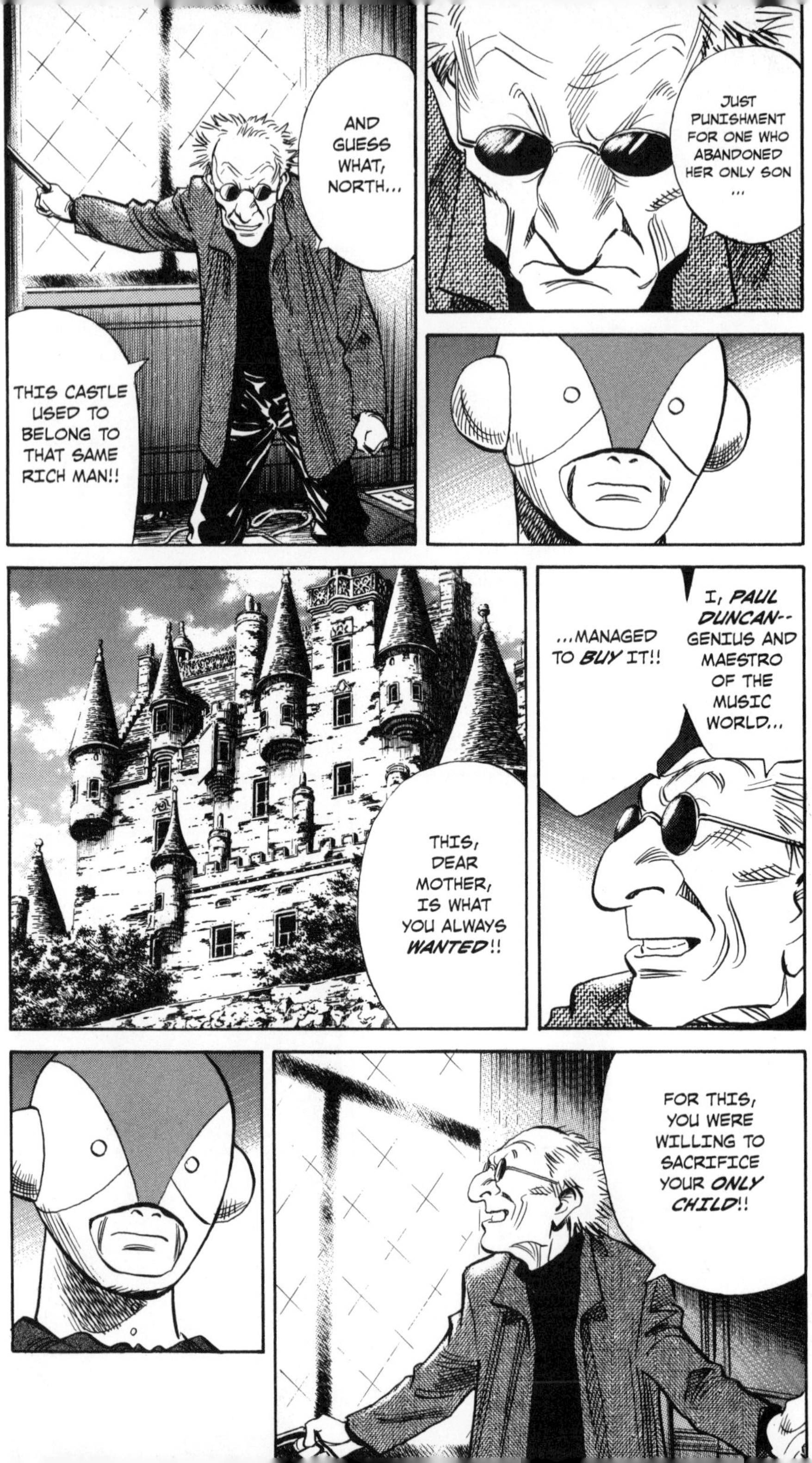
JUST PUNISHMENT FOR ONE WHO ABANDONED HER ONLY SON ...
AND GUESS WHAT, NORTH...
THIS CASTLE USED TO BELONG TO THAT SAME RICH MAN!!
I, *PAUL DUNCAN*-- GENIUS AND MAESTRO OF THE MUSIC WORLD...
...MANAGED TO *BUY* IT!!
THIS, DEAR MOTHER, IS WHAT YOU ALWAYS *WANTED*!!
FOR THIS, YOU WERE WILLING TO SACRIFICE YOUR *ONLY CHILD*!!

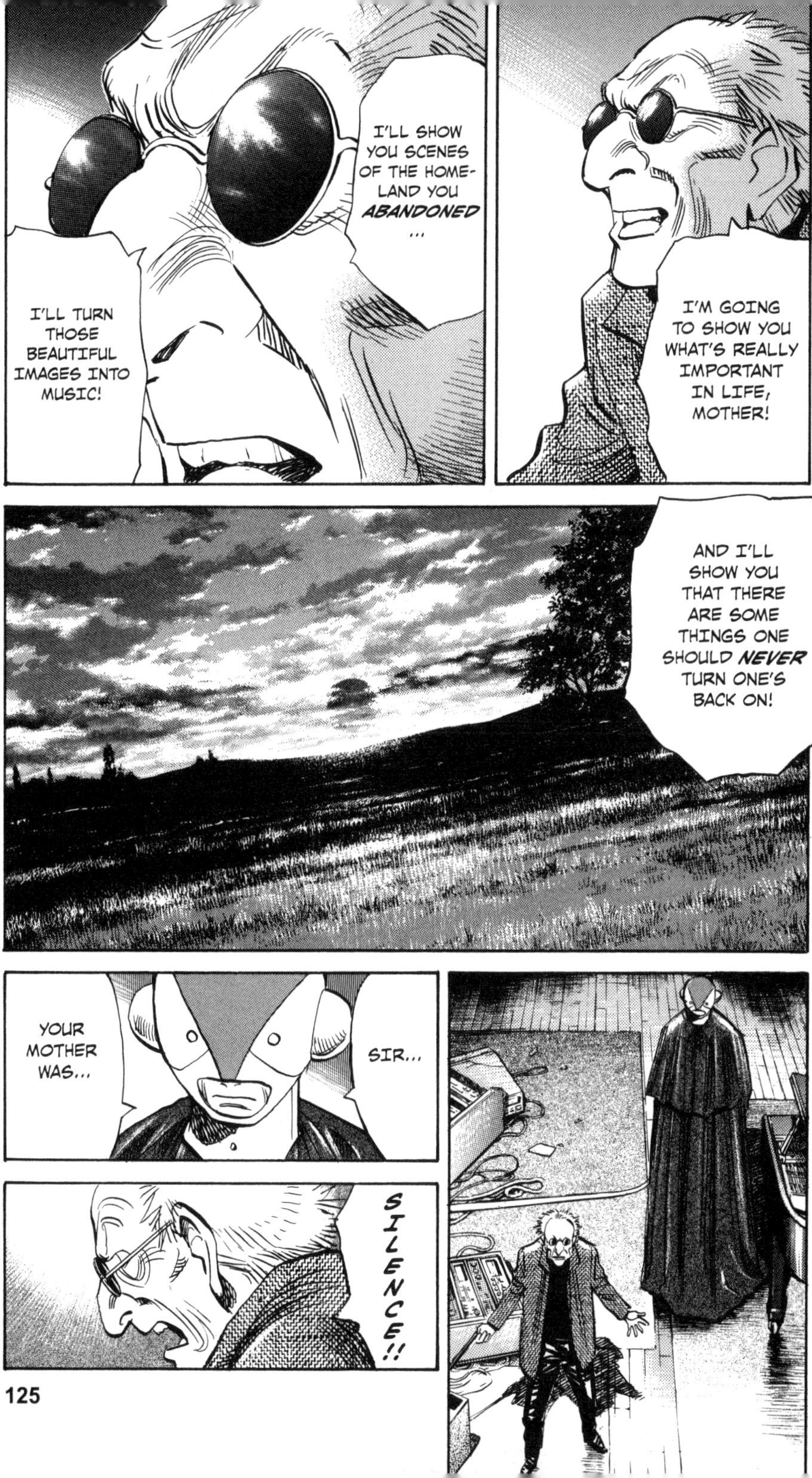
I'M GOING TO SHOW YOU WHAT'S REALLY IMPORTANT IN LIFE, MOTHER!
I'LL SHOW YOU SCENES OF THE HOME-LAND YOU ***ABANDONED*** ...
I'LL TURN THOSE BEAUTIFUL IMAGES INTO MUSIC!
AND I'LL SHOW YOU THAT THERE ARE SOME THINGS ONE SHOULD ***NEVER*** TURN ONE'S BACK ON!
SIR...
YOUR MOTHER WAS...
SILENCE!!

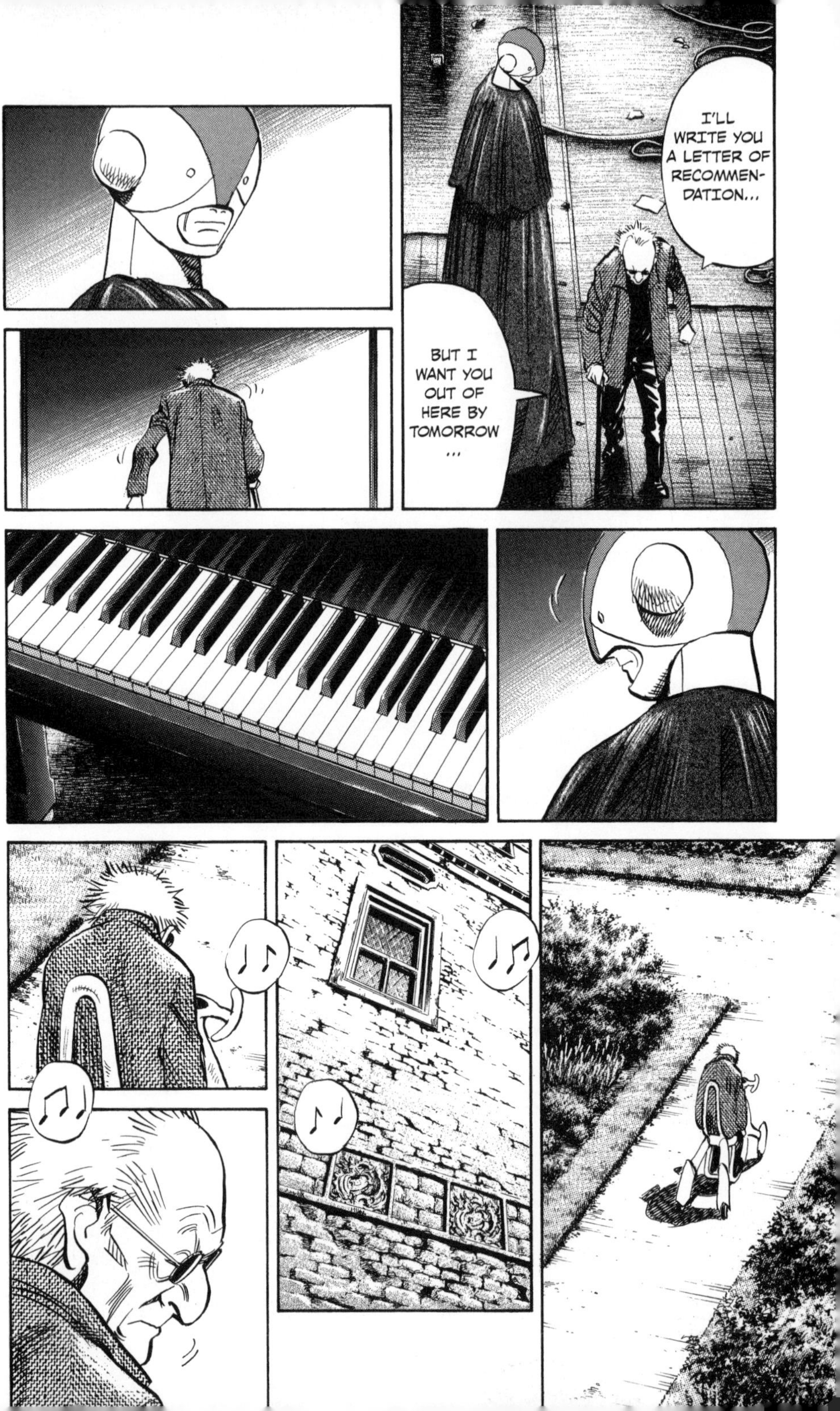
I'LL WRITE YOU A LETTER OF RECOMMEN-DATION...
BUT I WANT YOU OUT OF HERE BY TOMORROW ...

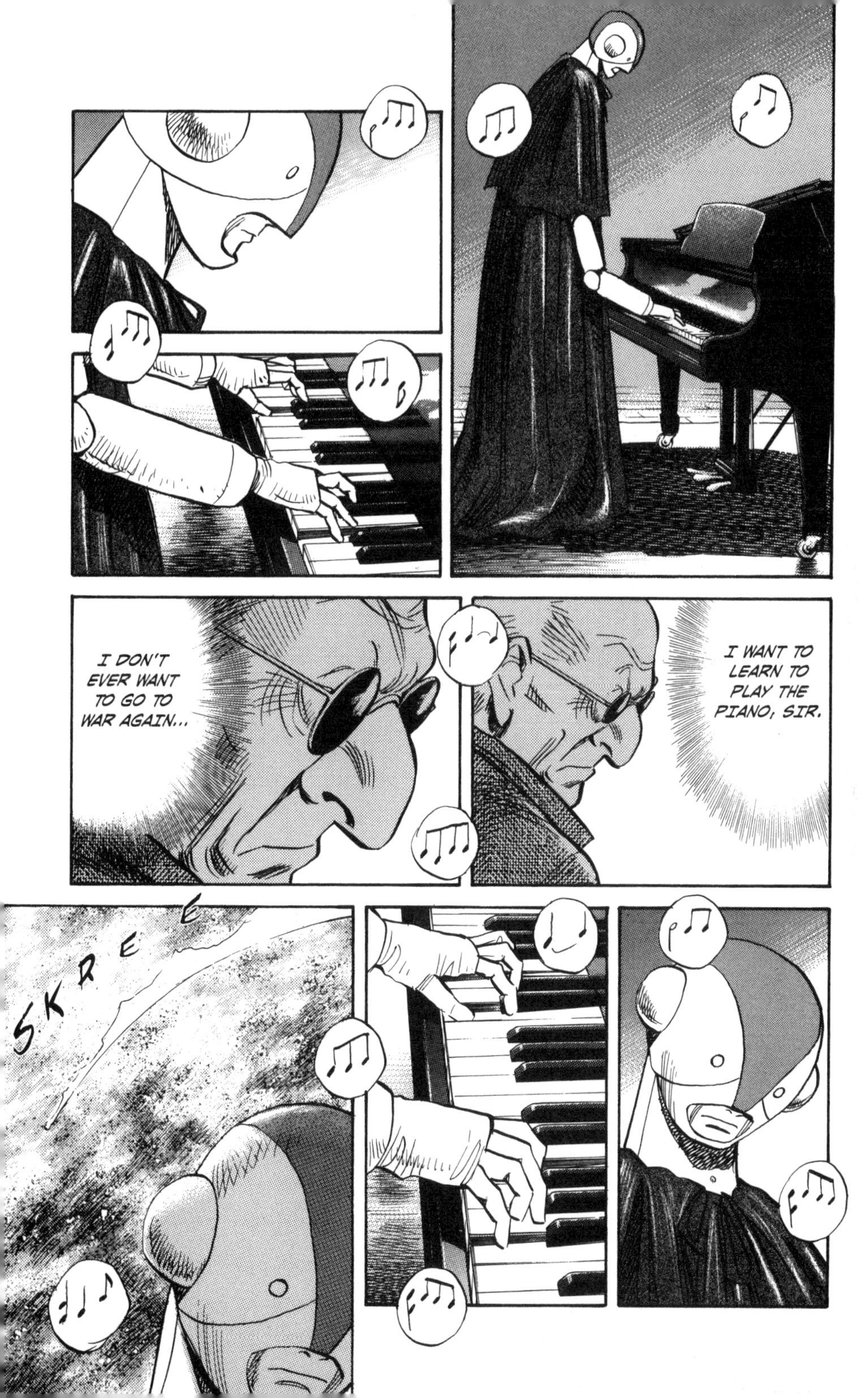
I WANT TO LEARN TO PLAY THE PIANO, SIR.
I DON'T EVER WANT TO GO TO WAR AGAIN...
SKREE

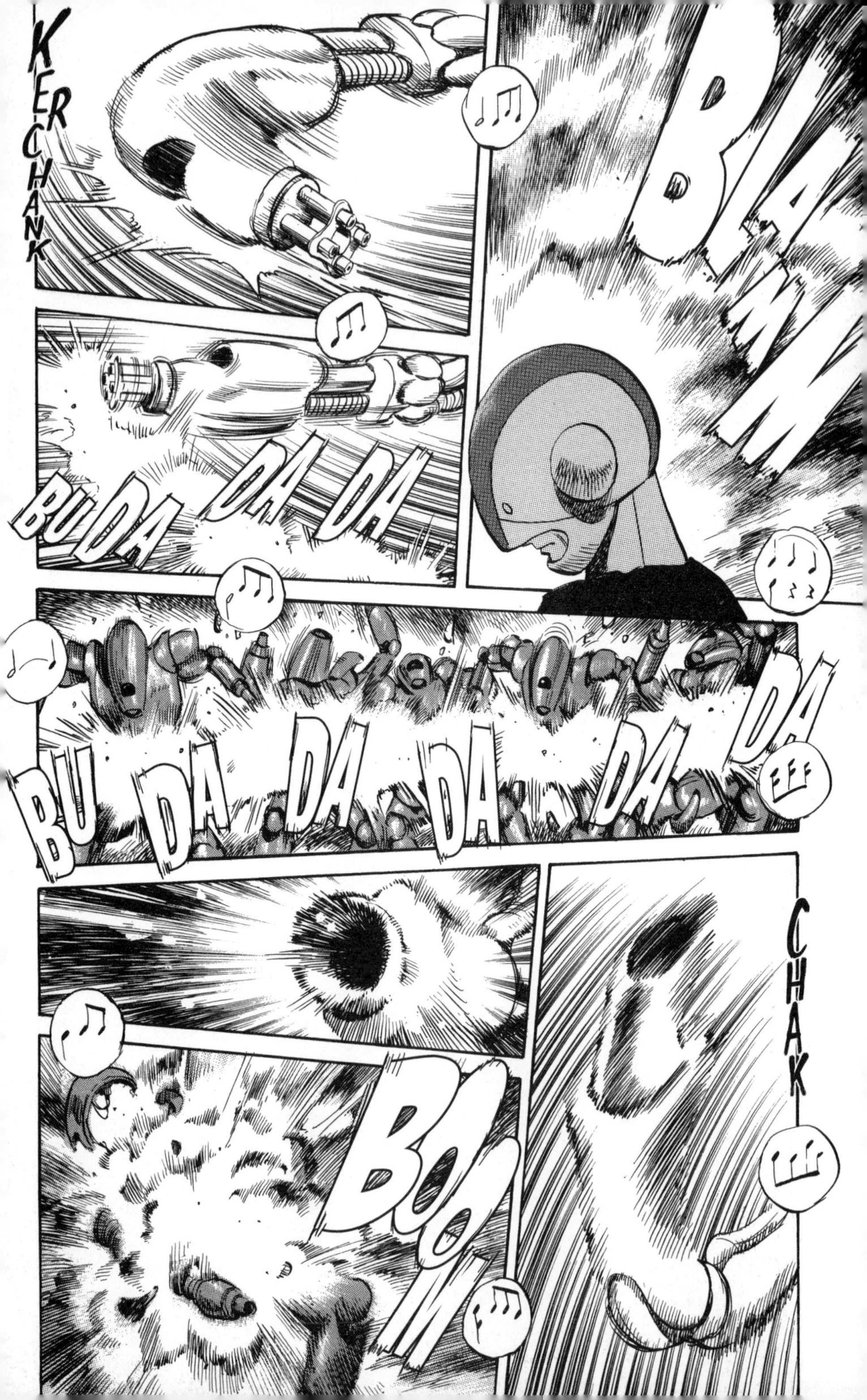
BLAM
KERCHANK
BUDA DA DA
BU DA DA DA DA DA
CHAK
BOOM

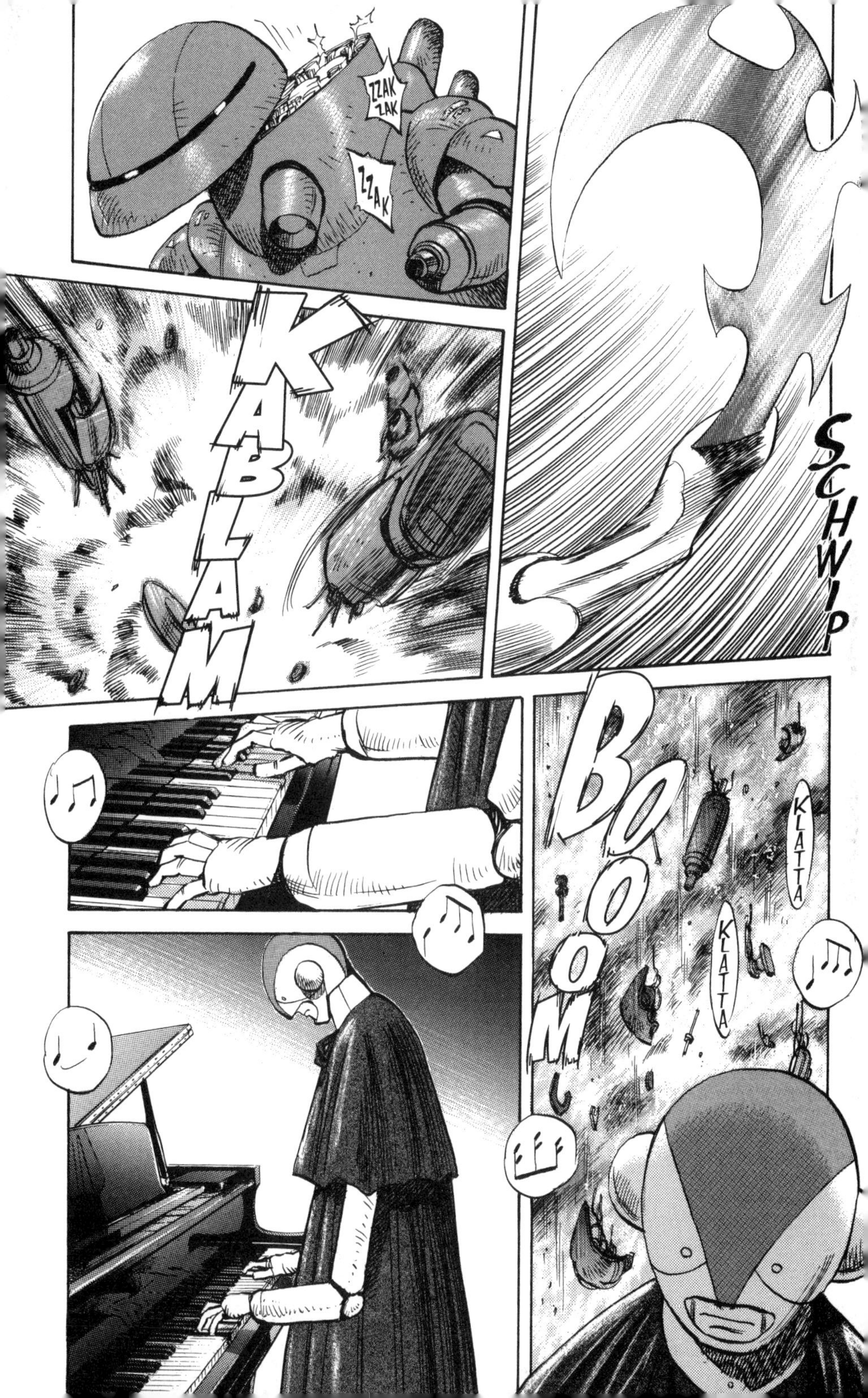
SCHWIP
ZZAK ZAK
ZZZAK
KABLAAM
BOOOOM
KLATTA
KLATTA

I HAVE TO ADMIT... HE *IS* GETTING A BIT BETTER...

HMPH!

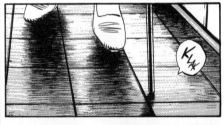

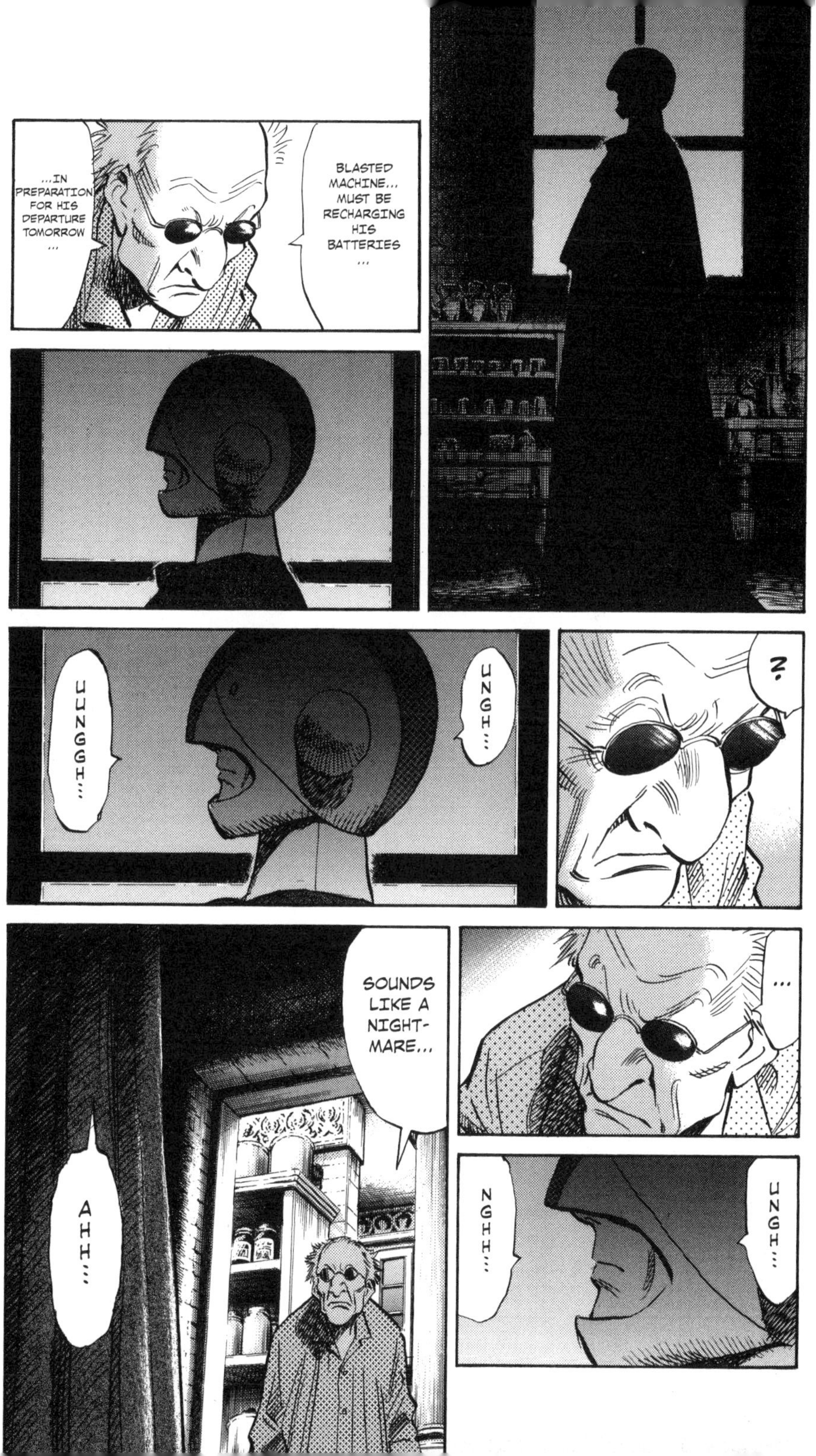
BLASTED MACHINE... MUST BE RECHARGING HIS BATTERIES...
...IN PREPARATION FOR HIS DEPARTURE TOMORROW...
?
UNGH...
UUNGGH...
...
UNGH...
NGHH...
SOUNDS LIKE A NIGHT-MARE...
AHH...

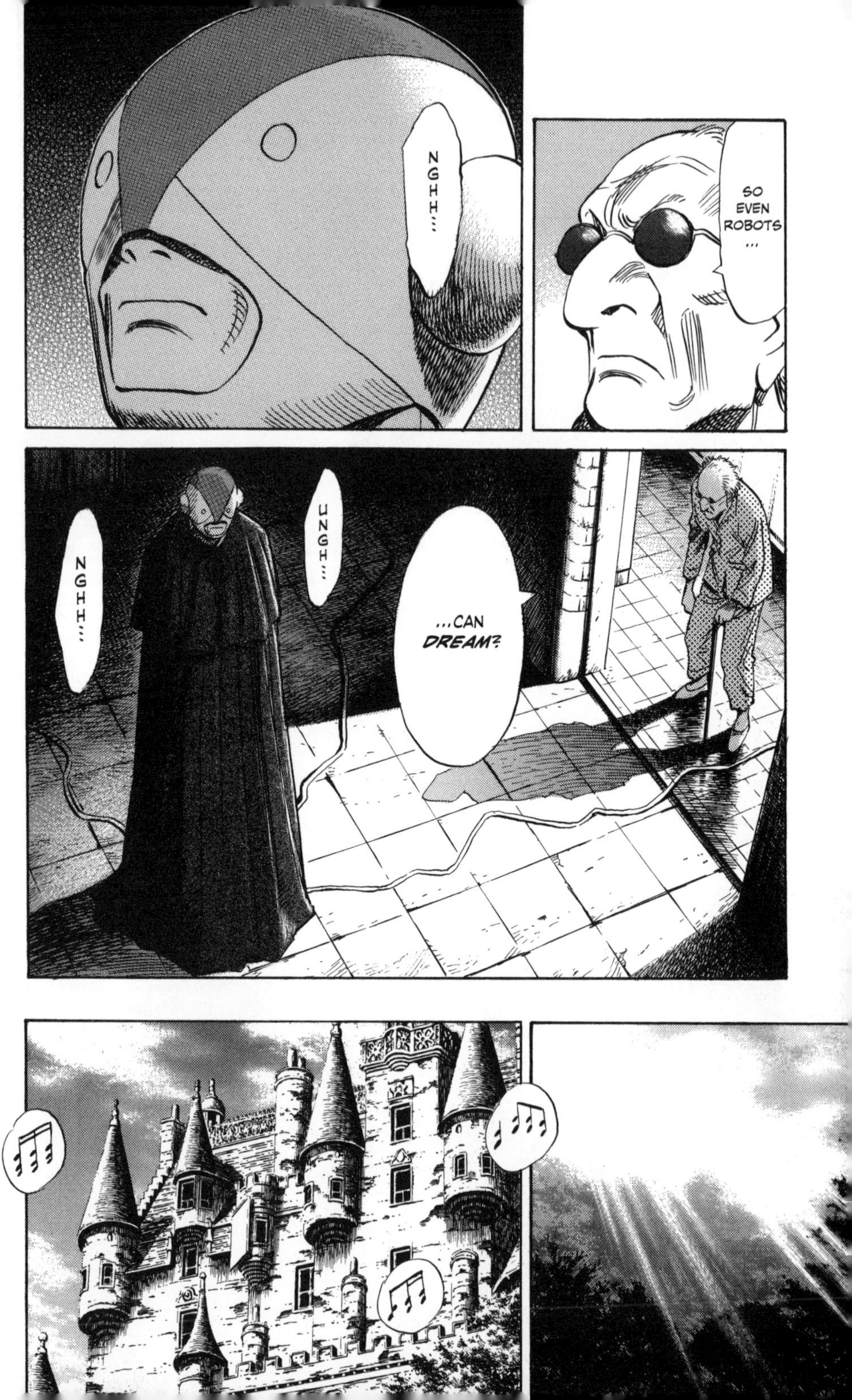
SO EVEN ROBOTS ...
NGHH...
...CAN DREAM?
UNGH...
NGHH...

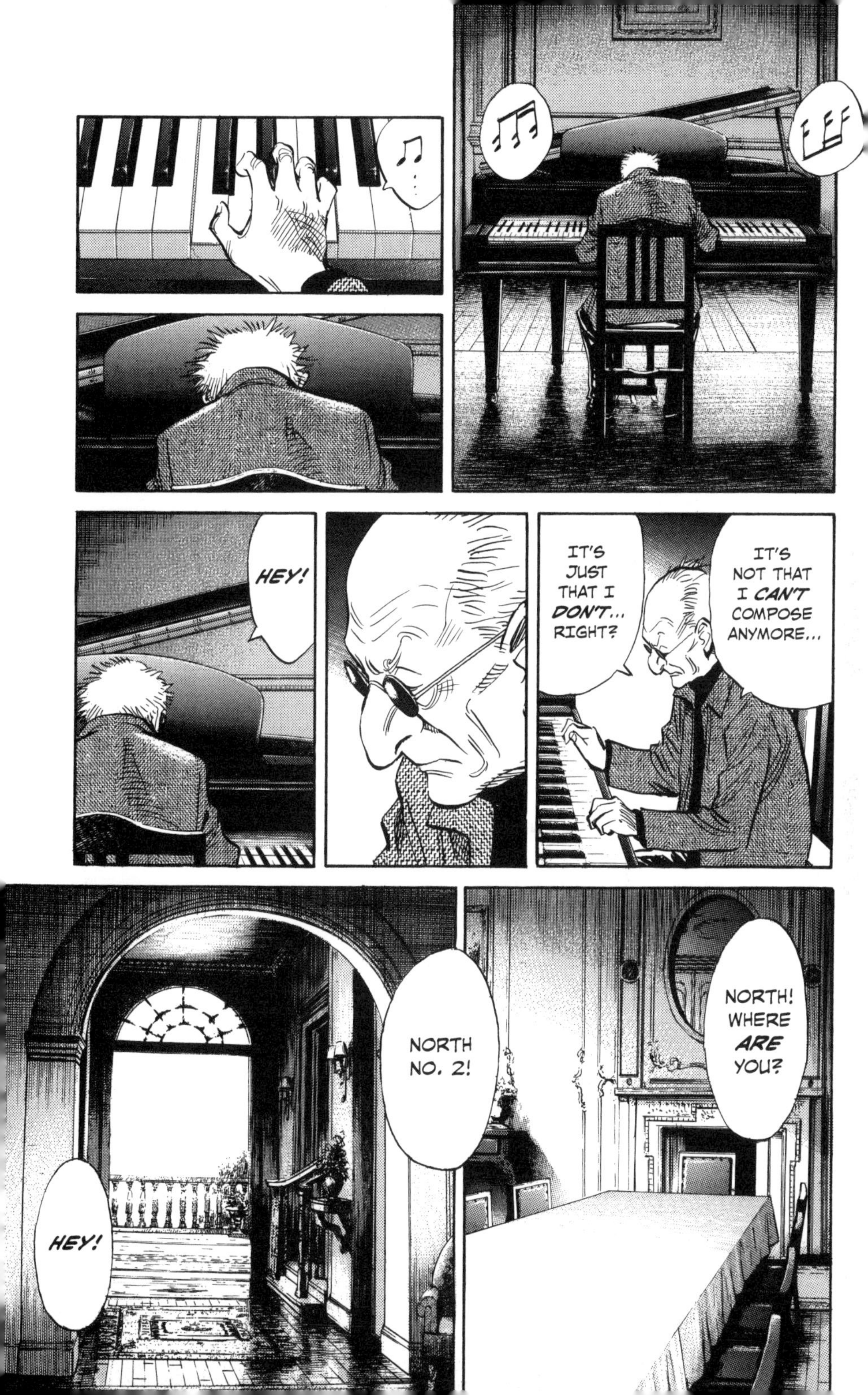
IT'S NOT THAT I *CAN'T* COMPOSE ANYMORE...
IT'S JUST THAT I *DON'T*... RIGHT?
HEY!
NORTH! WHERE *ARE* YOU?
NORTH NO. 2!
HEY!

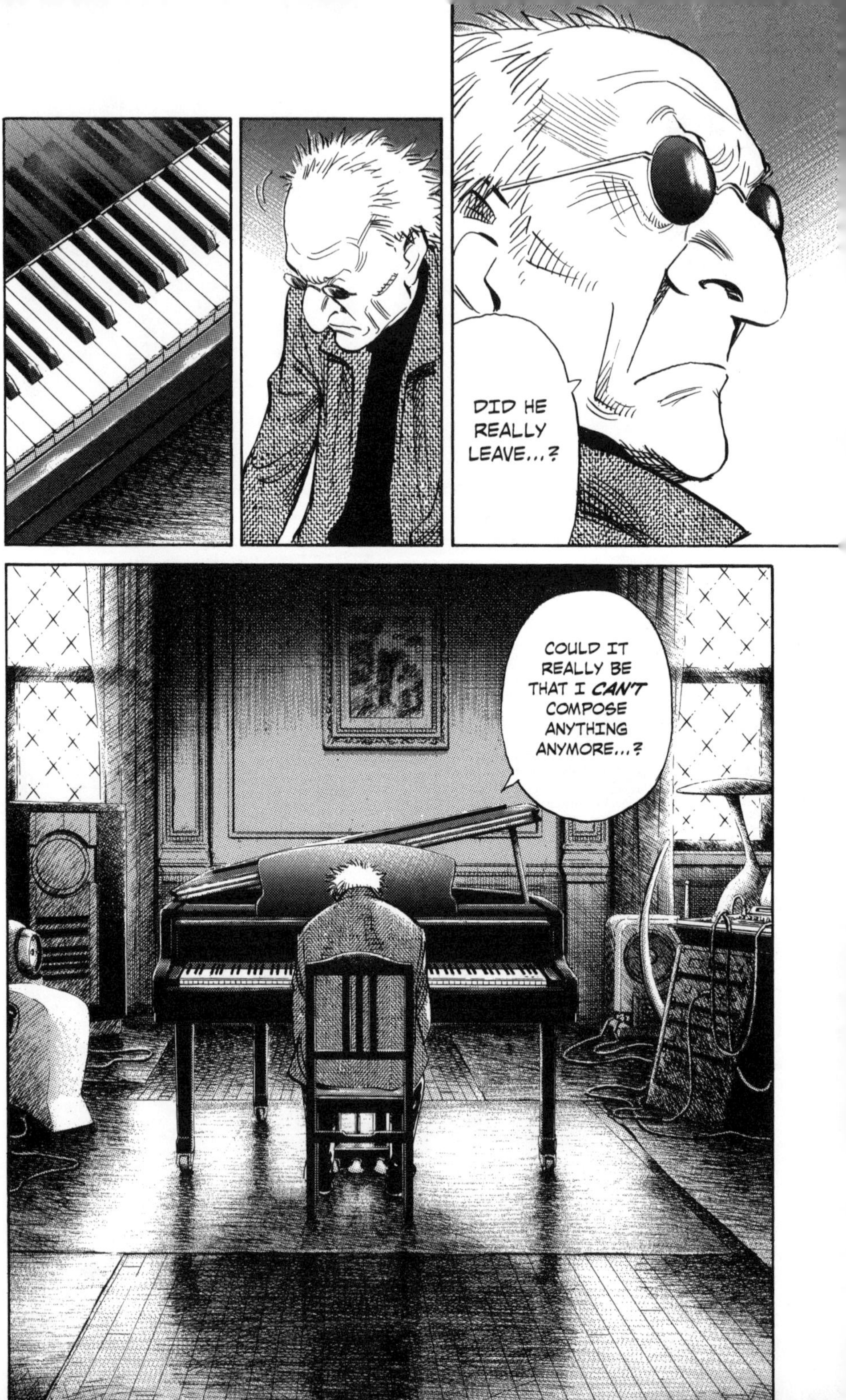
DID HE REALLY LEAVE...?
COULD IT REALLY BE THAT I *CAN'T* COMPOSE ANYTHING ANYMORE...?

Act 6 NORTH No. 2 (Part 3)

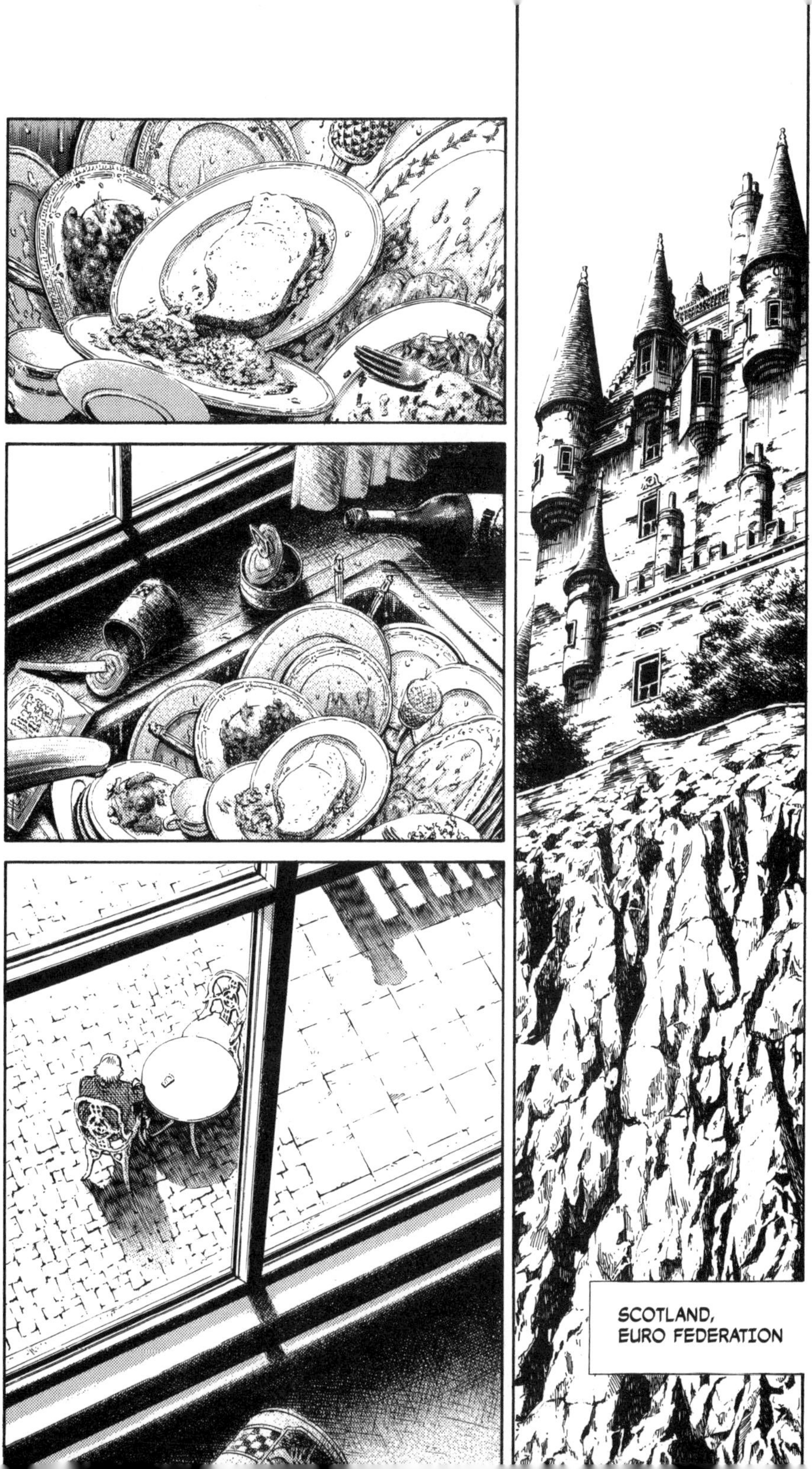
SCOTLAND,
EURO FEDERATION

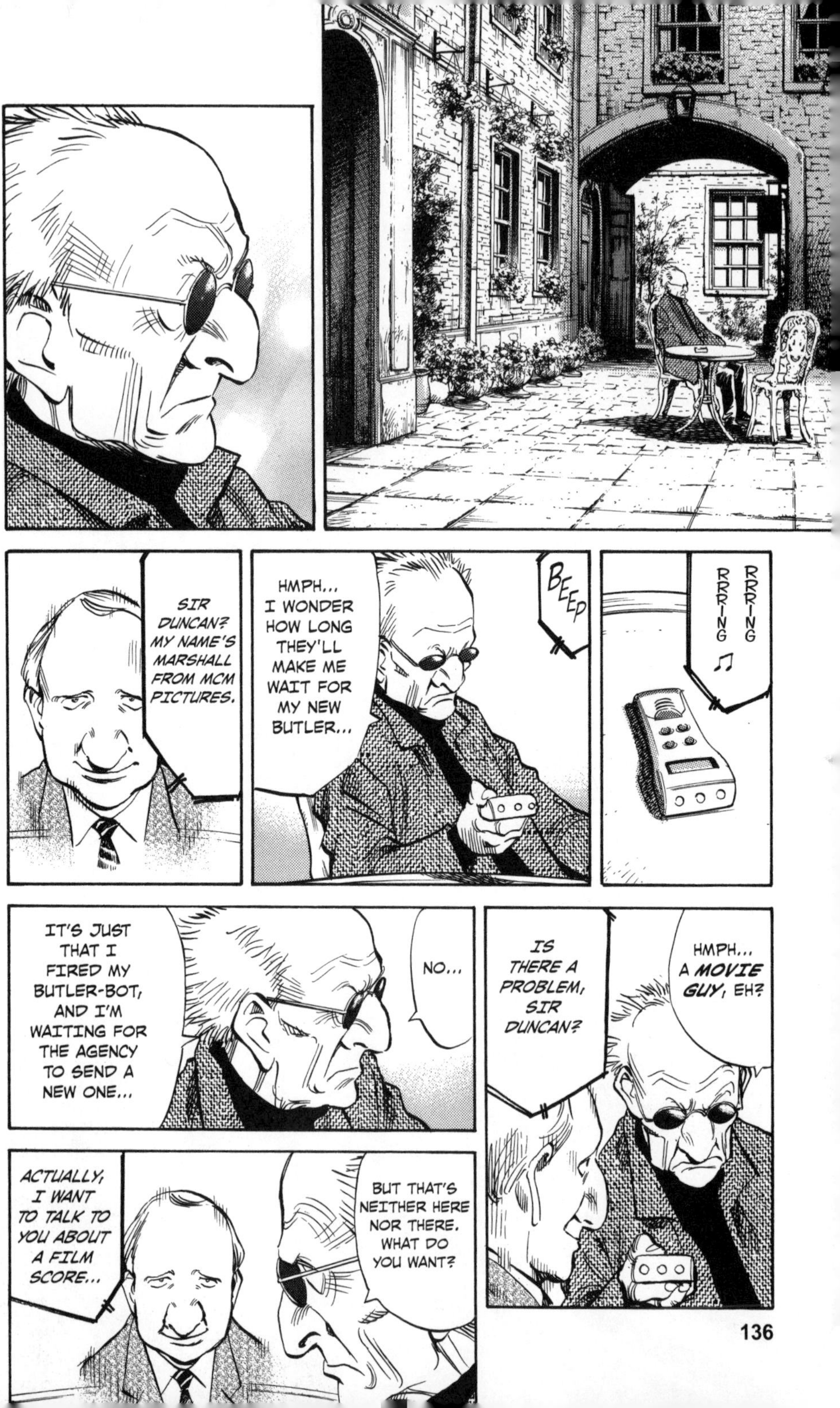
RRRING RRRING ♫
BEEP
HMPH... I WONDER HOW LONG THEY'LL MAKE ME WAIT FOR MY NEW BUTLER...
SIR DUNCAN? MY NAME'S MARSHALL FROM MCM PICTURES.
HMPH... A **MOVIE GUY**, EH?
IS THERE A PROBLEM, SIR DUNCAN?
NO...
IT'S JUST THAT I FIRED MY BUTLER-BOT, AND I'M WAITING FOR THE AGENCY TO SEND A NEW ONE...
BUT THAT'S NEITHER HERE NOR THERE. WHAT DO YOU WANT?
ACTUALLY, I WANT TO TALK TO YOU ABOUT A FILM SCORE...

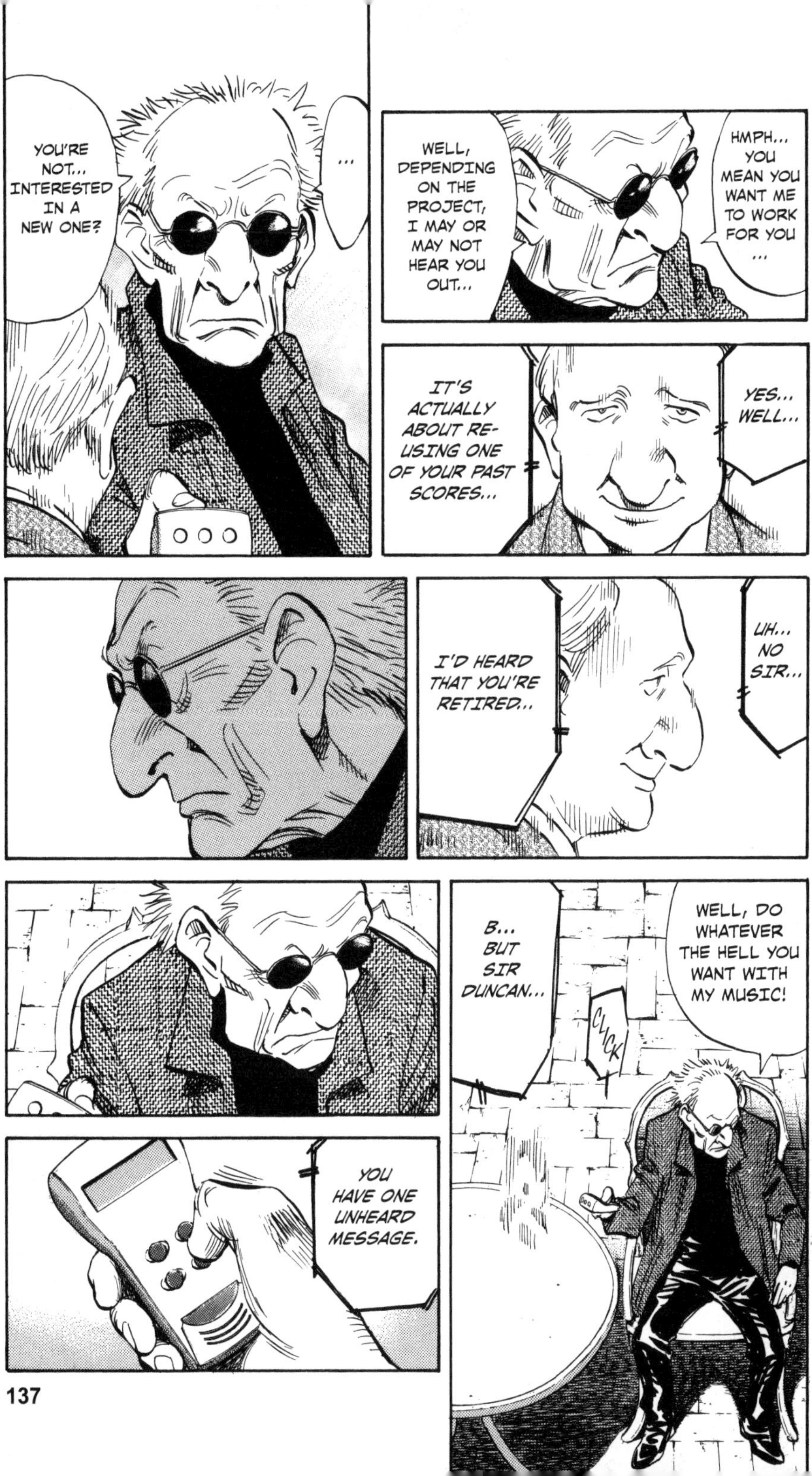
HMPH... YOU MEAN YOU WANT ME TO WORK FOR YOU ...
WELL, DEPENDING ON THE PROJECT, I MAY OR MAY NOT HEAR YOU OUT...
YES... WELL...
IT'S ACTUALLY ABOUT RE-USING ONE OF YOUR PAST SCORES...
...
YOU'RE NOT... INTERESTED IN A NEW ONE?
UH... NO SIR...
I'D HEARD THAT YOU'RE RETIRED...
WELL, DO WHATEVER THE HELL YOU WANT WITH MY MUSIC!
B... BUT SIR DUNCAN...
CLICK
YOU HAVE ONE UNHEARD MESSAGE.

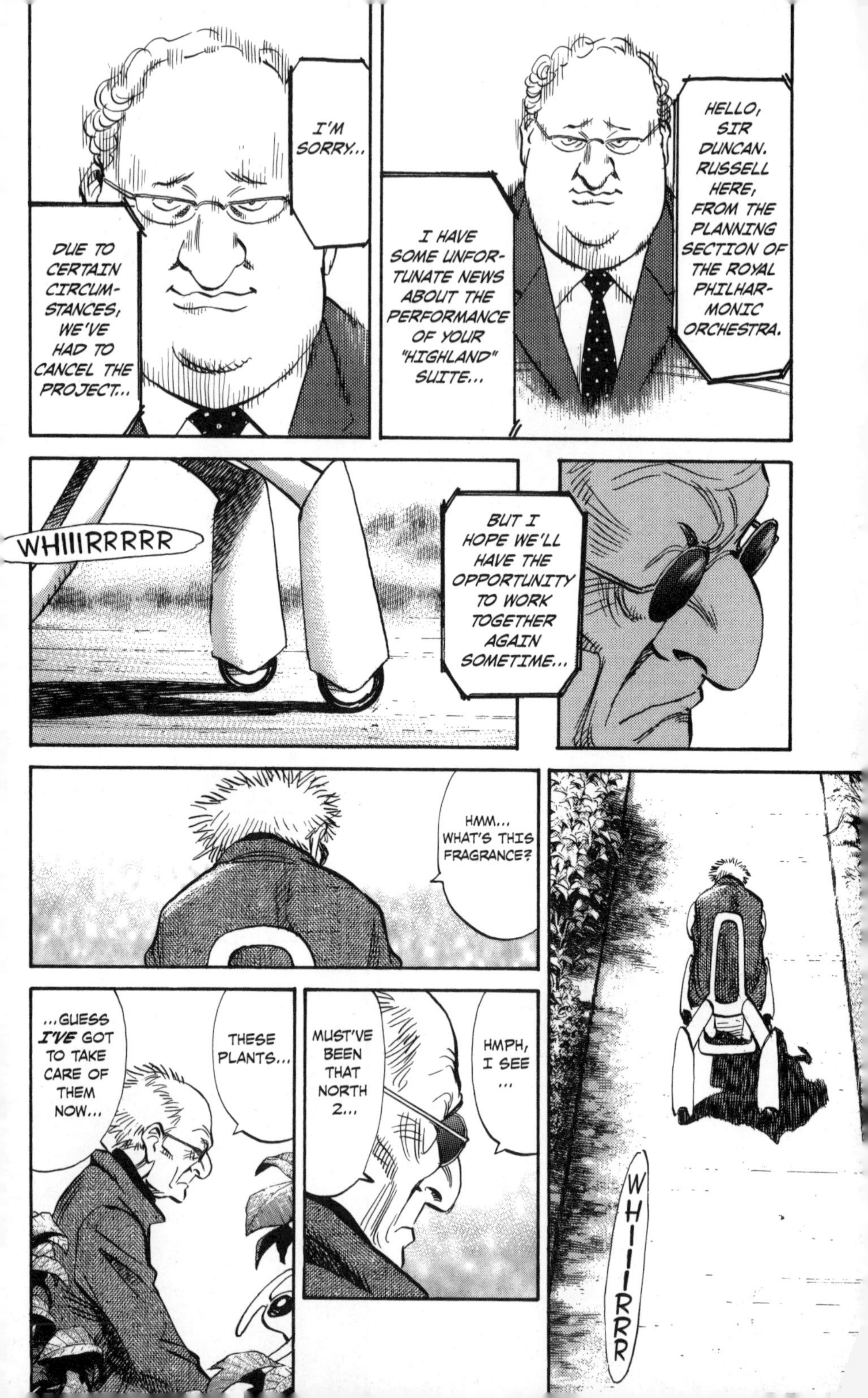
HELLO, SIR DUNCAN. RUSSELL HERE, FROM THE PLANNING SECTION OF THE ROYAL PHILHARMONIC ORCHESTRA.
I HAVE SOME UNFORTUNATE NEWS ABOUT THE PERFORMANCE OF YOUR "HIGHLAND" SUITE...
I'M SORRY...
DUE TO CERTAIN CIRCUMSTANCES, WE'VE HAD TO CANCEL THE PROJECT...
BUT I HOPE WE'LL HAVE THE OPPORTUNITY TO WORK TOGETHER AGAIN SOMETIME...
WHIIIRRRRR
WHIIIRRR
HMM... WHAT'S THIS FRAGRANCE?
HMPH, I SEE...
MUST'VE BEEN THAT NORTH 2...
THESE PLANTS...
...GUESS *I'VE* GOT TO TAKE CARE OF THEM NOW...

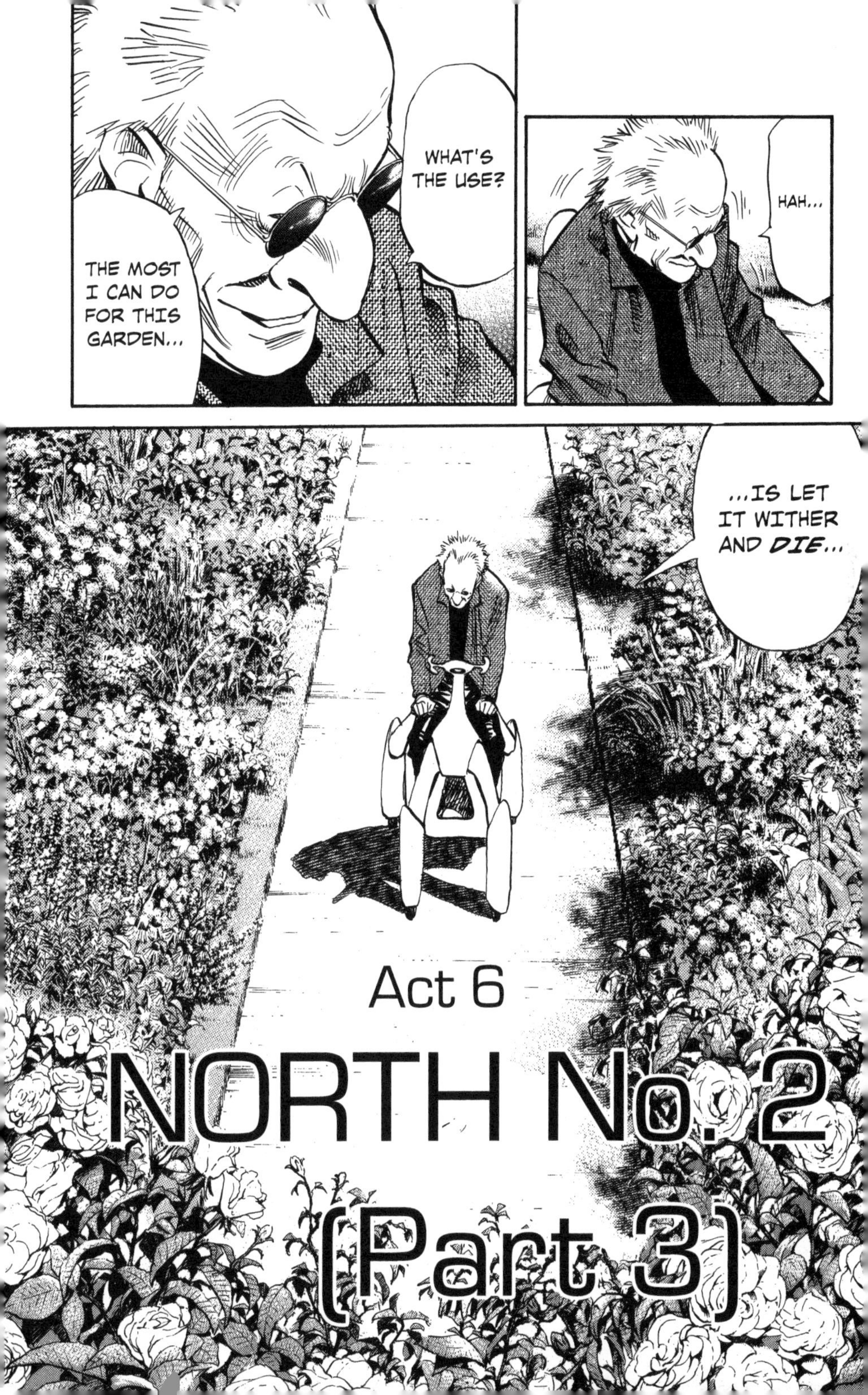
HAH...
WHAT'S THE USE?
THE MOST I CAN DO FOR THIS GARDEN...
...IS LET IT WITHER AND *DIE*...
Act 6
NORTH No. 2
(Part 3)

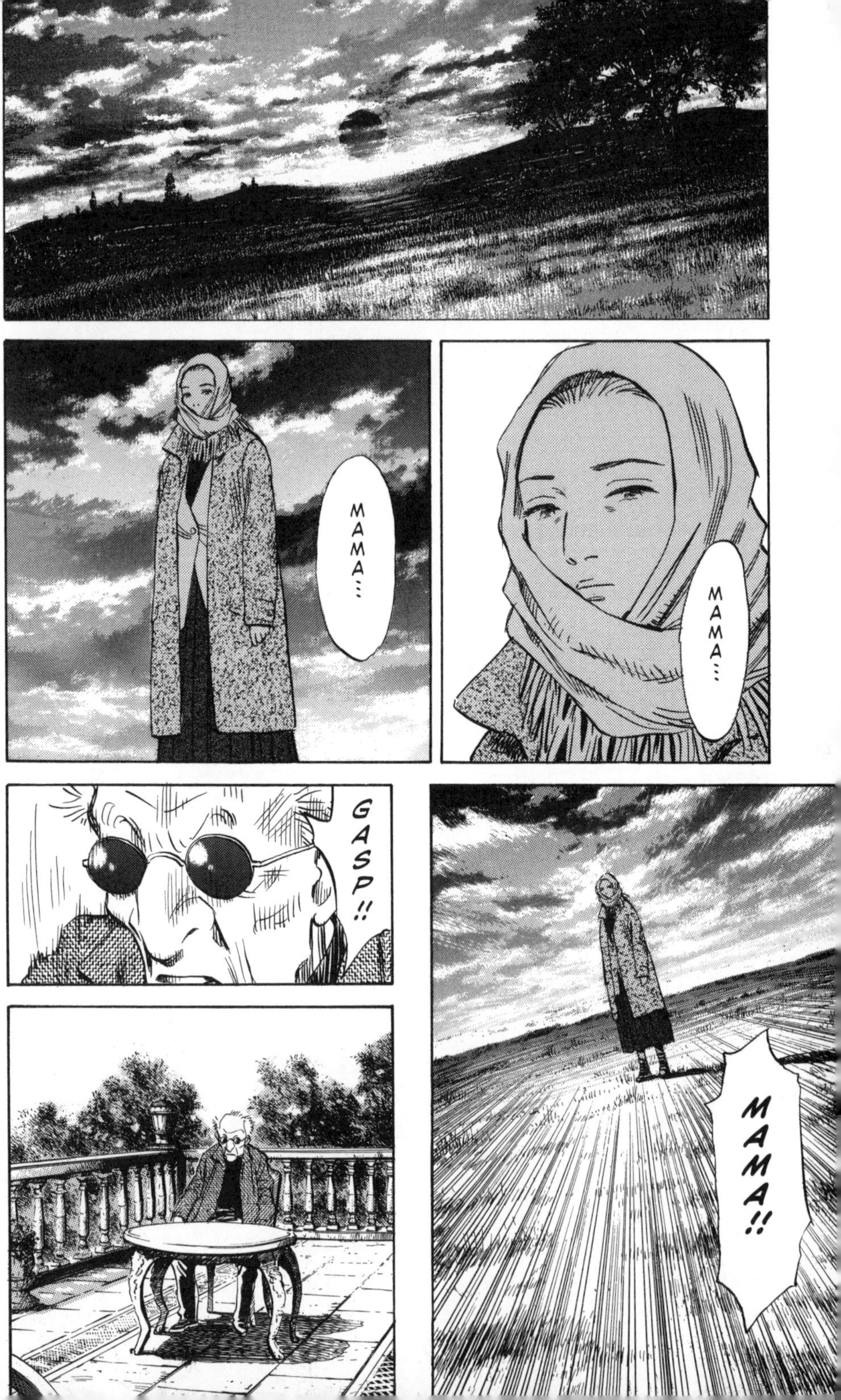
MAMA...
MAMA...
MAMA!!
GASP!!

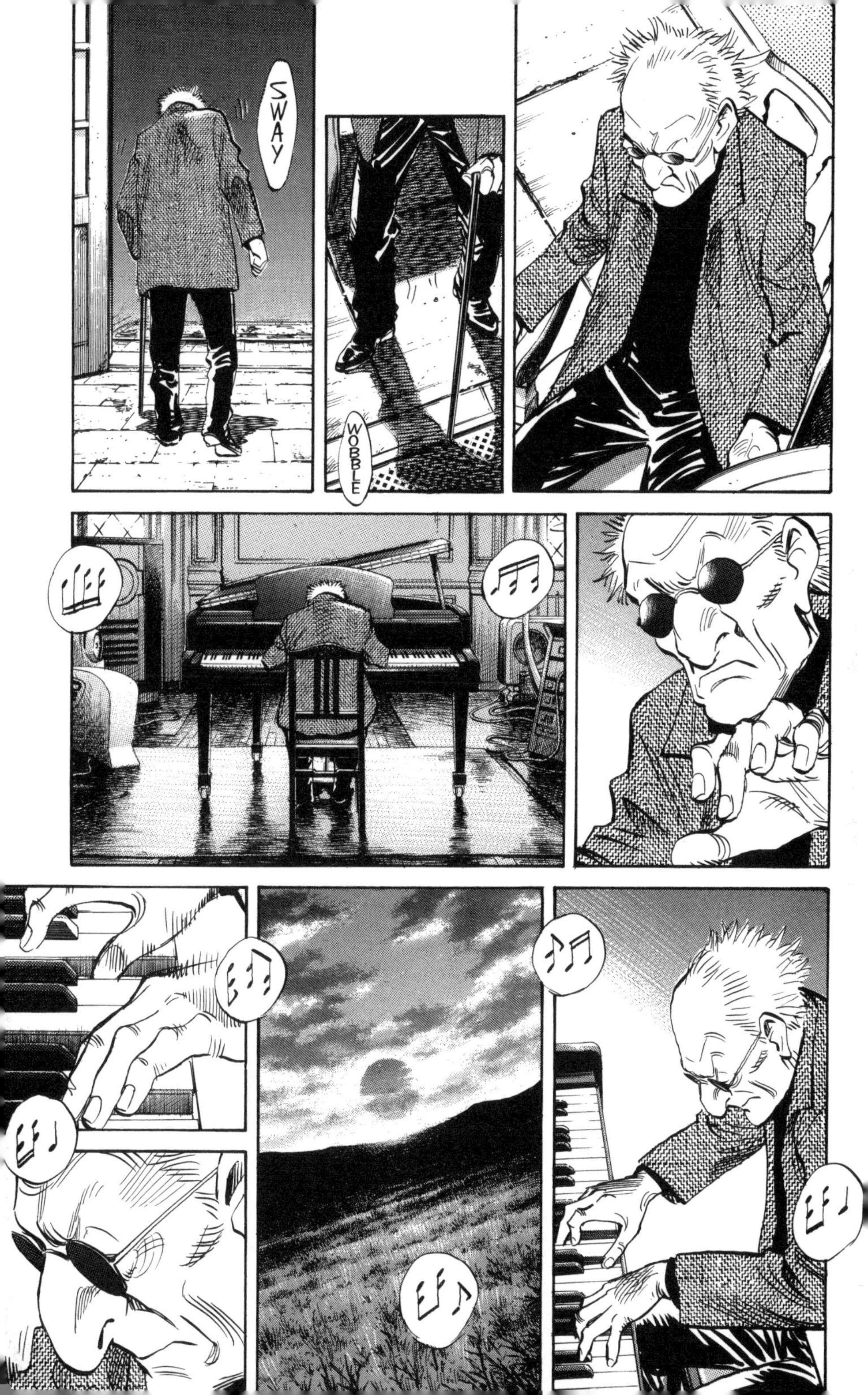
WOBBLE
SWAY

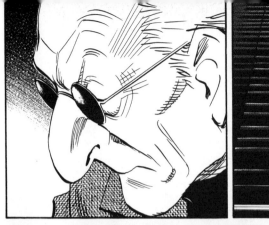

BANNG

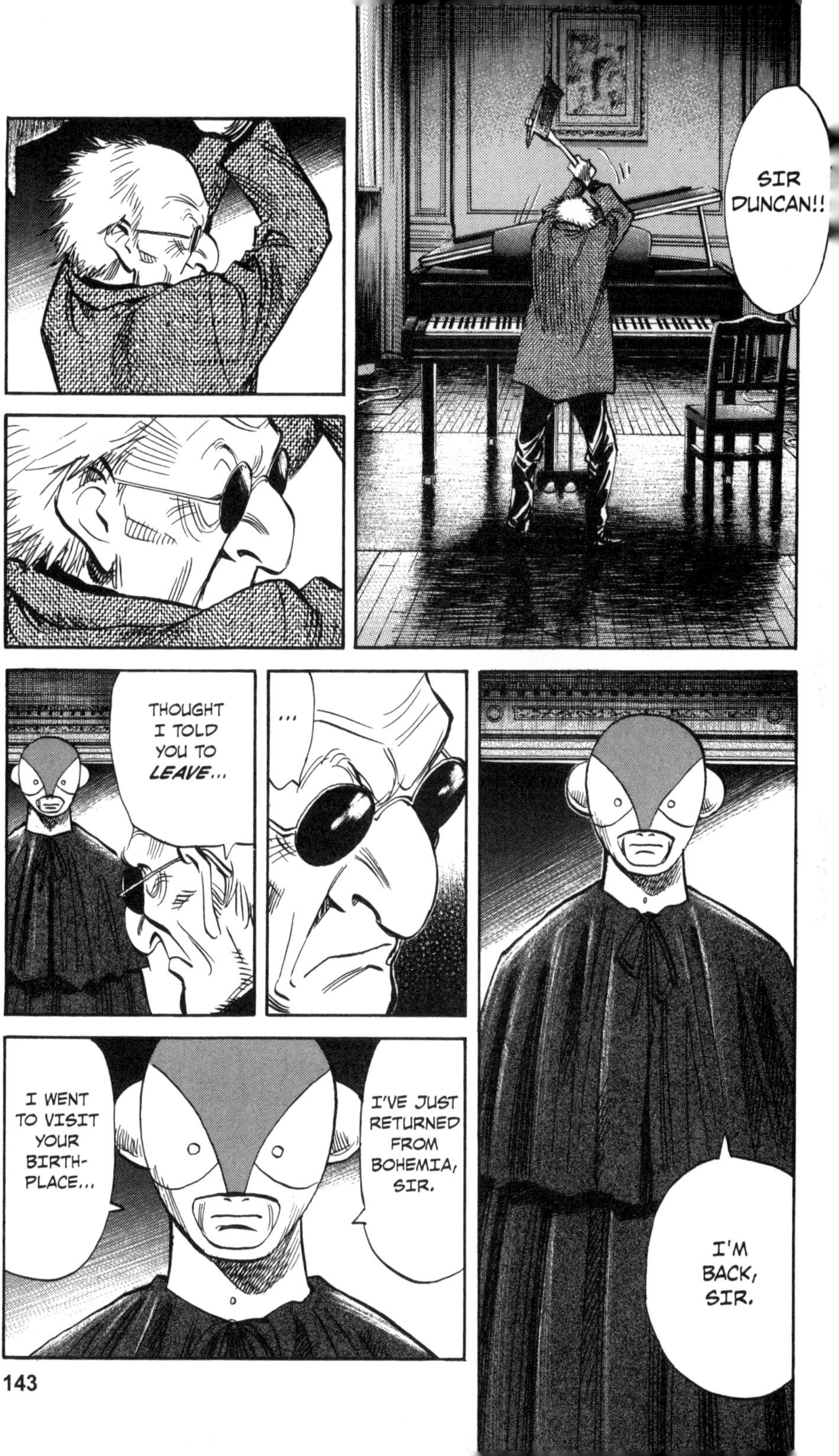
SIR DUNCAN!!
I'M BACK, SIR.
...
THOUGHT I TOLD YOU TO *LEAVE*...
I'VE JUST RETURNED FROM BOHEMIA, SIR.
I WENT TO VISIT YOUR BIRTH-PLACE...

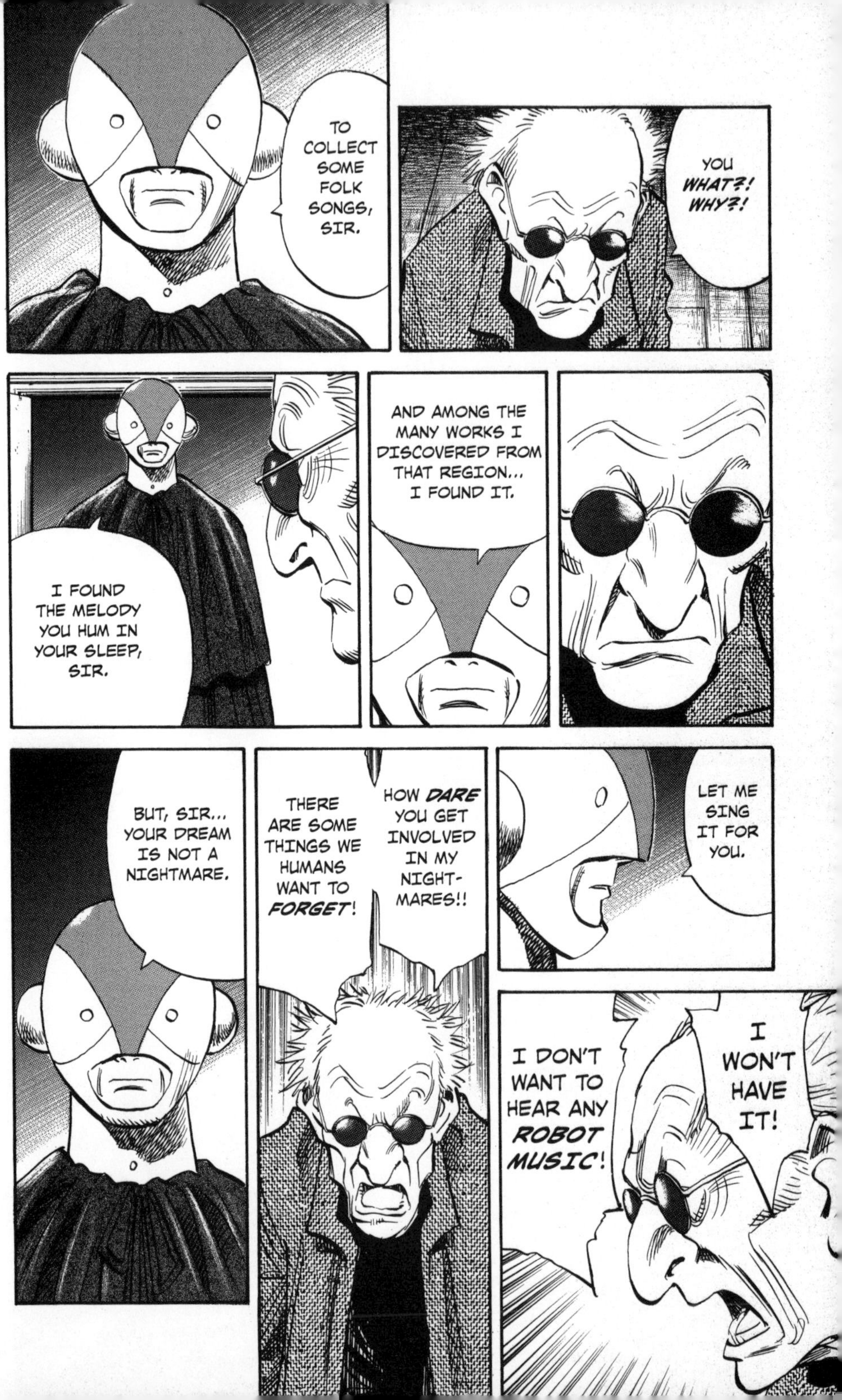
YOU WHAT?! WHY?!
TO COLLECT SOME FOLK SONGS, SIR.
AND AMONG THE MANY WORKS I DISCOVERED FROM THAT REGION... I FOUND IT.
I FOUND THE MELODY YOU HUM IN YOUR SLEEP, SIR.
LET ME SING IT FOR YOU.
I WON'T HAVE IT!
I DON'T WANT TO HEAR ANY ROBOT MUSIC!
HOW DARE YOU GET INVOLVED IN MY NIGHTMARES!!
THERE ARE SOME THINGS WE HUMANS WANT TO FORGET!
BUT, SIR... YOUR DREAM IS NOT A NIGHTMARE.

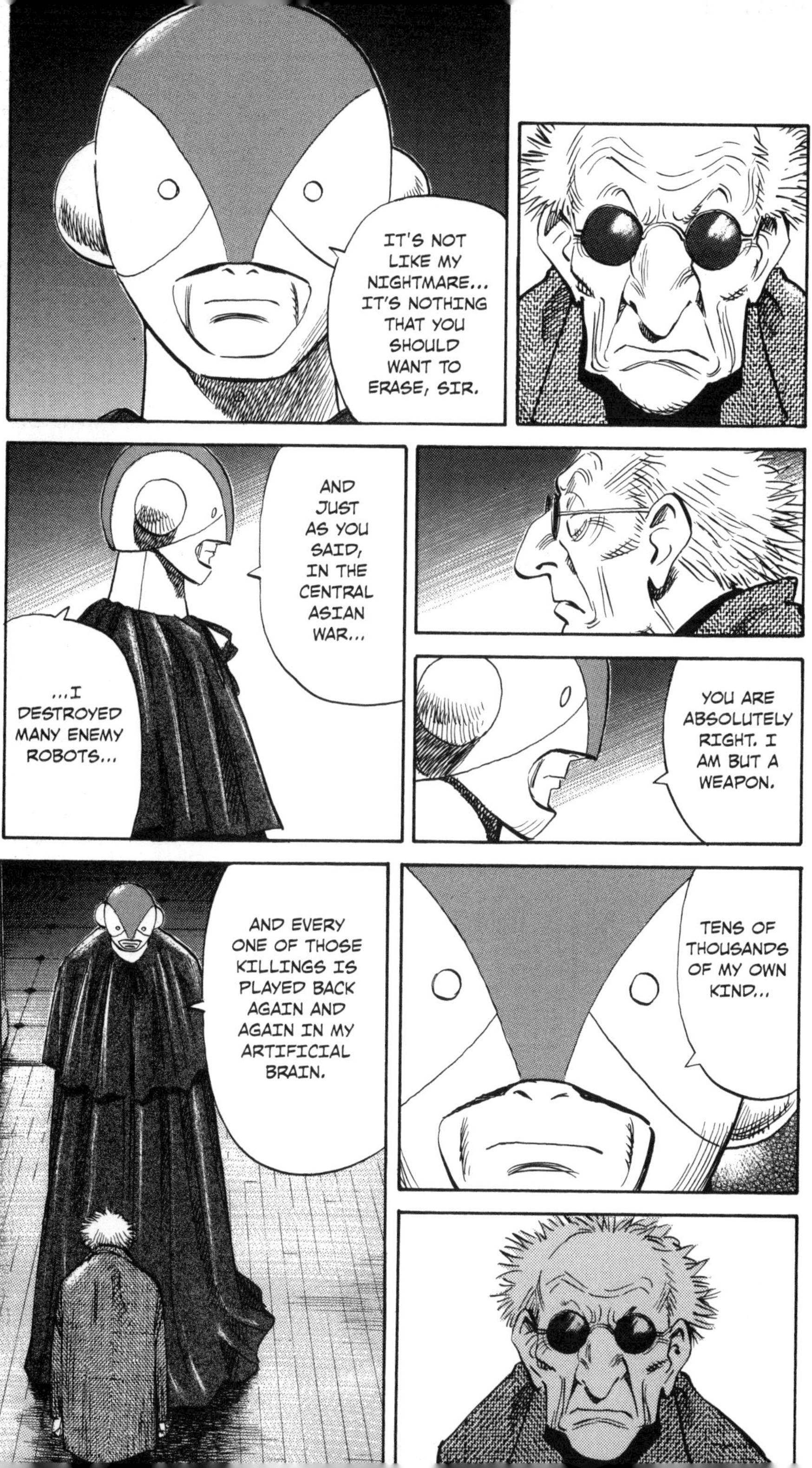
IT'S NOT LIKE MY NIGHTMARE... IT'S NOTHING THAT YOU SHOULD WANT TO ERASE, SIR.
YOU ARE ABSOLUTELY RIGHT. I AM BUT A WEAPON.
AND JUST AS YOU SAID, IN THE CENTRAL ASIAN WAR...
...I DESTROYED MANY ENEMY ROBOTS...
TENS OF THOUSANDS OF MY OWN KIND...
AND EVERY ONE OF THOSE KILLINGS IS PLAYED BACK AGAIN AND AGAIN IN MY ARTIFICIAL BRAIN.

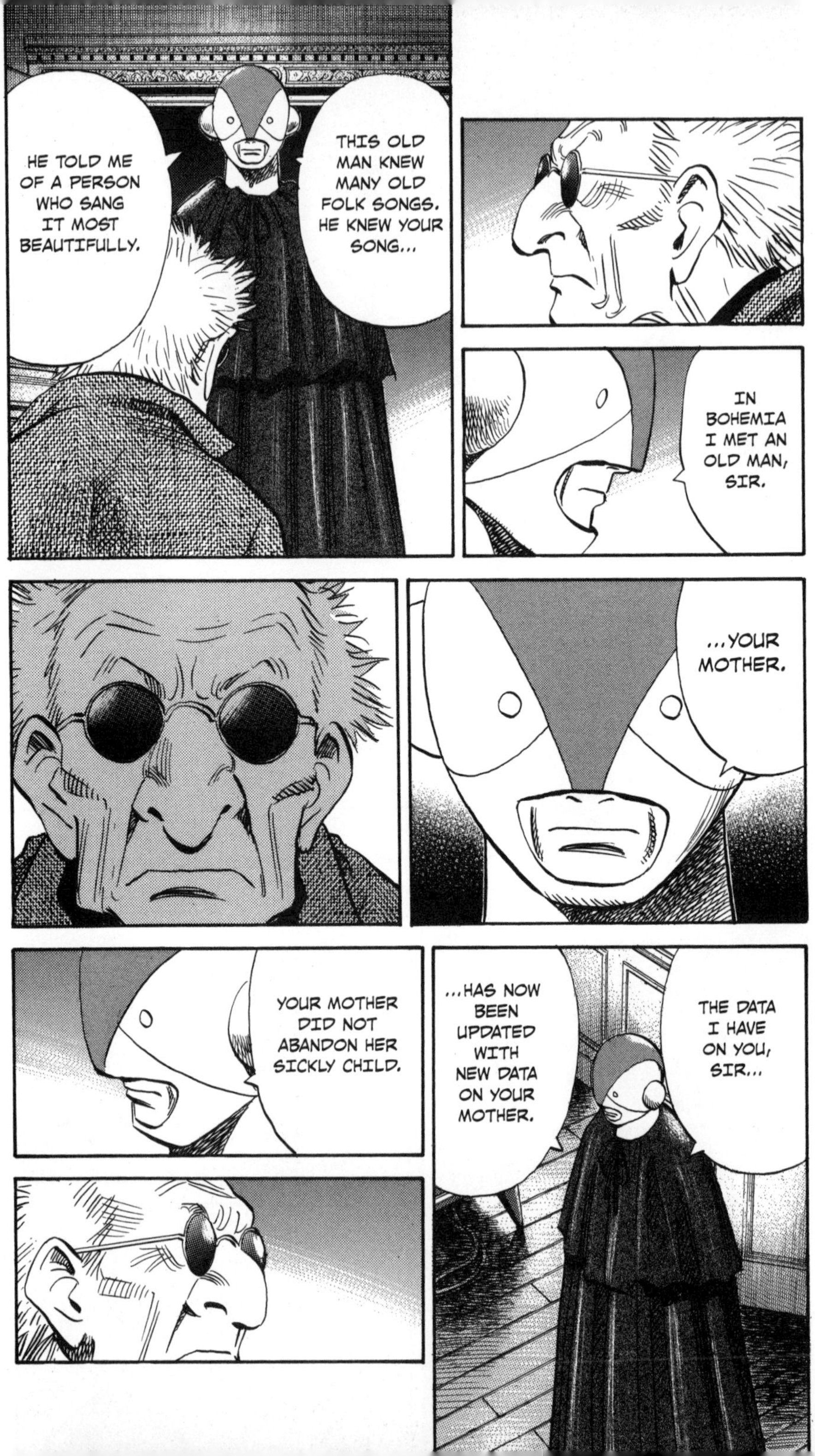
IN BOHEMIA I MET AN OLD MAN, SIR.
THIS OLD MAN KNEW MANY OLD FOLK SONGS. HE KNEW YOUR SONG...
HE TOLD ME OF A PERSON WHO SANG IT MOST BEAUTIFULLY.
...YOUR MOTHER.
THE DATA I HAVE ON YOU, SIR...
...HAS NOW BEEN UPDATED WITH NEW DATA ON YOUR MOTHER.
YOUR MOTHER DID NOT ABANDON HER SICKLY CHILD.

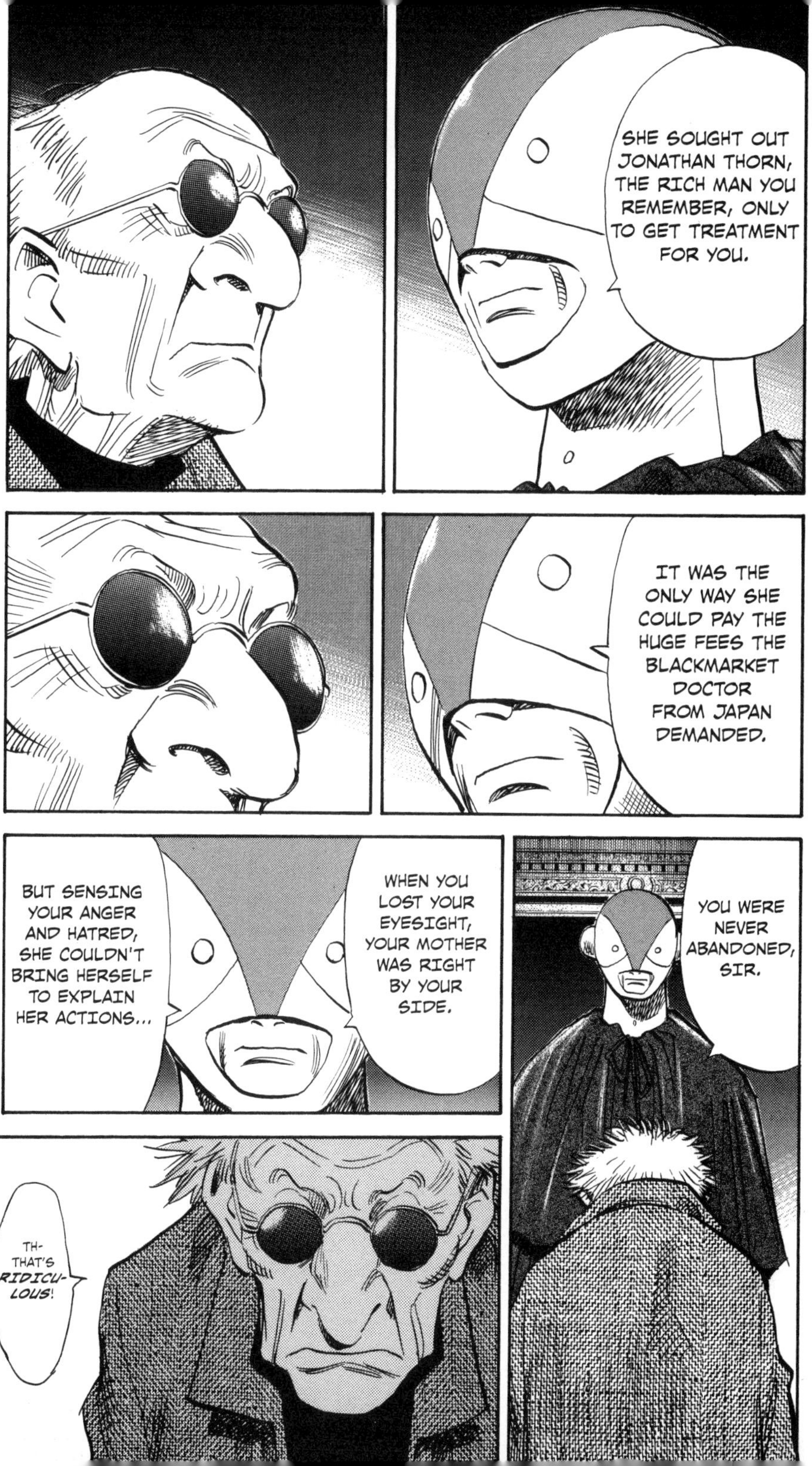
SHE SOUGHT OUT JONATHAN THORN, THE RICH MAN YOU REMEMBER, ONLY TO GET TREATMENT FOR YOU.
IT WAS THE ONLY WAY SHE COULD PAY THE HUGE FEES THE BLACKMARKET DOCTOR FROM JAPAN DEMANDED.
YOU WERE NEVER ABANDONED, SIR.
WHEN YOU LOST YOUR EYESIGHT, YOUR MOTHER WAS RIGHT BY YOUR SIDE.
BUT SENSING YOUR ANGER AND HATRED, SHE COULDN'T BRING HERSELF TO EXPLAIN HER ACTIONS...
TH- THAT'S RIDICULOUS!

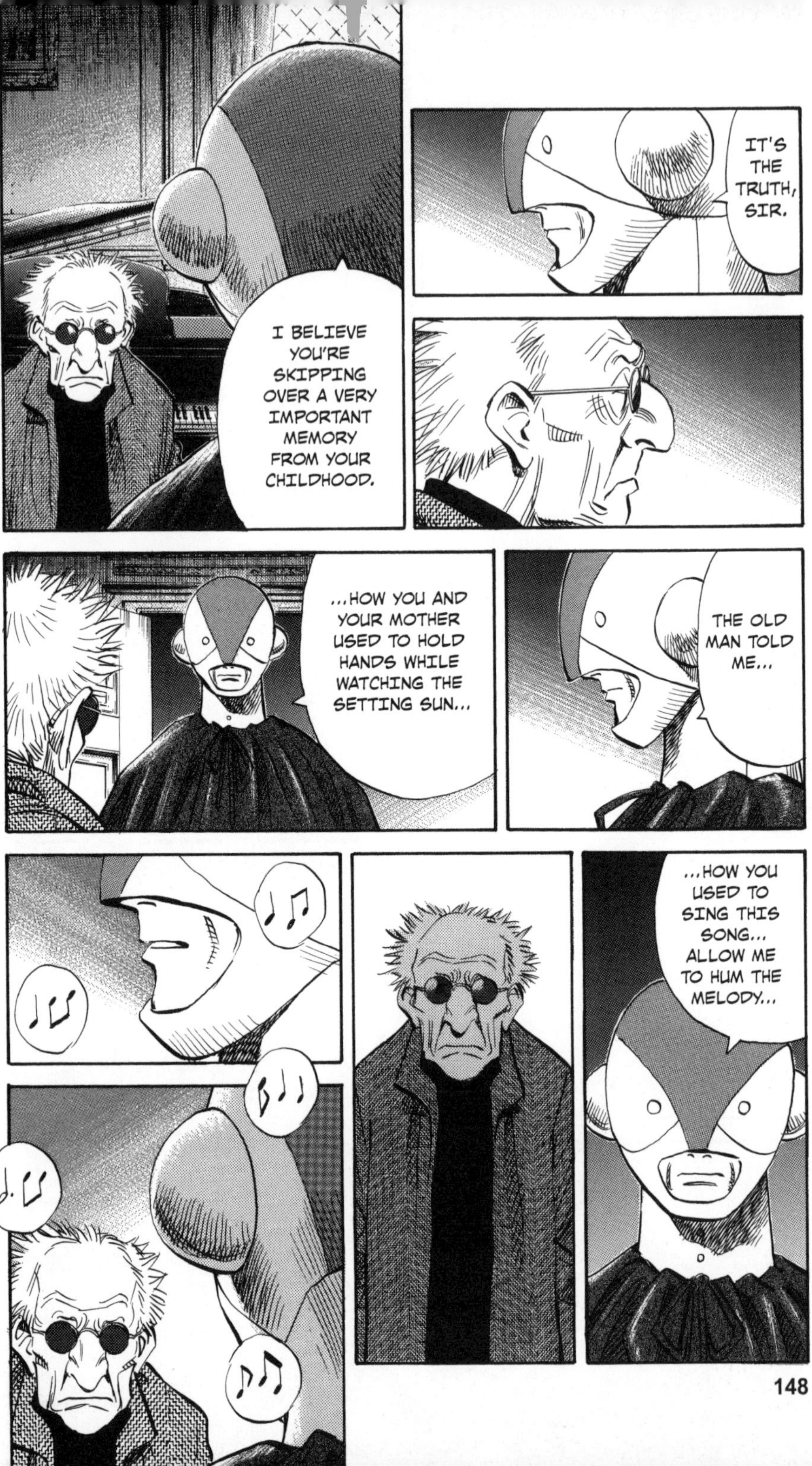
IT'S THE TRUTH, SIR.
I BELIEVE YOU'RE SKIPPING OVER A VERY IMPORTANT MEMORY FROM YOUR CHILDHOOD.
THE OLD MAN TOLD ME...
...HOW YOU AND YOUR MOTHER USED TO HOLD HANDS WHILE WATCHING THE SETTING SUN...
...HOW YOU USED TO SING THIS SONG... ALLOW ME TO HUM THE MELODY...

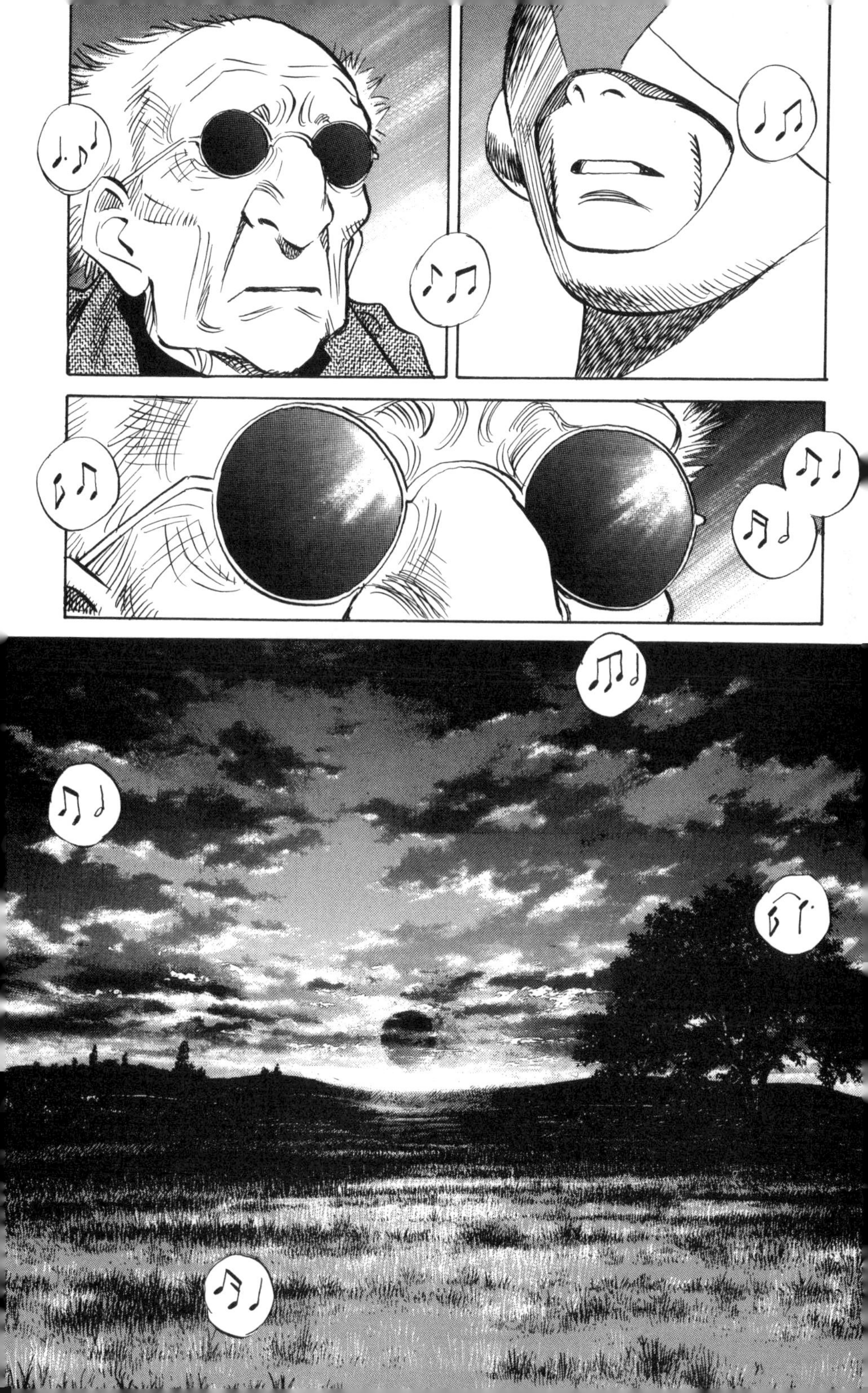

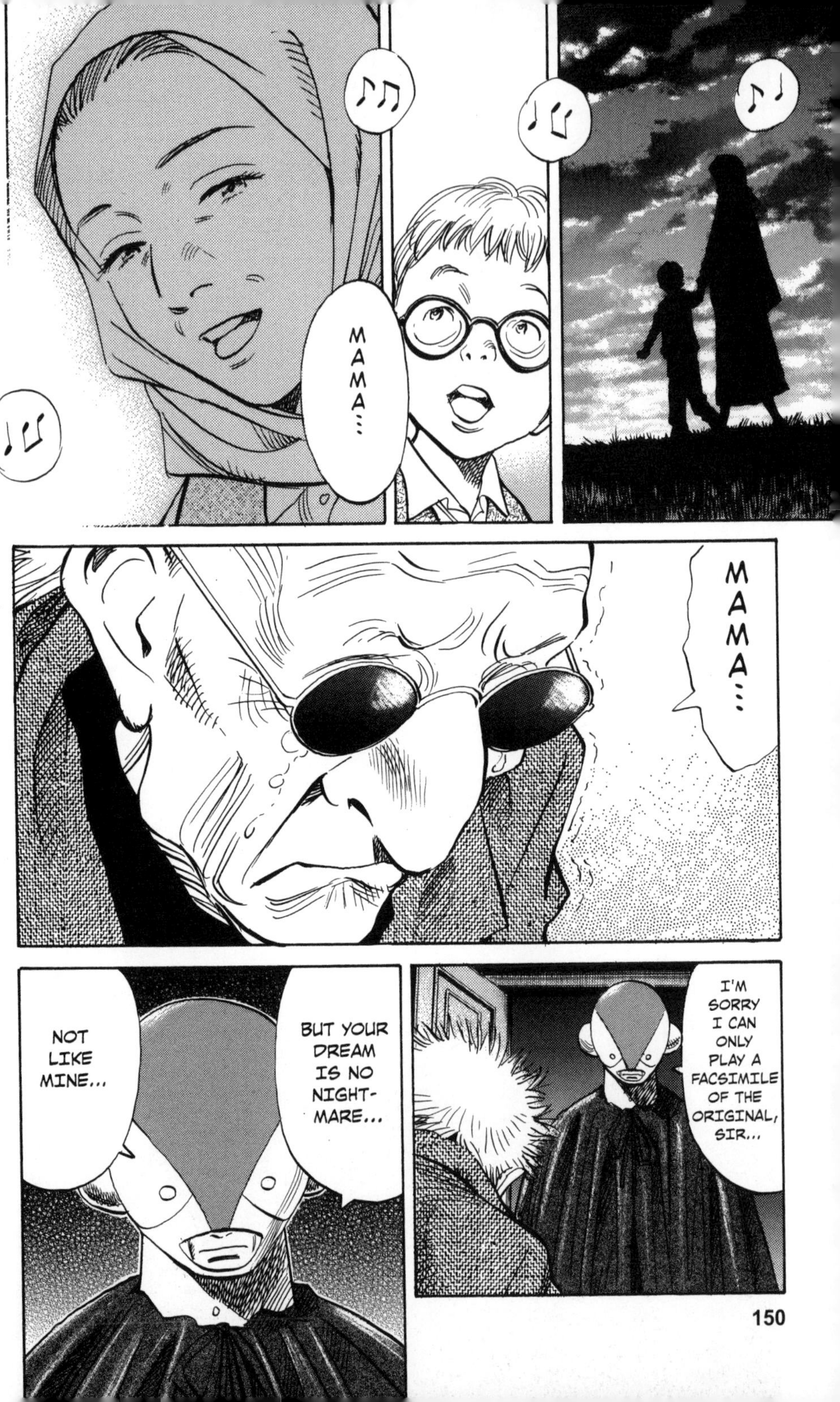
MAMA...
MAMA...
I'M SORRY I CAN ONLY PLAY A FACSIMILE OF THE ORIGINAL, SIR...
BUT YOUR DREAM IS NO NIGHTMARE...
NOT LIKE MINE...

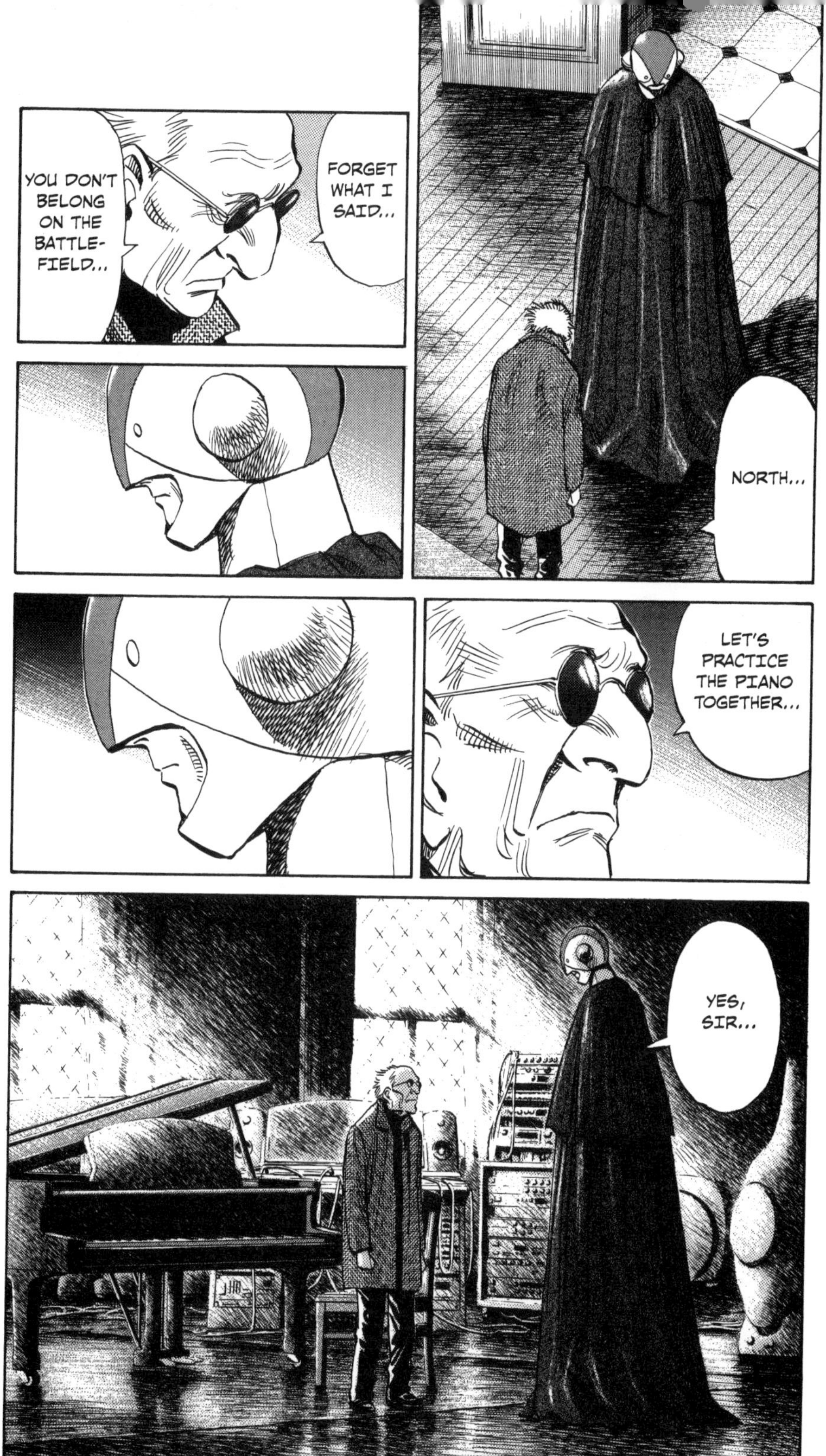
NORTH...
FORGET WHAT I SAID...
YOU DON'T BELONG ON THE BATTLE-FIELD...
LET'S PRACTICE THE PIANO TOGETHER...
YES, SIR...

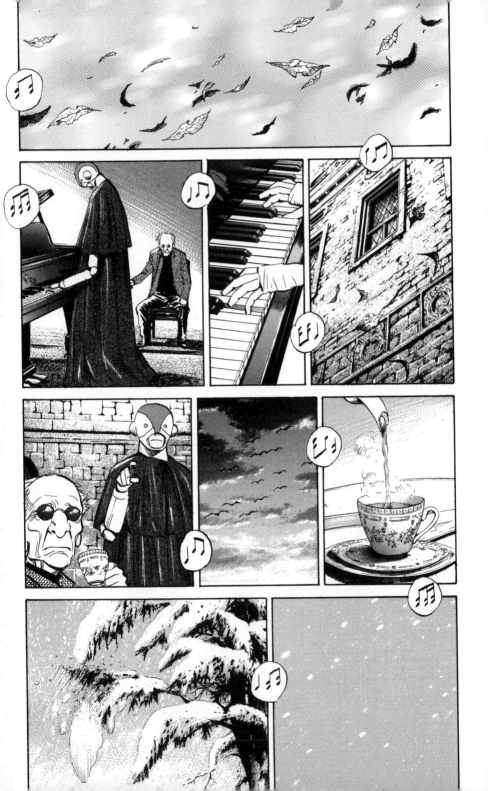

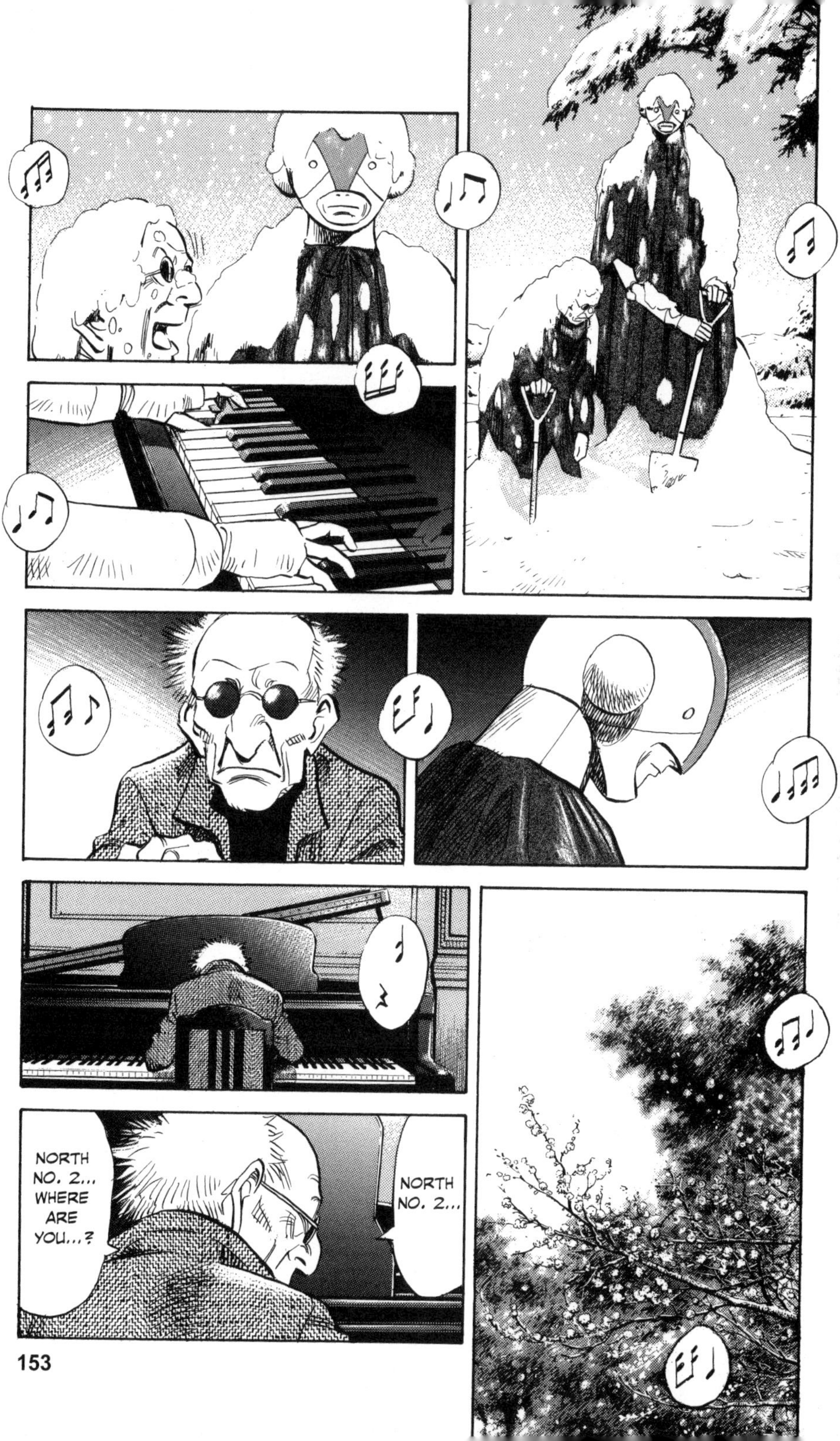
NORTH NO. 2...
NORTH NO. 2... WHERE ARE YOU...?

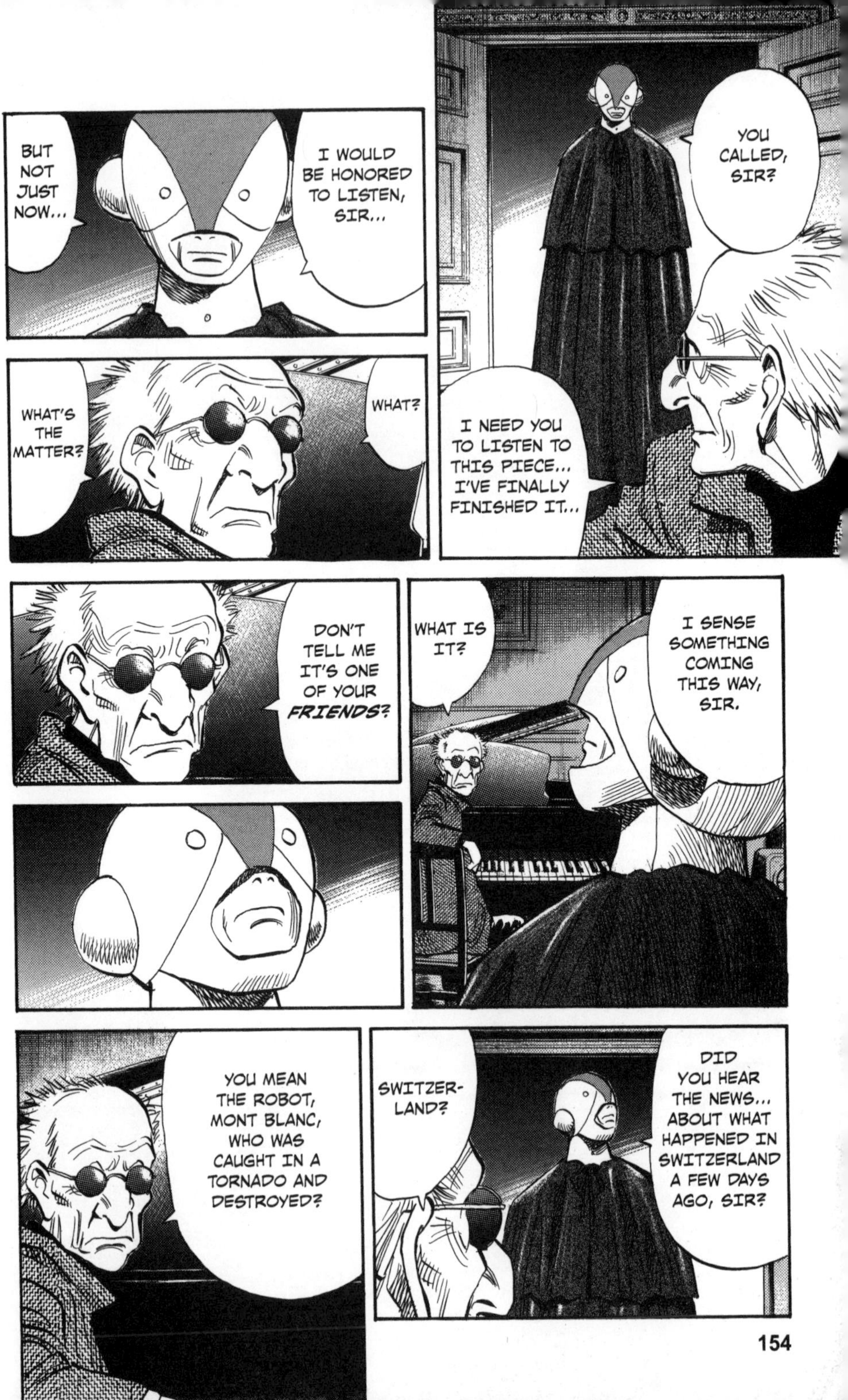
YOU CALLED, SIR?
I NEED YOU TO LISTEN TO THIS PIECE... I'VE FINALLY FINISHED IT...
I WOULD BE HONORED TO LISTEN, SIR...
BUT NOT JUST NOW...
WHAT?
WHAT'S THE MATTER?
I SENSE SOMETHING COMING THIS WAY, SIR.
WHAT IS IT?
DON'T TELL ME IT'S ONE OF YOUR *FRIENDS*?
DID YOU HEAR THE NEWS... ABOUT WHAT HAPPENED IN SWITZERLAND A FEW DAYS AGO, SIR?
SWITZER-LAND?
YOU MEAN THE ROBOT, MONT BLANC, WHO WAS CAUGHT IN A TORNADO AND DESTROYED?

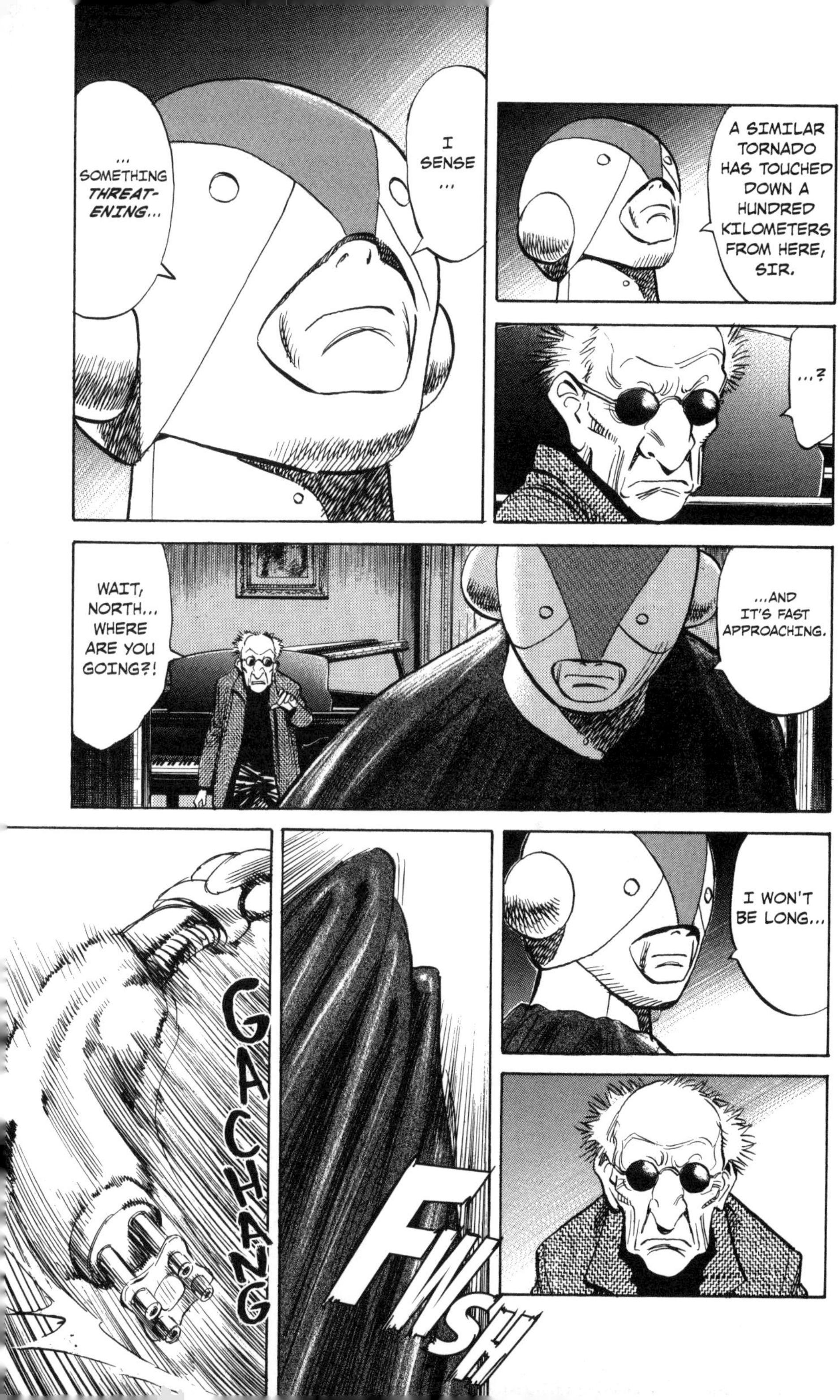
A SIMILAR TORNADO HAS TOUCHED DOWN A HUNDRED KILOMETERS FROM HERE, SIR.
...?
I SENSE ...
... SOMETHING *THREAT-ENING*...
...AND IT'S FAST APPROACHING.
WAIT, NORTH... WHERE ARE YOU GOING?!
I WON'T BE LONG...
FISH
GACHANG

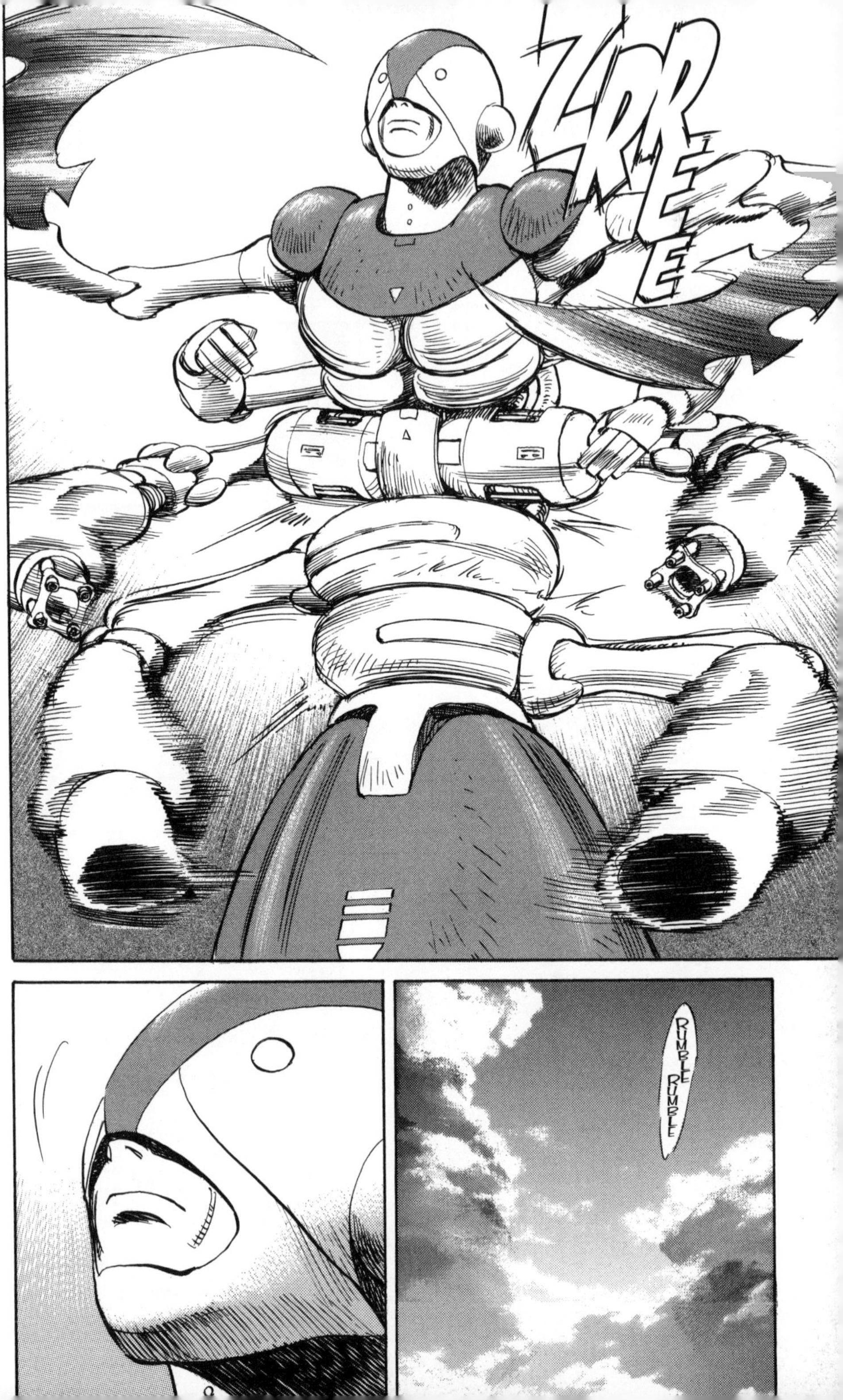
ZRRREEE
RUMBLE RUMBLE

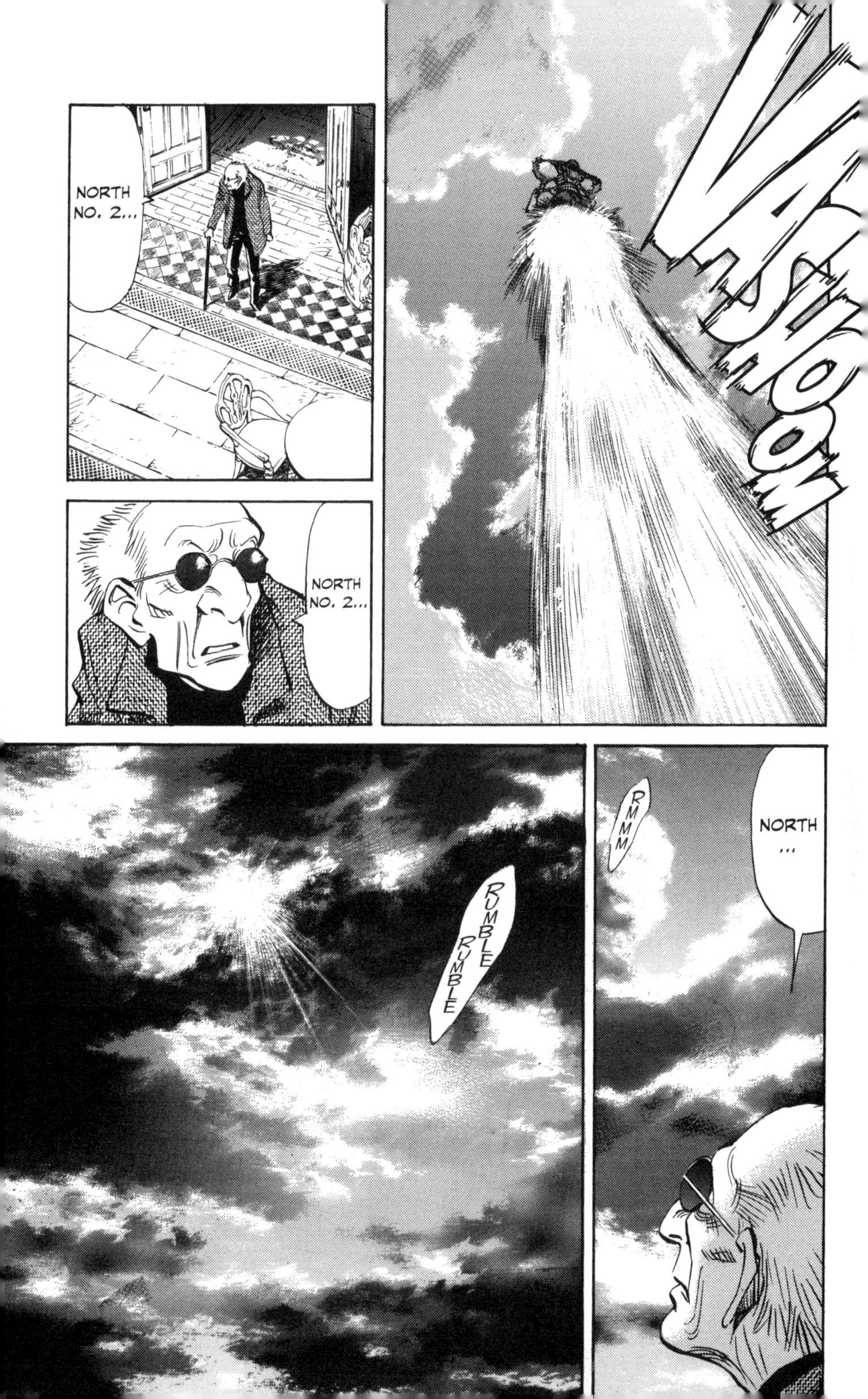
VASHOOM
NORTH NO. 2...
NORTH NO. 2...
NORTH ...
RMMM
RUMBLE RUMBLE

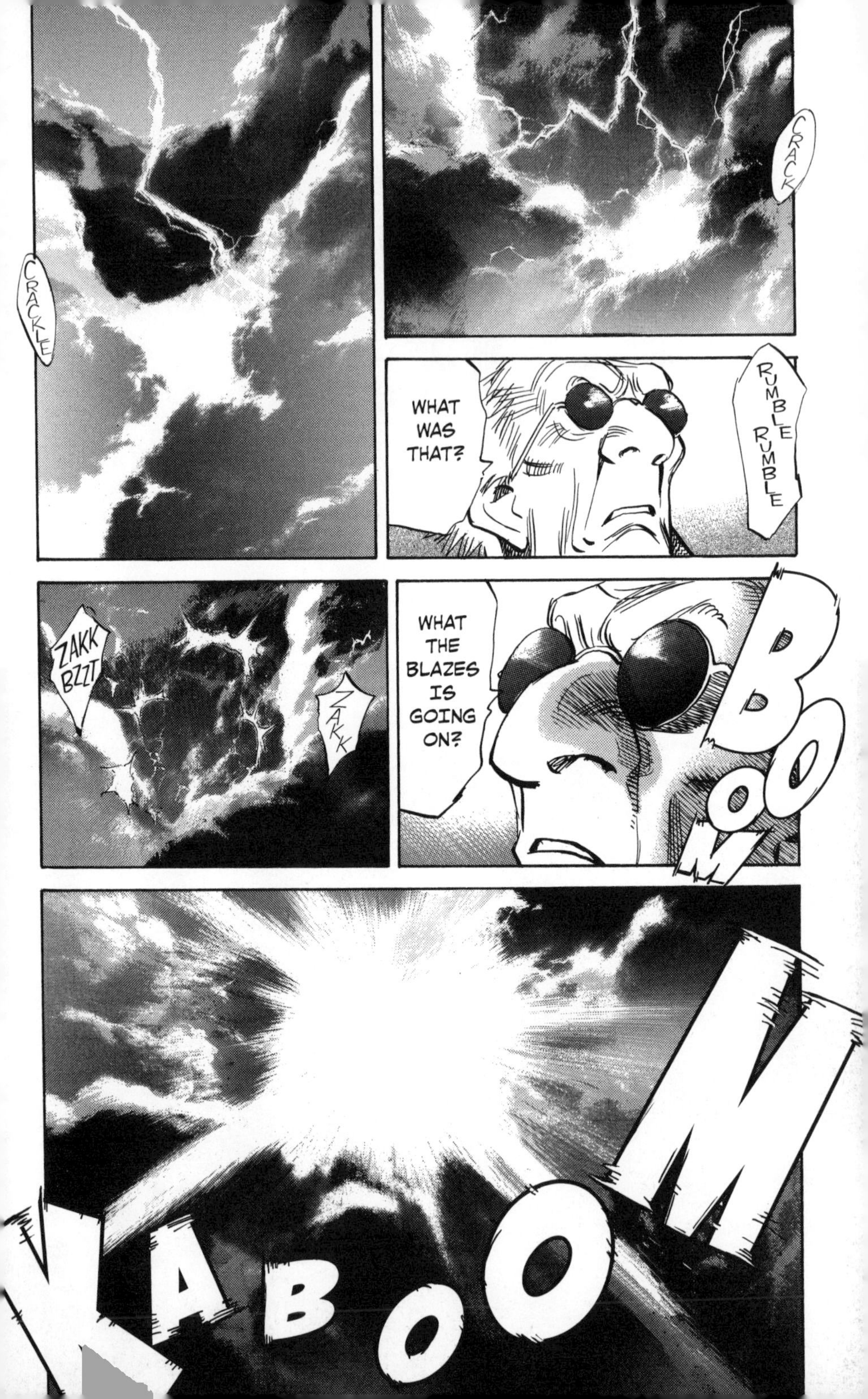
CRACK
RUMBLE RUMBLE
WHAT WAS THAT?
CRACKLE
BOOM
WHAT THE BLAZES IS GOING ON?
ZAKK
ZAKK BZZT
KABOOM

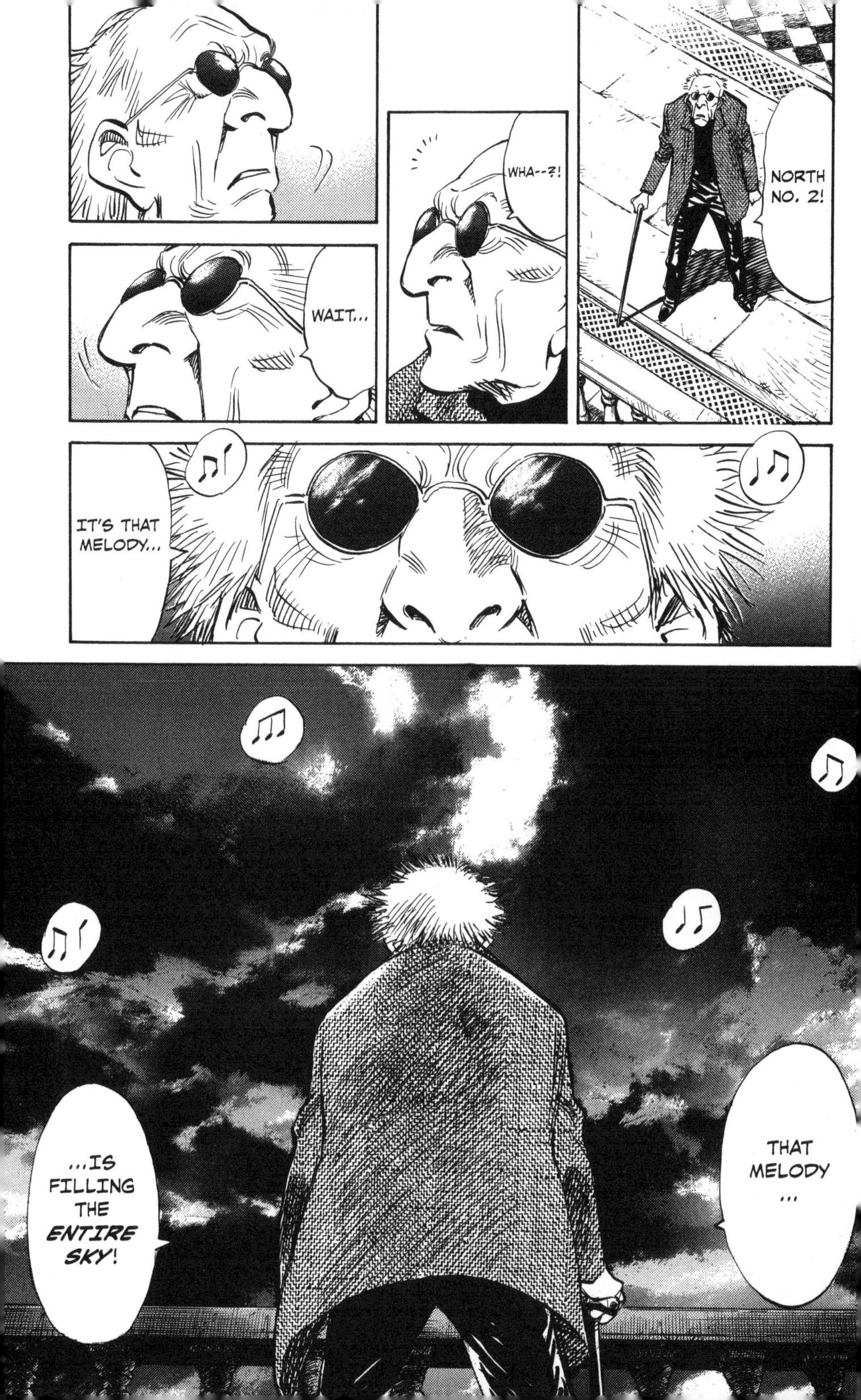
NORTH NO. 2!
WHA--?!
WAIT...
IT'S THAT MELODY...
THAT MELODY ...
...IS FILLING THE *ENTIRE SKY*!

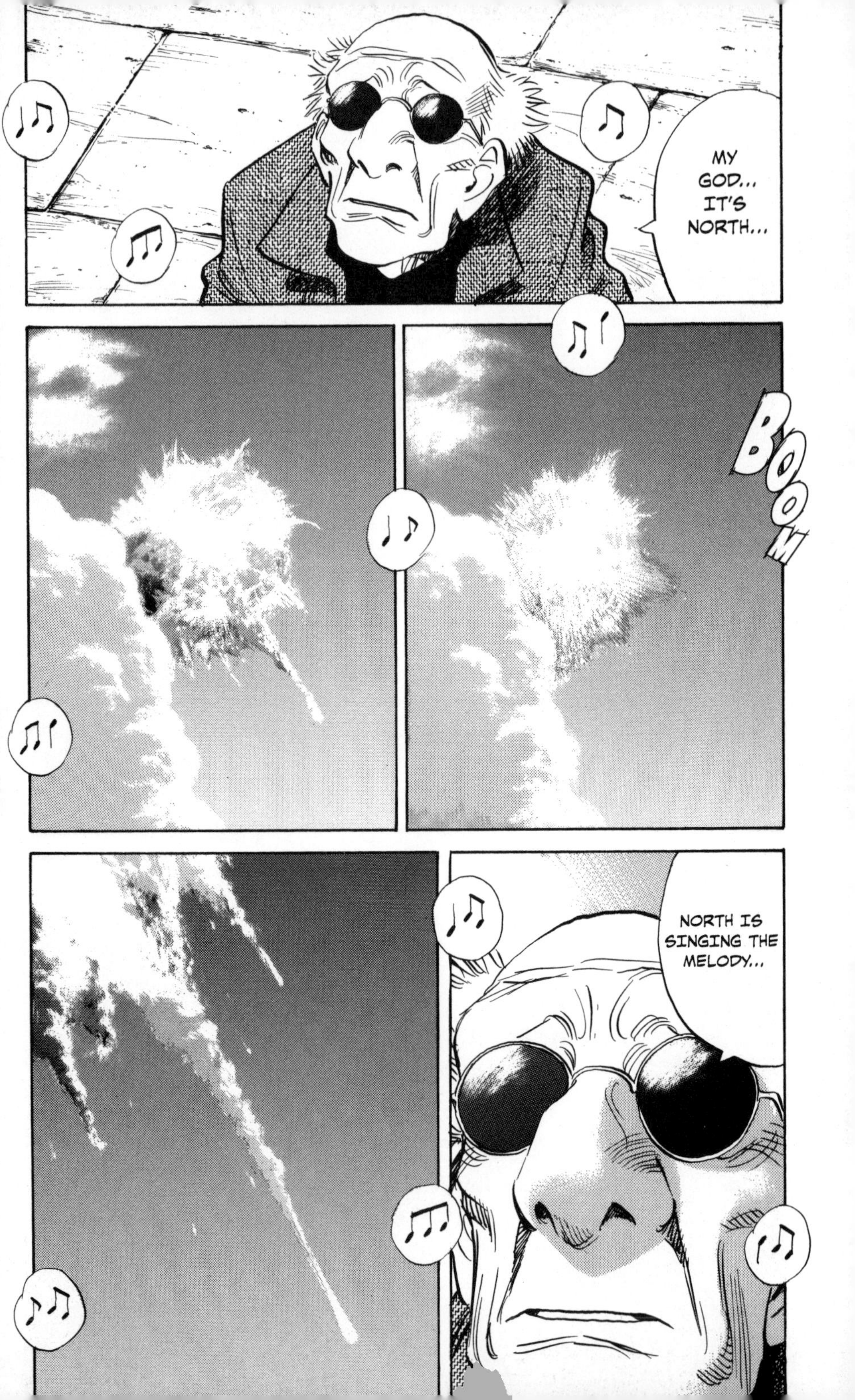
MY GOD... IT'S NORTH...
BOOOM
NORTH IS SINGING THE MELODY...

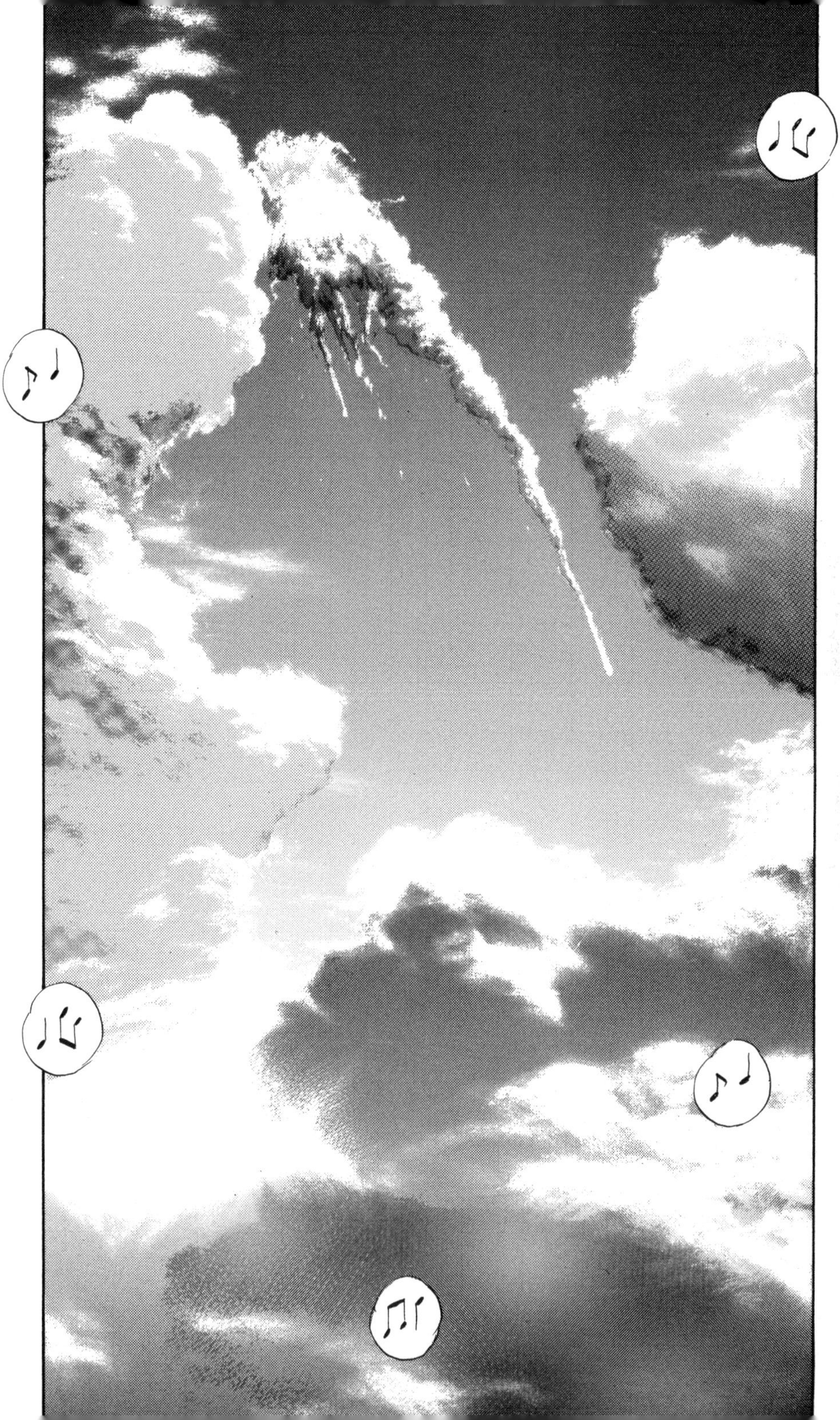

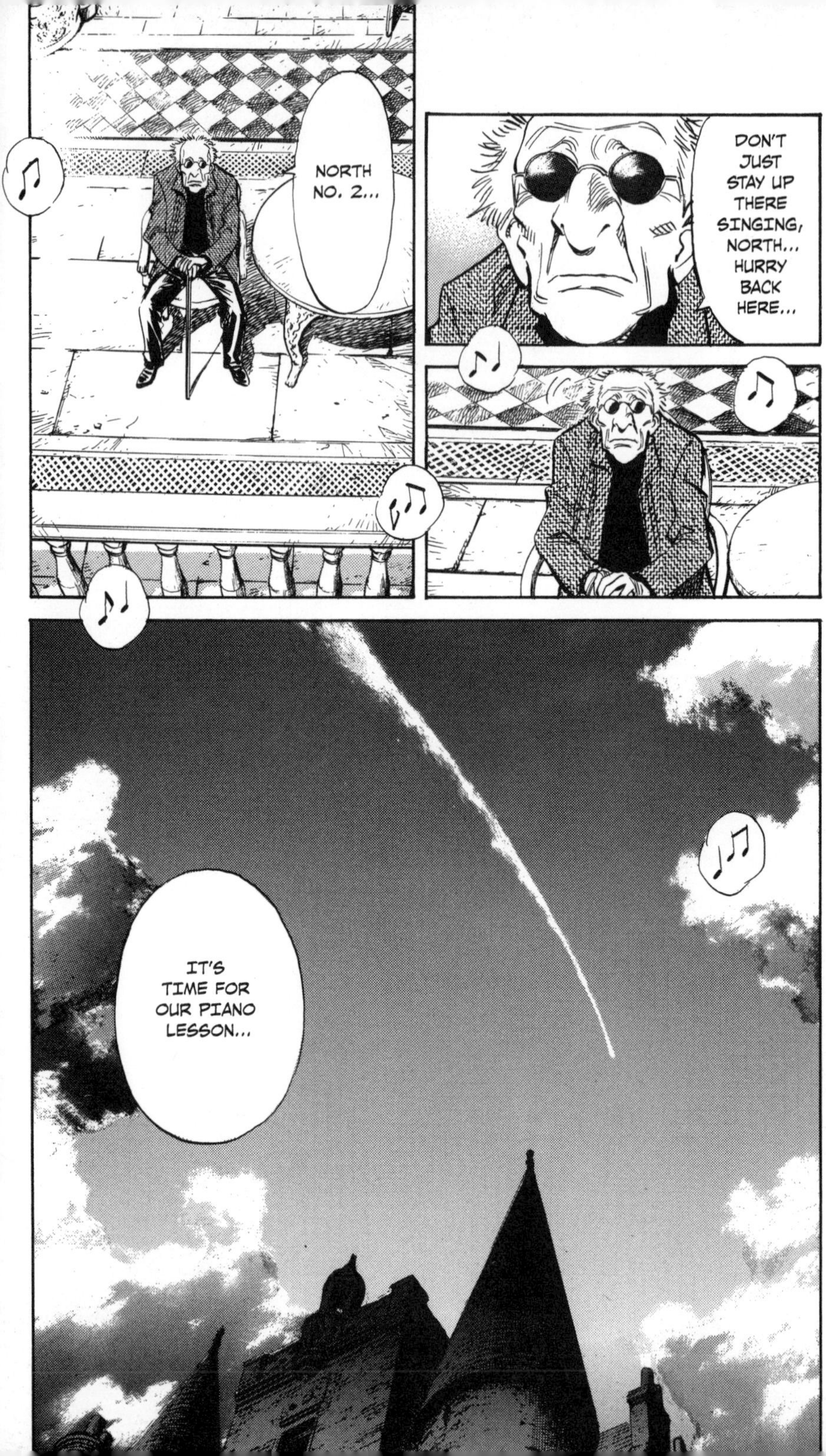
DON'T JUST STAY UP THERE SINGING, NORTH... HURRY BACK HERE...
NORTH NO. 2...
IT'S TIME FOR OUR PIANO LESSON...

Act 7 BRANDO

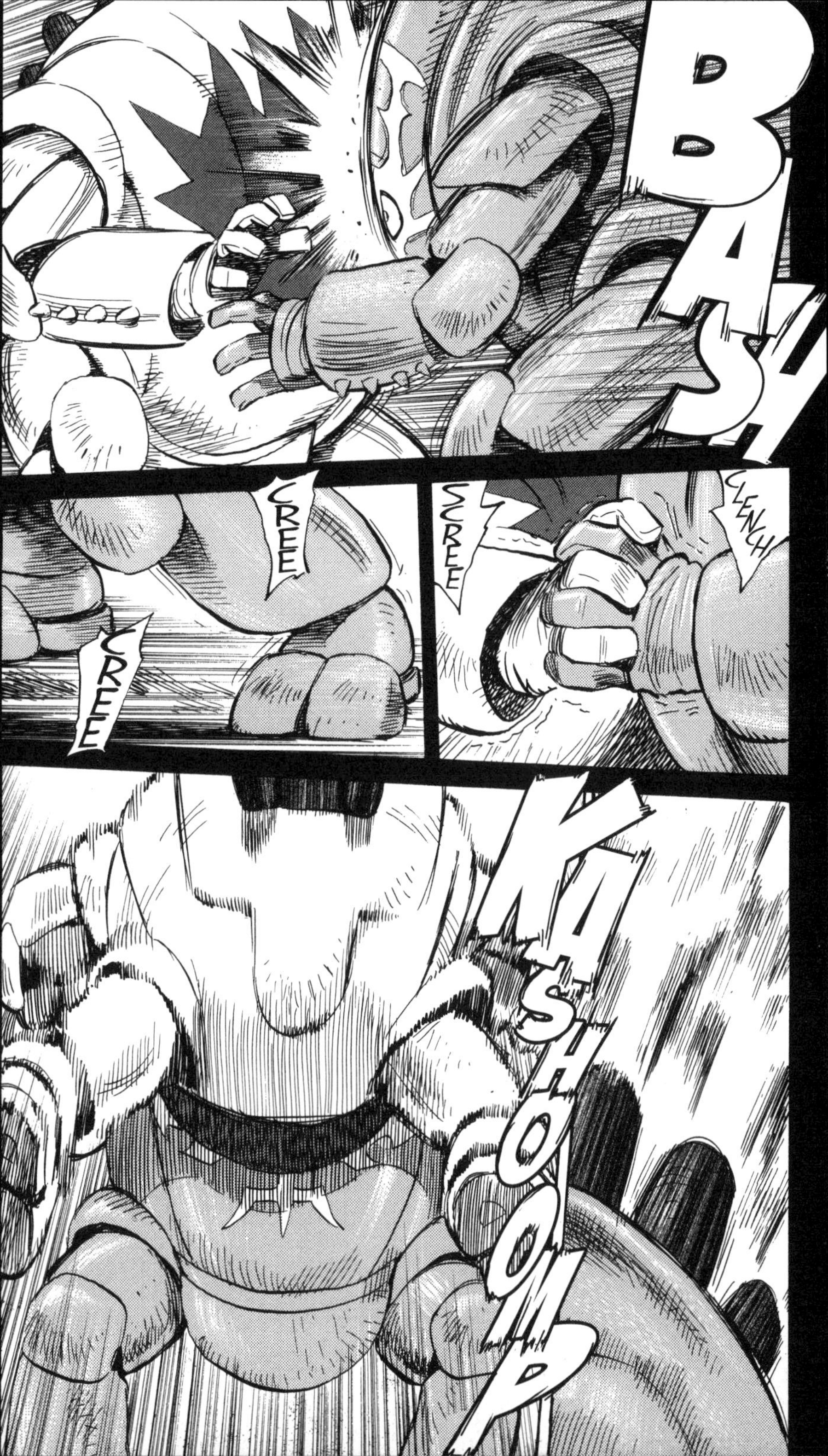
BASH
CLENCH
SCREE
CREE
CREE
KASHOOMP

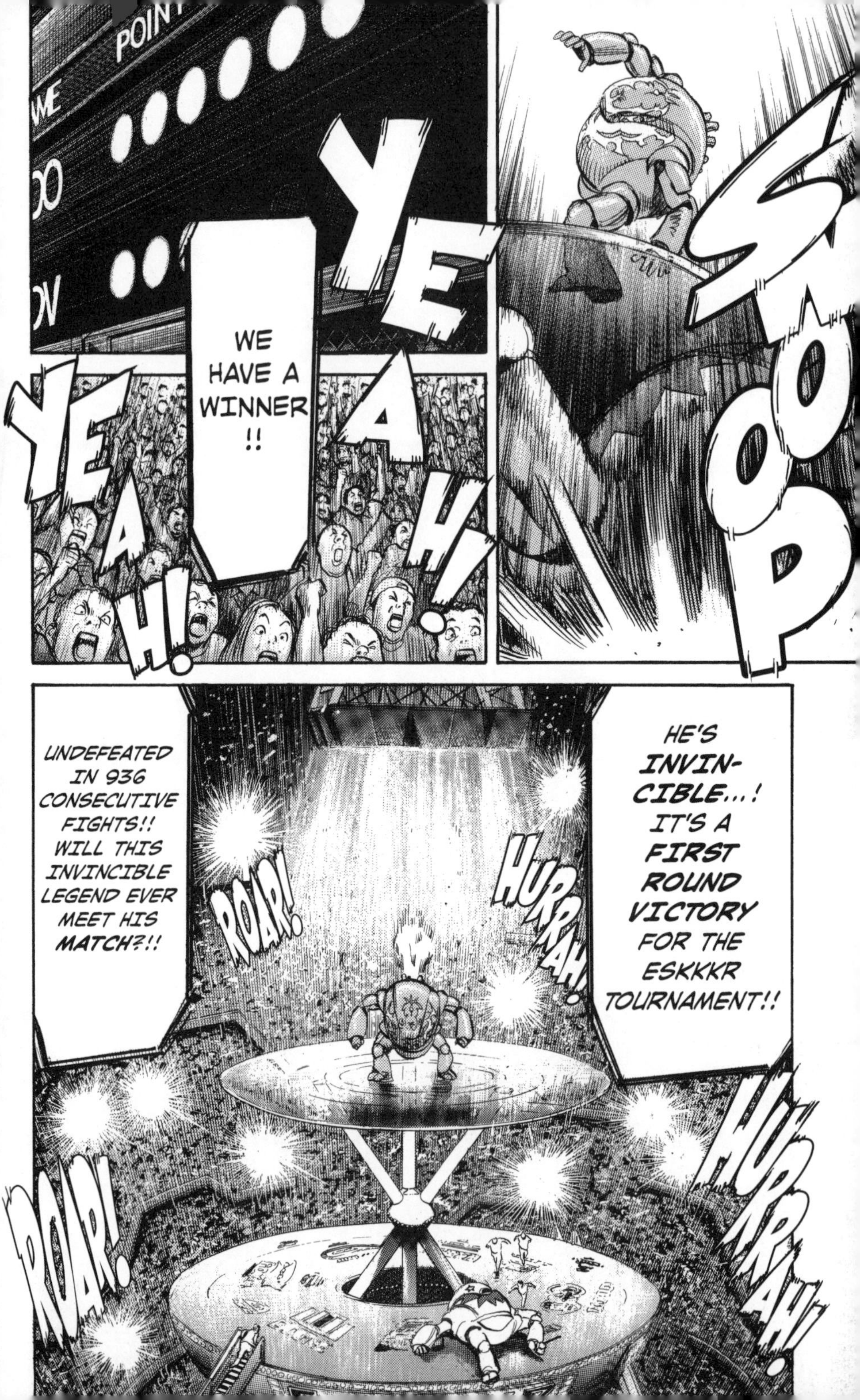
STOOP
YEAH!
WE HAVE A WINNER!!
YEAH!
HE'S INVINCIBLE...! IT'S A FIRST ROUND VICTORY FOR THE ESKKKR TOURNAMENT!!
HURRAH!
ROAR!
UNDEFEATED IN 936 CONSECUTIVE FIGHTS!! WILL THIS INVINCIBLE LEGEND EVER MEET HIS MATCH?!!
HURRAH!
ROAR!

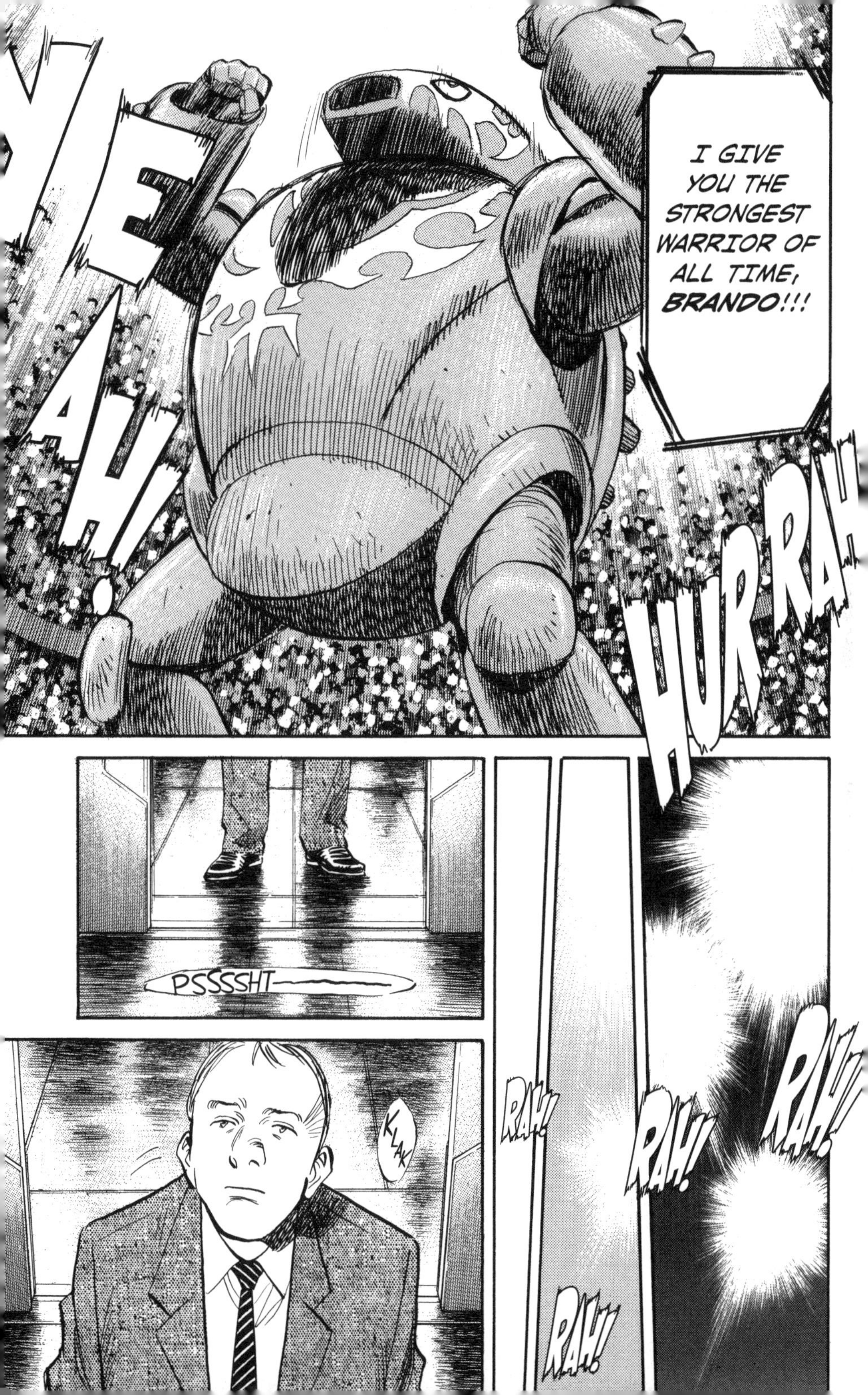
I GIVE YOU THE STRONGEST WARRIOR OF ALL TIME, **BRANDO!!!**
YEAH!
HURRAH
RAH!
RAH!
RAH!
RAH!
PSSSSHT
KLAK

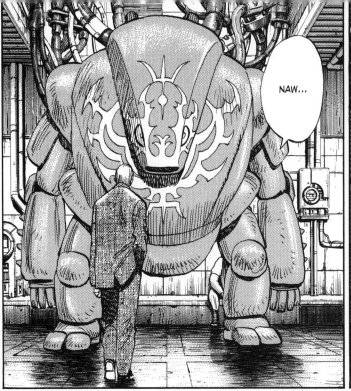

NAW...

THAT WAS AN IMPRESSIVE MATCH, BRANDO...

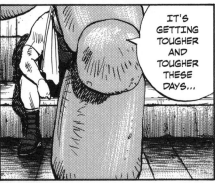

IT'S GETTING TOUGHER AND TOUGHER THESE DAYS...

LATELY, AFTER EVERY MATCH, I GOTTA SIT DOWN AND REST BEFORE I CAN MOVE AGAIN...

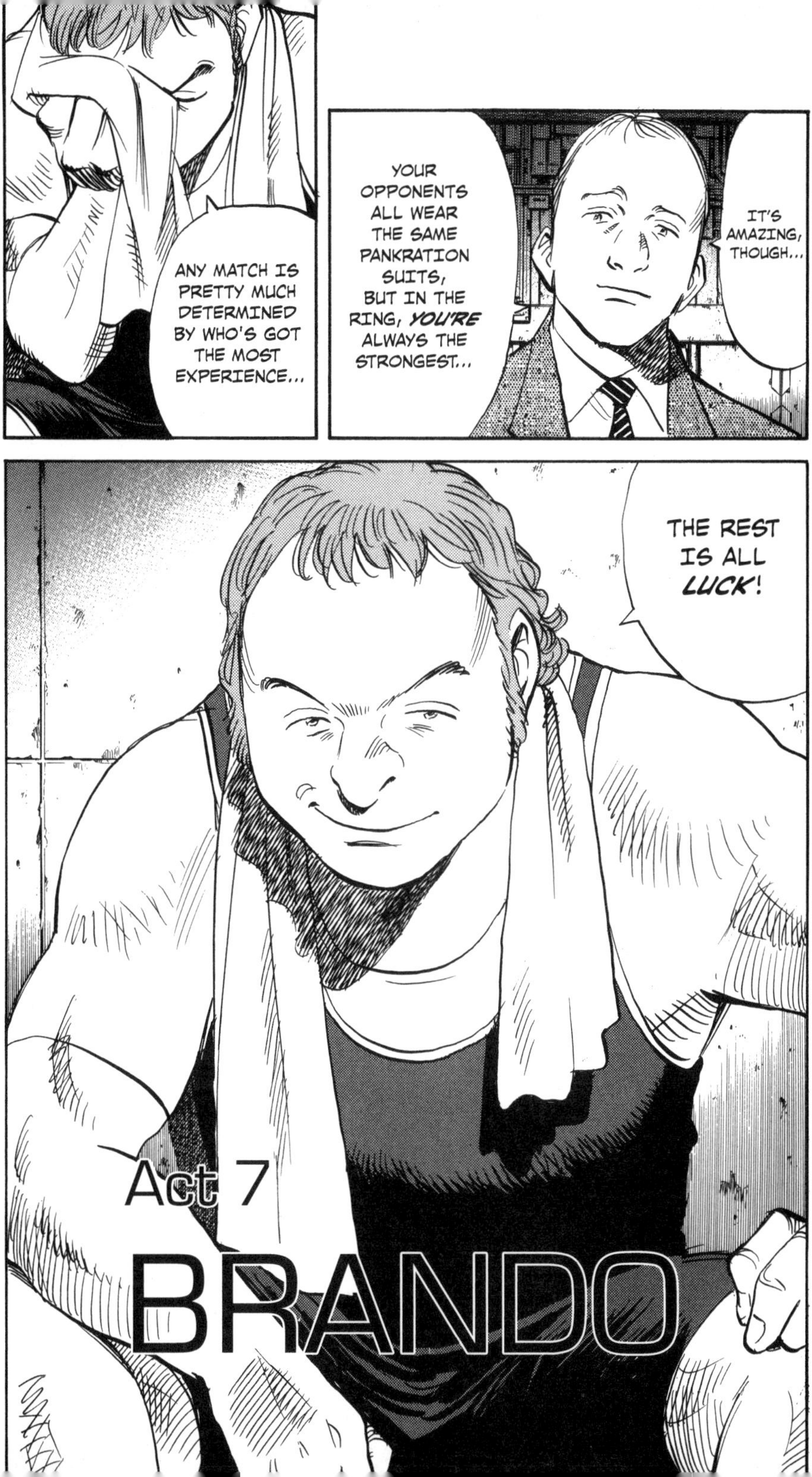
IT'S AMAZING, THOUGH...
YOUR OPPONENTS ALL WEAR THE SAME PANKRATION SUITS, BUT IN THE RING, YOU'RE ALWAYS THE STRONGEST...
ANY MATCH IS PRETTY MUCH DETERMINED BY WHO'S GOT THE MOST EXPERIENCE...
THE REST IS ALL LUCK!
Act 7
BRANDO

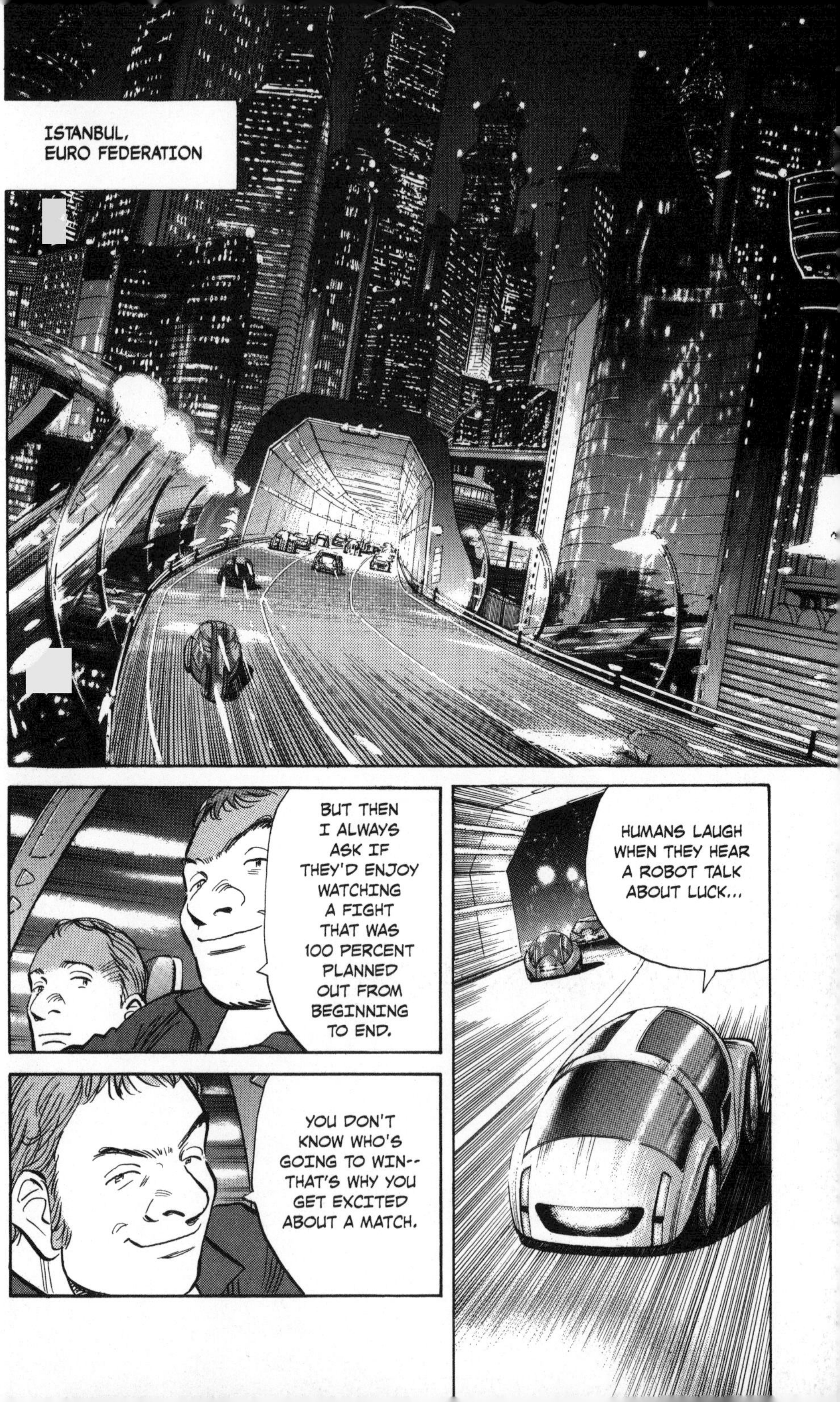
ISTANBUL, EURO FEDERATION
HUMANS LAUGH WHEN THEY HEAR A ROBOT TALK ABOUT LUCK...
BUT THEN I ALWAYS ASK IF THEY'D ENJOY WATCHING A FIGHT THAT WAS 100 PERCENT PLANNED OUT FROM BEGINNING TO END.
YOU DON'T KNOW WHO'S GOING TO WIN--THAT'S WHY YOU GET EXCITED ABOUT A MATCH.

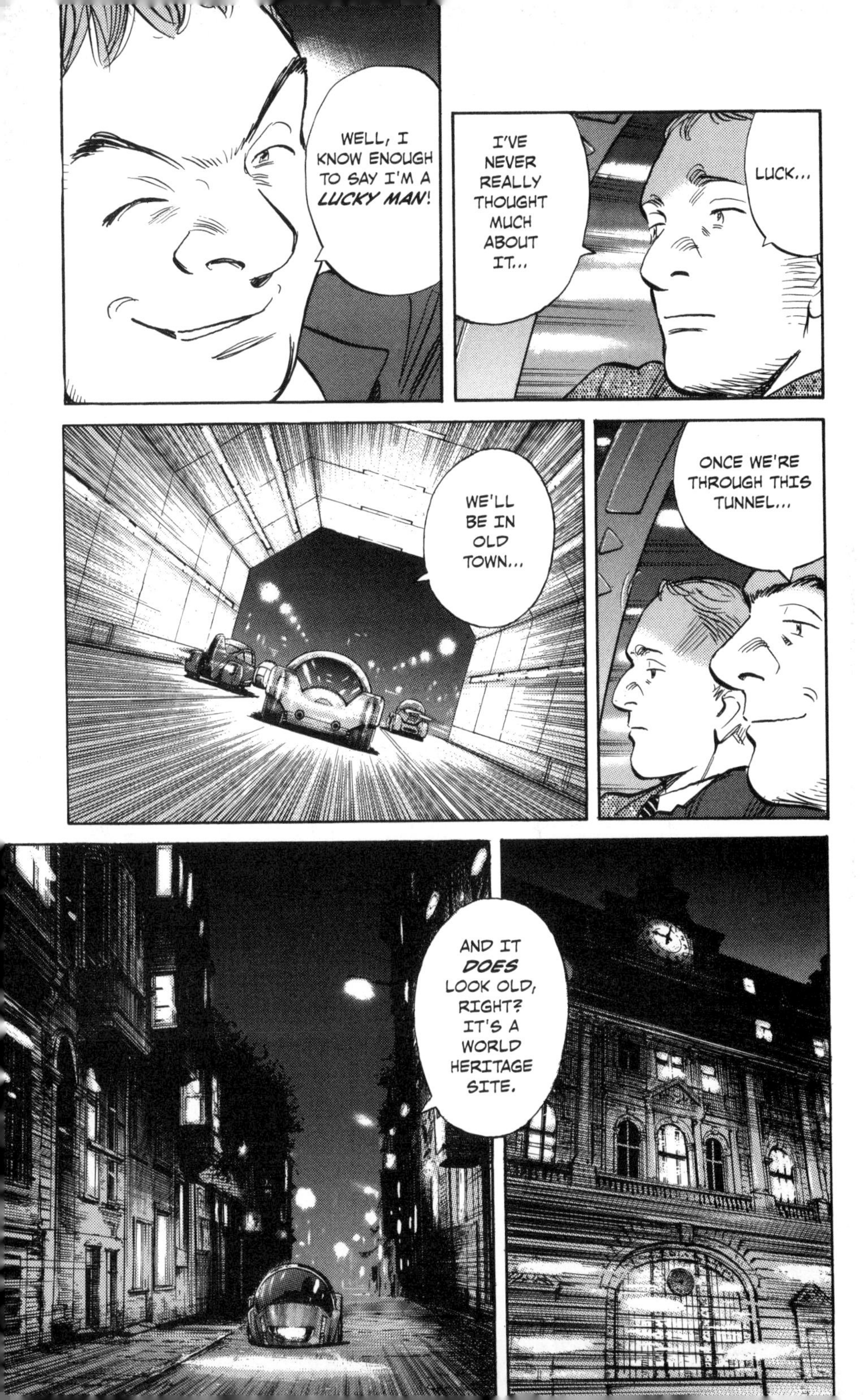
LUCK...
I'VE NEVER REALLY THOUGHT MUCH ABOUT IT...
WELL, I KNOW ENOUGH TO SAY I'M A *LUCKY MAN*!
ONCE WE'RE THROUGH THIS TUNNEL...
WE'LL BE IN OLD TOWN...
AND IT *DOES* LOOK OLD, RIGHT? IT'S A WORLD HERITAGE SITE.

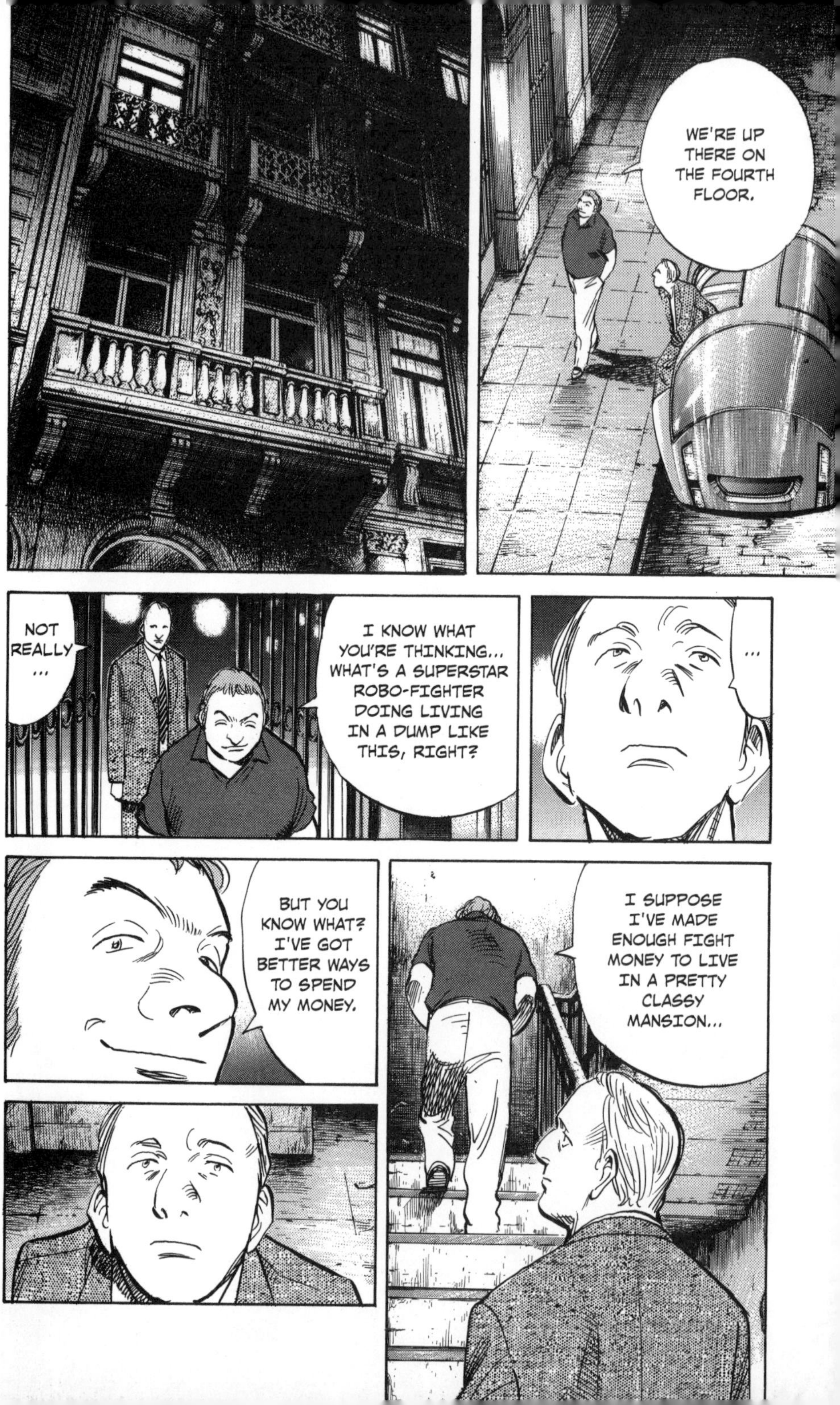
WE'RE UP THERE ON THE FOURTH FLOOR.
...
I KNOW WHAT YOU'RE THINKING... WHAT'S A SUPERSTAR ROBO-FIGHTER DOING LIVING IN A DUMP LIKE THIS, RIGHT?
NOT REALLY...
I SUPPOSE I'VE MADE ENOUGH FIGHT MONEY TO LIVE IN A PRETTY CLASSY MANSION...
BUT YOU KNOW WHAT? I'VE GOT BETTER WAYS TO SPEND MY MONEY.

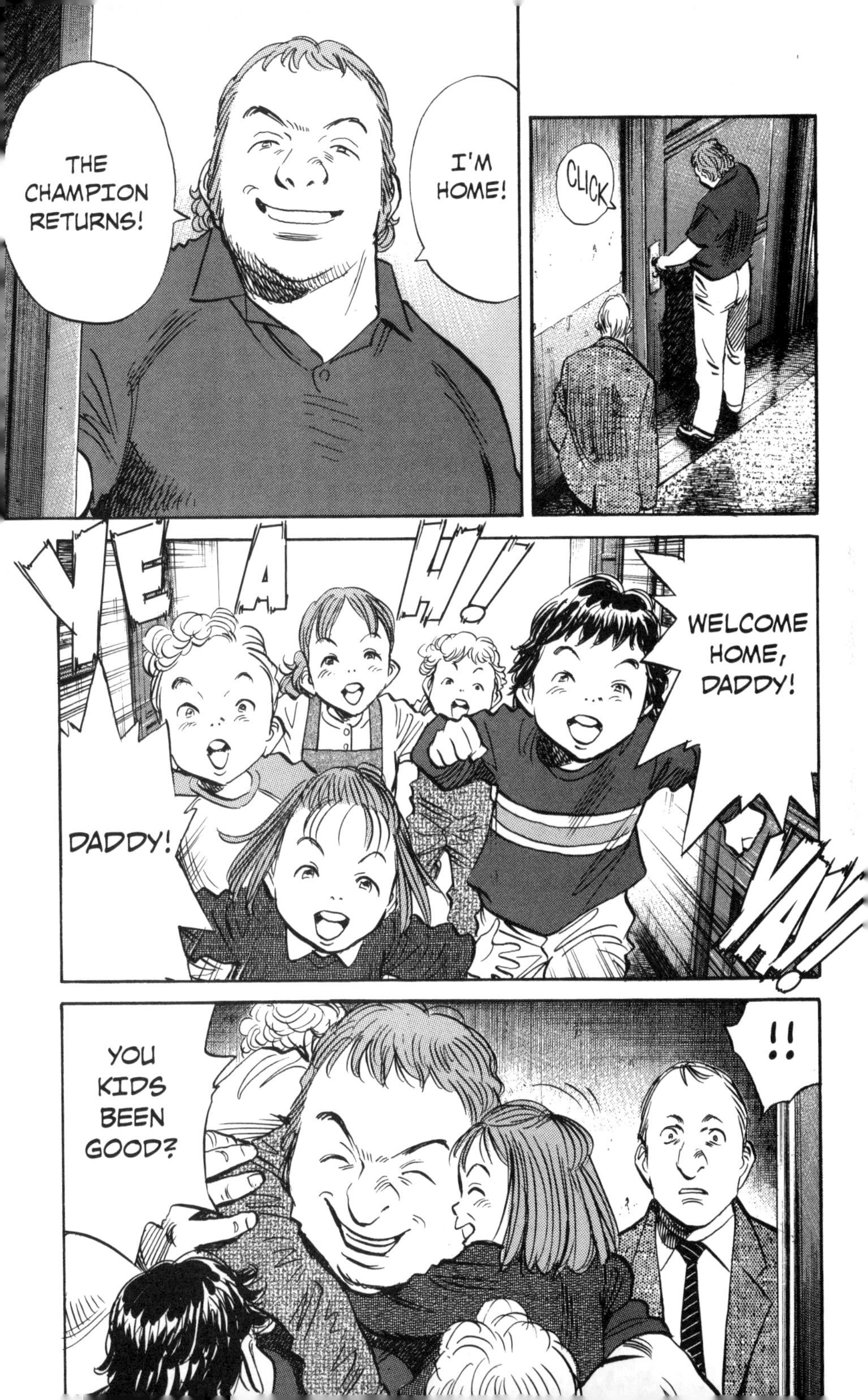
CLICK
I'M HOME!
THE CHAMPION RETURNS!
WELCOME HOME, DADDY!
YEAH!
DADDY!
!!
YOU KIDS BEEN GOOD?

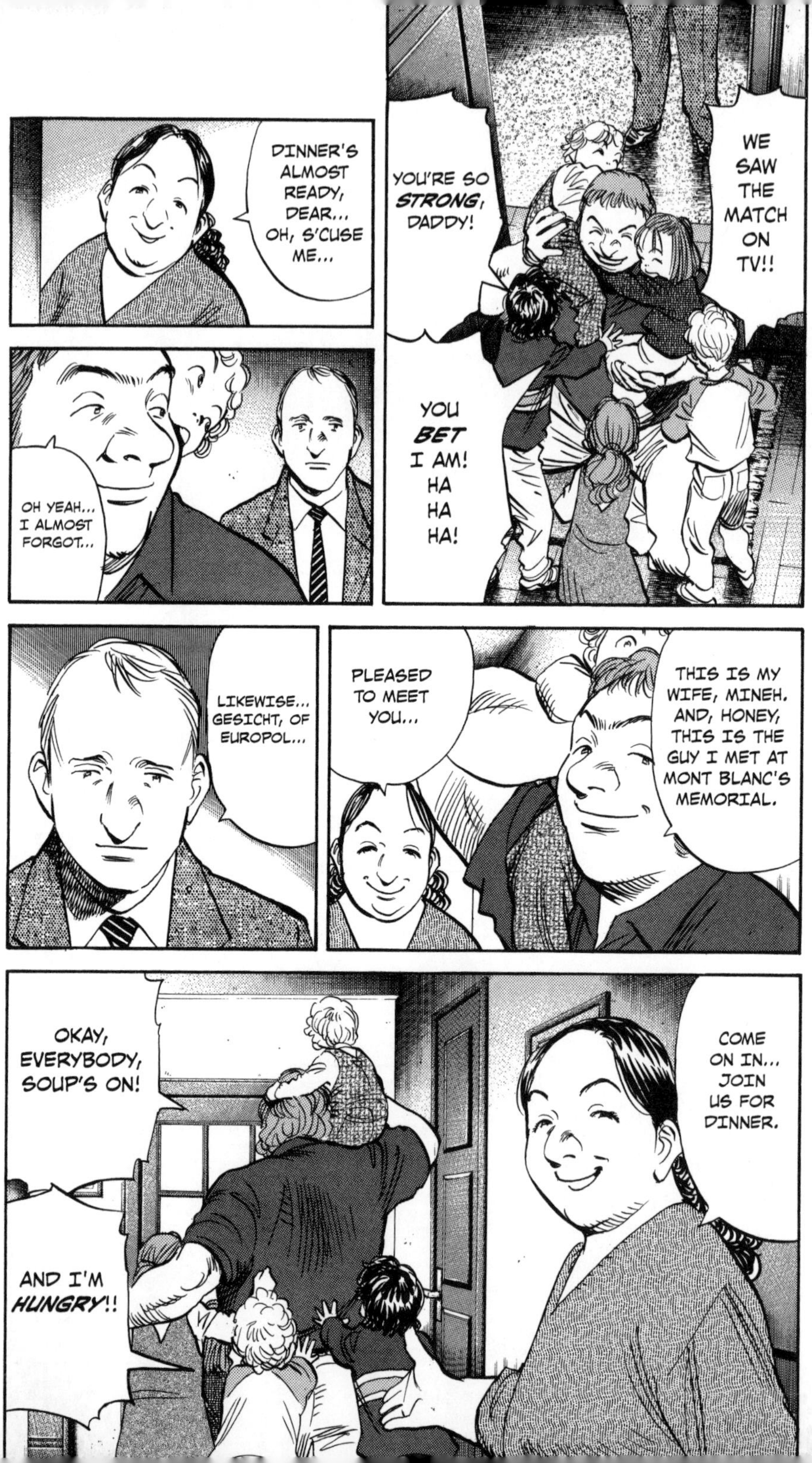
WE SAW THE MATCH ON TV!!
YOU'RE SO *STRONG*, DADDY!
YOU *BET* I AM! HA HA HA!
DINNER'S ALMOST READY, DEAR... OH, S'CUSE ME...
OH YEAH... I ALMOST FORGOT...
THIS IS MY WIFE, MINEH. AND, HONEY, THIS IS THE GUY I MET AT MONT BLANC'S MEMORIAL.
PLEASED TO MEET YOU...
LIKEWISE... GESICHT, OF EUROPOL...
COME ON IN... JOIN US FOR DINNER.
OKAY, EVERYBODY, SOUP'S ON!
AND I'M *HUNGRY*!!

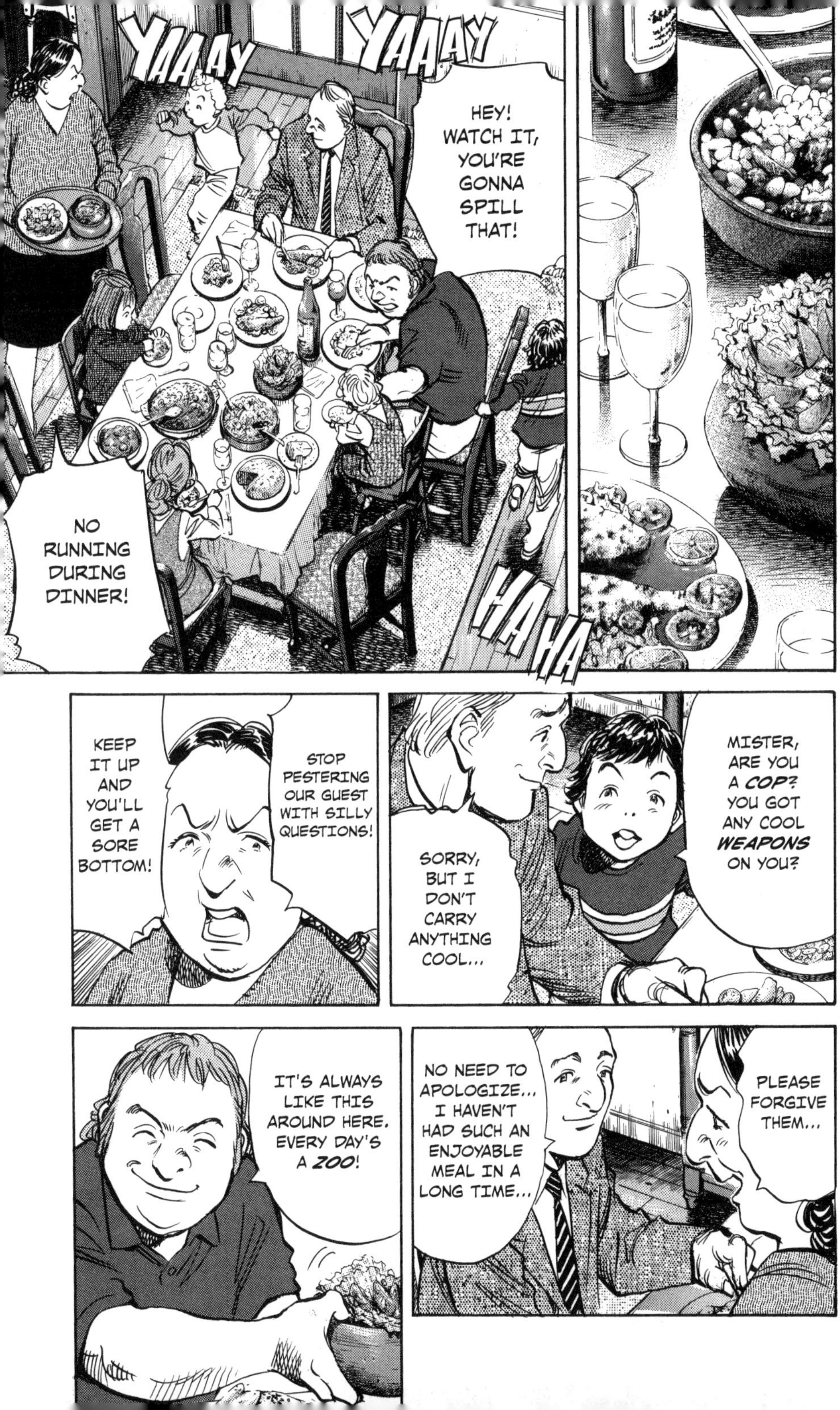
YAAAY
YAAAY
HEY! WATCH IT, YOU'RE GONNA SPILL THAT!
NO RUNNING DURING DINNER!
HAHA
MISTER, ARE YOU A COP? YOU GOT ANY COOL WEAPONS ON YOU?
SORRY, BUT I DON'T CARRY ANYTHING COOL...
STOP PESTERING OUR GUEST WITH SILLY QUESTIONS!
KEEP IT UP AND YOU'LL GET A SORE BOTTOM!
PLEASE FORGIVE THEM...
NO NEED TO APOLOGIZE... I HAVEN'T HAD SUCH AN ENJOYABLE MEAL IN A LONG TIME...
IT'S ALWAYS LIKE THIS AROUND HERE. EVERY DAY'S A ZOO!

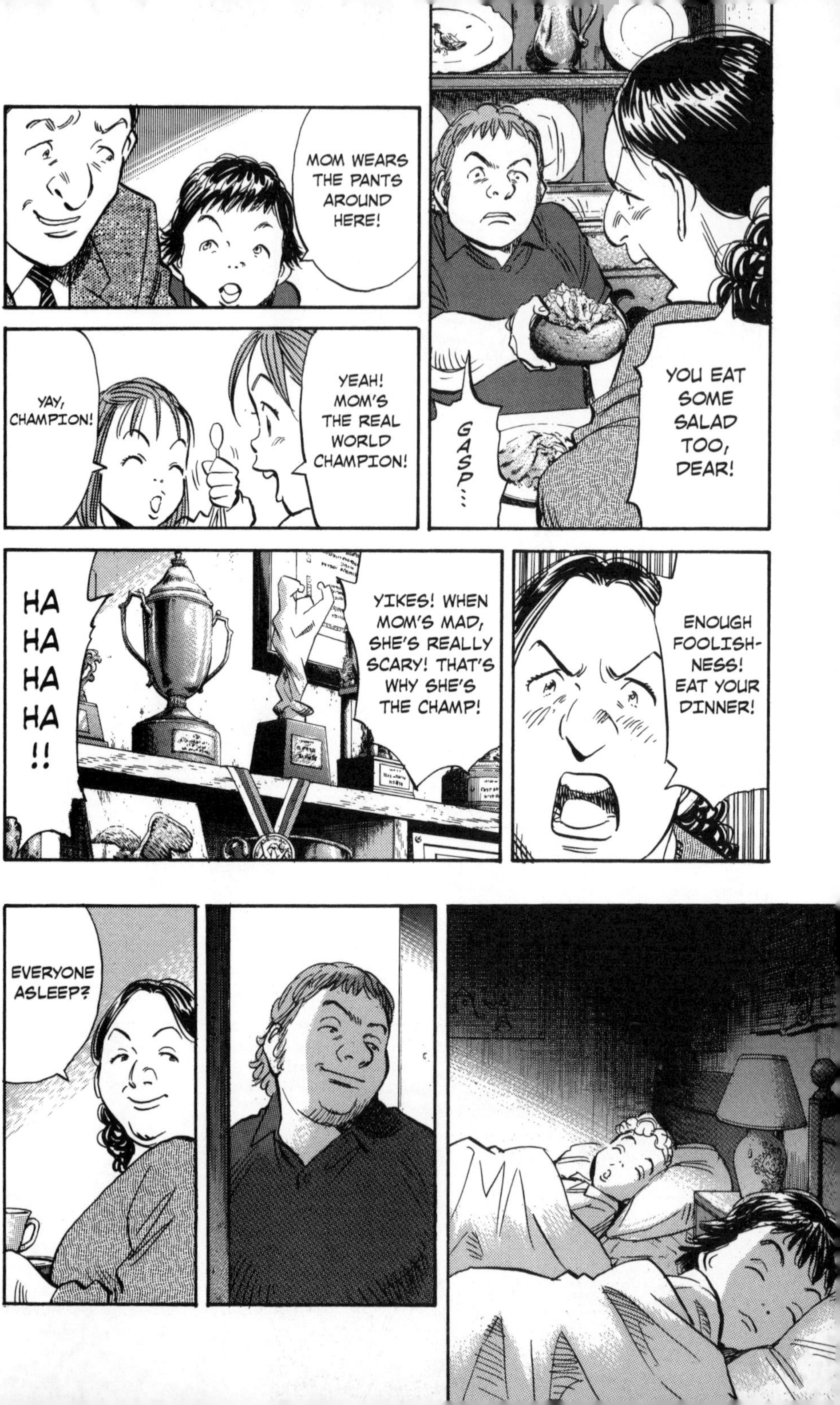
YOU EAT SOME SALAD TOO, DEAR!
GASP...
MOM WEARS THE PANTS AROUND HERE!
YEAH! MOM'S THE REAL WORLD CHAMPION!
YAY, CHAMPION!
ENOUGH FOOLISHNESS! EAT YOUR DINNER!
YIKES! WHEN MOM'S MAD, SHE'S REALLY SCARY! THAT'S WHY SHE'S THE CHAMP!
HA HA HA HA!!
EVERYONE ASLEEP?

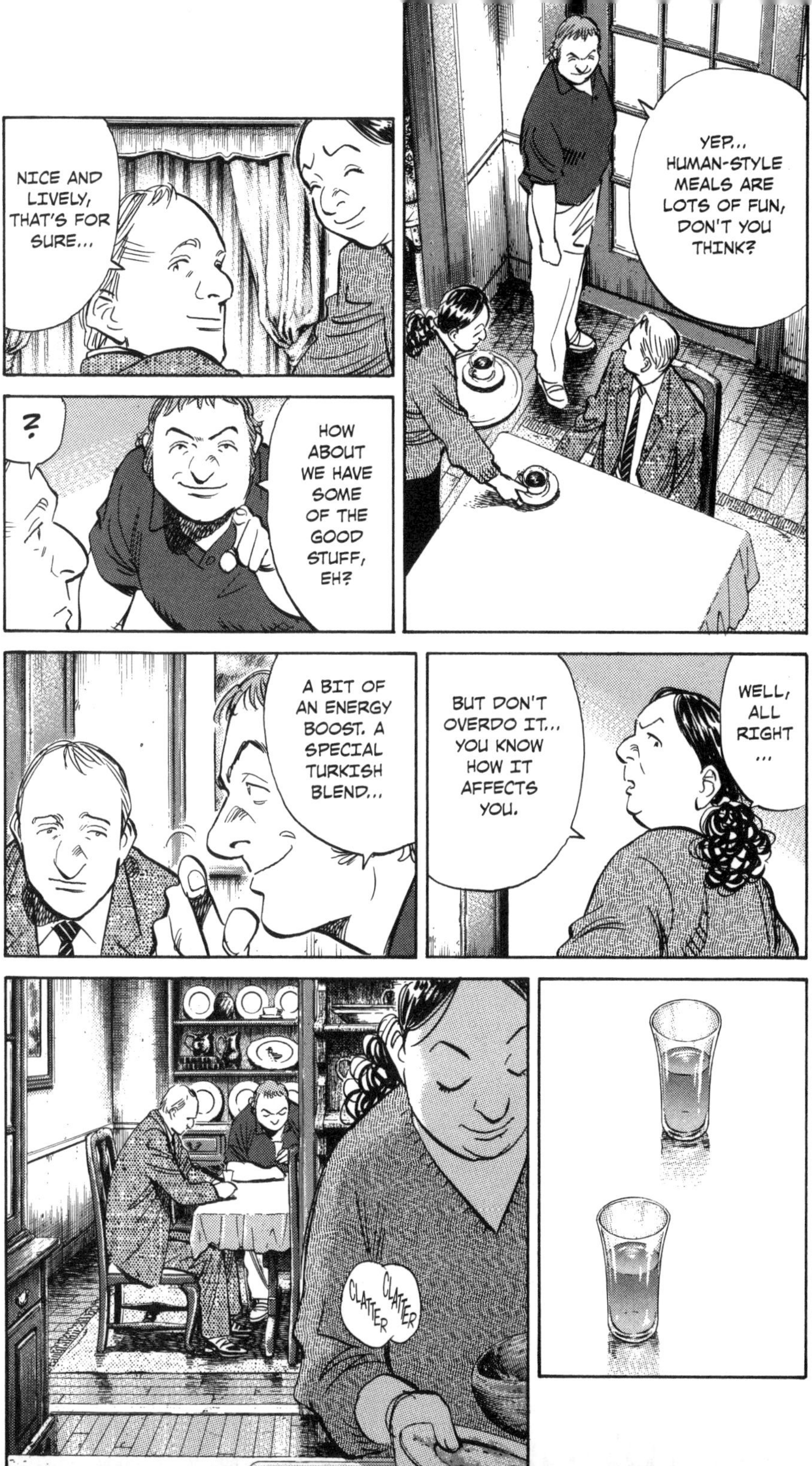
YEP... HUMAN-STYLE MEALS ARE LOTS OF FUN, DON'T YOU THINK?
NICE AND LIVELY, THAT'S FOR SURE...
HOW ABOUT WE HAVE SOME OF THE GOOD STUFF, EH?
?
WELL, ALL RIGHT ...
BUT DON'T OVERDO IT... YOU KNOW HOW IT AFFECTS YOU.
A BIT OF AN ENERGY BOOST. A SPECIAL TURKISH BLEND...
CLATTER
CLATTER

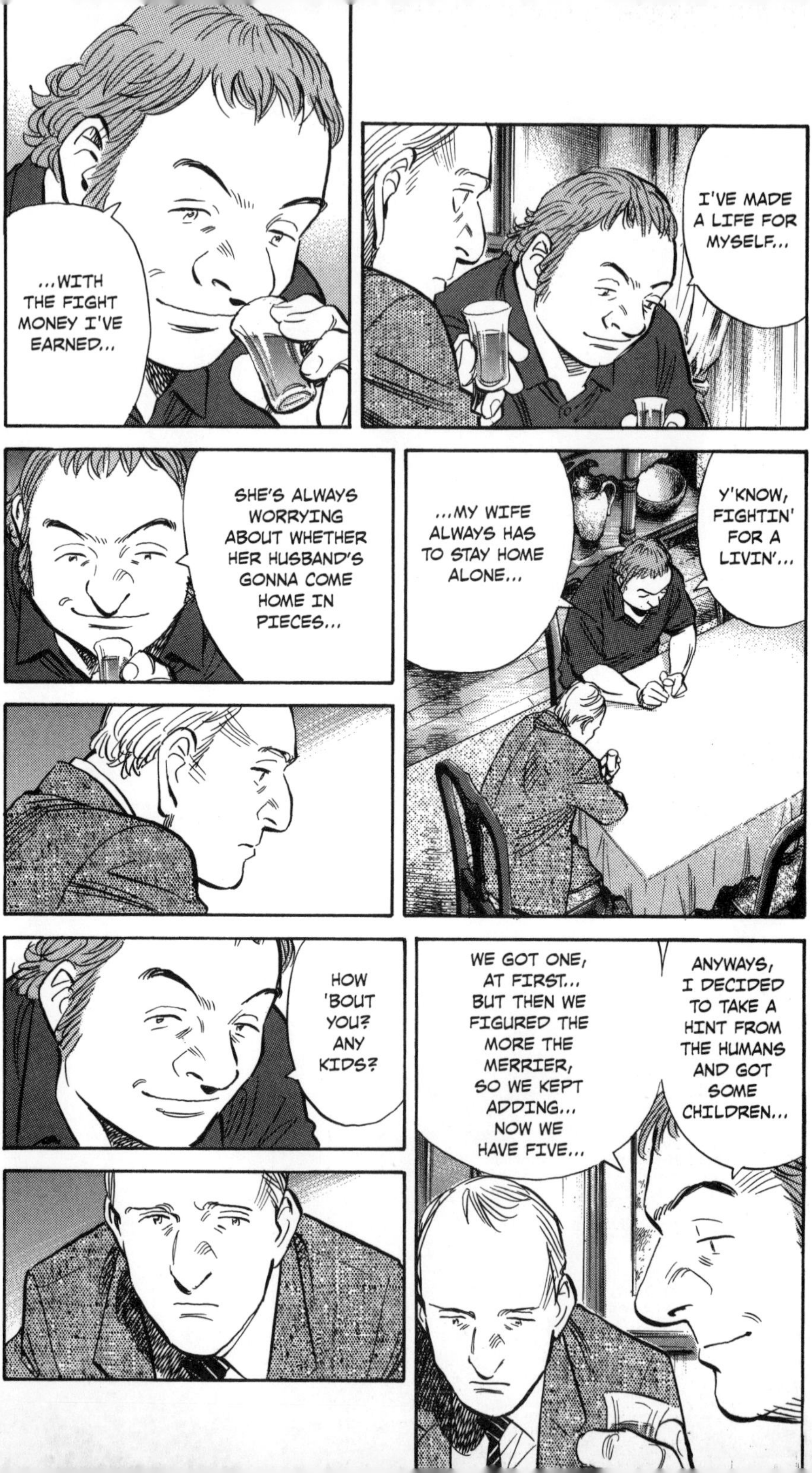
I'VE MADE A LIFE FOR MYSELF...
...WITH THE FIGHT MONEY I'VE EARNED...
Y'KNOW, FIGHTIN' FOR A LIVIN'...
...MY WIFE ALWAYS HAS TO STAY HOME ALONE...
SHE'S ALWAYS WORRYING ABOUT WHETHER HER HUSBAND'S GONNA COME HOME IN PIECES...
ANYWAYS, I DECIDED TO TAKE A HINT FROM THE HUMANS AND GOT SOME CHILDREN...
WE GOT ONE, AT FIRST... BUT THEN WE FIGURED THE MORE THE MERRIER, SO WE KEPT ADDING... NOW WE HAVE FIVE...
HOW 'BOUT YOU? ANY KIDS?

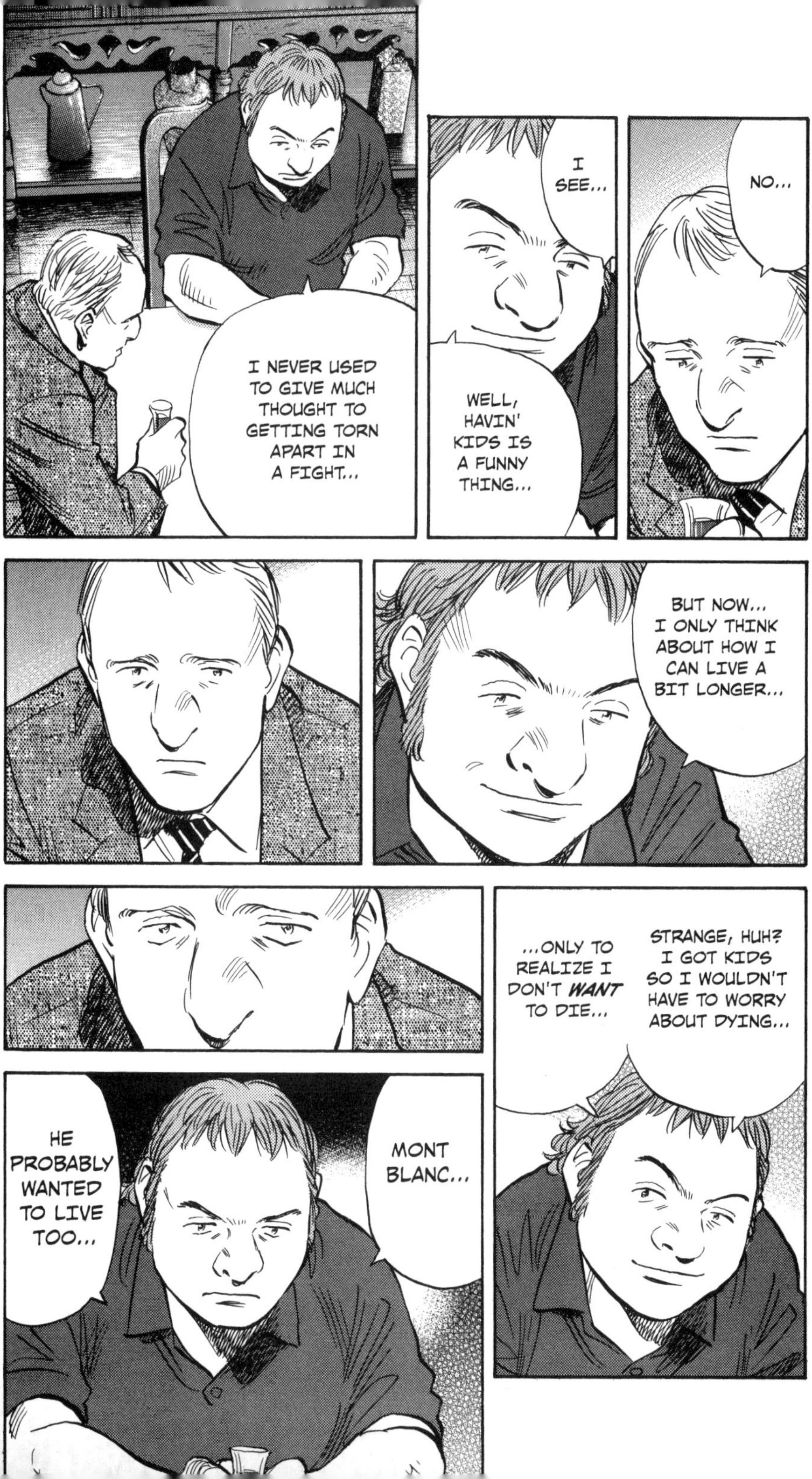
NO...
I SEE...
WELL, HAVIN' KIDS IS A FUNNY THING...
I NEVER USED TO GIVE MUCH THOUGHT TO GETTING TORN APART IN A FIGHT...
BUT NOW... I ONLY THINK ABOUT HOW I CAN LIVE A BIT LONGER...
STRANGE, HUH? I GOT KIDS SO I WOULDN'T HAVE TO WORRY ABOUT DYING...
...ONLY TO REALIZE I DON'T *WANT* TO DIE...
MONT BLANC...
HE PROBABLY WANTED TO LIVE TOO...

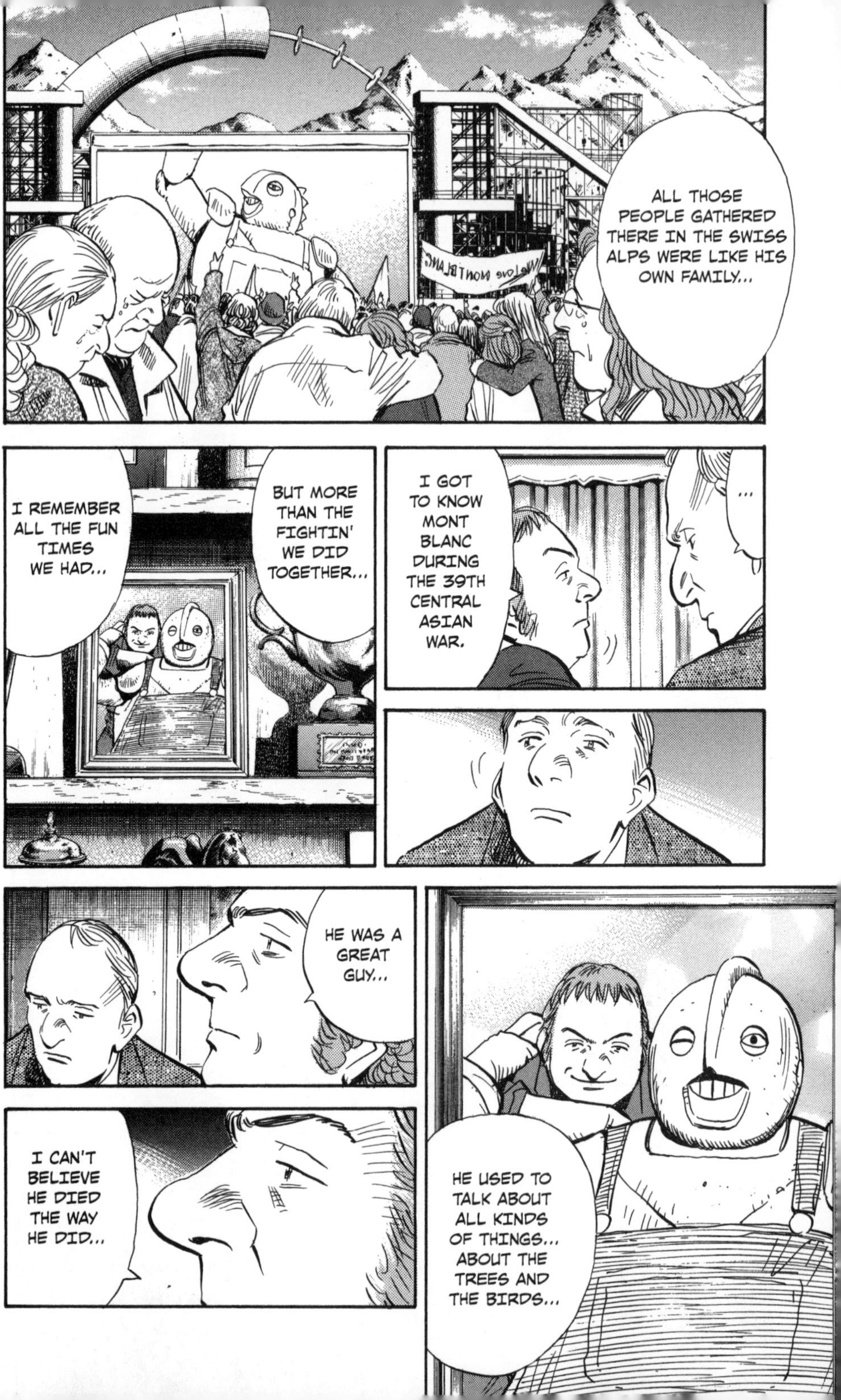
ALL THOSE PEOPLE GATHERED THERE IN THE SWISS ALPS WERE LIKE HIS OWN FAMILY...
...
I GOT TO KNOW MONT BLANC DURING THE 39TH CENTRAL ASIAN WAR.
BUT MORE THAN THE FIGHTIN' WE DID TOGETHER...
I REMEMBER ALL THE FUN TIMES WE HAD...
HE USED TO TALK ABOUT ALL KINDS OF THINGS... ABOUT THE TREES AND THE BIRDS...
HE WAS A GREAT GUY...
I CAN'T BELIEVE HE DIED THE WAY HE DID...

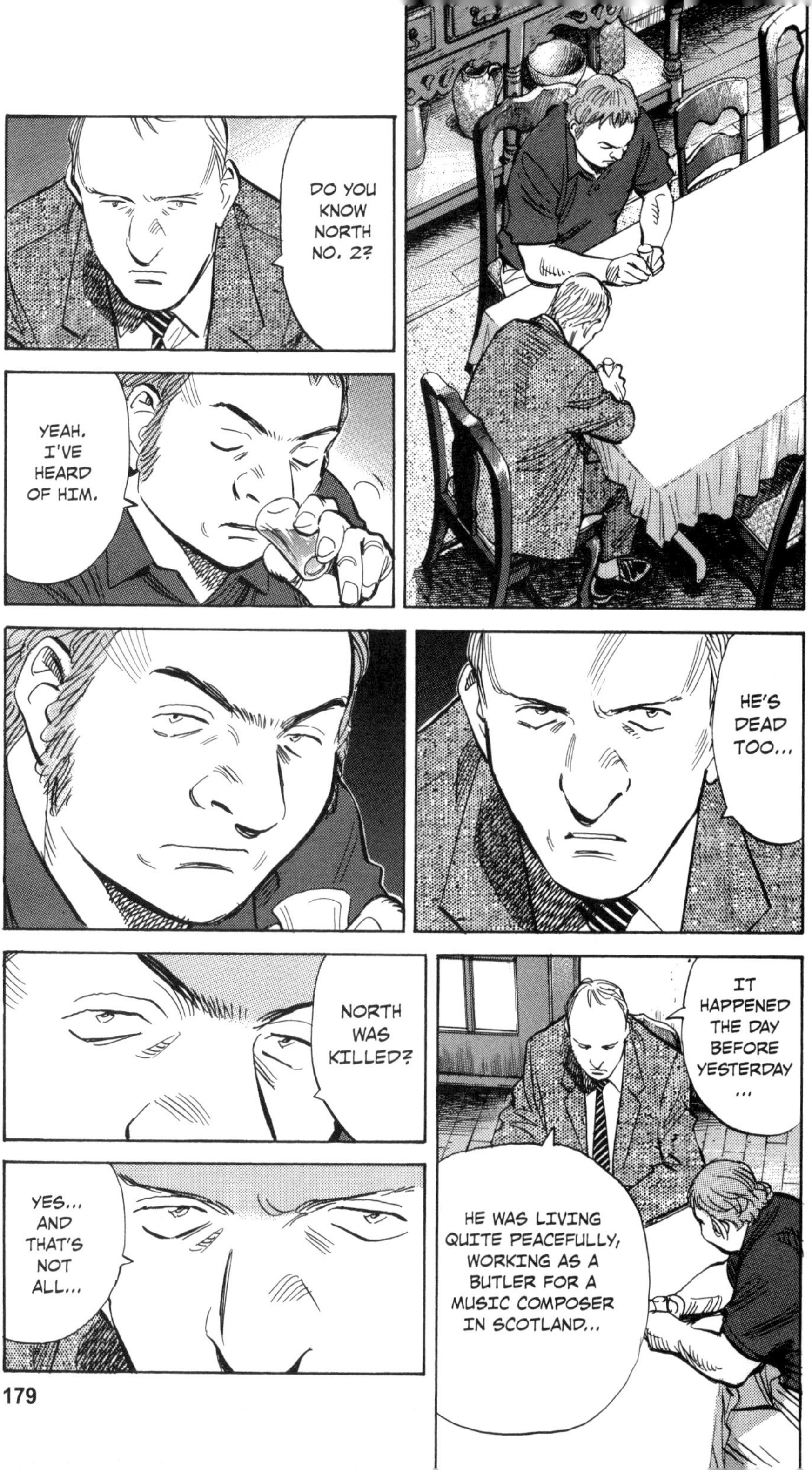
DO YOU KNOW NORTH NO. 2?
YEAH. I'VE HEARD OF HIM.
HE'S DEAD TOO...
IT HAPPENED THE DAY BEFORE YESTERDAY...
HE WAS LIVING QUITE PEACEFULLY, WORKING AS A BUTLER FOR A MUSIC COMPOSER IN SCOTLAND...
NORTH WAS KILLED?
YES... AND THAT'S NOT ALL...

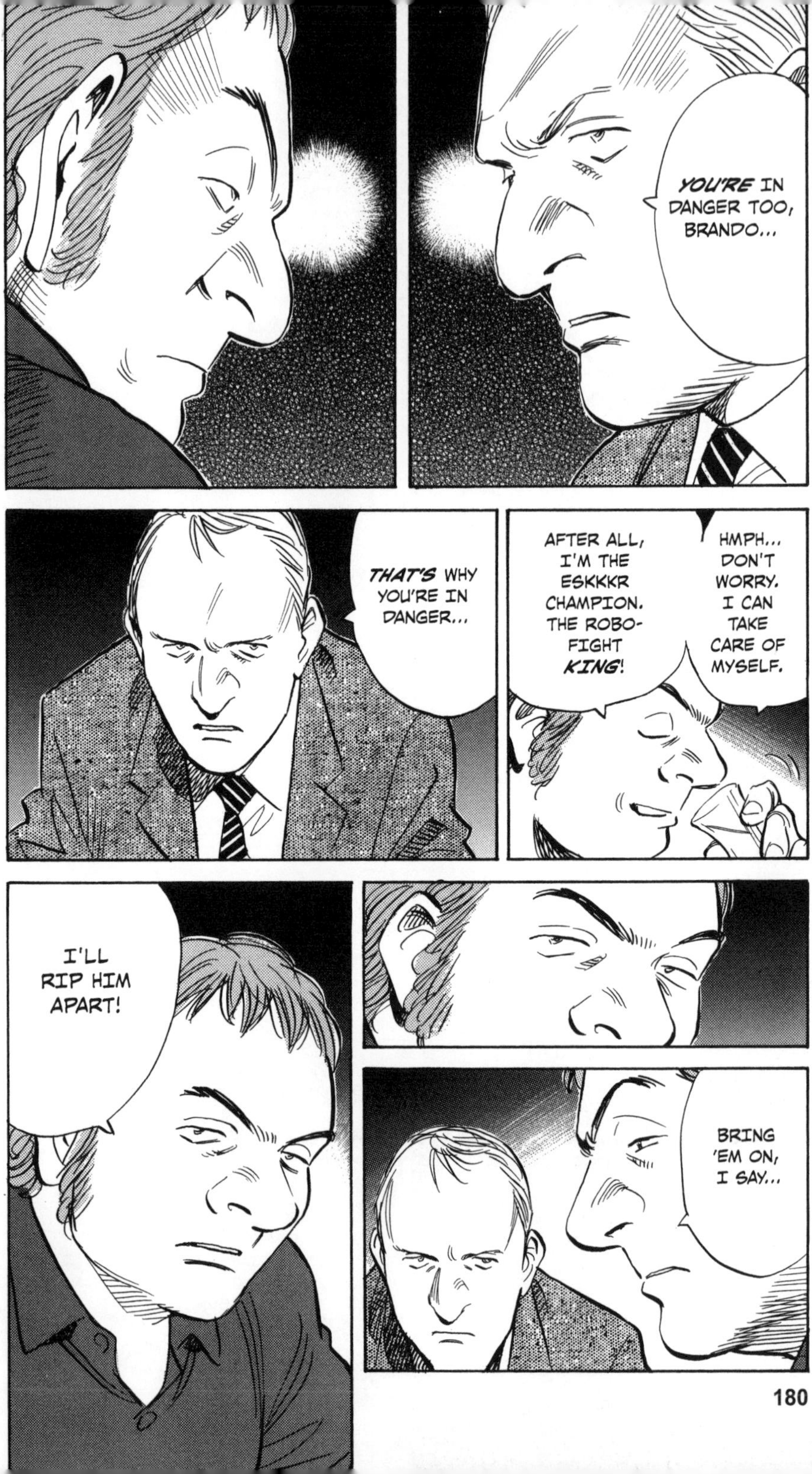
YOU'RE IN DANGER TOO, BRANDO...
HMPH... DON'T WORRY. I CAN TAKE CARE OF MYSELF.
AFTER ALL, I'M THE ESKKKR CHAMPION. THE ROBO-FIGHT KING!
THAT'S WHY YOU'RE IN DANGER...
BRING 'EM ON, I SAY...
I'LL RIP HIM APART!

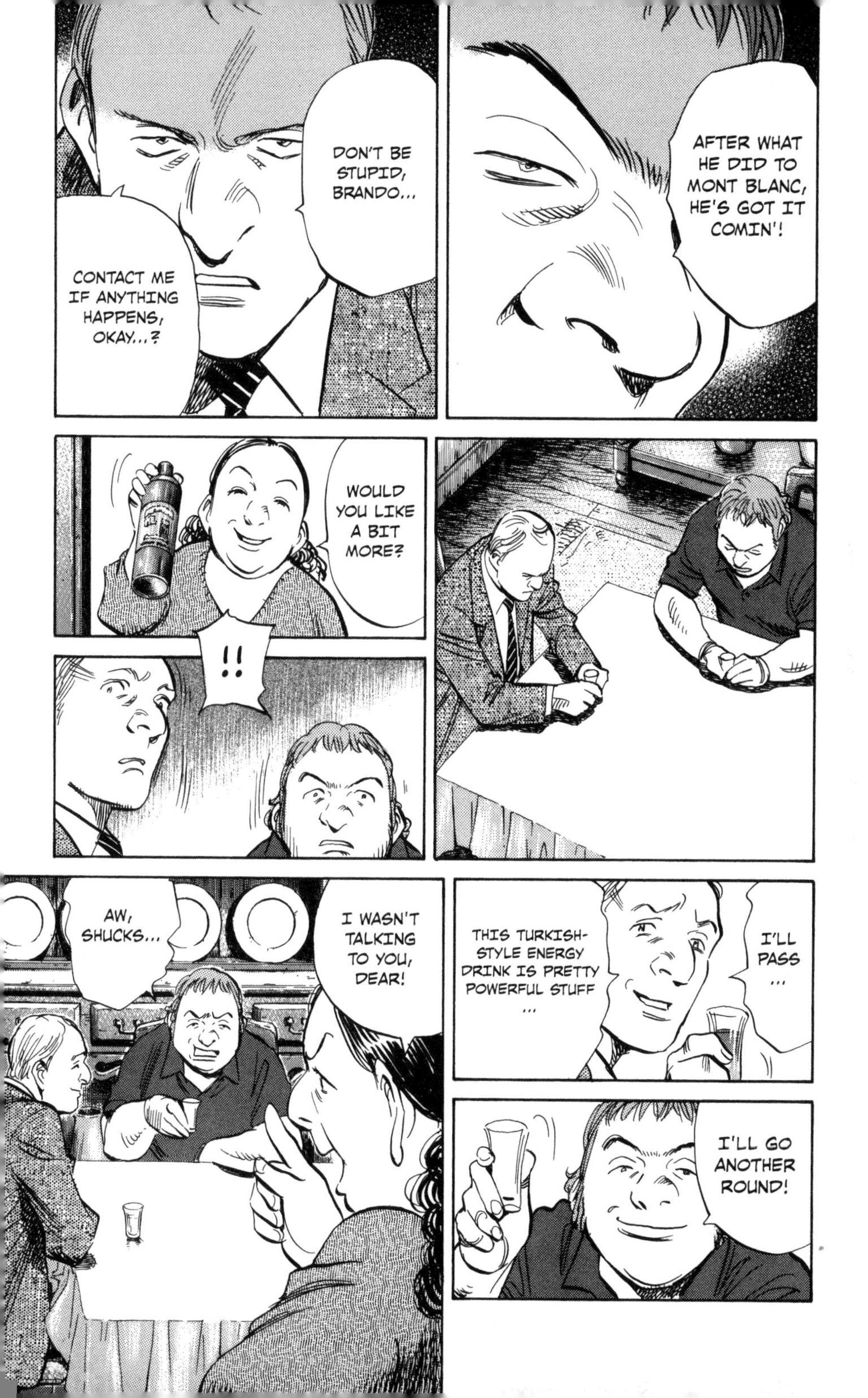
AFTER WHAT HE DID TO MONT BLANC, HE'S GOT IT COMIN'!
DON'T BE STUPID, BRANDO...
CONTACT ME IF ANYTHING HAPPENS, OKAY...?
WOULD YOU LIKE A BIT MORE?
!!
I'LL PASS ...
THIS TURKISH-STYLE ENERGY DRINK IS PRETTY POWERFUL STUFF ...
I'LL GO ANOTHER ROUND!
I WASN'T TALKING TO YOU, DEAR!
AW, SHUCKS...

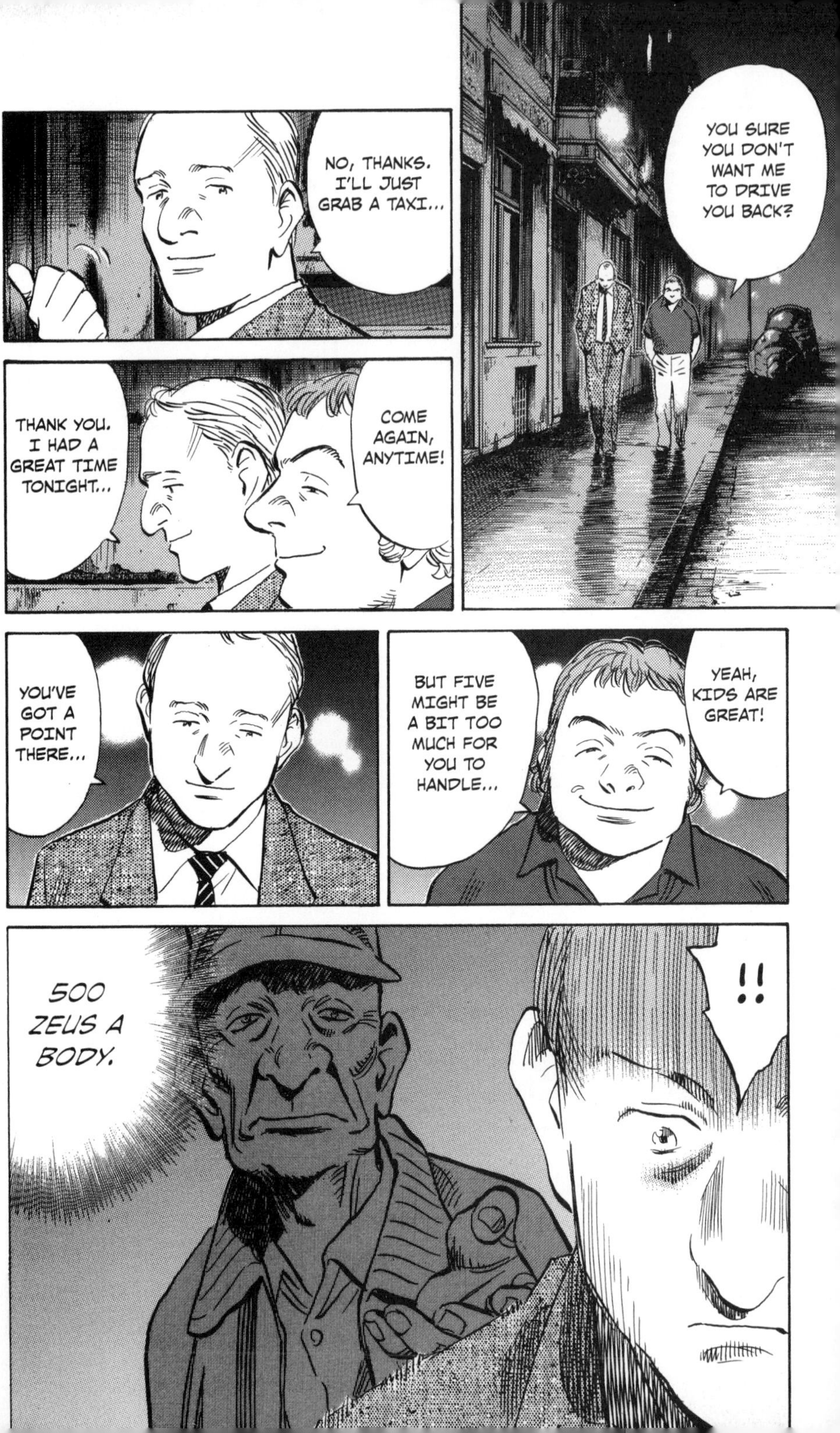
YOU SURE YOU DON'T WANT ME TO DRIVE YOU BACK?
NO, THANKS. I'LL JUST GRAB A TAXI...
COME AGAIN, ANYTIME!
THANK YOU. I HAD A GREAT TIME TONIGHT...
YEAH, KIDS ARE GREAT!
BUT FIVE MIGHT BE A BIT TOO MUCH FOR YOU TO HANDLE...
YOU'VE GOT A POINT THERE...
!!
500 ZEUS A BODY.

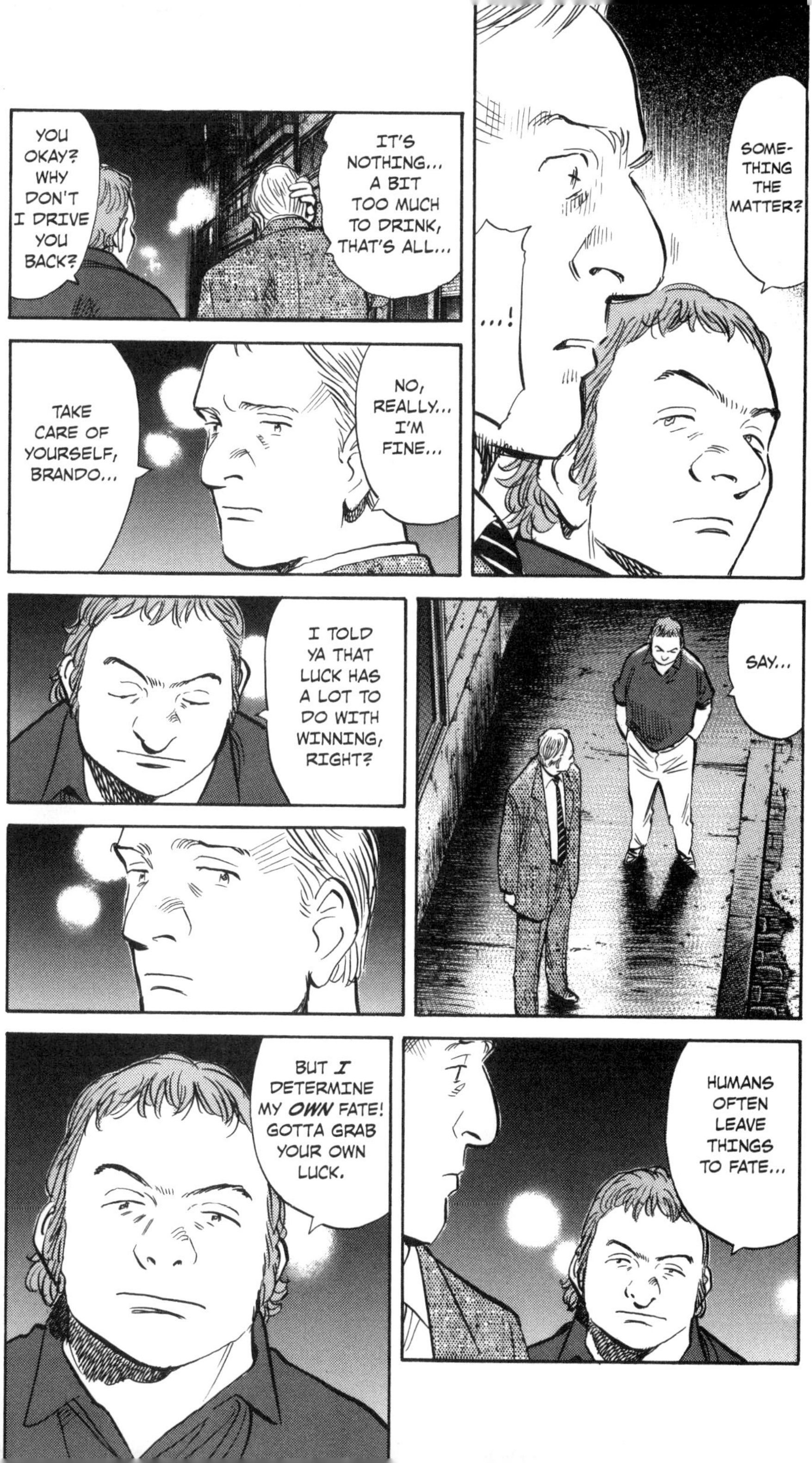
SOME-THING THE MATTER?
...!
IT'S NOTHING... A BIT TOO MUCH TO DRINK, THAT'S ALL...
YOU OKAY? WHY DON'T I DRIVE YOU BACK?
NO, REALLY... I'M FINE...
TAKE CARE OF YOURSELF, BRANDO...
SAY...
I TOLD YA THAT LUCK HAS A LOT TO DO WITH WINNING, RIGHT?
HUMANS OFTEN LEAVE THINGS TO FATE...
BUT *I* DETERMINE MY *OWN* FATE! GOTTA GRAB YOUR OWN LUCK.

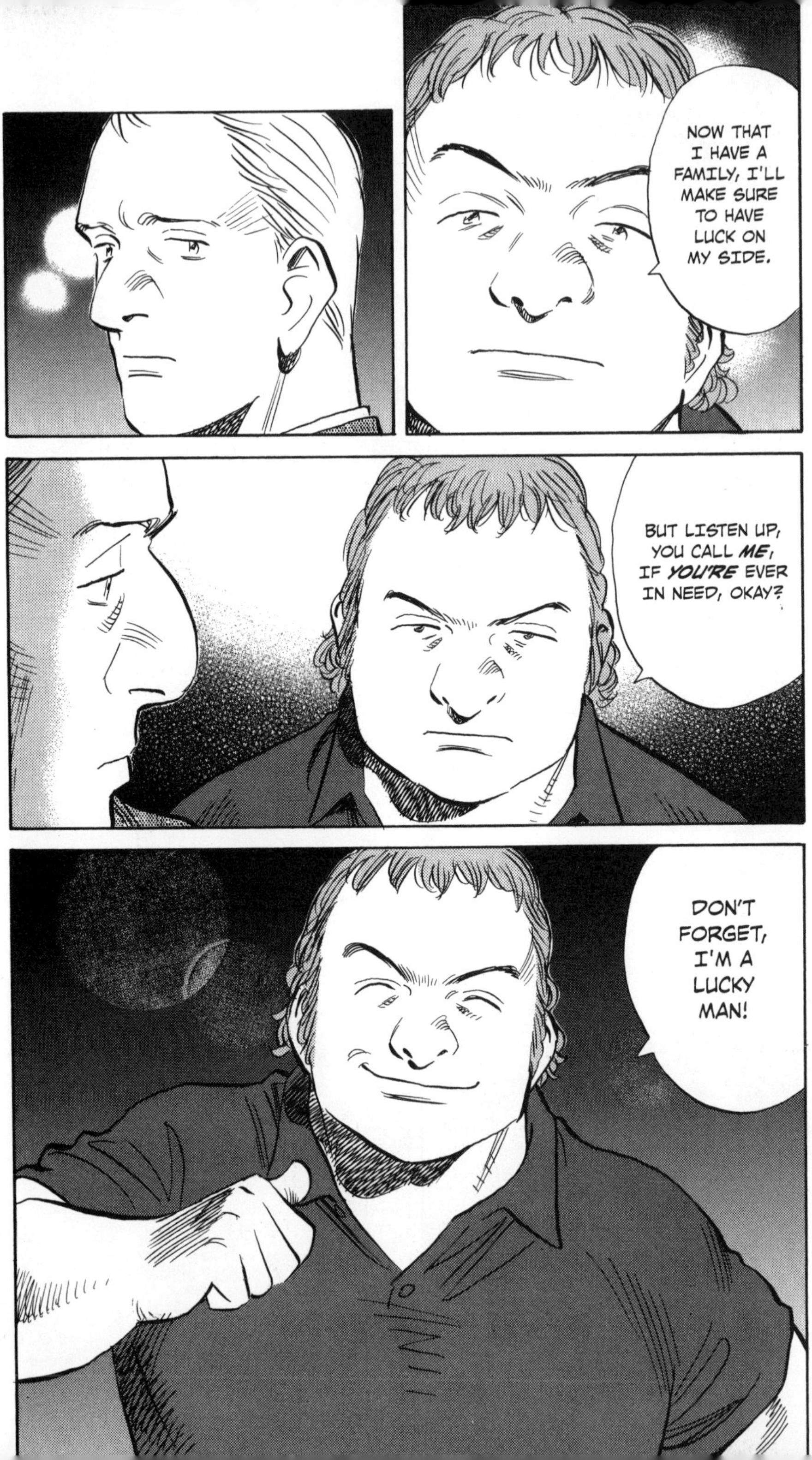
NOW THAT I HAVE A FAMILY, I'LL MAKE SURE TO HAVE LUCK ON MY SIDE.
BUT LISTEN UP, YOU CALL *ME*, IF *YOU'RE* EVER IN NEED, OKAY?
DON'T FORGET, I'M A LUCKY MAN!

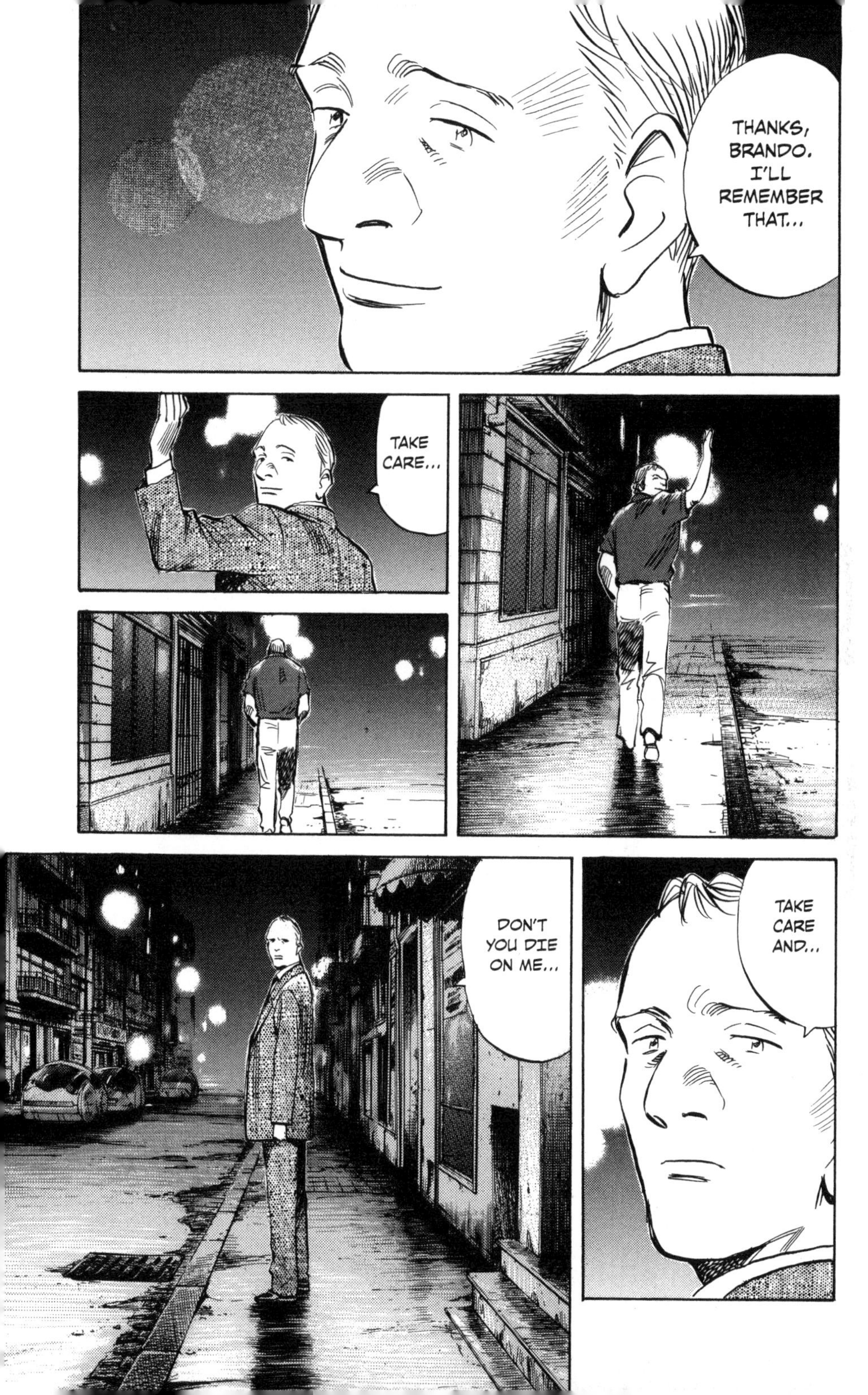
THANKS, BRANDO. I'LL REMEMBER THAT...
TAKE CARE...
TAKE CARE AND...
DON'T YOU DIE ON ME...

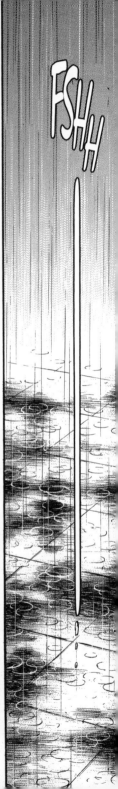

UH-OH
...

BNK

SORRY,
MISTER...

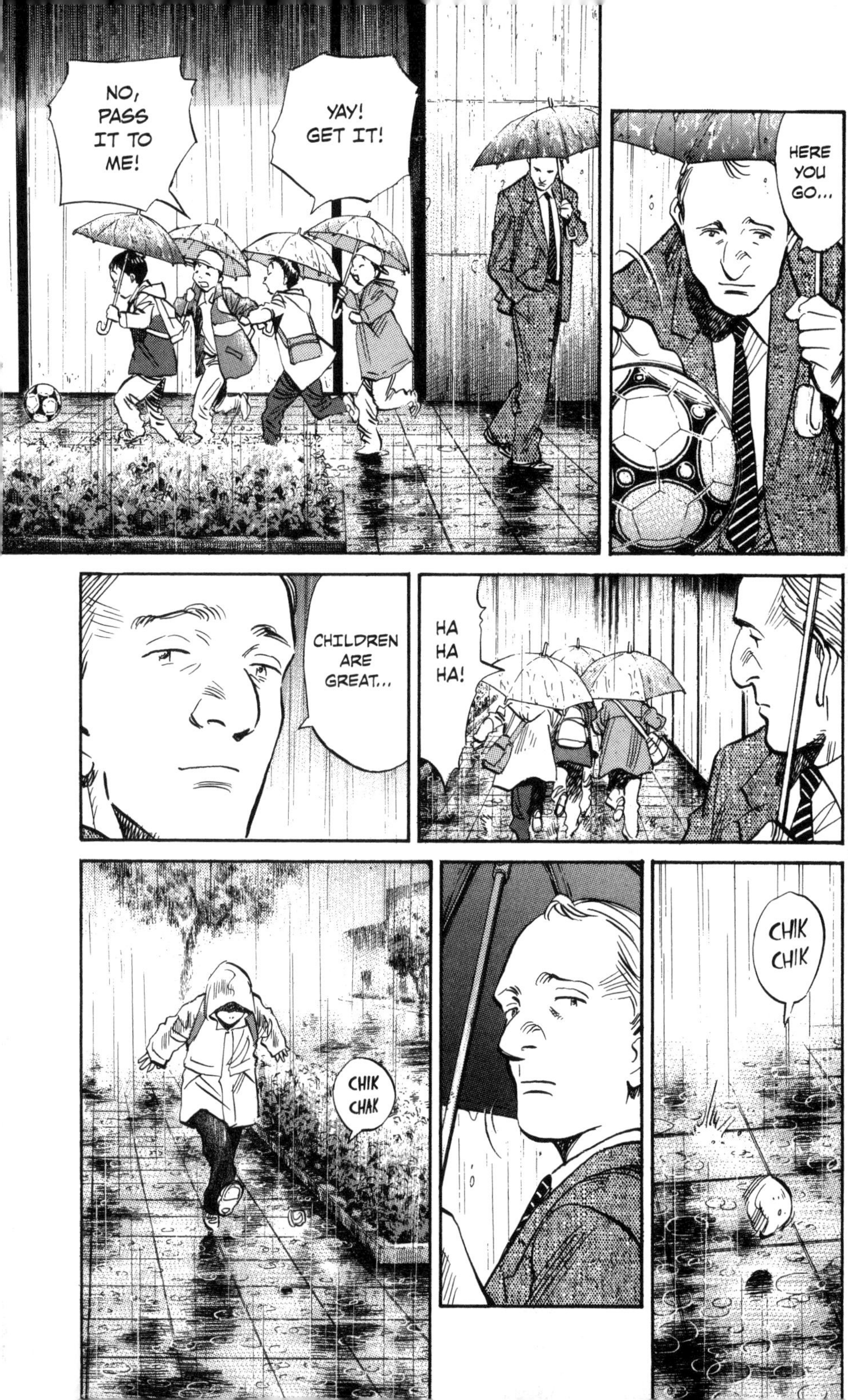
HERE YOU GO...
YAY! GET IT!
NO, PASS IT TO ME!
HA HA HA!
CHILDREN ARE GREAT...
CHIK CHIK
CHIK CHAK

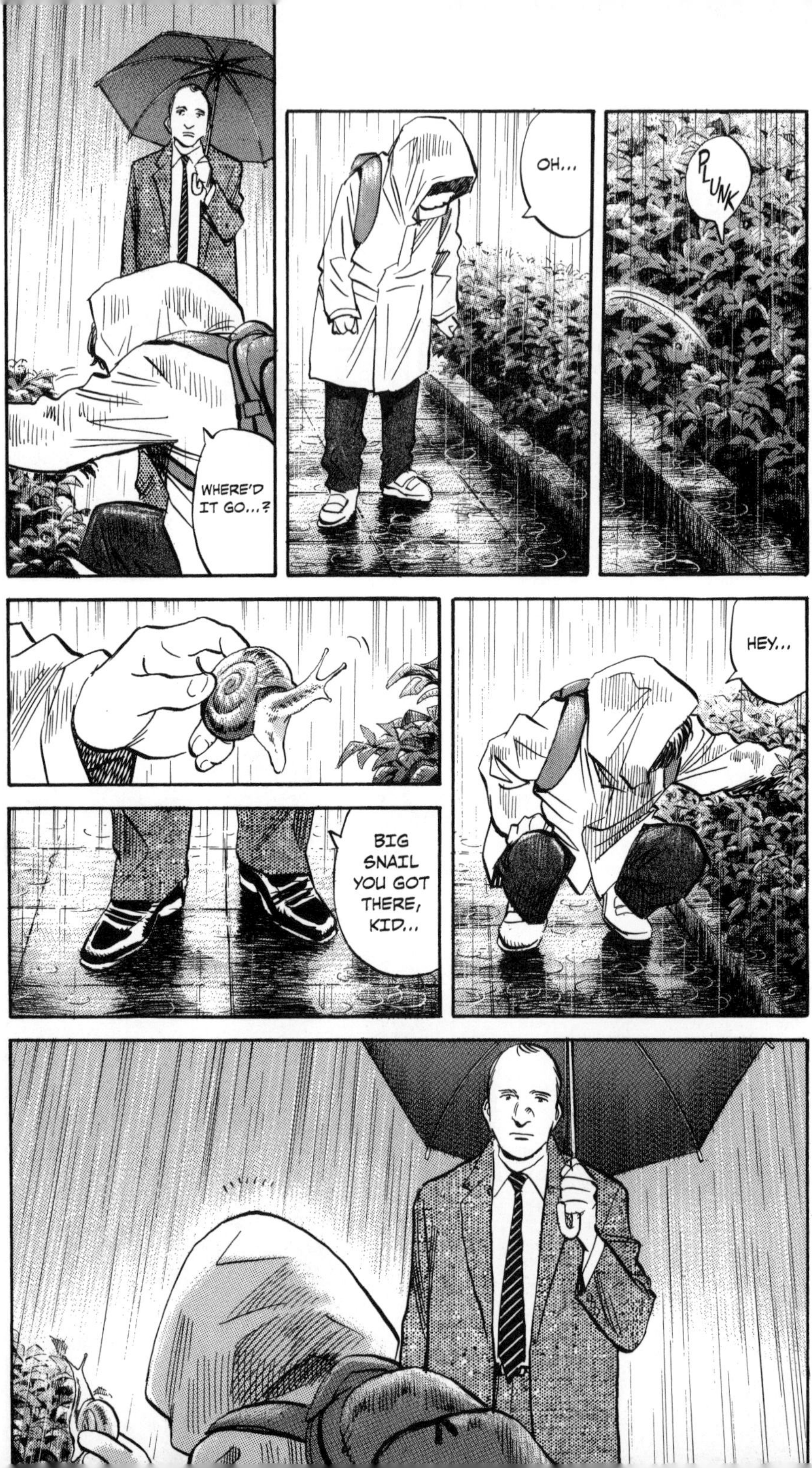
PLUNK
OH...
WHERE'D IT GO...?
HEY...
BIG SNAIL YOU GOT THERE, KID...

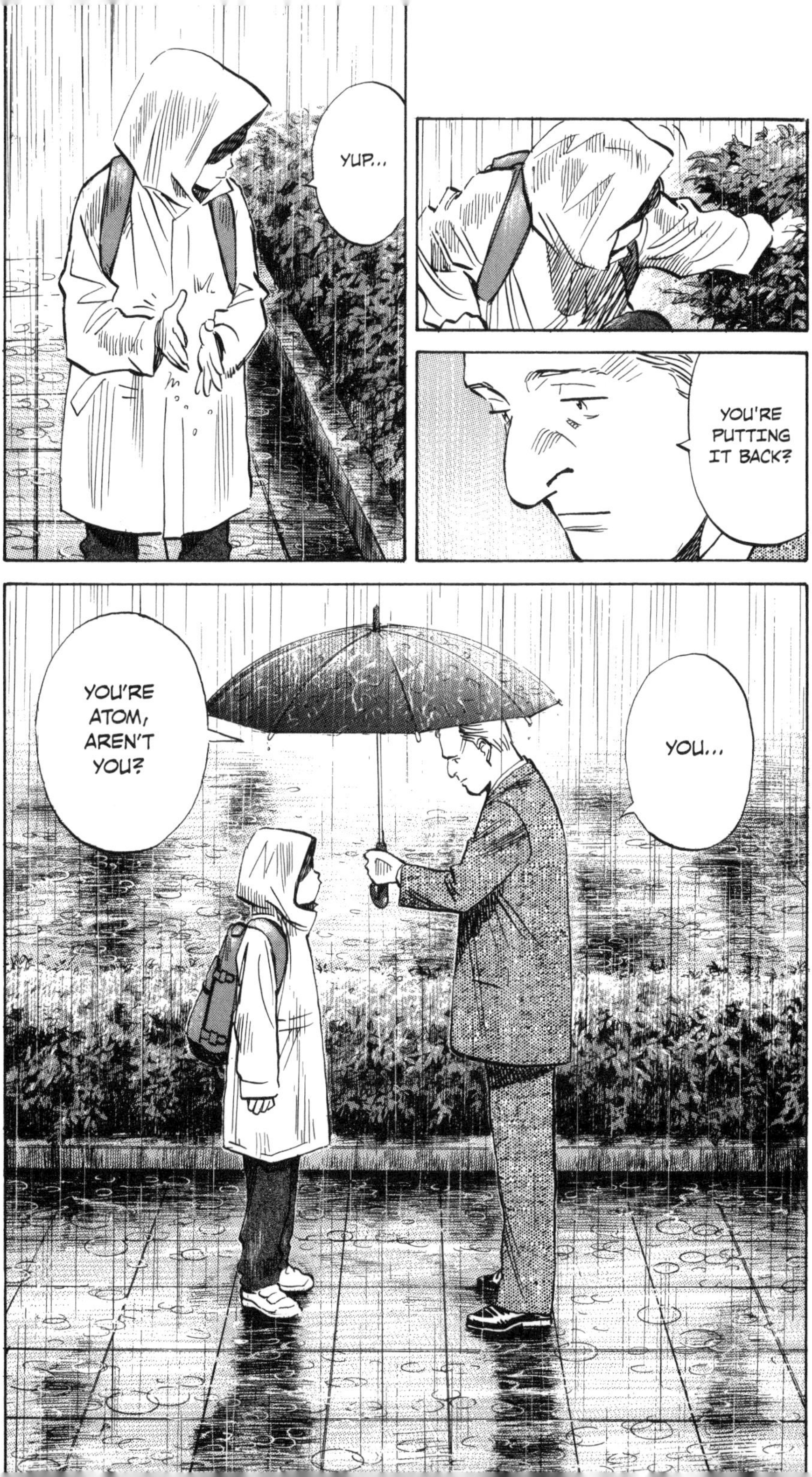
YOU'RE PUTTING IT BACK?
YUP...
YOU...
YOU'RE ATOM, AREN'T YOU?

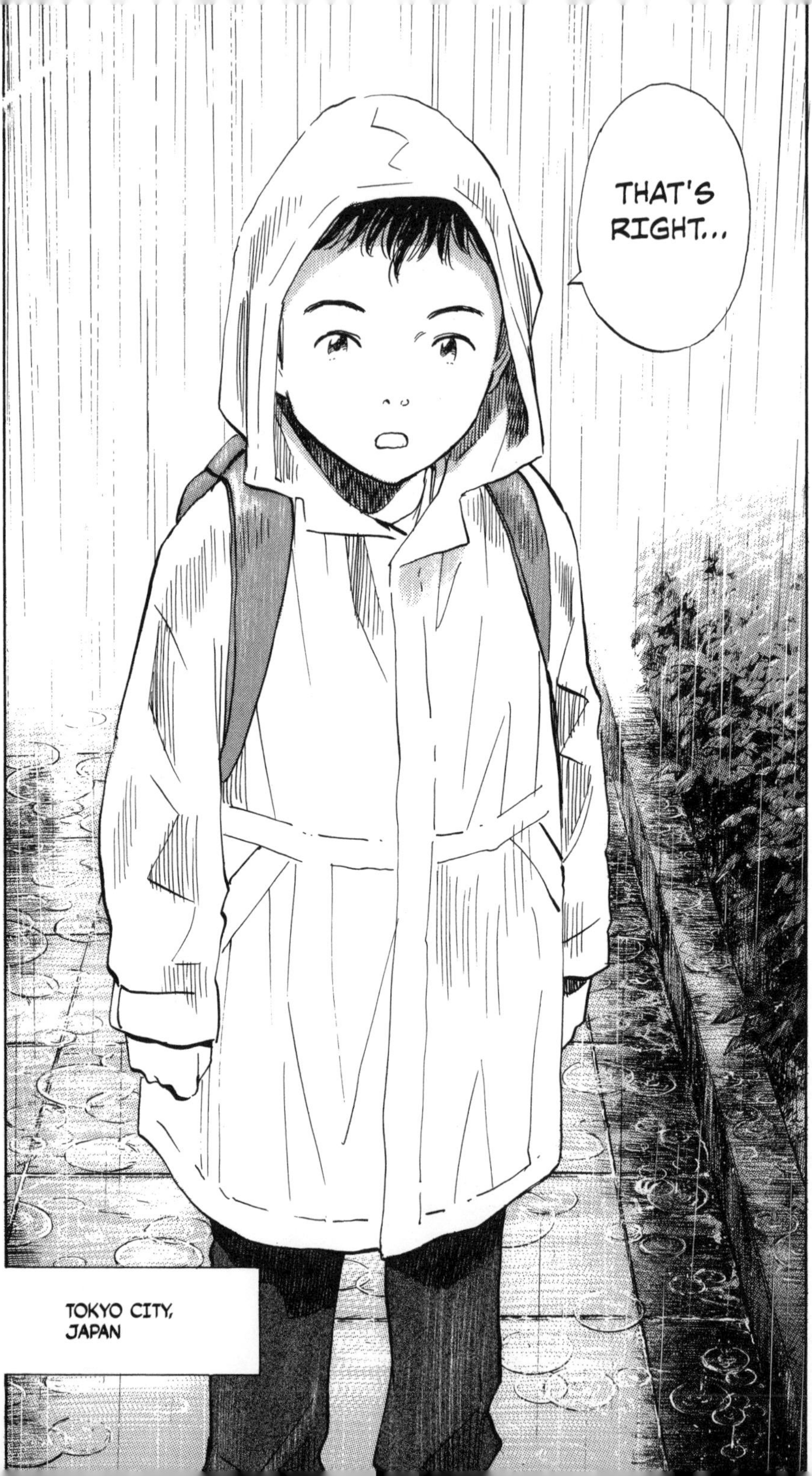
THAT'S RIGHT...
TOKYO CITY, JAPAN

THE LEGACY OF ASTRO BOY:
A Discussion Between Naoki Urasawa and Macoto Tezka

1928   Osamu Tezuka, the genius who would eventually become known as the "God of Manga," is born.

1951   Tezuka creates a narrative set in a futurish society about a boy robot whose machine body houses a soul. Children throughout Japan go wild over the story.

2003   Naoki Urasawa challenges himself to create the ultimate tribute to the God of Manga!

NAOKI URASAWA Manga Artist

Born in Tokyo in 1960. Finalist in the 1982 Shogakukan New Artist Competition. Debuted the following year, 1983, with *BETA!!* His works include *Monster*, *20th Century Boys*, *Pineapple Army*, *Yawara!*, *Master Keaton* and *Happy!*. In 1990 *Yawara!* won the 35th Annual Shogakukan Manga Award. *Monster* was awarded the 1st Annual Media Arts Festival prize in the Manga division in 1997, the grand prize for Manga for the 3rd Annual Osamu Tezuka Cultural Award in 1999, and the 46th Annual Shogakukan Manga Award in 2001. *20th Century Boys* was awarded the 25th Annual Kodansha Manga Award in 2001, as well as the 48th Annual Shogakukan Manga Award in 2003. Urasawa is generally regarded as one of the key manga artists of his generation.

MACOTO TEZKA Visualist

Born in Tokyo in 1961. Started to shoot 8mm movies while in high school and was praised by such luminaries as film director Nagisa Oshima. While in college, pursued the career of a visualist, making radical films based on his unique visual perspective. His works go beyond a single classification, ranging from short experimental films to HD and CG projects, as well as short fiction, event planning, concerts, CDs and multimedia productions. In 1999, his film *The Idiot* saw its theatrical release – a culmination of ten years of planning – and received the Venice Film Festival's digital award. We can expect his future visual statements to create waves of unprecedented size in the Japanese filmmaking world.

*This discussion first appeared in the September 5, 2003 issue of *Big Comic Original*.
Composition **TAKASHI NAGASAKI**   Text **BIG O (SATO)**   Photography **TAKESHI NONOSHITA**
With the cooperation of Tezuka Productions

SOMEONE HAS TO STEP UP TO THE PLATE AND CHALLENGE OSAMU TEZUKA.

[M. TEZKA]

INTERVIEWER: To start off, I'd like to ask you both how you first encountered Osamu Tezuka's work and in particular his *Astro Boy* series.

URASAWA: That must be a question for me, right?

TEZKA: Right, I'm not quite sure how I can respond to that...

URASAWA: I was probably four or five years old. We were moving to another house or something, and I was staying with my grandparents for a while. Thinking they'd get me something to help pass the time, they bought me some *Astro Boy* books, including the stories "The Greatest Robot on Earth" and "The Artificial Sun." *Astro Boy* was therefore my first experience with manga. After reading the books over and over, I started to copy the artwork. I actually got pretty good at it. I even copied Osamu Tezuka's signature...

TEZKA: As for me, I grew up watching my father draw his manga right in front of me at home, so I naturally thought that everybody else's dad drew manga too. I can't even recall if I first saw his animated works on TV or in the studio where they were being screened. It's all a bit vague in my memory.

URASAWA: Wow. Being the first kid to see Astro before anyone else in the world...That'd be like a dream come true...

INTERVIEWER: What did you think, Macoto, when Naoki Urasawa first contacted you with the idea of creating a new work loosely based on the Astro Boy story, "The Greatest Robot on Earth"?

TEZKA: I was really shocked. I thought, "Wow, this guy's really bold to even think of something like this." If it'd been a proposal from some unknown artist, it would have been easy to deal with, but this was from none other than the famous Naoki Urasawa. I figured it would be rude to turn him down right then and there, so I agreed to at least get together with him and discuss his idea.

URASAWA: It being the year of Astro Boy's "birth" in the original story, we first discussed the idea of me doing something with the Astro Boy character

"THE GREATEST ROBOT ON EARTH" HAS BEEN ENSHRINED AS A CENTERPIECE IN THE LITERATURE OF OUR GENERATION. [URASAWA]

on a very limited basis. But since he is such a special, unique character, I suggested that, rather than do a short, one-off piece using him, it'd be a lot more interesting to do something more serious and more hard-hitting, to really take this on as a long-term challenge. Early on though, I used talk about it as if someone else was going to do it.

TEZKA: Oh, is that how it was?

URASAWA: Sure, the way I remember it is that I suggested that if anyone were going to do something with *Astro Boy*, that they ought to really go for it, and try to take on something like "The Greatest Robot on Earth" – which happens to be my all-time favorite Astro Boy story. Then other people started getting excited about the idea. It's understandable, of course, because "The Greatest Robot on Earth" has been enshrined as a centerpiece in the literature of our generation. But then I realized that I really did want to get personally involved and draw it myself! Of course, once I said this out loud, I also started having some second thoughts.

TEZKA: Everyone of a certain generation has probably had the feeling, at least once, that they'd like to take on Osamu Tezuka. Someone has to take up the challenge sometime. But that stated, I've never thought that I should be the one to do it. After all, I'm Osamu Tezuka's son and we share the same blood. If I tried to do something with one of his original works, I'd just end up invisible...

LET ME SHOW YOU THE IDEA FOR "THE GREATEST ROBOT ON EARTH" THAT I'VE BEEN FORMULATING INSIDE MY HEAD. [URASAWA]

INTERVIEWER: You've got the same genes, after all.

TEZKA: So I started to think, "Who could I get to stand in for me on this?" Speaking metaphorically, there are many other sons of Osamu Tezuka out there, so I figured there must be someone who would take up the challenge. And of course Naoki Urasawa was the first one to volunteer to do so. But you know, there aren't many artists who can go mano-a-mano like this. It's a no-holds-barred kind of challenge, one that allows any kind of trick or subterfuge. So I have high expectations and I'm really looking forward to it.

INTERVIEWER: Macoto, have you ever come upon this kind of challenge in the film world?

TEZKA: Well, in terms of adapting another artist's work, it was a challenge for me to bring Ango Sakaguchi's novel *Hakuchi* (The Idiot) to the big screen. It's a true work of literature, but I had to use some tricks such as computer graphics to pull it off. When you work with a veteran crew, you've got to be really committed, or it shows...

URASAWA: What do they pay most attention to?

TEZKA: Well, directors are often evaluated by how unreasonable they are. For example, say you have a location where you want to have the camera cross over a small river. That might require building a bridge to support rails for a special dolly shot. Now, that becomes a big deal for the production. So what you do is express your needs in as humble a way as possible, without using the command voice so often associated with directors. You

WHO IS GOING TO GO HEAD-TO-HEAD WITH OSAMU TEZUKA?

say, "If we could only do it this way, we'd get our shot...but that's out of the question, right...?" Then you get a response like, "No, wait a minute, sir..." and before you know it, the staff has the bridge up and you get your shot. When the crew is naturally motivated to do their best possible work, the quality of the film improves. This is something the viewer is unaware of; it's just an example of what happens on location. So I'm happy to give Naoki Urasawa a free hand, even if it means he's going to be somewhat self indulgent.

URASAWA: On rereading "The Greatest Robot on Earth," I felt that there were scenes missing and also that some scenes were different than I remembered. Over the years, I guess I'd actually fleshed out my own version of the story in my head.

TEZKA: That's what makes Osamu Tezuka's work so intimidating. It's amazing how he could condense so much emotion and time into a single frame. And that's what gets expanded in readers' minds. There are so many stories that aren't necessarily visible on the surface. But Urasawa takes this a step further. He has another version of "The Greatest Robot on Earth" in his head that goes beyond what the average reader sees. It's that new version that I'm really looking forward to.

INTERVIEWER: Did you consider Osamu Tezuka's fan base when you approved of this project?

TEZUKA'S VIBRANT LIVING WORKS STILL RESONATE TODAY.

TEZKA: Well, if we were talking about music, countless covers have been made of Beatles songs, right? And if something new and interesting comes out of a new arrangement, that's good, right? And say a listener from the younger generation is inspired by the new arrangement to go back and listen to the original Beatles tune, well, that listener will have the pleasure of making a new discovery. I only hope that we can achieve the same result with this project.

URASAWA: That's right. I really hope the younger generation will go back and read Osamu Tezuka's original material, not as precious treasures to be displayed on a pedestal, but as vibrant living works that still resonate today. ⊠

ASTRO BOY
AND THE GREATEST ROBOT ON EARTH

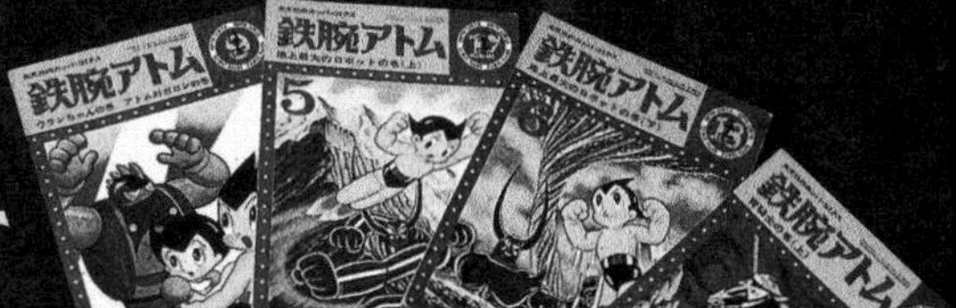
鉄腕アトム
鉄腕アトム
鉄腕アトム
鉄腕アトム

Kobunsha
KAPPA-COMICS

Astro Boy, the 100,000 horsepower boy robot with seven special powers, is a national hero who needs no introduction. He appeared on the scene fifty years ago as the robot boy in the story called *Atom Taishi* (Ambassador Atom), which was serialized in *Shonen Magazine* from April 1951 through March of the following year. He later became the hero of the manga series *Tetsuwan Atom* (Mighty Atom), followed by a thirty-minute animated TV series of the same name that aired from 1963. The most famous and popular story among all the episodes was "The Greatest Robot on Earth." In this episode, the villain, Pluto, had such an overpowering presence that his character gained a popularity far exceeding that of the usual bad-guy robot. In *Pluto*, Naoki Urasawa recasts the original story of "The Greatest Robot on Earth" in a new and exciting way.

POSTSCRIPT

Takayuki Matsutani, President of Tezuka Productions, Inc.

I have to confess, I am amazed to see how the original *Astro Boy* story has been turned into such an interesting concoction as *Pluto*.

As many readers may be aware, *Astro Boy* was born on April 7, 2003. In other words, when Osamu Tezuka began creating his *Astro Boy* manga series over half a century ago, he made April 7, 2003 Astro Boy's official "birthday" in the story.

In the weeks and months leading up to April 7, 2003, Tezuka Productions was intensely busy working on a new *Astro Boy* animation series and also a variety of commemorative events, but around that time we were also visited by an editor from the publisher Shogakukan, as well as Naoki Urasawa and Takashi Nagasaki, who works as Mr. Urasawa's producer. These gentlemen said that they wanted to create a new manga based on the original *Astro Boy* episode titled, "The Greatest Robot on Earth," and that they wanted to make one of the characters in the story – the very humanlike German robot detective, Gesicht (or Gerhardt in Dark Horse's English release of *Astro Boy*), who is himself a victim of discrimination – the hero.

At the time, I found the idea of making the new story's protagonist not Astro Boy but one of the original story's supporting characters very interesting. This was especially true because the man creating the new manga (which would of course be based on Tezuka's original work), would be none other than the remarkably talented Naoki Urasawa – famed for series such as *Monster* and *Yawara!*, and the recipient of innumerable manga awards, including the Osamu Tezuka Culture Award.

I immediately discussed the matter with Osamu Tezuka's oldest son, Macoto. He was fortunately not only willing to have his father's story adapted but, as it turned out, also willing to participate in the production in a supervisory role. And sure enough, only a year after the new story began serialization in a manga magazine, we had accumulated enough pages to compile them into a paperback volume. And the response has been so favorable that I have been asked to write the postscript to the volume you are now reading.

Naoki Urasawa has created one hit manga series after another, starting with his judo manga series *Yawara!*, which was so popular that it presumably led to Ryoko Tani – the female judo champion who won two gold medals for Japan in the Athens Olympics – being affectionately nicknamed "Yawara-chan." Ever since his popular series *Monster* in particular, Urasawa has created truly unique world visions all his own. But at this point, I am already convinced that *Pluto* will become one of his most representative works.

Naoki Urasawa and Osamu Tezuka are thirty-two years apart in age. Urasawa made his professional debut as a manga artist at the age of twenty-two or three, so it is also interesting to note what Osamu Tezuka was doing at the same time in life. In 1950–1951, although Japan had still not recovered from the devastation of World War II, some children were of course already reading long, narrative "story manga," and a line-up of monthly boys manga magazines had just been established. Tezuka had abandoned his plans of becoming a physician and plunged himself into the manga world, where he began drawing furiously. In addition to serializing *Jungle Taitei* (Kimba, the White Lion), and *Astro Boy*, as well as a variety of girl's manga stories, in magazines, he was also creating one-off paperback volumes.

By the time Tezuka reached the age that Urasawa is now, his animation production company, Mushi Pro, had gone bankrupt, and his career was truly in a mess. But if we look at his schedule for the following year, 1973, and the year after that, he had already started serializing his *Black Jack* stories, as well as *Mitsume ga toru* (The Three Eyed One), and *Big Comic Magazine* was serializing *Barubora* and *Shumari*. By December of 1974, he seems to have been almost possessed, drawing a huge volume of serialized works for four weekly manga magazines, one biweekly, three monthlies, and a variety of one-shot pieces. I'm trying not to overemphasize what Tezuka did at this point in his life. Artists and writers are all different by nature, and there is little point in boasting about quantity for the sake of quantity, but quantity does mean something. In any field, the ability to work hard, and the ability to continue to work, can be a huge asset for a creator.

Nowadays, even non-Japanese refer to Japanese comics with the word *manga*, which has grown in popularity to become a very international term. It is a reflection of the fact that in the fifty or more years since the war ended, Tezuka and the Tokiwaso group of manga artists, as well as many others, were able to develop and help evolve manga into a truly amazing medium of expression. Yet today manga seems to have reached a turning point. In tandem with Japan's booming postwar economy, manga sales grew at an extraordinary, unconditional pace until recently, but there are clouds on the horizon that hint of future problems. Nonetheless, as a medium of expression, manga still has an almost infinite potential. And it has a nearly infinite potential to develop even further. As such, I would like to make an earnest entreaty of Mr. Urasawa. Please continue to create works that lead and guide the rest of the manga industry. Please continue to create, not only for the sake of people of the past, but also the future.

AUGUST 2004

The late Osamu Tezuka, a manga artist for whom I have the utmost respect, created the series *Astro Boy*. This timeless classic has been read by countless numbers of fans from when it was first created in the fifties to now. As a child, "The Greatest Robot on Earth" story arc from *Astro Boy* was the first manga I ever read that really moved me and inspired me to become a manga artist. With *Pluto* I've attempted to infuse that story with a fresh new spirit. I hope you enjoy it.

NAOKI URASAWA

Manga wouldn't exist without Tezuka Osamu. He is the Leonardo da Vinci, the Goethe, the Dostoevsky of the manga world. Naoki Urasawa and I have always felt that his achievements and work must not be allowed to fade away. Tezuka wrote that Atom, the main character of his most representative work *Astro Boy*, was born in 2003. This was the same year that we re-made "The Greatest Robot on Earth" story arc from the *Astro Boy* series. Who was Osamu Tezuka and what was his message? For those of you readers who are interested in *Pluto*, I highly recommend you read it alongside Tezuka's original work.

TAKASHI NAGASAKI

PLUTO: URASAWA × TEZUKA
VOLUME 1
VIZ SIGNATURE EDITION

BY Naoki Urasawa & Osamu Tezuka
CO-AUTHORED WITH Takashi Nagasaki
WITH THE COOPERATION OF Tezuka Productions

TRANSLATION Jared Cook & Frederick L. Schodt
TOUCH-UP & LETTERING James Gaubatz
COVER ART DIRECTION Kazuo Umino
LOGO & COVER DESIGN Mikiyo Kobayashi & Bay Bridge Studio
VIZ SIGNATURE EDITION DESIGNER Courtney Utt
EDITOR Andy Nakatani

EDITOR IN CHIEF, BOOKS Alvin Lu
EDITOR IN CHIEF, MAGAZINES Marc Weidenbaum
VP, PUBLISHING LICENSING Rika Inouye
VP, SALES & PRODUCT MARKETING Gonzalo Ferreyra
VP, CREATIVE Linda Espinosa
PUBLISHER Hyoe Narita

Printed in the U.S.A.

Published by VIZ Media, LLC
P.O. Box 77010
San Francisco, CA 94107

10 9 8 7 6 5 4 3 2 1
First printing, February 2009

www.viz.com store.viz.com

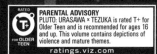

ASTRO BOY

Osamu Tezuka's iconic *Astro Boy* series was a truly groundbreaking work about a loveable boy robot that would pave the way for all manga and anime to follow. Tezuka created the manga in 1951 and in January of 1963 adapted it to become the first weekly animated TV series ever to be broadcast in Japan. In September of that same year, it became the first animated TV series from Japan to hit the airwaves in the United States. The series and its title character were originally known in Japan as *Tetsuwan Atom*, which translates to "mighty Atom" – or for the more literally minded, "iron-arm Atom" – but was released in the U.S. as *Astro Boy*. Decades later, in 2000, Dark Horse Comics brought the manga for the first time to English readers, also under the title *Astro Boy*.

Within the context of the story for this English edition of *Pluto: Urasawa × Tezuka*, the precocious boy robot will be referred to as "Atom" in the manner in which he has been known and loved in Japan for over fifty years. Elsewhere, such as in the end matter, the series will be referred to as *Astro Boy* as it has been known outside of Japan since 1963.